THE OLDEST CITY

PRESS PORCÉPIC

THE OLDEST CITY

The Story of St. John's, Newfoundland

by

Paul O'Neill

Published by Press Porcepic, 70 Main Street, Erin, Ontario, NOB ITO, in October of 1975 with the assistance of the Canada Council and the Ontario Arts Council.

Printed in Canada by
Web Offset Publications Limited

ISBN 88878-070-2

Distribution:

CANADA
Musson Book Company
30 Lesmill Road
Don Mills, Ontario
M3B 2T6

U.S.A.
Books Canada Inc.
33 East Tupper Street
Buffalo, New York
14203

U.K.
Books Canada Ltd.
1 Bedford Road
London N2
England

Canadian Shared Cataloguing in Publication Data

O'Neill, Paul, 1928—
The oldest city: the story of
St. John's, Newfoundland.

1. St. John's, Nfld.—History.
2. Newfoundland—History. I. Title.

F5447.S14.073   971.8
F1124.S14.0
ISBN: 0-88878-070-2

For John

This Book Is Yours; With A Lifetime Of Affection

BOOKS BY PAUL O'NEILL

"Spindrift and Morning Light"
"The City in Your Pocket"
"Legends of a Lost Tribe

Publisher's Preface

The story of St. John's was originally conceived by the author as a single volume covering the whole range of the city's history: political, social, economic, and personal. Because of the detail of the treatment and the historical span involved, the work when completed would have been fourteen hundred pages long. The publisher believed, too, that a great deal of the book's value and charm lay in the thoroughness and detail of the research.

Our decision to publish the book in two parts thus arose from our desire to produce a work that would be easy and pleasant to handle, to dip into, to use for research or to read for pleasure. The first part then is essentially a study of St. John's political history and its colourful people, the second part covers its social and military history. There is a great deal of overlapping in these categories, of course, and the decision may be somewhat arbitrary, for we believe that each part can stand alone as a fascinating historical work.

Each part will contain a detailed table of contents; the first part will include the bibliography, the second the index. Together or singly they make up the first historical study of Canada's oldest city, and should provide a valuable addition to Canada's history.

Acknowledgements

This work is history in a particular pattern. Because it is the first history of St. John's ever to be compiled, I feel it would have been extremely difficult to have told the story in chronological order and include the mass of information and detail these volumes should contain.

For those wanting a complete picture of the life and history of the town at any specific period the work will be frustrating as they will have to refer to many chapters. However, for those interested in the numerous small details, events, dates, and human interest happenings that tell of the story of entertainment, education, sport, religion, and other facets of life, in the development of St. John's, I hope the book will prove a satisfaction.

The historical evolvement of each sphere covered by this book has been investigated exhaustively. Wherever possible, sources, dates, etc., have been carefully checked and counterchecked. Unfortunately, much valuable material has been lost in the numerous fires that have swept St. John's. What errors are to be found in the manuscript are due to the vagueness of sources, contradictory information, or the author's own inability to recognize an inaccuracy. Sources quoted in the chapters may be checked in the bibliography. It was the author's intention to compile rather than interpret the events recorded in this work. What is important is that they are now available in a single source. My concern has not been to startle, but to unify. A search on two continents for unpublished diaries, letters, reports, drawings, photographs, and other material, has proven to be generally unavailing.

The quest for confirmation of certain facts and stories was often exasperating and frequently time consuming. Some cherished myths had to be exploded for the sake of historic fact. The frustrations of my quest were relieved by the generous assistance of many people and especially the following.

I am most deeply indebted to Claire Pratt for such a thorough job of editing and an indefatigable determination not to let any of my inadvertent errors slip by. For introducing me to Press Porcepic and bringing to an end my publishing woes I offer my sincere gratitude to Clara Thomas.

In Ireland I should like to thank the staffs of the National

Library in Dublin, the Waterford City Council and Chamber of Commerce, and the staff of the Library at the University of Cork. I am also indebted to Helen Maher of the Galway Public Library, Father Ryann of Carrick-on-Suir, the Reverend Mother Columbanus of Blackrock, Marcus Bourke of Dublin, the Reverend Brother W. B. Cullen of Callan, and Mr. McQuillan, J. J. Ryann, the Reverend Dr. Marsh, Tom Murphy, and the rector of old St. Patrick's Church, all of Waterford. Special thanks for special favours to Thomas O Duinn of Wexford, Colonel Sidney Watson of Clonmel, Sister Mary Magdelene of Shantalla, Galway, and Father Benignus Millet, OFM, for making available the archives of the Franciscan House of Studies, Killiney, and to Father Bartholomew Egan, OFM, who helped conduct the search there. I have a special obligation to thank my dear friend Marie Stephens of Limerick for her invaluable assistance during my search through Ireland. Her deft perusal of letters, manuscripts, and files saved me an immense amount of work.

In Scotland a thank you goes to the staff of the Scottish National Library, Edinburgh, for assistance with the Cochrane papers, and to a kind informant at Tobermory, Isle of Mull, Inner Hebrides, for some important leads.

In St. Helier, Jersey, Channel Islands, a word of particular thanks goes to the Local History Librarian, Mr. Raymond Falle, who was most helpful in several ways before, during, and after my visit. Also an acknowledgement for cooperation goes to the Société Jersiase and Dr. J. T. Renouf.

In England I owe a debt of gratitude to Alan O. Wills and J. E. C. Clarke for making available the archives of the Society of Merchant Venturers, Bristol, without restriction, and to Commander Walter Raleigh Gilbert of Compton Castle, Devon, for new insights into Sir Humphrey Gilbert and permission to reproduce a painting of his famous ancestor. Special thanks go to G. M. Hayward of Phoenix House, London, for many hours of invaluable assistance in combing the archives of his company. My thanks as well to Dr. Helen Wallis who opened the British Museum to my quest. I am indebted also to the helpful staffs of the British Museum, the National Newspaper Library, the Public Records Office, the British Theatre Museum, and the Royal College of Music. In Devon, I am grateful to P. A. Kennedy of the Devon Record Office, Exeter, Walter Pearse of Ashburton, Mr. Atwell of Broadhempston, and Michael Hope of Shrewsbury, Shropshire. At Newstead Abbey, near Nottingham, the guide was kindness itself. Thanks also to Mr. Sykes of the Nottingham Public Library. I cannot forget my deep gratitude for helpful aids to my cousin in London, Margaret Buckingham.

In the United States of America a word of thanks is owed to the co-operative staffs of the New York City Public Library, the Boston

Public Library, and the Archives Division and State Library in the State House of the Commonwealth of Massachusetts, especially Miss Sheerin and Leo Flaherty. My thanks as well to John Willis of Theatre World, Paul Myers, and Frank Campbell of the Library & Museum of the Performing Arts, and to Melvin Parks of the Museum of the City of New York. A thank you to Francis Robinson of the Metropolitan Opera, Quaintance Eaton, Tony Randall, and a true friend, Michael Cashin.

· In Canada my special thanks goes to the staff of the Public Archives of Canada, in Ottawa, and especially to Madeleine Major-Fregeau, Lawrence Earl, E. H. Dahl, and Peter Kaellgren who took the time to aid my search. Also, my thanks to J. Hunter of Ottawa's National Gallery of Canada. A word of appreciation, too, for the helpfulness of the staffs of the Halifax Public Library, the Nova Scotia Provincial Archives at Dalhousie University, and to Gordon McLean and the staff of the New Brunswick Provincial Archives in Fredericton.

In Newfoundland I am indebted to many people and cannot possibly name them all. First of all I must express my gratitude for their aid and encouragement to Premier Frank D. Moores; the Honourable John Crosbie, former Minister of Finance; and the Honourable Tom Doyle, former Minister of Tourism. Without their active involvement the work would probably never have been published. For valuable assistance I would especially like to thank F. Burnham Gill, John Greene, David Davies, and the other members of the staff of the Provincial Archives; Agnes O'Dea and her staff in the Newfoundland Room, Memorial University Library; Grace Butt, Kitty Power, Stephanie Edwards, Mona Cramm and all of the extremely helpful staff at the Provincial Reference Library—Newfoundland Section; Sal Mac-Donald of the Registry of Deeds, Confederation Building; City Clerk Rupert Greene and Noel Vinnicombe of the staff of City Hall; Mayors William Adams and Dorothy Wyatt for access to and permission to copy old photographs; and Bobbie Robertson of the Newfoundland Historical Society for special favours. Marion Stone and Nish Collins have my gratitude for greatly easing my research work. For other help I must thank Sister Mary Patricia, Addison Bown, Maurice Devine, Wilfrid Ayre, Brother H. B. French, W. C. Woodland, John O'Reilley, Tom Cahill, Dr. Louise Whiteway, E. E. Knight, Eugene Young, Francis Rowe, Sister Theresa Tobin, Monsignor Patrick Kennedy, Arthur Fox, Leo P. Hynes, Don Morris, Dorothy Harries, Magistrate Hugh O'Neill, John Puddester, Sister Mary Francis, Frank Petten, Andrew Horwood, Bill Squires, Judy Curtis, Eugene Ozon, Brother J. B. Kean, Jean Murray, Edward Casey, Paul Sparkes, Gordon Duff, Shane O'Dea, Brother F. R. Foran, Sylvia Wigh, Ignatius Rumboldt, Sylvia Snow, Daisy (Myrick) Collins, Captain Douglas Fraser, Monsignor Alphonsus Penny,

Genevieve Allen, the Reverend, J. S. S. Armour, Harold Morris, Aubrey MacDonald, Mary Martin, Lewis Brookes, Bill Pushie, George Baggs, Kevin Jardine, Major P. J. Cashin, Vieva Edison, Dr. S. MacKenzie, John Fagan, John Carter, and the Chief Justice the Honourable R. S. Furlong. I am grateful to Frank Graham and Michael Harrington for special leads and most valuable assistance. I was also fortunate to have the co-operation of many people who supplied information on their families and businesses. They were too numerous to list here. For their generous help I acknowledge my debt.

My thanks to the Hutchinson Publishing Group Ltd., London for permission to quote from *My Air Armanda* by Air Marshal Balbo and to Charles Scribner's Sons, New York, for permission to quote from *The Spirit of St. Louis* by Charles A. Lindbergh.

Among those who kindly helped by their encouragement were Lewis and Phyllis Brookes who planted the seed for this book in my mind. Kay Breen, Jean Neary and Jim Long listened with patience and criticized most helpfully. My mother was often forced to dredge nearly forgotten facts from the depths of her memory to satisfy my impatience for accuracy and I am grateful.

Lastly, I am under a special obligation to mention my debt to the Most Reverend J. M. O'Neill, D.D., and Dr. A. B. Perlin, who by their advocacy of my cause, enabled me to obtain Canada Council aid for research. This project was completed with the assistance of a Canada Council grant under its Canadian Horizons Program. A. B. Perlin has been most generous with his help, which was always as close as the nearest telephone.

I would also be remiss if I did not here record the memory of a beloved little dog Toby, who looked on with patient sympathy night after night, year after year, as the story slowly took shape. He listened in devoted silence as I read aloud the troublesome chapters, winced with me when my frustrations became too much to bear, and often licked encouragement when I felt near defeat. He died, age fifteen years, one month to the day before the work was completed. With him I buried at Briarcliff many of the memories of trying to compile this work.

Briarcliff, Bay Bulls.
St. John's, Newfoundland.
May 9th, 1973.

Contents

List of Illustrations

1

On the Side of a Hill

Sir Humphrey Gilbert lands at St. John's, Newfoundland, 5 August 1583. Gilbert claimed the island for Queen Elizabeth of England. (From the Confederation Life Gallery of Canadian History)

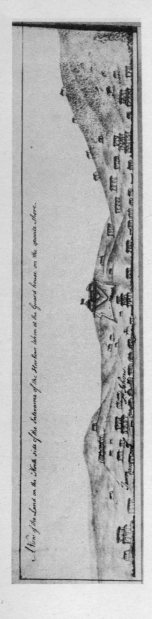

A View of the Land on the North side of the Entrance of the Harbour taken at the Guard House on the south shore.

The oldest known sketch of St. John's. A view of the town in 1762 as seen from the Frederick Battery on the south side of the harbour. Fort William is in the centre. The platforms are flakes for drying codfish. (Courtesy Public Archives of Canada)

A view of St. John's in 1786 from the Log Book of H.M.S. *Pegasus*. Fort Townshend is on the crown of the hill. The Church of England chapel can be seen beneath the fort. (Courtesy Public Archives of Canada)

The Narrows from Duckworth Street east. This painting on stone by Lt. A. Thompson was first published in 1842.

6

The only known sketch of downtown St. John's prior to the Great Fire of 1846. Water Street looking west from King's Beach (site of the Newfoundland War Memorial) in 1837. Drawing by William Gosse.

Looking out the Narrows from St. John's harbour, 1798. At the left is the original Blockhouse atop Signal Hill. Between the rows of fish flakes and fishing stages below the hill is Waldegrave Battery. (Courtesy British Museum)

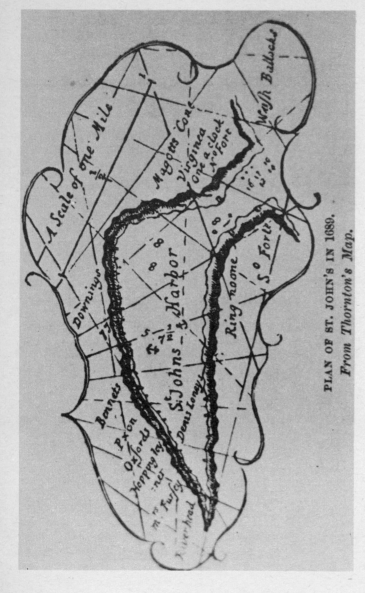

PLAN OF ST. JOHN'S IN 1689.
From Thornton's Map.

The oldest known map of St. John's, 1689.

9

Sir Humphrey Gilbert, half brother of Sir Walter Raleigh, founded the British Empire in St. John's, 5 August 1583, by taking formal possession of the island of Newfoundland in the name of Queen Elizabeth I. (Courtesy Commander Walter Raleigh Gilbert)

Gower Street and the roofs of St. John's from Hotel Newfoundland. The towers of the Roman Catholic Basilica are in the background. (Courtesy Newfoundland Tourist Development Office)

11

New Gower Street looking west towards Barter's Hill, circa 1900. City Hall is now on this site. (Courtesy St. John's City Hall)

These tilts, photographed at Pouch Cove around 1880, are typical of the houses built at St. John's during the 17th and possibly early 18th centuries.

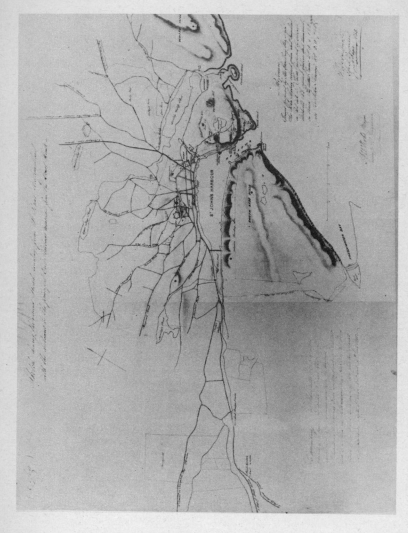

A sketch showing the various roads leading from St. John's to the out harbours in 1845. Prepared to accompany Major Robe's letter to Inspector General Fortificationas and several memoranda to Governor Sir John Harvey.

St. John's in 1798 from a water colour by R. P. Brenton. Fort Townshend is above the town with the Church of England chapel in the centre. On the right is the courthouse and jail. The ship at the left is moored beside Ayre's Cove. Just above the cove is the Roman Catholic chapel and residence of Bishop O'Donel. (Courtesy Public Archives of Canada)

15

St. John's from Signal Hill in 1831. This water colour was made for Governor Cochrane. On the right Government House can be seen. The court house and various churches are in the centre with Fort Townshend above them. (Courtesy Public Archives of Canada)

16

Looking east along Duckworth Street from the foot of Cathedral Street (1848). The "Patriot" office is on the left. The Bank of British North America, to the right of Free St. Andrew's Kirk, is the only building in this sketch still standing today. Next to the bank Dr. Carson rented a house and surgery from his next door neighbour, Robert Prowse. Prime Minister Little's law office is on the right. (Courtesy Public Archives of Canada)

17

Water Street looking east from Adelaide Street (circa 1885). Photographed by S. H. Parsons, the noted St. John's photographer and "the Brady of Newfoundland". (Courtesy CBC—St. John's)

Water Street looking east from in front of the court house. All these buildings were destroyed in the Great Fire of 1892. Second from the right is Walter Grieve & Co. (circa 1885). [Courtesy CBC — St. John's)

19

A winter's morning on Water Street around 1885, looking west towards the Market House. David Sclater's shop is on the left. (Courtesy St. John's City Hall)

The S.S. *Vanguard* and another sealing ship being towed through pack ice on her way to the seal hunt around the turn of the century. Sealers line the rails and rigging. (Courtesy St. John's City Hall)

21

St. John's from Riverhead, circa 1880.

22

Ayre's wharf and ice blocking St. John's harbour shortly after the turn of the century.

23

Underneath the flakes. This photograph taken at Quidi Vidi shows what Water Street and other St. John's lanes looked like in the days when the harbour waterfront was covered by fish flakes. Most of them were ordered removed after the Great Fire of 1817.

24

Outport schooners dry their sails in St. John's harbour following a rainstorm around the turn of the century.

25

St. John's harbour from the Southside in the early days of the present century.

26

The streetcar tracks on Water Street west, opposite the Railway Station, following a snowstorm around the turn of the century. (Courtesy St. John's City Hall)

27

George M. Barr's mercantile premises on the St. John's waterfront in the 1930s. In the foreground Mr. Barr watches men from the schooners weighing up dried, salted codfish which was purchased for shipment to world markets in the casks shown lying on their sides. In late fall each year schooners from coastal villages all around the island crowded every wharf in St. John's unloading salt cod and loading winter supplies for the outports. (Courtesy St. John's City Hall)

St. John's today. This view taken from the Southside shows ships of the Portugese White Fleet moored in the harbour. The Anglican Cathedral is on the right and the Roman Catholic Basilica in the centre with St. Bonaventure's College to the left of it. (Courtesy Newfoundland Tourist Development Office)

St. John's Harbour taken from the air. In the foreground is the dry dock, once the largest in the world. At the left, Harbour Drive and Water Street snake eastward. The Narrows are in the upper right hand corner. (Courtesy Newfoundland Tourist Development Office)

On the Side of a Hill

The town is beautifully situated on the side of a hill; you cannot conceive anything more romantic . . . .
SISTER MARY MAGDALENE, *Letter from St. John's—1833*

The claim of St. John's, Newfoundland, to being the oldest city in North America is based on a mixture of legend and fact. Although it cannot be proven, it is probably the oldest city site on the continent to be chosen by and continuously occupied by the white man. The title of oldest city generally goes to Mexico City, founded as Tenochtitlan on two islands in Lake Texcoco in the year 1325.

Vera Cruz, the first city in North America to be established by the white race was founded by Hernando de Cortes, 21 April 1519, as La Villa Rica de la Vera-Cruz (The Rich City of the True Cross), on a site that was already that of an Indian village.

The oldest city in the United States is St. Augustine, Florida, founded in September 1565 by Mendez de Aviles, on the site of an Indian village, near where Ponce de Leon landed in 1513. Both Vera Cruz and St. Augustine can prove they were occupied as townsites by settlers of European origin before St. John's appears in the records of history. The same is true of Mexico City and other communities in Spanish North America. All these places, however, were developed on sites previously occupied by Indians.

The harbour of St. John's has probably been frequented by Europeans from about the year 1500. We know that by the summer of 1527 it was already a popular rendezvous for Frenchmen fishing the waters of the West Atlantic. From this it would appear that there were summer residents in the area soon after the Cabot discovery, but the construction of a house for permanent residence cannot be proven before 1605.

The story of St. John's begins with the discovery of Newfoundland by John Cabot, 24 June 1497, or 3 July by our calendar. Historians ever since have argued over the exact site of his landfall. Cabot was the first white man since the Vikings to set foot on the mainland of either of the Americas. Columbus did not land on the mainland of South America until the following year.

31

The explorer's landfall has been placed everywhere from Labrador to Maine. Nothing can be conclusively proven from the fragmentary evidence that exists. A letter from John Day, an English wine merchant in Bristol during 1492-93 and later a resident of Seville, addressed to the Very Magnificent and Honourable Lord, the Lord Great Admiral (beyond doubt Columbus), discovered in the Spanish archives at Simancas in 1956, is the latest evidence that seems to give the honour of being "Prima Tierra Vista" to Newfoundland.[1] A majority of those who have worked on the puzzle also believe the discovery to have taken place somewhere on the coast of Newfoundland. One of the most plausible of recent theories is that presented by the American historian, Samuel Eliot Morison, in his book, *The European Discovery of America*. Admiral Morison claims the community of Griquet, on the northeast coast of Newfoundland, as Cabot's landfall.

The claims of Cape Breton in Nova Scotia cannot be dismissed. It appears that Sebastian Cabot, the imp-tongued son of the great Venetian explorer, was the first to be responsible for the theory of a landfall on Cape Breton Island. However, when the boastful Sebastian had his portrait painted in later life, the inscription read: "Sebastian Cabot, Venetian Knight, first discoverer of Newfoundland under Henry VII, King of England." If his vanity had not prevented him from usurping his father's claim to the discovery, it would certainly not have stopped him from claiming to be the first discoverer of Canada, rather than Newfoundland, had he been sure of a Cape Breton landfall.

Historical documents, as well as tradition, generally favour Newfoundland rather than Nova Scotia. For example, there is a report in the British Museum to Their Excellencies the Lord's Justices, dated Whitehall, 11 September 1719, which, in rejecting Spanish claims to Newfoundland waters, states: " . . . it is notorious that the island was first discovered by John Cabot, anno 1497, and at the charge of King Henry the Seventh, and he took possession thereof in the name and for the use of His said Majesty. It appears likewise that King Henry the Eighth sent one Bute to make a settlement in Newfoundland and that several voyages were made thither in that reign by Mr. Hoare and other merchants."

Perhaps the controversy will never be settled. The site of Cabot's landfall is immaterial to this book. It is enough to know the few facts of which we can be sure. John Cabot, or Giovanni Cabota, was a naturalized Venetian in the pay of King Henry VII of England, who discovered the mainland of the Americas, 3 July 1497, or 24 June by the old calendar. For this he was granted a yearly pension of £ 10 for life by the king. Within a year or two of his discovery Cabot vanished from history and is thought to have been lost on a second voyage.

Moderns tend to sneer at the pension. In the context of its time it seems to have been a generous gesture. The official yearly salary for a ship's captain, provided he was employed for fifty weeks, was £8.3.17. What ship's captain even today, would not be delighted with a yearly pension for life nearly 20 per cent higher than his regular salary?

Thanks to Sebastian Cabot's efforts to claim for himself the honours due his father, the Cabot voyage is shrouded in misinterpretation and legend. One popular myth has it that St. John's was so named by John Cabot when he sighted its almost perfect landlocked harbour on St. John's Day, 24 June 1497. Wherever the old mariner landed on Discovery Day it was almost certainly not St. John's. He did commemorate the feast by naming his landfall "The Isle of St. John" but, as has been pointed out, it is impossible to identify or locate this site from existing evidence. In the many disputes among historians none has ever put forward a claim that the landfall was the site of what became the city of St. John's.

Admiral Morison, in the aforementioned book, says that, having discovered Newfoundland on June 24, John Cabot sailed his ship *Matthew* to the south and " . . . Possibly she investigates the completely land-locked harbour which to-day nourishes St. John's, the Newfoundland capital . . . ." This is as close an association with John Cabot as the city can claim.

In 1502 Hugh Elliot and Thomas Ashehurst, merchants of Bristol, obtained from Henry VIII letters patent for the establishment of a colony in Newfoundland. There is no further information to be found regarding this venture, but subsequent developments in the colonization of the island indicate the harbour of St. John's as the site for the intended colony.

The origin of the name of the city is as much a mystery as the landfall, and just as open to dispute. It seems likely that it was the gift of an early Portuguese explorer, possibly Gaspar Corte-Real, on his first voyage in 1500. Corte-Real brought back to Portugal, from that voyage, fifty-seven Beothuck Indians captured in Newfoundland. He also brought with him a sword found on the shores of the island which seems to suggest a connection with John Cabot. An observer, living in Lisbon at the time, wrote: " . . . There has been brought hence a piece of broken sword inlaid with gold which we can pronounce to have been made in Italy and one of the [Beothuck] children had in his ears two pieces of silver which appear to have certainly been made in Venice—which induces me to believe that the country belonged to that continent."

The Corte-Real sword, discovered three years after the voyage of Cabot, would certainly seem to link the Italian explorer with Newfoundland. It is unlikely that some unknown person with a sword made in Italy would have visited the place in such a short period of time. The weapon would seem to have been either broken and abandoned or forgotten and left behind by someone on the *Matthew* who had gone ashore.

If the sword had been forgotten, then it was probably smashed by Indians. They were fairly numerous all over Newfoundland, even on the Avalon Peninsula, until after 1618, when a mysterious disease, probably smallpox brought from Europe by the white man, wiped out many thousands from Newfoundland to Long Island Sound.[2]

The possibility that Corte-Real gave St. John's its name is given some validity by the fact that the earliest record of the place appears on a Portuguese map by Rienel, in 1519, as Rio de San Johem. Most likely, Corte-Real, or one of his contemporaries, paid a brief visit to the harbour; saw the distant Waterford River, then many times its present width, empty into the bay, which he took to be the mouth of a large river; named the place Rio de San Johem (St. John's River); and sailed away. The headland to the north was called Capo de Sa Francisco (Cape St. Francis) and the one to the south of the harbour Capo de Espera (Cape of Hope—now Cape Spear).

The name of St. John's varied considerably during the following years of the sixteenth century. Some of the names which followed Rienel's Rio de San Johem are: Haven of St. John (Rut, 1527), Sam Johem (Freire, 1546), Sainct Johan (Le Testu, 1555), St. John's (Parkhurst, 1578; also Hayes, 1583), S Jones (Velasco, 1610), Saint Johns (Mason, 1620), St. John's (Whitbourne, 1588-1622), St. Ieans Harbour (Visscher, c. 1680), and St. Johns Harbour (Thornton, 1689).[3] It would seem that Anthony Parkhurst was the first person to record the spelling that has become common usage. Parkhurst was an English merchant who made four voyages to Newfoundland in the 1570s. He reported that he found the place much frequented by "Vile Portingals, descending of the Jews and Judas kind." There is also the possibility that the community was given its name by one of the early English mariners. Within a stone's throw of the Bristol dock from which John Cabot sailed, stands the Church of St. John the Baptist, known as St. John's-on-the-Wall. Built in 1174 and rebuilt in 1400 St. John's is the last survivor of five churches that were in or on the old city wall of Bristol. A bridge stretched across the head of the quay from the Church to Froom Gate, the dock used by Cabot and others who sailed to Newfoundland around 1500. Many of the sailors on these early vessels must have come from the Bristol parish of St. John's. The church was certainly known to all of them. In some manner they may have named the popular haven in the West Atlantic for their home parish.

The last word on the subject will be left with G.R.F. Prowse, a son of the noted historian, Judge Prowse. He presents a very reasonable explanation for the origin of the name. Prowse says we know that Cabot called his landfall the Isle of St. John's in commemoration of the feast day on which it was discovered. Based on years of study of this point, Prowse's conclusion is that the name St. John's Isle became associated with an indefinite part of the east coast of Newfoundland. He says the name could only have had a short life but it may have lasted long enough among sailors to cause its transference to the landlocked harbour which from earliest times was usually their first and last port of call. Prowse maintains that it would probably have been known as the "harbour of St. John's Island," which could account for the possessive form, St. John's, instead of St. John.

On 3 August 1527 John Rut reached the place in command of one of Henry VII's wine ships, *Mary of Guildford*. After sailing along the coast of Labrador and encountering some icebergs, Rut abandoned the task assigned him by Cardinal Wolsey of finding a northwest passage to Cathay and headed south for the more agreeable waters of the Caribbean. On the way he paused at St. John's long enough to write a letter to Henry VIII, and to wait six weeks off Cape Spear, as prearranged, for another vessel in the expedition, the *Samson*, which had become separated during a storm. The *Samson*, however, did not turn up and was never seen or heard of again.

Rut's letter is quoted in Chapter 2. At the time of his visit the port of St. John's was already a popular gathering place for European fishermen. He reported to the king: "We found Eleuen [eleven] saile of Normans and one Brittaine [Breton] and two portugal Barks all fishing. . . ." The fact that not one of the fourteen ships Rut found in the harbour was English shows that the place was held in low esteem by British fishing interests. Having discovered the island, the English neglected to exploit it until the middle of the sixteenth century. By 1548, however, English trade with Newfoundland seems to have become fairly common. Richard Hakluyt writes of the period: "St. John's was a very popular place during summer but in winter given over to the fruition of birds and wild animals." Rut's letter indicates that soon after 1519, when Spanish eyes were dazzled by seeing Mexico City in all its Aztec glory, St. John's was already much frequented by Normans, Bretons, and Portuguese.

In the middle of the sixteenth century England began to take a real interest in the potential of Newfoundland. The Dutch appeared on the scene in the last quarter of the century. Rivalry between England and France for possession of the island began in 1624 with the capture, in Newfoundland waters, of French ships by English pirates.

What has been described as the first organized tourist cruise to the New World was arranged in 1536 by Master Richard Hoare (Hore) "and divers other gentlemen," who seem to have been inspired by Cartier's first voyage to the New World. A group of thirty members of the Inns of Court and of the Chancerie booked for the ill-starred adventure for which Henry VIII may have contributed some of the money. Hoare picked two vessels, the *William* and possibly the *Trinity*. The passengers were "all mustered in warlike manner at Gravesend, and after receiving of the sacrament they embarked themselves in the ende of April, 1536." The wonder is not so much that the young barristers sailed off on the voyage but that any of them returned. They had no qualified pilot, were so badly victualled that in the end they fell to eating each other, and finally took to piracy. When they reached home, the uneaten lawyers were in rags and tatters and on the verge of starvation.

Arriving in the New World, the tourists rubbernecked the Straits of Belle Isle but soon suffered their first hardship on the coast of Labrador, Cartier's "Land God Gave to Cain." The *Trinity* appears to have been lost with all on board. Alain Moyne, a Breton pilot who was to have taken them into the Gulf of St. Lawrence, sailed down the east coast of Newfoundland instead. There was most certainly a stopover at St. John's before rounding Cape Race and cruising along the rugged south coast. When their food ran out the gentlemen killed birds, robbed nests and resorted to "raw herbes and rootes in the fields and deserts." When this supply proved insufficient they cast lots and began to devour each other; why they could not have survived on the plentiful supply of lobster, cod, trout, and other fish is a mystery.

In the end they succeeded in capturing a French ship, "Well furnished with vittaile," that was watering in a Newfoundland cove. After plundering the French vessel they set sail for home and reached St. Ives around the end of October 1536. The king compensated the Frenchmen and a lawsuit was instituted against Master Hoare by the owner of the *William*, who claimed he had been defrauded.

The next visit of importance to the growing community of St. John's was that of Jacques Cartier in June 1542. He was on his way home to France from his third voyage up the St. Lawrence where he had been sent with five ships the previous year. Cartier had wintered at the fort of Charlesbourg Royal where he was instructed to wait for his superior, Jean-François de la Rocque, sieur de Roberval. Roberval, who had never been to sea, held a commission which promoted him over Cartier and he had complete authority over the new lands and every Frenchman in them.

King Francis I issued an invitation to all and sundry to emigrate to "les terres neufves" and Roberval was swamped with applicants anxious to escape the agonies of domestic poverty. Meanwhile, Cartier waited for him at Charlesbourg Royal, but he never came. By spring there was signs that the natives were restless so Cartier resolved to abandon the place and return to France.

As the great explorer entered St. John's harbour he found, to his surprise, the tall ships of Roberval lying at anchor. They were three in number and bore two hundred persons, among whom were a number of women. Roberval had experienced some difficulty in departure and did not leave La Rochelle until 16 April 1542. He had reached St. John's on June 8, a few days before Cartier's arrival. A member of Roberval's party wrote:

> The 8th of this month we entered into the road of St. John, where we found seventeen fishers. While we made somewhat long abode there, Jacques Cartier and his company, returning from Canada, whither he was sent with five vessels the year before, arrived in the very same harbour. Who, after he had done his duty to our general, told him that he had brought certain diamonds and a quantity of gold ore which was found in the country; which ore the Sunday next ensuing was tried in a furnace and found to be good.[6]

Cartier's *La Grande Hermine*, a craft that ranks with the *Santa Maria* and the *Matthew* as one of the three great ships of early North American history, was accompanied by *L'Émerillon*, and an unnamed boat. The explorer's memoirs indicate that when his ship entered St. John's he found twenty vessels at anchor in the port: probably the seventeen that Roberval had found there a few days earlier plus Roberval's three ships. This would have meant a port population of somewhere around 1,500 persons.

If reports are accurate, Cartier had on board seven quintals (700 lbs) of pearls, ten barrels of gold and seven of silver. Roberval ordered the explorer to return with him to Canada but the cunning mariner decided to desert his leader and, in the dark of night, "stole privily away" with his three ships and reached St. Malo in mid-October 1542.

The Devon county records in Exeter show that by 1560 ships from Topsham, Exmouth, and Kenton were regular visitors to St. John's. The references are brief. For example, 8 September 1565, the return is noted of the *Gratias Deo*, out of Dartmouth. There is no indication of permanent settlers in Terra Nova, as the island was then called.

In 1566 Sir Humphrey Gilbert proposed a voyage to discover a northwest passage to China, and he included a scheme for establishing colonies in the New World. It was 1578 before he finally got under-way. Humphrey Gilbert's parents were Otho and Katherine Gilbert of Compton Castle, Devon. When the boy was eight years old his widowed mother married Walter Raleigh of Fardell, Devon, and moved to Hayes Barton, where her son, the future Sir Walter, was born in 1552. Humphrey, born in 1539, was the eldest of five brothers. The Gilbert and Raleigh boys grew up wild, impetuous, irascible, with a strong feeling for music and poetry. They were carried away by speculations and projects to explore, not only the mind, but the sea as well. In 1569 Humphrey, a thirty-year-old soldier-adventurer, put down an uprising in the Irish province of Munster with such brutal cruelty that his name was hated in Ireland for generations. The following year he was given a knighthood.

Back in England, Gilbert dug out his plans for the New World and decided to found a colony on the totally unsuitable island of Anticosti, in the St. Lawrence, a place he had never seen. Queen Elizabeth did not think much of the proposal but she was very devoted to the Gilbert-Raleigh brothers and granted Sir Humphrey letters patent, 11 June 1579. For this he has been styled by some historians the "Father of British Colonization."

A man of extraordinary talents, courage, and enterprise, Gilbert set out in 1578 on an abortive voyage to North America, with six ships and a band of "Musitians." The fleet sailed on September 26 and was soon being hurled about the Atlantic by westerly autumn gales. When insubordination threatened to become mutiny the squadron returned to Dartmouth where the undaunted knight intended to make a fresh start the following year. However, the Privy Council forbade his leaving in 1579 because of the piracies of some of his fleet. The payment of fines for these miscreants stripped Gilbert of most of his financial resources.

Funds for a second voyage to North America were raised from such men as Sir Francis Walsingham and the Merchant Adventures of Southampton. In return Gilbert promised to direct all the trade to and from the capital of his new colony through that port.

Queen Elizabeth passed word along to Gilbert, through Sir Francis, that she did not wish Sir Humphrey to depart on the venture. The Queen very wisely observed that he was a man "of not good happ by sea."[7] In spite of this clear-sighted vision by his fellow redhead, Gilbert was determined to proceed with his plans. At Compton Castle, tucked away in the hills of Devonshire, he sat down with his half-brother, Sir Walter Raleigh, and the two discussed and prepared for the expedition. The rooms in which they dreamed dreams they hoped might astonish the world, confound Spain, and bring great glory to the England of Elizabeth I have been faithfully restored since 1930, by Commander Walter Raleigh Gilbert, who is now living on the estate which he has turned over to the National Trust.

For his second adventure on the high seas Gilbert organized a fleet of five ships. The largest of them was the 200-ton *Raleigh*, owned by its namesake, with a commander named Butler, and Robert Davis of Bristol as master. At the last minute, illness prevented Sir Walter Raleigh from boarding his ship for the voyage. Next in size was the

Delight, 120 tons, owned and commanded by William Winter, who was to be relieved at St. John's by Capt. Maurice Browne. There were two 40-ton vessels: the *Golden Hind*, commanded by Edward Hayes, with William Cox as master, and the *Swallow*, which Gilbert had seized from John Callis, for an act of piracy, with Browne as captain. The pinnace *Squirrel* owned by Gilbert and captained by William Andrews, was only 10 tons.

The total complement on board the vessels was something over 260 men including another band of "Musitians." Hayes writes, in his narrative of the voyage, " ... we are provided of Musike in good variety not omitting the least toyes, as Morris Dancers, Hobby horses, and Many like conceits to delight the Savage people, whom we intended to winne by all faire means possible."

The fleet sailed from Plymouth Sound, 11 June 1583. Within two days a contagious disorder was said to have broken out on board the *Raleigh* and she returned to port. The real reason for the desertion is thought to have been Butler's wish to avoid mutiny by a crew that feared it was underprovisioned. The action infuriated Gilbert but there was nothing he could do about it.

On August 3 the four remaining vessels rendezvoused off St. John's. There were thirty-six ships of various nations in port. At first they refused Sir Humphrey admittance, thinking him to be a pirate. Somewhat put out by this reaction to the arrival of one of the Queen's favourites he displayed his commission and was placated by having a salute fired in his honour. As he grandly sailed through the Narrows, the *Delight* grounded on a rock and had to be towed free by long-boats.

On August 5 Gilbert went ashore to take formal possession of the New Found Land in the name of Queen Elizabeth. Most histori-ans have accepted the tradition that this ceremony was held near the present War Memorial, in the vicinity of what was called the Beach. There is nothing to support this claim. In fact, it seems a most unlikely spot. Eye-witnesses speak of the event taking place on the side of a hill overlooking the harbour so that it could be watched from the decks of the various ships in port. It is more probable that the hill spoken of was Hill o'Chips, and the site of the ceremony atop the cliff, opposite Cavendish Square, just west of Devon Row.

Some historians, including Judge Prowse, have claimed the hon-our for the area of Garrison Hill, stating that Feaver's Lane, an old pathway from the waterfront to Fort Townshend (still existing between Gower Street and Bond Street), is the oldest cross street in St. John's. This is not correct. The existence of Feaver's Lane, before the con-struction of Fort Townshend in the 1770's, cannot be proven. Hill o'Chips, mentioned by that name in the earliest Colonial correspond-ence, was just a short walk from the waterfront and seems a most likely hillside location for Sir Humphrey, a showman at heart, to have paraded his men and his musicians and performed his ceremonial duties.

Wherever the site, the act of taking possession was brief and to the point. It began with a ceremony of homage which took place in a tent erected on the hillside. Hayes tells us: " . . . he took possession of the said lande in the right of the Crown of England by digging up a turfe and receiving the same with a hazell wand delivered unto him after the manner and the lawe and customs of England." Gilbert then emerged from the tent and, amidst a flutter of flags and a blare of music, ordained and established three laws: (1) Public worship was to be according to the Church of England. (2) Any attempt prejudicial to Her Majesty's right and possession of the territory was to be punished as in a case of high treason (hanging, drawing, and quartering). (3) Anyone uttering words of dishonour to Her Majesty should "loose his eares and have his ship and goods confiscate."

How the Catholic subjects of Spain, France, and Portugal, forcibly assembled on the hillside, privately reacted to this promulgation we can only imagine. Publicly they went along with the show, probably in the hope of soon being rid of the knight adventurer. A round of entertainments occupied the next several days. Stephen Parmenius of Buda, a Hungarian poet who was possibly acting as Gilbert's secretary, wrote to Richard Hakluyt after the reading of the proclamation: " . . . At the moment we are regaling ourselves rather more cheerfully and sumptuously."[8]

All the captains were entertained on board Gilbert's ship with wine and music. They, in turn, invited their new governor to more revels on shore. This would seem to indicate that some kind of seasonal dwellings had been erected, for it is unlikely the feasting and drinking would have taken place on the beach. Another indication that there were houses of some kind in the community is the fact that Gilbert took to sleeping on shore, which almost led to the desertion of one of his shops.

William Winter of the *Delight* and William Andrews of the *Squirrel* claimed to be ailing and said they could go no further. This may have been true, as dysentery and other diseases had already claimed some of the crews. Several died on board the *Delight* while the vessel was in St. John's harbour. Gilbert put his two ailing masters, and other mariners "sicke of fluxes," on board the *Swallow* and they set sail for home with letters for Hakluyt and others. These communications are now an invaluable record of the ill-fated voyage.

In their narratives Hayes and Parmenius fail to mention flakes, stages, or human habitations, but they do speak of inhabitants. It seems unlikely these would have been Indians. Gilbert is thought by some to have had women among the people on his ships since his idea was to colonize, but there is nothing to support this presumption. When he sailed from England Sir Humphrey had the intention of colonizing farther south than Newfoundland. However, before leaving St. John's, he changed his mind and said to Hayes: " . . . I am now become a northern man altogether, and my heart is set on Newfoundland."

On Tuesday, 20 August 1583, the fleet, now reduced to three vessels, sailed from St. John's on a southward course. The first stop was intended to be Sable Island, off Nova Scotia, where they were to stock up with fresh meat because almost all their provision of pickled beef had been expended partying at St. John's. When day broke, on August 29, the master of the *Golden Hind* reported seeing cliffs ahead in the haze and rain. He signalled a warning to the Delight, but she was " . . . keeping so ill watch that they knew not the danger before they felt the same too late to recover it." Only a few survived the shipwreck including the master, Richard Clarke. Maurice Browne and Stephen Parmenius were numbered with the lost.

Gilbert had no choice but to sort out the men and provisions that were left and return to England. A man of foodhardy obstinacy, the headstrong leader insisted, against the better judgement of others, on staying aboard the tiny *Squirrel*, instead of the more seaworthy *Golden Hind*. Off Cape Race he came on board the larger ship to have a wound dressed in his foot that had been caused by a rusty nail. On another fair day, so Hayes tells us, the general came on board again "to make merry together with the captain, master and company, and continued there from morning until evening." It is also reported that the loss of some charts and mineral samples caused him to "beat his boy in a great rage."

Monday, September 9, was a rough day at sea. Hayes wrote:

" . . . In the afternoon the frigate was neere cast away, oppressed by waves, yet at that time recovered; and giving forth signs of joy, the General sitting abaft with a book in his hands, cried out unto us in the *Hind* (so oft as we did approach within hearing), we are as neere to heaven by sea as by land. Reiterating the same speech, well beseeming a souldier, resolute in Jesus Christ, I can testify he was . . . ."

Hayes goes on: "That same Monday night, about twelve of the clocke, or not long after, the Frigat being ahead of us in the *Golden Hind*, suddenly her lights went out, whereof it were in a moment, we lost the sight, and withall our watch cried, 'The Generall was cast away', which was too true. For in that moment, the Frigat was devoured and swallowed up of the sea." The Newfoundland historian, Archbishop Howley, found charity a most elusive virtue in writing of Sir Humphrey Gilbert. His Irish blood could not forgive the general his savage repressions in Ireland. Instead of mourning "a souldier, resolute in Jesus Christ," it was Howley's claim that "By a merciful dispensation of Divine Providence this unscrupulous ruffian" was removed from further brutal depredations.

Archibishop Howley was not alone in his opinion. The adventurer was a man both loved and hated by his contemporaries. In St. John's he laid the cornerstone on which the British Empire, the greatest known to history, was built. Admiral Morison, in his history of the Atlantic voyages, has called him the "Pathfinder of the English Empire . . . . Sir Humfry Gilbert pointed the way to New England and Virginia."[9]

After the drowning of his half-brother at the age of forty-eight, Sir Walter Raleigh obtained a grant of a large plantation in Newfoundland. According to the Jersey historian, A. C. Saunders, when Raleigh became governor of the Channel Island of Jersey in 1600 he induced the sailormen of Jersey to start fishing in and around St. John's, "a territory over which he was Lord."[10] Had Sir Humphrey not drowned, and Sir Walter not been executed for treason, the story of the colonization of Newfoundland might have been greatly accelerated.

In 1615 Captain Richard Whitbourne, one of the captains who had welcomed Gilbert to St. John's, wrote a discourse on Newfoundland in which he spoke so highly of the potentialities of the "Newland" that King James took all possible means to encourage his people to settle there and develop the great potential of the fisheries.

Exactly when the Colony of St. John's was established we do not know. In writing of the founding of Quebec in 1608 one account states that there were already dwellings at St. John's. There is a mention of the place, as a colony of permanent inhabitants in the Bristol archives for the year 1623. However, we know there were settlers long before that.

In 1584 Edward Hayes formed the Newfoundland Company with the intention of establishing a permanent settlement on the island. He hoped to centre his colony at St. John's but the plans do not seem to have materialized. Professor C. M. MacInnes, the noted Bristol historian and a specialist in matters pertaining to John Guy's venture at Cupids, states that "Guy chose Conception Bay as the best site for his colony, presumably to avoid the fisheries settlements round St. John's."[11]

In 1610 John Guy, an important promoter of the Newfoundland Company and an enemy of western adventurers, started the first officially sanctioned colony in North America at Cuper's Cove (now Cupids), Newfoundland. There were already colonies as far south as Virginia but these were begun by private individuals. Guy's Colony was sponsored by the Society of Merchant Venturers of Bristol. Somehow St. John's escaped the control of the Newfoundland Company and grew up wild and ungoverned.

In 1616 a man named William Payne put in a tender for the St. John's lot. That same year, Sir Percival Willoughby, a member of the Newfoundland Company, tried to obtain the lot for John Browne, a partner of his son-in-law. Some eleven years later, in the spring of 1627, Payne called it "the principall prime and chief lot in all the whole country." He tried to interest Sir William Conway in development of the settlement: "as it now standes the yce being broken and some howses allready built it will require no great change." Payne claimed the lot was providing him with much profit in fish, furs, and sarasparilla and there were great hopes of iron and silver. He owned nine of the twelve shares in the lot and, in spite of his claims for the plantation, was trying to unload six of these on Conway.[12] With this exchange of letters Payne vanishes from history.

During his stay at St. John's, in August 1583, Sir Humphrey Gilbert had made some grants of land in the community to the merchants and captains he found in the harbour. In time these may have become the traditional ships' rooms upon which settlers were forbidden to intrude. Ships' rooms were locations on shore for the curing and drying of fish. They were set apart at intervals along the shore of the harbour and preserved exclusively for the use of fishing ships. While no one dared encroach upon them they were not vested rights but a common property on which no permanent building could be erected.

The presence of these ships' rooms retarded the orderly growth of the St. John's waterfront until the end of the eighteenth century. There were nine of them located on the north slope of the harbour. From west to east these were Pye Corner (or Rotten Row), Darkuse's, Lady's, Gallows Hill, Burst-Heart Hill, Church Hill, Hudson's, Admiral's, and Isle of Chips.[13]

Pye Corner was at the foot of Prince's Street, Darkuse's was west of Steer's Cove and Waldegrave Street, Lady's was in the area of Queen Street, and Gallows Hill was at the junction of Duckworth Street and Queen's Road. Burst-Heart Hill included Beck's Cove, Bates Hill, and Carter's Hill, and the ships' room was probably in the cove. Church Hill originally ran down to the waterfront and included the area we now call Court House Steps. Hudson's ships' room is now Hunter's Cove. Admiral's extended from St. John's Lane almost to Cochrane Street, and Isle of Chips was at the foot of Hill o' Chips. In spite of official attempts to protect these locations for fishery purposes there were encroachments from time to time and the offending buildings were always ordered torn down.

In spite of obstacles and drawbacks settlement in Newfoundland was ahead of New England. It was not until 15 May 1602, that

Captain Bartholomew Goswold became the first white man on record to set foot in New England.[14] Two days later he landed at Martha's Vineyard. By 1609 St. John's was already a place of trade and commerce. That year Henry Hudson, the ill-fated navigator and explorer, called in for supplies. He did the same in 1614.[15]

It is recorded of Newfoundland that " . . . expeditions multiplied so rapidly, that in the year 1615 upwards of two hundred and fifty English vessels, carrying altogether more than 15,000 tons, were employed on the coasts. Fixed habitations were formed which gradually extended on the eastern side from St. John's and Thorne Bay [Torbay] to Cape Race."

The grant of the province of Avalon to Sir George Calvert (afterwards Lord Baltimore), 7 April 1623, mentions " . . . a little harbour weh boundeth upon ye South part of ye Plantacon of St. John's." The habitations of "ye Plantacon" were probably not actual houses but structures known as tilts. Tilt houses were common among northerners, including Scandinavians, until recent times. They were especially popular with sodbusters on the prairies. Of simple construction, they were built of logs set vertically into the ground and covered on the outside with sods. There was a door, a glassless window, and a hole in the roof, above an open-fire pit, to permit smoke to escape. Later, chimneys of fieldstone were added. The floor was of tramped earth or flat stones.

The first permanent resident of St. John's whose name is known to us was Thomas Oxford. We assume from his writing that he was born in the community. In a petition seeking redress for depredations committed against him by western adventurers in 1675-76, Oxford claimed that " . . . he and his predecessors have been possessed of houses, stages, etc. in the said Harbour of St. John's for about seventy years."[16] If this statement is factual then the Oxford family settled in St. John's around the year 1605. According to Thornton's map of 1689 their property was in the area of Adelaide Street. Thornton's map shows seven plantation owners from Magotts Cove (Hoylestown) to Riverhead. They are: Downings (Cochrane Street), Bennetts (Prescott Street), Pxons (McBride's Hill), Oxfords (Adelaide Street), Joyners (Queen Street), Denis Loneys (Waldegrave—Prince's Street) and Mrs. Furzey (Springdale Street). These locations are approximations and the plantations were probably separated from one another by ships' rooms.

William Hinton was a Stuart family hanger-on who was several years abroad in exile with Charles II. It was his claim "that he never asked the King for anything but the governorship of Newfoundland which His Majesty had promised him several times."[17] In one of his several petitions for the position, entitled "Reasons for the Settlement of Newfoundland," Hinton wrote about the year 1670: " ... The inhabitants of St. John's build houses and make gardens and orchards in places fitt for cureing and drying fish, which is a great hinderance and not to be suffered."

He was siding with the west country merchants who were determined to uproot the colonists. These men set about to malign the country and accused the peaceable settlers of crimes that were more often their own. They claimed in a petition to the British government that the inhabitants debauched the fishermen with rum and bad women, and said: " ... The country is not the least improveable whereby to give subsistance to ye inhabitants, it being nothing but woods, boggs and rockes."

In 1675 they succeeded in having Sir John Berry sent out from England to remove the settlers from Newfoundland. Berry's mission delighted the west country merchants who would then have no competition in the fishery from permanent inhabitants of the island. However, on his arrival Sir John was converted to the cause of the colonists by such men as Thomas Oxford and John Downing. He decided to support the rights of the settlers to stay in Newfoundland and ordered the first census of the island to show the extent of permanent settlement.

The census of 1675 reveals that St. John's had a population of 185 persons (300 years later its metropolitan population was over 150,000). The community consisted of 48 boats, 23 stages, and 155 head of cattle, with some sheep. The most affluent citizen was John Downing, a man whose role in Newfoundland history has been greatly underrated. He owned two houses, probably one at the foot of Cochrane Street and another in Quidi Vidi, where his considerable fishing premises were located. Downing also had a farm in the area of Virginia Water. He employed 25 men and owned 5 boats and 2 stages. The census tells us Thomas Oxford was married, with 3 sons and 4 daughters, 4 boats, 1 stage, a bunkhouse for his fishermen, 2 gardens, a cod-oil vat, and 2 flakes. He employed 13 men and 2 women.

Next in importance came Denis Loney and Mrs. Ffuze (Furzey). They each owned 4 boats and 2 stages. Loney employed 16 men, and Mrs. Ffuze, a widow, employed 18 men. Bennett possessed 3 boats, 1 stage, and employed 15 men. Richard Hoppingly, who seems to have taken over the Joyner property, employed 4 men. Andrew Exon (Pxon) appears to have been more interested in farming than fishing. He owned 1 boat, 1 stage, 1 vat, 1 flake, 3 gardens, and 15 pigs. Exon also had a wife, 3 daughters, 4 male servants and a female servant.

Another census was taken in 1677. This one shows a total population of 249 which included 24 property owners, 15 wives, 17 sons, 25 daughters, 159 male servants, and 9 female servants. There were 27 dwellings, 45 stages, 29 boats and 8 horses. Richard Horton of Horton's Plantation was added to the list of major property owners which still included Downing, Oxford, Hoppingly and Exon.

Two years earlier, in 1675, John Downing, Thomas Oxford, and several others took ship to England to fight the deportation orders given Sir John Berry. Their battle took two years against strong opposition. In 1677 they returned to St. John's with word that planters and settlers would be able to keep their plantations and houses until further notice. The major contributor to this victory was John Downing. By then cleared land, permanent houses, well-kept kitchen gardens, and ornamental trees were a part of the growing town. The triumph of Downing and his associates over the rapacious greed of the west country merchants assured the community of survival. By 1677 there were 523 settlers living in 28 communities scattered about the island of Newfoundland.

The tilt dwelling eventually gave way to the small stone cottage which was, in turn, replaced by the bow house, and finally by the single, and two-storey, saltbox house. This is a style of residence peculiar to Newfoundland, Nova Scotia, and New England. The true saltbox was a two-storey structure in front with a gable roof that sloped down to a single storey at the back. Very few of these old houses still exist in St. John's but they are fairly common in many outports. The craft of the stonemason died out in Newfoundland because settlement was barely tolerated. There were almost no legal grants to property, and a building could be burned or pulled down at the whim of a governor or military official. Building a substantial dwelling in stone was an expensive and risky venture. A wooden house was less costly and could be more easily replaced. It was also found to be warmer in winter, especially during the period when indoor chimneys were forbidden by law. Local timber was used in the construction of these houses but much was also imported from the American colonies. Downing wrote in his *Brief Narrative of 1676* that the practice of rinding trees was not done by the inhabitants, whose "stages and houses are covered with New England and the country's boards."[18]

The sacrosanct ships' rooms prevented the development of streets so that St. John's grew in a most disorderly manner with houses scattered all over the hillside. A resistance to civic neatness and planning is still apparent in most of the outports of Newfoundland where houses are erected facing in any and every direction on a crazy-quilt pattern of lanes and fields.

By 1681 St. John's had 27 property holders, including 17 wives, 32 children, and 2 widows. There were 221 servants and 49 boats. The leading employer was William Serjeant who had 4 boats and 20 servants. After him came John Juitt, on the Holdsworth property, with 15 servants. Philip Bard was the only one listed as a merchant and old John Downing was still around. The population totalled 299 persons.

A trade was growing with Ireland. Many of the vessels brought out immigrants from the Emerald Isle seeking a better life, free of the oppression in their tragic homeland. British ships frequently called in at Irish ports on their way to Newfoundland. For example, in 1690 the merchants requested the Newfoundland convoy to call at Cork, for forty-eight hours, to take in a supply of provisions, manufactures, and youngsters—young men in their late teens or early twenties who were employed at the Newfoundland fishery for a summer, a winter, and a summer before being sent back home. This was called a Newfoundland season.

Capt. Jos. Crowe, commander-in-chief of Her Majesty's ships in Newfoundland, in 1711 sent a report to the Lords of Trade, in which he said that the people living in St. John's had no benefit from deer, beaver, martin, fox, etc., because of "these beasts retiring to the woods frightened by the great number of people that resort there more than to other places."[19] He added that a great many encroachments were daily made upon beaches, stages and ships' rooms by planters who built dwelling houses there. He ordered the planters dispossessed according to the intent of the Act of Parliament of 1675.

Crowe, who brought a Church of England minister with him, found the church in disrepair and Sunday a time of much merriment. He says: "Before my arrival the Lord's Day was nothing at all regarded neither by the inhabitants nor the common sailors who spent it generally in houses of entertainment in drinking and swearing and the most disorderly actions, living without sense of religion, and profaning the day to that degree that a stranger could never believe they had heard of Christianity nor indeed of God, except by the oaths, curses, blasphemous expressions and horrid imprecations."

He commented on the diet of the townspeople: "They feed their men in the summer season mostly with fresh cod, with some salt pork and a little beef and brisket. They catch all their cod with hooks and line, but some of them with baits and nets, and other with hooks by bobbing."

In an attempt to remedy the disorderliness of the town he gave orders "for suppressing drunkenness, cursing and swearing with fines and punishment...." He tried to make the place safe for body as well as soul by demanding that a group of "seamen and others should keep guard in the night and patroul along the back sides of the harbour of St. John's to prevent the mischiefs frequently committed by the spyes of the enemy and others upon the inhabitants." This might be called the first attempt at forming a local police force.

Crowe ordered "That the houses in Fort William of St. John's are not to be sold or let for hire but in case the person that built it or otherwise purchased the same for some time past does not inhabitant therein themselves, the said houses are at the disposal of Governor Collins to put therein such persons as are destitute of habitation in the said fort." Five men from each ship in the harbour were to go into the woods to cut stockades and palisades to repair the works of the fort. A 1709 map shows nine gardens of inhabitants within the fort area.

The houses of the town did not impress Christopher Lilly. In 1715 he noted: "The habitations which (except about half a dozen) are but little value, no better than such huts as us'd to be built in the army during winter campaigns." At the time Lilly wrote, St. John's had already been burned several times by French invaders.

With the advent of peace between France and England the place began to grow. There were 42 private houses and 16 taverns by 1735. Three years later the number of dwellings reached 82, and 94 acres of land were under cultivation. By 1751 more than 40 acres were cultivated and the number of houses was placed at 158. The 1764 census reveals that the town contained 125 acres of cultivated land and 226 dwellings.

In 1762 the governor, Admiral Graves, had written the Board of Trade in London to complain of the inconveniences of the port of St. John's. He commented on the benefits to commerce likely to result from fortifying Ferryland Head.

Four years later, in 1766, Sir Joseph Banks came to St. John's and his journal contains some valuable impressions of the community. He wrote:

> It is very difficult to compare one town with another tho that probably is the Best way of Conveying the Idea. St. John's, however, Cannot be Compared with any I have seen. It is Built upon the side of a hill facing the Harbour, Containing two or three hundred houses and near as many fish Flakes interspersed which, in summer time, must Cause a stench scarce to be supported. Thank heaven we are only there spring and fall, before the fish were come to the Ground and after they were all gone off. For dirt and filth of all Kinds St. John's may, in my opinion, Reign unrivalled as it Far Exceeds any Fishing town I ever saw in England. Here is no regular Street, the houses being built in rows immediately adjoining to the Flakes, Consequently no Pavement. Offals of Fish of all Kinds are strewed about The remains of the Irish men's chowder who you seek making it and skinning and gutting fish in Every Corner. As Everything here smells of fish You cannot get anything that does not Taste of it . . . ."

In a flight of literary fancy he has the hogs, poultry, game, and even the cows' milk tasting of fish.

Sir Joseph confided: "St. John's, tho the most disagreeable town I ever met with, was for some time perfectly agreeable to us." He admitted that in June "the weather was as hot or hotter than Ever I knew it in England." His desire to procure a Newfoundland dog was frustrated. "Those I met with were mostly Curs with a Cross of the Mastiff in them."

In a note on a piece of paper, which he pasted on the fly leaf of his Journal, Banks adds:

> St. John's Contains about 300 houses. In winter 1765-66 its inhabitants were 1,100 viz., 750 men, 350 women & children. In some Years the number of returning fishermen have increased the number of inhabitants of this place only, to the number of 10,000. The number of Irish in this Place are recorded in winter to double the number of English .... In the year 1762 when the French took this Place 700 Irish immediately entered into their service. The number of winterers in the whole island are recorded at 10,000. The Harbour here is remarkably fine Capable of Containing 200 Sail of Vessels. Secure from every wind that can blow.

The summer population of St. John's in 1766 was nearly half the entire population of Tennessee, almost twice that of Illinois, and three times that of Michigan. It made it one of the largest towns on the continent. In winter the story was entirely different.

The last quarter of the eighteenth century, following the final settlement of French claims in North America, brought shiploads of emigrants to the shores of the island. It was in this period that the trade links were forged between St. John's and Waterford, Ireland.

Thomas Covey, writing in 1770, says of Waterford that it was the third port of trade in the kingdom at that time. He adds that the merchants were "also fair traders and as such a set of most useful men to the welfare of society. There are more ships sent from this port to Newfoundland yearly than are sent from all ports in the Kingdom." Most of these vessels docked at St. John's and almost all brought out settlers, in addition to porter, coarse linen, other provisions, and "cheese called mullahawn."[20]

The laws of 27 January 1676, forbidding immigration and ordering ship's captains not to carry settlers to Newfoundland, were ignored. In 1701 Capt. Arthur Holdsworth had been accused of bringing out 236 passengers. No particular punishment seems to have been meted out to him or to the other captains who continued to violate the law. Even Governor Dorril's burning of Irishmen's houses in 1775 and his orders that they be expelled and forcibly returned to Ireland did not stem the tide. The edict was unworkable and his successor abandoned the plan in favour of trying to regularize life in the colony.

The archives of the Phoenix Fire Office, London, contain a letter from one Theophilus Pritzler, dated 18 May 1785. It reads: "Some time since a Friend of mine was in Town who trades to Newfoundland . . . he mentioned there were a great number of new buildings at Saint Johns but which were built in such a manner that he thought they would communicate in case of fire and there was a probability of the whole town being destroyed in one fire." Pritzler's letter shows us that it was in the 1780s that the place began to grow and take on the appearance of a town with "a great number of new buildings" going up.

In 1798 *The Times* of London gave its readers the following description of the community:

> The town of St. John [sic] is situate on the west side of the harbour. The houses are irregular and scattered. In the fishing season, which begins in May, and ends in September, there are perhaps 5,000 people there; but many of them return to England annually with the ships, which in time of war rendezvous here to meet the convoy. In the harbour there are some very convenient wharves or keys, which large vessels may lie alongside of to take in their cargoes, few of the ships in this trade exceeding 300 tons burthen. The houses are built of wood, and covered with shingles; should a fire happen, the consequences must be dreadful. The adjacent country admits of very little cultivation, on account of the summer being short and the winter very severe; indeed, there is very little open ground, for the country is covered with woods, which are impenetrable, except by beaten paths. The plain land is usually used for pasture, though some little grain is produced; but the crops are generally very thin.[21]

We gather from this that Newfoundland housing had changed considerably since 1663 when the Plymouth surgeon, James Yonge, observed: "The houses are made of a frythe of boughs, sealed inside with rinds, which look like planed deal, and covered with the same, and turfs of earth upon, to keep the sun from raning them."[22] A "frythe of boughs" refers to a hedge of boughs and a deal is a slice about 6' x 9" x 3" sawn from a log. Between 1663 and 1697 these sod tilts were replaced by shingle or clapboard houses.

By 1796 the population of St. John's had reached 3,742: 670 men, 514 women, 732 boys, 642 girls, 572 male servants, 136 female servants, and 475 dieters (seasonal workers). Of the total population, 1,430 were Protestant and 2,312 were Roman Catholic. There were a number of trades to serve the people's needs, such as shoemakers, watchmakers, tinkers, hairdressers, auctioneers, tailors, coopers, blacksmiths, and three schoolmasters. There was even a gardener, Daniel Condon. In 1798 Governor Waldegrave warned the sheriff, on pain of his instant removal from office: "You will take good care that Jeremiah Marroty and John Fitzgerald do not erect chimneys to their sheds, or even light fires in them of any kind." The sheds were likely their homes.

If life seemed hard in the colony it was probably better than life back home where "manners were rigid and morals lax." The ordinary Londoner lived in "stews of filth and wretchedness." Crime was commonplace and the only consolation of the poor was in drink. The motto of the grog shops was "Drunk for a penny. Dead drunk for tuppence. Free straw." Men, women, and even children were burned for theft in England until 1794 when the law was repealed. Corpses dangled from gibbets, and the lash and pillory were commonplace. The lust for blood was also satisfied by bull-baiting, cock-fighting, and bare-knuckle boxing. Violence and disease were a way of life amongst a "starving rabble herded into crowded tenements amidst the squalor and stench of filth and disease."[23]

As late as 1844 weavers in the north of England were at work fourteen to sixteen hours a day, six days a week, for eight or nine shillings. In the mines, nude children, regardless of sex, were chained to ore carts and never saw the light of day. They laboured on their hands and knees in a hell of water, cold, rats, and darkness. Naked chimney sweeps were prodded up chimneys. If they hesitated, a fire was burned in the grate to force them up the flues where some roasted to death or were suffocated. These boys and girls from orphanages and poor houses were sold into a seven-year apprenticeship for as little as thirty shillings.[24] In an age of such unspeakable brutalities at home it is small wonder that many preferred to take their chances in St. John's and the other communities of the North American colonies.

By the year 1807 the population of the town had reached 5,057. That same season saw 670 immigrants land in the harbour, five-sixths of whom came from Ireland. Charles Fox Bennett, who became Prime Minister in 1870, recalled St. John's as he first saw it in 1806:

> At that time the town . . . was little more than a fishing settlement. The whole area was nearly covered with flakes on which to dry fish . . . . Water Street was so narrow in some places that a cart could barely pass . . . . All the ground westerly of [Springdale Street] was covered with flakes as far as Radford's [Bambrick Street] . . . and west of that the country was covered with alder bush and scrub to the point where the two roads [Crossroads] take their departure, one for Topsail and the other for Bay Bulls . . . beyond this was the forest with good

size timber growing thereon. In like manner the Southside Hill was covered with timber down to the entrance of the Narrows, as was Signal Hill and the ground lying between Quidi Vidi Lake and Signal Hill. Duckworth Street was little better than a path running under the flakes and not extending beyond Holdsworth Street, being there intersected by a very wet marsh. The houses, if they could be called such, were, with very few exceptions, of a temporary character. Their height was limited to about seven or eight feet between the ground floor and the roof floor. There were some moderately spacious stores built over the water. The exceptionally good houses were within the two garrisons.[25]

In 1811 an Act of the British Parliament empowered the granting of private property in Newfoundland, including ships' rooms, which had become a nuisance to the governors. By this Act a kind of legal settlement was at last tolerated. The growth of the colony had been retarded for more than a century and a half beyond that of the rest of British North America.

Governor Sir John Duckworth granted tenure to many who sought land titles, and with property came the right to build substantial dwellings without fear of loss. The abolition of the ships' rooms meant that Water Street could develop as a mercantile area, and shops began to spring up from King's Beach west to Springdale Street. A downtown started to emerge as the population rose to ten thousand people.

In 1811 the merchants wrote to the king: "We beg leave to state to your Royal Highness that the town of St. John's, with the exception of one house, is built of wood; that the principal street is, in one place not more than six feet wide, that all our streets are narrow, unpaved, and unlighted."

That year Governor Duckworth had the ships' rooms divided into a number of lots which were put up on public auction, on leases of thirty years, renewable at expiration upon payment of a sum equal to three years' rent, if built on with timber, or one year's rent if built on with stone or brick. Party walls between adjoining lots were to be built of brick or stone, of twenty inches thick, and to stand equally on each lot. Downtown buildings were to be two storeys high or not less than eighteen feet from wall-plate to sill. No encroachments were to be made on the streets by bow windows, porches, or other erections. Proper drains were to be provided by the lessees, and on the Admiral's Ships' Room (King's Beach) a common sewer was to be made at the joint expense of the lot holders.

The historian, Anspach, writing soon afterwards, says these improvements would most effectually contribute to introduce cleanliness, salubrity, and even elegance into a town hitherto remarkable for a confined and unwholesome atmosphere, where the slightest contagion assumed at once the character of the most inveterate and obstinate pestilence; and where the habitations, made of timber, without any order, regularity, or regard to the public safety, conveyed to the mind the idea of universal and unavoidable destruction in the event of fire.[26]

Miss Isabella Durnford, who came to St. John's in 1809 with her father, kept a journal of her impressions of the town.

Unfortunately the present whereabouts of this document are unknown, and only some passages have been quoted. She remarked of the Southside Hills: "The heights overlooking the entrance to St. John's are covered almost from waterline to summit with fir and spruce and planted with [gun] batteries romantically situated." To assist in keeping up the morale of the troops during the severe winter of 1812, Miss Durnford says, a mock battle was fought on the ice-covered surface of Quidi Vidi Lake. She also notes that the game of hurley was encouraged whenever the harbour was frozen or otherwise ice-bound.

The Durnfords had a piano in their quarters which was tuned for them by Sir William Parker, a Lieutenant attached to the flagship of the admiral. Another who took part in their musicales was the purser on a frigate in St. John's, a brother of Sir Henry Bishop, the celebrated English composer. His opera *Clari; or The Maid of Milan*, includes the air "Home Sweet Home."

Lt. Edward Chappell, in *Voyage of H.M.S.* Rosamund *to Newfoundland*, a pompous and supercilious work, published in 1818, said the capital of 1813 consisted of one very narrow street with very few handsome or even good-looking edifices. He said that Water Street stood

upon very irregular ground, and is not paved. . . . There are a great number of small public houses, but scarcely one tolerable inn; the London Tavern, however, has a good billiard room attached to it. Shops of all descriptions are very numerous, but most commodities are extravagantly dear. . . . The number of wharves for lading ships is remarkable. . . . [It was Chappell's opinion that] the State of Society in St. John's is such as might be expected in a place where the majority of the principal inhabitants have risen from the lowest fishermen. The vulgar arrogance of these upstarts is sometimes both ludicrous and offensive. Literature and polished manners are here unknown; and a stranger must not be surprised to observe a constant violation of the most ordinary rules of speech.

The Lieutenant said that the president of the Committee of Merchants (Major Macbraire) was an Irishman of low origin. Of the fires which took place following his visit in 1813, he commented: " . . . if there be the least taste displayed in rebuilding, the Capital of Newfoundland cannot fail to be greatly improved by the catastrophe." Sir Richard Keats, who also arrived on the *Rosamund*, as governor, had a different opinion. He found the town attractive and promising; Keats wrote: "St. John's seemed to have grown out of its original situation and changed its character from a fishery to a large commercial town."

A census of St. John's taken in the summer of 1815 shows that there were 10,018 people living in the community. That summer no less than 11,000 Irishmen came to St. John's, but in the fall many of them went to Prince Edward Island or the United States. It was not a good year for business. Some forty merchant houses, big and small, had to declare insolvency.

Gaslight, and even kerosene oil lamps, were in the future. At night, light was provided the poor by cod-oil lamps, and the well-to-do by candles. Most people dipped their own candles. There were no friction matches, and many persons kept live coals in a heap of ashes under an upturned pot overnight. There were no stoves. The merchants had Dutch ovens, and the fishermen open fireplaces with pothooks. Only the wealthy used coal. Wood for winter fuel was cut along Forest Road, so named for the fact that it was once well wooded with fir and birch from King's Bridge Road to Quidi Vidi. North of Gower Street there was little but marshland. Military Road was still a footpath across the marsh, linking Fort William and Fort Townshend. In 1818 Governor Hamilton aided settlement of the higher levels by granting his gardener, Thomas Cooke, a tract of land at the head of Long's Hill, and south of Freshwater Road, that became known as Cookstown.

At the time of the famine conditions and disastrous fires of 1817-18, it was suggested that as many as 2,400 individuals should be removed from the community of St. John's, but nobody knew quite where to send them.

When Governor Cochrane arrived in 1824 he erected a substantial Government House and also acquired a country residence at Virginia Water. The merchants and the well-to-do soon followed his example and both town and country houses began to flourish.

However, as late as 1829 the Chief Justice was able to complain that he found only two houses suitable and available for his residence. They were Government House and the Commissariat Office, a building on King's Bridge Road, restored in 1973 by the federal government. The Chief Justice complained bitterly:

> . . . the Buildings in St. John's must be of a very poor description. The fact is that it hardly contains any houses affording

those advantages which the severity of the climate calls for: and the few which approach nearest to this Character are in the hands of individuals who require them for their own use. An officer of the government, therefore, must, unless he is furnished with Quarters by the Public or can erect them for himself, be worse lodged in this colony than perhaps he would be in any other portion of the British Empire.

Although Governor Duckworth had leased a number of ships' rooms in 1811 it was not until 1824 that the right to hold property in Newfoundland was given full legal acknowledgement. Even at that late date there were those who vociferously opposed settlement in the island and fought to discourage it.

A memorandum of government transmitted to the House of Assembly on 10 January 1833 gives a very good pen picture of conditions in St. John's before the fire of 1846.

A very dense population for the extent of the town is collected within it—the houses generally are of a very wretched description and filthy in the extreme—and while a succession of fires has led to a widening of the principal streets, many are too confined. . . . The streets are generally extremely dirty, which is partly caused by there being no means of carrying off the filth by proper conduits. They are very improperly undermined by numerous cellars. . . . In the spring of the year many parts of the town are scarcely habitable in consequence of the effluvia from seal oil vats—the public coves are a receptacle for every sort of nuisance.

In spite of the horrors indicated by the memorandum, the Presentation Sisters, who arrived from Galway in 1833, seemed to like the place. On September 22 Sister Mary Xaverius Lynch wrote home:

We are agreeably surprised at the appearance of the country which we heard so terrific an account of. The view of the harbour and surrounding country from the Bishop's House [Henry Street] is most picturesque and beautiful on whatever side you turn and appears to be in a perfect state of cultivation. The harbour is covered with vessels and small boats which has a beautiful appearance. All around there is to be seen hills and mountains, perfectly green, interspersed with houses, green fields and small gardens. At the foot of these hills, at the very edge of the water there are houses and gardens and as far as the eye can carry you on the tops of these hills and mountains there are houses and cows and trees and the water underneath gives the whole a most romantic and beautiful appearance. In fact you would never be tired with the scenery. We are delighted with it and every day we discover fresh beauties. . . . The town appears to be very large and there are great valleys.[27]

The only fault the sisters found with St. John's was the severe cold. In January 1834 Sister Xaverius wrote:

> The sky is beautiful and clear and while the frost is most intense and ready to freeze your limbs off you are cheered by the most beautiful atmosphere. . . . The people here make use of the most curious things for walking according to the weather. In snow they wear a kind of thing called Moggissons. They are made either like shoes or boots made of wood. They are worn over their shoes. In frosty weather they wear a kind of thing called creepers. . . . The gentlemen use long poles higher than themselves to keep themselves from falling. . . . Bone setters are in great demand. . . . Everything is very dear in this country. As to cream and butter they are a luxury and eggs are 6/—a dozen, fresh meat is the greatest rarity in winter, a turkey 30/—and fowl a great treat. . . . This puts me in mind of giving you a description of the houses here. They are all built of wood the roofs not slate but covered with wood and built in such a manner that they can be moved from one place to another being built up from the ground and on wheels. It is not unusual here when one does not like the situation of their house to move it to another place.[28]

The building of houses on stilts appears to have been an enduring tradition. In 1711 Capt. Jos. Crowe mentions Capt. Arthur Holdsworth's house as "standing upon stakes and shores." Until recent years most outport houses were built in this manner with a front door suspended as much as eight or ten feet above a garden. These doors had no steps leading from them and there were no verandahs.

Sister Mary Magdelene, writing 24 November 1833, says of the children of St. John's:

> . . . they improve upon acquaintance, are very docile and most anxious to come to school. . . . They are fond of dress-wear, necklaces, ear-rings, rings, etc. so that from their appearance you would scarcely think you are teaching in a poor school. No such thing as a barefoot child to be seen here, how great a contrast between them and the poor Irish! . . . The town is beautifully situated on the side of a hill: you cannot conceive anything more romantic, the houses built (you would think at a distance) over each other, for the foundation of one will be just on the level with the top of another. . . . They have vehicles particularly suited for this season called sleighs or trolleys. They are very low, drawn by horses and sometimes by dogs (which are as useful as horses in this country) but they must

have bells fastened to their necks otherwise they might be lost in the snow.[29]

The next view of the town comes from Hon. Thomas Talbot, a famous educator, who taught at St. Bonaventure's College when it first opened. He describes St. John's in the late spring of 1837.

> The houses presented a rough . . . sombre aspect thrown together in irregular clusters without order or arrangement of any kind . . . fish flakes or stages ranged along either side of the harbour or port. There were some good shops or stores in the line of street along the water's edge, and some few detached private residences . . . and very nasty, ugly paths too, with poor, dirty, miserable houses lining them on either side. The houses were all wooden—I cannot remember one that was of stone or brick except the Government House.[30]

The historian, Rev. Philip Tocque, says: "Since 1839 St. John's has been called a city, owing to a Protestant Bishop being at that time appointed. . . . " Some three years later, in 1842, Sir Richard Bonnycastle saw the place as being full of very narrow streets and some superior shops. Queen Street, he said, had good stone houses on one side and was improving. Cochrane Street was

> laid out wide, but not yet much built upon. Duckworth Street, the next great parallel to Water Street, is also improving . . . by the addition of stone and brick houses; but altogether, St. John's has not yet arrived at much architectural embellishment, and it will be many years before the thickly crowded little wooden tenements will give way to a better and safer class of buildings, owing to the expense of importing cut stone, brick and lime.

Sir Richard found the Public Hospital "very prettily situated near the river head . . . ," but St. John's Church was a "large dilapidated wooden building." The Roman Catholic chapel was in the same condition but was "now being replaced by a very fine stone cathedral, which, when finished, will rival or surpass that of Montreal." The architectural disasters over which Bonnycastle and others grieved were all wiped out in the Great Fire of 1846, and a new town, looking almost identical to present-day Waterford or Wexford, in Ireland, rose out of the ashes. Even before the fire, improvements seem to have been taking place. On 1 September 1845 the *Morning Courier* reported to its readers:

> Go where you may in the most public part of the city and the carpenter's handiwork strikes the eye. No convenient place that admits of the foundation of a house is now unoccupied.

The ground is becoming very valuable and the rents are very high so that those who build on their own land, or those who build on rented land, are equally the gainers. If this state of things is to continue ... who that left here some 40 years ago will know the city in its manhood? 'Twas then little more than a straggling village covered from the water's margin to the centre of the city with insignificant dwellings and flakes. Then we had no public buildings. Now we have public buildings of various kinds.

Many new streets were laid out in the 1850s. These included Darling (now Bond Street), Victoria, Cathedral, and Chapel Streets. In 1859 Bannerman Street and Colonial Street were finished. Bishop Mullock and others petitioned the House in 1866 for a sum of money to complete LeMarchant Road, which then turned down what is now Patrick Street, as far as the Hamilton Avenue intersection. Freshwater Valley was opened up in 1873, when a road was constructed along the sides of Mount Ken to Topsail Road. A report at the time said of this road: "It will be most useful to the people of Freshwater as well as to the inhabitants of St. John's generally. It will shorten the distance to Topsail considerably and will make a most beautiful summer drive. Besides it will open up a fine tract of agricultural country." That fine tract is now an industrial park and the summer drive is the Kenmount Road section of the Trans-Canada Highway.

By 1873 Water Street was in serious need of rebuilding. It had not been levelled and in many places the road was higher than the wooden sidewalks. Extensive repairs followed Inspector Dennis O'Brine's statement that "The great and increasing traffic to which the street is subjected necessitates the use of material of a more durable kind than any gravel; and this being the main artery of the metropolis, too much cannot be done to make it in good travelling condition."

The previous year, 1872, David Kennedy, Jr., a passing stranger, had written his impressions of St. John's, while awaiting the Allan boat. The city then had a population of 23,000. Kennedy calls it

A queer place ... full of heights and hollows, corners and angles, and not so substantial in its buildings. [He said it was composed of by-streets and lanes] and a nebulous collection of wooden huts perched higgledy-piggledy upon the stony braes. The better class of houses are of brick, some faced with plaster, too many with an old, unwashed appearance. If the folk used whitewash or paint upon their houses it would wonderfully brighten up the town. The larger shops are very respectable and do a deal of quiet business, St. John's being the emporium for the whole island.

You will see one shop ornamented with the sign of a white polar-bear, another with a big black seal, here a dog over a door, there a golden codfish. One noticeable thing is the startling frequency of drinking-shops. Every second store seems to be "Licensed to sell Ale, Wine and Spiritous Liquors".

Through the streets drive little fish carts drawn by diminutive, shaggy horses. Burly, red-whiskered men in blue guernseys walk along trailing heavy cod in their hands. A knot of bulky, black dogs are snarling over some fish refuse. There are scores of dogs. You see them prowling about the streets, romping with the children or sunning themselves in the doorways. No matter where you go you are always knocking against some bass-voiced dog or other. Everybody owns one.
...

You walk on rough cobble pavements, and climb steep, foul by-ways, with rocks cropping up in the middle of them. You see rickety houses all out of the straight, shored up with long poles. . . . You come upon long rows of squalid dwellings, the narrow doors cut in half, with only the lower leaf shut.

No matter how decayed or wretched the house, it possesses a little shop for the sale of confectionery and tape. Hens dance in and out behind the counter. Nets, sails, oil-tuns and anchor-chains lie on all hands. Long legged pigs, goats and scraggy cows dispute supremacy with bare-legged, bareheaded children who play at "ringba-jing" and other games in the middle of the street. Down at the shore the fishermen are drying and mending their nets, and at wooden stands erected on the wharves people are buying cod, salmon and halibut.[31]

Kennedy's St. John's, like the dancing hens, is a one-sided exaggeration of the truth. Some twenty years later Tocque described the street life of the town as "a picturesque and striking scene. . . . " In speaking of its frequent devastation by fire, the clergyman says that "like the Phoenix, it always rises better, brighter and more triumphant from its ashes." He noted it was "build on a succession of hills rising from the waterside, and much like the hilly part of the upper town of Quebec."[32]

The harbour shrank considerably over the years. The north shore was pushed out nearly a hundred yards into the water. Captain Robinson, a former harbour master, reported in 1883:

It is not only probably, but a matter of history, that Water Street has attained its present breadth by encroaching on the harbour; the filling in process took place after every conflagration, the object was exceedingly reasonable; an attempt to get as far away from other houses as possible. And it must be remembered that the North Side of the Street was very steep. . . . Consequently the debris of the blasting of the North Side of the street has been used as filling, this can be plainly seen under the wharves of several mercantile premises, and the Queen's Wharf in particular.

In spite of the disparaging remarks of such transients as Lieutenant Chappell, Sir Richard Bonnycastle, and David Kennedy, there were some handsome buildings in and around St. John's. Many of these old homes, erected during the first thirty years of the last century, are still standing. They include "Winterton," the house of Chief Justice Furlong, 8 Winter Avenue; 42-44 Power's Court behind St. Joseph's Convent, off Signal Hill Road; the Newfoundland and Labrador Press Club Building, 1 Springdale Street; 14 Kenna's Hill; and the stone house below it which was built by Hon. Patrick Keough; and the commissariat building, behind St. Thomas's Church, on King's Bridge Road. As mentioned before, this house is now being restored. It was probably begun in 1818 and finished in 1819.

The houses of Victorian St. John's sported latticed verandahs, curling eaves, and gothic windows. The interiors glowed with the darkness of polished mahogany. Many of the furniture pieces were decorated with turrets, minarets and flying buttresses. Mahogany was in railings, chairs, tables, sideboards, beds, dressers, and chests. Buttoned and dimpled, black horsehair sofas stood against sombre velvet window drapes that trailed heavily on the floor. Flock wallpapers of garish floral designs or monstrosities in moiré silk were all the rage.

These homes could not be maintained were it not for an army of housemaids who yearly made their way to the city from the outports. To go into "service" in St. John's was the dream of many a fisherman's daughter. Most went in service at the age of fifteen or sixteen years. Within a year they were almost unrecognizable having been deloused with a fine-tooth comb, given a permanent wave, and fitted with false teeth and eyeglasses. Some of these outport maids married well and became society matrons as their husbands rose to positions of influence and wealth.

Those who had to remain in service faced a day of backbreaking tasks. They cleaned, dusted, scrubbed, washed, ironed, polished silver, cleared grates, and set the fires. They carried in kindling, coal and birch junks, lugged hot water up to the bathrooms and slops down the numerous stairs, washed out chamber pots, filled kerosene lamps, washed lamp chimneys, prepared and served three full meals a day, and then tumbled into bed, under the low roof of an attic. A very good salary for a housemaid in Victorian times was ten dollars a month.

If the housing conditions of the poorer classes in St. John's left much to be desired, they were not unique. In 1885 there were fourteen thousand families living in substandard dwellings in Edinburgh, one of the better-off cities in Britain. Mary Preston, in an article on Victorian homes of England, says that "home" was often a single room in a large tenement house, with one water tap and not a single indoor toilet. Royal commissions reported that many farm labourers' cottages

60

had only two rooms and one of these was a bedroom, six or seven feet high, where whole families slept with water seeping in from above and below.[33] The St. John's housemaid, secure in her garret bed, was frequently better off than many of her kindred in the mother country, and seat of empire.

The year of Captain Robinson's report on the harbour, 1883, the historian, Rev. Moses Harvey, presented a much more glowing description of the city than was the custom. Harvey spoke of the Narrows, the approach to the port, as

> a scene which for grandeur and sublimity is not surpassed along the entire American coast.... The city is built on the northern side of the harbour on a site which could scarcely be surpassed.... The facilities for drainage are all that could be desired ... the city presents a very picturesque appearance.... There is ample space in every direction for expansion. Already, on the summits overlooking the business parts of the city, houses of a superior description are erected; and these will ere long grow into crescents and squares, and form the fashionable quarter. Water Street, the principal business street, presents a very substantial though not handsome appearance, the houses being of stone or brick. Shops, stores, and mercantile counting-houses occupy the ground floors, while the merchants and shop keepers live in the upper stories.... Many of the shops present a very handsome appearance. In other parts of the city the houses are for the most part built of wood and many of them are dingy and commonplace. Of late years, however, taste has been developing and houses have been built of a superior description. Gradually the wooden buildings will be replaced by houses built on the best models.... In due time St. John's will be transformed into a handsome city, for the magnificent site it occupies admits of the introduction of the best improvements of modern times ... perhaps there are few towns of equal size in which so much business is transacted and money made in the course of a year.
> St. John's enjoys the immense advantage of possessing an abundant supply of the purest water ... is rarely visited with epidemics, and is one of the healthiest cities on the American side of the Atlantic.... It is a thousand miles nearer England than New York, and but sixteen hundred and forty miles from the Irish coast.

In 1892 Prometheus once more hurled destruction on the community and St. John's was burned to the ground. The rebuilt city is the one we know today. People were, are, and probably always will be, of many minds regarding this most ancient habitation of the white man in the New World. Perhaps the most apt description is that of a visitor who has called it "Dublin on the Isle of Skye."

St. John's has been sneered at and held in deep affection. It engenders hostility and love. Few who ever become involved in the life of the place remain indifferent. It has a brazen charm that overflows in the boundless hospitality for which it has become world famous. The city does not hide the scars of its centuries of neglect and hostility any more than it hides its haphazard streets quietly poked away from the rush and roar of a commercialized world. St. John's is flesh and blood, obstinate insecurity, warm humour, small, brave, untidy, and undereducated. It has survived four and one-half centuries of handicaps that have challenged its existence. Often naïve, frequently cheeky, it is among the few truly interesting cities on the North American continent.

2

A Military Animal

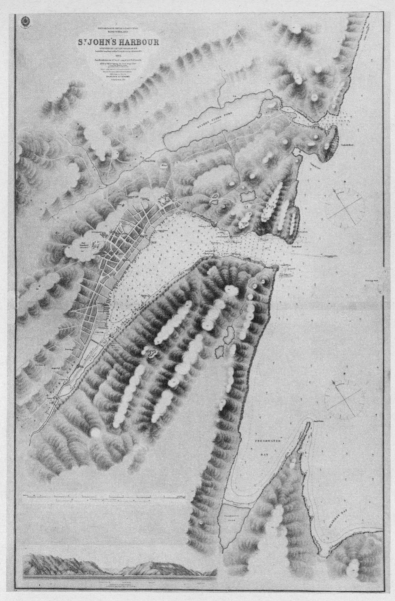

Captain Orlebar's survey map of St. John's harbour made in 1862. The map shows Fort William looking like a maple leaf and Fort Townshend on a height of land beside the Roman Catholic Cathedral. Riverhead is at the upper end of the harbour in the lower left portion of the map. (Courtesy Public Archives of Canada)

Quidi Vidi village as it looked in the late 19th century. Christ Church dates from 1842. The building to the right of the church was used as a field hospital in the Battle of Signal Hill (1762) at the end of the Seven Years War.

Approach to the harbour of St. John's. From a water colour by N. Pocock, circa 1810. (Courtesy Public Archives of Canada)

St. John's seen from outside the Narrows, 1798. Fort Townshend is in the centre of the picture with the Church of England chapel below it. (Courtesy British Museum)

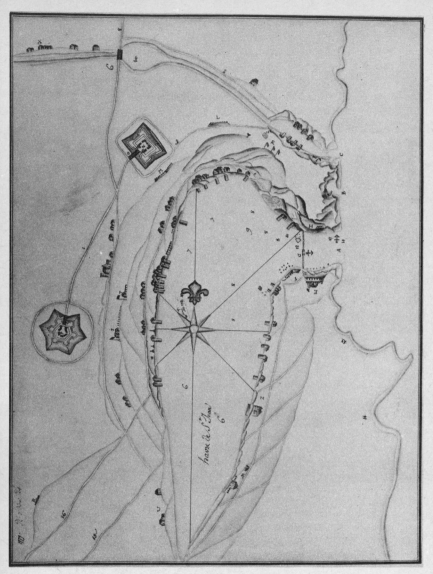

St. John's from a French map of 1779. Fort William is on the right and Fort Townshend on the left. The building flying a flag below the fort is the Church of England chapel. The courthouse, also flying a flag, is to the right of the church. The boom from Chain Rock to Pancake Rock can be seen across the Narrows in the centre foreground.

Military Road looking east towards Cavendish Square before the erection of Hotel Newfoundland at Fort William. Canon Wood Hall is on the left. The Ethel Dickinson Memorial in the intersection has been moved to a site further south in the square. The ruins behind the monument are the abandoned foundations of Sir Robert Reid's Avalon Hotel. (Courtesy St. John's City Hall)

70

Fort Townshend can be seen behind the house on the left. This is the only overall view of the fort in existence and shows the junction of Garrison Hill, Harvey Road, Bonaventure Avenue and Military Road in 1891. Mount St. Francis monastery is visible behind the trees. The building on the right is the old Roman Catholic Palace which was destroyed by fire. (Courtesy Public Archives of Canada)

H.M.S. *Briton* (later H.M.S. *Calypso*) moored at the Southside in St. John's shortly after her arrival from England to be used as a training ship for the Royal Newfoundland Naval Reserve in 1902. The last of the wooden warships, she was converted into a coal and salt storage hulk and eventually towed to Lewisporte in the late 1940s. Today her abandoned hulk rots on a northeast coast beach. (Courtesy St. John's City Hall)

72

St. John's Harbour, probably at the time of the visit of the Duke and Duchess of York in 1901. In the foreground is Waldegrave Battery which was re-activated in the days of World War I and manned by the Legion of Frontiersmen. (Courtesy St. John's City Hall)

Fort Pepperrell, the American military installation built at St. John's in 1941. It has since been renamed Pleasantville and now houses, apartments and government offices.

Fort Townshend as it appeared in 1904 when the ramparts were already filled in but many of the original fort buildings were still standing. (Courtesy Christian Brother Archives)

Private Tommy Ricketts of the Royal Newfoundland Regiment who won the Victoria Cross at the age of 17 years, becoming the youngest V.C. winner in World War One. (Newfoundland Provincial Archives)

The unveiling of the Newfoundland War Memorial at Haymarket Square, King's Beach, by Field Marshal Earl Haig, 1 July 1924. This monument stands near the supposed site of Sir Humphrey Gilbert's taking possession of Newfoundland, 5 August 1583, thereby founding the British Empire.

A Military Animal

Man is a military animal
Glories in gunpowder, and loves parades.
                    PHILIP JAMES BAILEY *Festus—A Metropolis*

No city in the Americas has fallen to invading foreign soldiers as frequently as St. John's. Four times it has known defeat and occupation by the enemy: 1696, 1705, 1708, and 1762. In addition there were various other threats and alarms, the most recent being in World War II when a Nazi U-boat attempted to fire its torpedoes through the Narrows.

As early as 1618 there is mention of a rude fort being built by the inhabitants of St. John's on a commanding height of land. Most historians agree this was probably in the area of Fort William. Before that there were various raids on shipping in and around the waters of the Avalon Peninsula.

The earliest enemy was not the French but the Spaniard. It appears that the first military-style operation launched in the vicinity of St. John's was a private raid in 1582 by Henry Oughtred, a Southampton merchant, with Sir John Perrot, on Spanish and Portuguese fishing ships in revenge for losses suffered by the merchant in Spain.[1] The raid was so effective that the Iberians moved their base of operations from St. John's to the south and west coasts of Newfoundland.[2]

In December 1585 there was a proposal in England for a raid on the Spanish in Newfoundland to "starve his [King Philip's] country and possess his mariners and shipping, wherein consists his chief strength." In 1587 Francis Drake and John Hawkins also made proposals for an attack on the ships of Spain in Newfoundland waters, but the Spaniard in America was left in relative peace until 1595, while England concentrated on a blockade in European seas. By that time the Spanish fishing industry was in decline and a new rival was increasing its activity in the West Atlantic—France.

English attempts to shake the French loose from the St. Lawrence area failed. On the high seas they had more success. English privateers plundered fishing vessels returning to Europe from Newfoundland and Canada. To protect their vessels Basque merchants obtained passports from the Lord Admiral of England, thus admitting English sovereignty over the island and fisheries of Newfoundland. As an example of this there is a record in the High Court of Admiralty in London of a Stephen de Herembilett, who testified that the Basque owners of the *St. Mary St. Vincent*, of Ciboure, procured such a passport for their voyage to Newfoundland in 1595. They obtained a second passport for the return journey from the English fishing admiral in St. John's harbour.

In 1628 the Marquis de la Rade cruised up and down the coast of Avalon with three ships and four hundred men, raiding English fishermen in St. John's and other communities. Lord Baltimore retaliated by capturing six French fishing ships in Trepassey Bay and sending them home to England as prizes.[3] In addition to French raids the scattered settlements of Newfoundland were threatened by the Barbary pirates, the Salee Rovers, and such pirate kings as Peter Easton, Sir Harry Mainwaring, and the Dutchman, Admiral de Ruyter.

In 1612 Easton, with nine ships and five hundred "of His Majesty's subjects taken from their honest trade of fishing," did £20,400 damage as he plundered the coast of Avalon.[4] He waited at Ferryland for news of a pardon which was granted but did not arrive until after he had fled to seek the protection of the Duke of Florence.

De Ruyter twice attacked St. John's successfully. He declared, when he captured the place, on 6 June 1665, that if there had been six mounted guns he would not have attempted to enter the port.[5]

Following this attack in 1665 Christopher Martin, a Devonshire captain who was vice-admiral of the Newfoundland convoy, erected a fort on the south side of the Narrows, known as the Castle. It was small, but very strong, and useful against ships trying to enter port. In 1673 Martin, with a force of thirty men, manned the Castle and successfully drove off an attack by the Dutch buccaneer, Capt. Jacob Everson, who attacked the community with four pirate ships.[6]

The English merchants of London and the west country waged a ceaseless battle against settlement in Newfoundland. To them the island was a summer fishery station only. The French, once they had established their claims, saw it as an integral part of their great plantation of New France. In 1604 they settled St. Pierre and Miquelon and, in 1627, included Newfoundland in their plans for colonization. Placentia was settled, fortified, and garrisoned in 1662. Families came out from France, and in 1672 a Royal Governor was appointed. St. John's, on the other hand, was intended only to be a fishing station protected by a British military garrison. There was considerable ignorance about the potential of the place in the English court of the seventeenth century.

As animosities grew between England and France it became apparent to the English planters living in Newfoundland that there was a distinct military threat of takeover from the thriving French community at Placentia. The first person to try to do something about this was Robert Robinson.

In 1669 we find Captain Robinson petitioning to be made governor of the little colony growing up around St. John's harbour.[7] He believed it was necessary to regulate abuses and prepare land defences for the community of scattered houses stretched out for a distance of a mile and a half along the waterfront. His bid found little sympathy in England and failed.

Undaunted by setbacks, in 1680 Robinson (by then Sir Robert), asked leave to have his crew raise fortifications at St. John's with no expense to the Crown except a little brandy with which to pay his men for their labour. Leave being granted, work was begun on battlements which were the beginning of what later became Fort William.

In the early summer of 1696 a strong French fleet, under the command of Chevalier Nesmond, attacked St. John's. The surprised settlers manned the Castle, Robinson's fort, and North Battery, which was erected above Chain Rock and later became the site of Waldegrave Battery. Nesmond's ships, as they tried to force the Narrows, received a pounding from these shore batteries. Finally the attack was given up and the fleet sailed off.[8] This warning of French intentions in Newfoundland had little effect on English military thinking. It was inconceivable that the enemy would march on the town from Placentia, and no attempt was made for an orderly defence against land troops.

On 12 September 1696 Pierre le Moyne, sieur d'Iberville, arrived in Placentia, having been sent there from Quebec by Governor Frontenac to further his grand design of driving the English from North America. D'Iberville, a French Canadian, then thirty-five years of age, had an outstanding reputation for military ability and was considered one of the finest soldiers in New France. That his arrival on the scene was resented by Governor de Brouillon was natural. The Governor was further embarrassed by the fact that his expedition, commanded by Nesmond, had failed to capture St. John's.

D'Iberville felt that the best plan of attack was by land. The Governor protested bitterly and refused to change his mind about the value of another sea attack. A compromise was reached whereby d'Iberville would lead a land force and de Brouillon would take the fleet to St. John's. There was more unpleasantness between the two commanders when the governor insisted that his orders from Frontenac allowed him all booty and spoils of battle. D'Iberville insisted on his right to keep all he took. This was resolved after much wrangling by an agreement to a fifty-fifty split.

On November 1, at the head of a disciplined force of four hundred soldiers, coureurs de bois, and Indians, d'Iberville left Placentia, crossed St. Mary's Bay, and marched on Ferryland. He found Lord Baltimore's old colony deserted, the inhabitants having all fled to Bay Bulls. After staying eleven days at Ferryland, the force proceeded in small boats to Bay Bulls. On seeing the French approach, the settlers abandoned the community, including a 100-ton vessel lying in the harbour. Word finally reached St. John's, on November 26, that a small French land force had taken Petty Harbour. A group was organized to go out and drive them off, only to find it faced a disciplined army. The English defenders hastily retreated. The deep snow presented them with difficulties for which d'Iberville's force was prepared and there was much loss of life.

Two days later the French reached the heights above Kilbride to find a party of one hundred English entrenched in the Southside Hills, attempting to defend the Waterford valley. The settlers put up a stout resistance but were no match for the professional French soldiers. Some of the survivors were taken prisoner, while the rest fled toward the town. It is said that d'Iberville, sword in hand, ran all the way, followed by about a hundred men. Within hours, only Robinson's crude fort remained in the hands of the English.

The French spent the next two days looting the homes of the planters. Some of them were very well-to-do men and the booty collected was considerable. It was loaded on board a ship for transport to Placentia. Anxious to get on with his campaign, d'Iberville had one of the Indians scalp a prisoner named William Drew who was then sent to the fort with a message to Governor Miners that all the defenders could expect a similar fate if they did not immediately surrender. The sight of the bloody scalp of their compatriot did the trick. Miners and four of the principal citizens came out of the fort under a flag of truce. They agreed to a surrender on condition that ships be provided to take them to England, or Bonavista, and that none of the defenders would be in any way molested. It is obvious from this demand that what valuables they had were hidden about their persons. The skirts of the women being especially useful in this regard. On the nights of January 29 and 30 a detail of sixty men burned the houses to the ground and, in mid-January, the French force abandoned the ravaged community to attack English settlements in Conception Bay.[9]

Late in 1697 a squadron under command of Admiral Norris, with 1,500 soldiers under command of Colonel Gibson, were sent out from England to recapture the island. When they reached St. John's they were greeted by blackened ruins, an abandoned community, and not a single inhabitant to be found. The soldiers were set to work to restore the fortifications and the population gradually drifted back from hiding in the woods. Instead of attacking the French in their Placentia stronghold the punitive expedition satisfied itself with some repairs and rebuilding, and sailed away leaving Captain Handyside and three hundred men to winter in the desolate community with little in the way of food, fuel, or clothing. All crops and stores had been destroyed by the enemy. The lack of provisions, the want of suitable shelter, and the bitterness of the long, hard winter which followed led to outbreaks of starvation and disease that caused the deaths of 214 of the 300 soldiers before spring relief arrived.[10]

The British government was finally forced into action by the west country merchants, who had suffered considerable financial loss, and by the New England colonies, which saw a threat to their own security in French possession of Newfoundland.[11] Attention was at last given to measures for the protection of British interests in the island. An order was issued in 1697 to strengthen the fortifications by erecting a proper fort at St. John's.

In that year Capt. Michael Richards was sent out from England in charge of a group of soldiers and others who were to see to the construction of King William's Fort. On 31 March 1698 the Privy Council gave an order for the placement of a permanent garrison at St. John's. Lieutenant Lilburne was dispatched with sixty soldiers and gunners, to replace the remnants of Handyside's perished force.

Richards set to work and soon had under construction officers' houses, four barracks, guardhouses, and a storehouse. By 1700 the job was in full swing. It was not, however, without its problems. The townspeople were reluctant to make their horses available for hauling wood from Long Pond where it was cut. Richards finally had to pay eighteen pence per day for each horse and there was an additional cost for the driver. It is obvious that horses were more valuable than men, for wood cutters only got sixpence a day each.

Two of the four carpenters working on the fort gave Richards some trouble. John Rendal and Robert Browne were discharged "for ill behaviour and frequent neglects of H. M. service" and all who hired them afterwards were required to make deductions from their wages of "2 shillings per day from each till further advice comes from England." Prospective employers were exhorted "not to fail therein."

Rendal obviously felt aggrieved for he forced the captain, by letter of attorney, to credit him with six pounds. Richards wrote to England hoping to have the payment stopped. The difficulties appear to have been ironed out, for the following year both men were back on the payroll.

By 1700 the fortification was being called Fort William and that year the well was dug. Labour problems continued to plague the Captain. He wrote to a friend that his workers were " . . . a bundle of shameful villainy. . . . I never saw so many barefaced scandalous actions as they dwell in and no reasoning but sword in hand, like the Polish Diet."

One of the expenses Richards had to report to England in 1700 was £206.12.0 for liquor, which was served only to those engaged in the work. Brandy was five shillings and sixpence a gallon, and the rum cost slightly less than six shillings a gallon.

Residents of St. John's, Quidi Vidi, and Torbay were required to work on the fort while those of Petty Harbour were made to supply firewood for the lime kiln. Horses were still hard to come by and on 21 November 1700 Richards ordered William Cliff and Thomas Johnson, churchwardens, to make their horses available to haul "sufficient timber to finish ye barracks" and to supply another day's firewood to the lime kiln. He figured this would take about three days.

Cliff and Johnson were busy men, for they were also charged with seeing that all persons not at church, or in their houses, on Sundays were taken up as vagabonds and turned over to the guard. The guard appears to have been a civilian one, for Richards ordered that anyone who did not report for guard duty, or get a friend to cover for him, should supply a night's firewood for the guard. He put them in charge of arresting all persons of either sex found abroad between midnight and dawn, and to "keep a keen eye on the tippling houses."[12]

For his efforts in building the fort Captain Richards appears to have been promoted to Major and returned to England in 1703.

Lt. Thomas Lloyd was posted to St. John's in 1700. He was to prove the most colourful figure in the military history of Newfoundland. There are so many conflicting reports about the man that, taken in the context of his times, it is difficult to make a true assessment of his character. He seems to have been brave, resourceful, gay, offhand, arrogant, unprincipled, amoral, loyal, and well able to protect his own interests. In an earlier age he would probably have been a cavalier. He was devoted to wine, women, and song (at least fiddle music) and was undoubtedly one of those charming scoundrels who enliven the pages of history with their unconventional antics and devil-may-care attitude.

On 24 September 1703 Lloyd, because he was the oldest lieutenant at the fort, succeeded Major Richards in command of the garrison. He found a crony in Col. John Roope, of the Royal Engineers, who had worked on building the fort with the unskilled and inefficient labour. Roope is thought to have become a plantation owner in the town, taking the property known as Roope's Room.

Lloyd, as a military man, resented the fact that the ranking naval officer in port was his superior. The officers and men of his garrison were on quarrelling terms with their naval counterparts, and drunken brawls were common among the lower ranks. Discipline became slipshod. There was discontent among the settlers as well. Matters came to a head when John Jackson, a Church of England clergyman stationed at St. John's, wrote to the Honourable Commissioners of Trade and Plantations, on 17 January 1705, to accuse Lieutenant Lloyd of abusing the soldiers, staging sex orgies within and without the fort, preventing people from attending church on Sundays, sadistic punishments, and other infamies.

Capt. Timothy Bridge, commodore of the Newfoundland convoy, arrived in St. John's in the summer of 1704 to find the community split into factions. Planters such as Capt. Arthur Holdsworth defended Lloyd while men such as Jackson thundered against his depredations.[13] In view of the seriousness of the charges made against the Lieutenant, he was advised by Bridge to return to England and clear himself of the allegations.

The behaviour of the authorities in England seems puzzling. The officer was found guilty of some of the charges. Given a reprimand, he bought back his commission and received a promotion to Major. He was returned to his command of the fort at St. John's in October 1705.

Meanwhile, all had not gone well with his replacement in command, Lt. John Moody. This young officer found Fort William a sorry military installation. It was built four square, without any bastion, and much of the interior was exposed. The parapet was too low so that the men upon the ramparts were not covered. Moody was forced to fix plants and throw up earth to cover the men and also to make long wooden troughs for carrying bombshells and grenades, to secure the ditch during attack. The platforms were all out of order and deficient. The carriages of the guns were mostly rotten and out of repair, as were the beds of the mortars. The place for the magazine was too slight, lying open, and not bombproof. The walls of the fort were only of loose earth, palisaded, and apt to fall down into the ditch.

The North Battery was of no use, the men being so exposed to the enemy's fire they could not stand by a gun. On the other side of the Narrows, the Castle, while stronger than the fort, was exposed by a platform built above it so that no man could stand by a gun if the platform came into the possession of an enemy. With these defences Moody faced a French land invasion by Subercase, governor of Placentia, who sent a mixed force of 450 men to take the town. After a forced march from Placentia they reached Bay Bulls. Their commander, Montigny, decided to continue to St. John's where the French troops arrived during the night of 21 January 1705. To ensure a surprise attack they were ordered to lie in the snow until a half-hour before daybreak. The intense cold from which they suffered put the French soldiers in such a bad mood that when the order was finally given to attack the town they revenged themselves by unspeakable brutalities against the men, women, and children whom they murdered in cold blood. The rest were made prisoners in the church. However, the French failed to press the attack on the fort, leaving Moody time to prepare his defences.

The English command was split by rivalries which existed as a result of Lloyd's dislike for Moody. John Roope had a letter from Lloyd placing him in charge of the North Battery and advising him that he did not have to obey Moody's instructions. Lt. Robert Latham, a master mason who had been placed in charge of the Castle, resented the appointment. In addition to these complications Colin Campbell, the prize agent, sided with Roope. The two were later accused of treachery by furnishing information to the French. It seems more probable that they were caught outside the fort and became subservient to the French in an effort to save what they could of their property and belongings.

After two weeks of futile attempts to overcome the resistance of Moody and forty men in the fort, and Latham with twelve men in the Castle, Subercase wrote to Moody urging him to surrender, telling him that he was no longer able to restrain the fury of the Indians. He attempted to trick Latham into coming out of the Castle by telling him that Moody intended to surrender. Neither ruse worked. A four-day truce gave both men an opportunity to strengthen their defences. Subercase's gift of a brace of partridge and a request for a personal interview had no effect on Moody. The Governor finally had to content himself with burning the houses and stores of the town on March 5 and returning to Placentia with two hundred prisoners, while Montigny and the Abenaquis Indians were sent with a force to murder, burn, and plunder in the settlements of Conception Bay. They continued as far north as Bonavista, capturing everything except Carbonear Island.[14]

When Lloyd left Newfoundland there were sixty-six officers and soldiers in the garrison. Immediately before his return there were fifty-six making it appear as if ten might have died in the battle with the French invaders. A few may have deserted. On his return Captain Lloyd brought with him from England about eighty soldiers with two drums and one officer. He immediately charged Moody with embezzlement of Her Majesty's provisions and with having "caused a woman to be whipped within the fort at St. John's, and otherwise ill used by the soldiers, that she died within fourteen days. . . ."

The whipping charge also involved the Reverend Mr. Jackson. It would seem that the affair had grown out of an incident involving the parson's wife. One morning after the departure of Captain Lloyd the Jacksons' maid was making the beds. The lady did not like the way it was done, stripped off the sheets and gave the girl a piece of her mind. Instead of being cowed by her mistress the maid returned

Madam Jackson's abuse with impudence. The matter was brought to the attention of the parson who lodged a complaint with Moody. He asked that the servant be put in her place by the garrison commander. It was an age when whipping posts and stocks were a fact of everyday life, so it was probably not unusual in the unruly town of the times when the girl was ordered whipped in Fort William. The whipping was administered on her bare back outdoors in freezing temperatures and cold water was thrown on the wounds so that it froze to the cuts. When the lashing was resumed the caked ice broke away tearing the flesh. The poor unfortunate was then turned out to fend for herself, and the townspeople were forbidden to render her any assistance. Some of the Lloyd faction, however, took the girl in, but she died within fourteen days. When Lloyd got back from England and heard of the affair he lost no time in revenge. The charges he pressed against both men resulted in their recall to England to defend themselves.

Moody and Jackson sailed on the vessel of the navy commodore, Captain Bridge, probably in some sort of custody. As they neared the English coast the vessel ran into quite a severe storm, was wrecked, and sank off the Isle of Wight. Everyone was saved including Madam Jackson and the couple's eight children, but they lost all their possessions and were in want for years afterwards.

When he reached London Moody faced trial. Some soldiers said in his defence that he kept the garrison in very good discipline during the five weeks and three days under seige at St. John's. They said they had been in great want of shoes, stockings, shirts, and other necessities and these had been supplied at the charge and expense of Moody. "Both day and night he exerted himself by his personal courage, conduct and bravery, countenancing and encouraging the soldiers and garrison, encouraging them and declaring with resolution, night and day, that he would stand by them and spend the last drop of his blood in defence of the garrison." Moody, at his own expense, had constantly furnished the soldiers with rum, brandy, and other liquors, undergoing great hardships and sufferings for Her Majesty's service. They said he had shown himself a brave and valiant commander through all five weeks and three days. They claimed that Mr. Latham had been disobedient to the commands of the officer and that he had not set a good example to the soldiers in the garrison.[15]

This declaration in support of Moody was upheld by the testimony of three of the leading merchants of St. John's and the wife of another. William and Abraham Taverner, Thomas Minshew, and Mary Benger, whose husband was said to have suffered great injustice at the hands of Lloyd, testified to Moody's brave defence of the fort. They claimed the inhabitants had been encouraged to re-erect their stages, ships' rooms, and habitations. They had cheerfully and successfully entered into business again, but to their unspeakable surprise and grief Moody was recalled and Lloyd, whom former irregularities had rendered odious, was sent in his stead, honoured with an increase in power that set him above the control of the navy commodores.

The merchants and Mrs. Benger said that the people, since the return of Lloyd, were worse used than before. They were compelled like slaves to go into the woods on Sundays to cut timber for him, were spit upon, kicked, beaten, wounded, overladen with unequal quartering of soldiers, and were dispossessed of their properties and inheritances.[16]

On the other hand John Templeman, a merchant of Bristol, stated that Lloyd, by then a major, had cultivated good understanding with all the inhabitants. He spoke of the good discipline he kept over his soldiers, and being an understanding man, was able to assist both ships and planters in any extraordinary circumstance. Templeman ended by saying, "He carrys himself in all respects as become (sic) a prudent and good governor...."[17]

According to the English Army List and Commission Registers for 1702-07, on 1 May 1705 Thomas Lloyd was "to be Captain to the Independent Company in Newfoundland and likewise to be commander of our Forts and Garrisons there." His promotion was rapid. Just over two months after being made captain, on 20 July 1705, the following notation was made, "Thos. Lloyd to be Major of Foot." The early use of the title "governor" refers to governor of Fort William and was not a governorship of Newfoundland.

Lieutenant Moody (or Captain as he then was) cleared himself of the charges with even more facility than Lloyd, for he was promoted to the rank of Lieutenant-Colonel and returned to Newfoundland as Lieutenant-Governor of Placentia, after the French were forced out of the community, as a result of their behaviour in 1708.

On the clear, moonlit night of 31 December 1707 all was tranquil in the rebuilt town of St. John's. The only sounds which disturbed the stillness of the quiet scene came from within Fort William where the officers and soldiers were welcoming the new year with liquor and song. Unseen by anyone, a French force from Placentia, under St. Ovide and de Costabelle, moved past the shuttered houses to within sight of the main gate at Fort William. As dawn was breaking, a sentry saw the approaching enemy. His musket misfired. His shouts alerted another sentry who fired off a warning shot.

A deposition of Capt. Benjamin Gosse[18], 18 April 1709 in the Massachusetts state archives at Boston, tells the story. In the deposition there is a letter from Mr. Burrows, "a considerable merchant of Exeter," to Mr. Symons in Barnstable:

> On New Year's Eve or New Year's day last in the night a force detached from Placentia (as is said not inconsisting of

> 150 men) attempted and took by surprise the fort at St. John's in Newfoundland without any manner of opposition. The Commander of enemies forces coming to the Governor in the fort at Newfoundland and took him by his hand (he the Governor then being in his morning gown) and said that he thanked him for his New Year's gift—and thereupon the garrison were made prisoners of war. . . .

On hearing this news from Newfoundland George Buck, a considerable merchant of Biddeford, proposed to lend the government of Great Britain such ships as were ready to transport forces to reduce or retake St. John's.

According to a French account, by Charlevoix, the force consisted of 164 men, including Indians. On the last day of December they reached to within fifteen miles of St. John's without being observed. About 4:00 a.m. the French attacked a sentry at the southwest corner of the fort. Leaving fifteen or sixteen men to guard the entrance, St. Ovide crossed the ditch and scaled the twenty-foot-high rampart, with two ladders and six men, three of whom were dangerously wounded by scattered musket fire. Within half an hour the engagement was over and the fort taken. In all, eight English soldiers were killed and seven wounded, and three French soldiers died.

Below Fort William about six hundred settlers were crowded into Fort St. George, where Devon Row stands today. A door connecting the two forts was locked and the keys were in Major Lloyd's house. The door proved too stout an obstacle to force. The commander was routed out of his bed and, in trying to get the drawbridge down and the door open between the forts, was wounded three times. Fort William had been protected by eighteen guns mounted, four mortars for bombshells, and twenty for grenades.

The Castle on the south side of the Narrows surrendered next day. Settlers on that shore of the harbour had fled there for protection but, finding themselves without an officer-in-command, they surrendered. St. Ovide sent a message to Costabelle informing him of his success. Word was sent to France, but Costabelle thought it was useless to await reinforcements from home so he ordered the forts destroyed and the French to return to Placentia at the end of March.[19]

John Collins, a merchant who was afterwards appointed English governor of Fort William, was at Mr. Winchen's house on New Year's Day and heard Sergeant Steel say that when the French entered the old fort only one man was on the works and that Major Lloyd came as far as the ramparts, cried "Fight, boys," and was never seen again. William Keen, the magistrate who was murdered in his bed years afterwards, said he saw Major Lloyd "very heavy eye'd and little notice was taken of him." The inhabitants were imprisoned in storehouses about five o'clock on the evening of New Year's Day. Keen and a few others were kept in their own houses.

On January 8 Major Lloyd, Lieutenant Phillips, and Engineer Vane with his wife were sent to Placentia by ship. On March 27 St. Ovide himself sailed away to the French capital, taking with him three hundred English prisoners, including William Keen and John Collins. On May 13 Lloyd and Phillips were shipped to Canada. The English merchants arrived back in St. John's on June 26. Lloyd was later transported to France where he is thought to have died fighting a duel.

On May 13 two hundred soldiers from France arrived at St. John's on board the man-of-war, *Fiddell*, only to find the town abandoned. They went on to Placentia where St. Ovide received news of being created Knight of St. Louis, and Governor of St. John's.

Little interest seems to have been taken by England in rebuilding Fort William. After 1708 the garrison was reduced to less than thirty men who spent most of their time trading with the planters, or fishing to augment their incomes. On 10 December 1712 Sir Nicholas Trevanion, Commander of H. M. Ships and Garrisons, and Governor-in-Chief at Newfoundland, confirmed "John Collins, Esq., Governor of Fort William, and it is appointed, during cessation, that twenty men lie in fort every night."[20]

With the coming of peace between England and France, and the signing of the Treaty of Utrecht in 1713, the shoddy fort was completely abandoned and allowed to fall into decay. The ramparts of Fort St. George were torn down and settlers' houses built on the commanding site. In the treaty it was agreed that the French would abandon all their claims to Newfoundland. Governor De Costabelle lost no time in sending off the Placentia garrison, and inhabitants, to Cape Breton. Some of the settlers objected but Costabelle urged all to go except idlers and vagabonds, whom he discreetly left as a legacy to his successor.

Placentia was placed under the rule of the governor of Nova Scotia, while the rest of Newfoundland was ruled by the commodore at St. John's. Moody returned to take up his duties as governor of Placentia where he and the other English officers bought the property of the departing Frenchmen.

From a military point of view St. John's slumbered until the outbreak of the War of the Austrian Succession in 1740, when England and France became enemies once more. Hasty repairs were carried out in an attempt to restore Fort William. In 1743 Capt. Thomas Smith arrived as military governor. He had with him a body of marines, and under his direction they carried out much of the work of restoration. From 1745 to 1750 Fort William, and the battlements nearby, were garrisoned by four companies of foot, a captain with about fifty men, forty pieces of cannon, and well-stocked stores.

In the spring of 1762, in what has been called the most inexplicable venture of the Seven Years' War, a French fleet of four ships of war, thirty-two officers, and nearly seven hundred troops, under the command of Count d'Haussonville, sailed from Brest in a thick fog, eluded the British cruisers of Sir Edward Hawke, and escaped to sea. The squadron, under Admiral de Ternay, took Bay Bulls on June 24 and marched on St. John's. They arrived three days later. Resistance against such an overwhelming force was useless by the handful of soldiers in Fort William. There was a Gramont sloop in port with trade from Ireland. She carried twenty-two guns, which were hastily mounted on shore. Without coming to action or obtaining a capitulation, the place surrendered on June 27 at the first summons.[21]

Having secured the town, the French commander set to work to improve the fortifications. He began work on the erection of a fort on Signal Hill and also on a defence battery at the mouth of Quidi Vidi harbour.

There were in Nova Scotia and Louisbourg about 1,500 British Regulars and Provincials. It was proposed they be employed immediately in endeavouring to remove the French from St. John's. No move could be made without orders from Major-General Sir Jeffrey Amherst, Commander-in-Chief in North America, who was in New York. A cartel brigantine with 140 prisoners sailed from St. John's for England on July 18, but finding itself badly provided for with water and provisions it changed course for Louisbourg. It brought with it news of the surrender of the town.

Lord Colville, the naval commander at Halifax, decided to take the *Northumberland* and the *Gosport* in hopes of joining the *Syren* and *Antelope*. The latter ship was carrying Captain Graves, the governor, to Newfoundland. Colville proposed to cruise off St. John's to cut off the enemy's supplies. He chanced upon a schooner and took her near the harbour mouth. She had been an English privateer, taken by the French, with eight carriage guns mounted, and was manned by thirty Frenchmen.

Colville learned that the enemy had sent away a great part of the inhabitants of St. John's—men, women, and children—by giving them vessels and provisions to carry them wherever they pleased. He met two of these, the Gramont sloop and a schooner, and took twenty-three single Irishmen to replace the squadron marines he had left at Placentia and Ferryland. The Irishmen told him there were others at Bay Bulls waiting to join the squadron, but during two days in the port not a man joined them.

Admiral Lord Colville frequently passed the harbour mouth at St. John's and could plainly see that Fort William was fortified all around with new works. He says "a redoubt or something like one was raised at Kitty Witty [sic]. The old battery on the Southside of the harbour's mouth was repaired with additional works, and a new one erected on the same side nearer the entrance."[22]

On September 8 he received by sloop express from Halifax letters from Sir Jeffrey Amherst at New York acquainting him that he had come to a resolution to muster all the troops he could from New York, Halifax, and Louisbourg in order to dislodge the enemy as soon as possible from St. John's and that his brother, Lt.-Col. William Amherst, would command these troops. On the 11th Colville was joined by William Amherst, with the troops in ten transport vessels. The Admiral proposed Torbay as the most proper place to land.

On September 12 they proceeded to Torbay. Next morning Colonel Amherst landed with the troops in the head of the bay, having only four men wounded by the enemy firing from a distant bush. He marched directly to Quidi Vidi and was master of that village by evening, without having a man killed. Everything belonging to the army was carried from Torbay to Quidi Vidi in shallops, escorted by boats from the squadron, under the care of Lieutenant Dugdale.

The French fleet was to have sailed from St. John's that morning leaving three hundred men to garrison the town for the winter. On seeing Colville's fleet they returned to port and landed their soldiers again.

Before daylight on the morning of September 15, in a cold drizzle and thick fog, Captain McDonnell led a party of British and American soldiers from Quidi Vidi to the cliffs at Cuckold's Cove where they scaled a steep ravine, passed the French sentries entrenched on Signal Hill, and were not discovered by the enemy until they reached the top of the hill. McDonnell was wounded in the attack and treated by Mrs. Horwood of Quidi Vidi, who can be called Newfoundland's first practical nurse.[23] Her house was used by the British as a field hospital for the treatment of their wounded. It is said to be the one still standing in the village, on the east side of the main road, immediately to the right of Christ Church. Though severely wounded, McDonnell recovered and returned to England. In the Battle of Signal Hill, Lieutenant Schuyler of the Royal Americans and about thirty men were killed.

The fog which aided the British in their capture of the heights also proved to be a blessing to the enemy. Under cover of the westward breezes and thick fog, the French fleet, consisting of the *Robuste* (74 guns), *L'Eville* (64), *La Garonne* (44), *La Sicorne* (30), and a bomb ketch, escaped into the Atlantic unnoticed by Colville's watch. The Admiral was somewhat put out to lose his prey. He wrote: "Thus, after being blocked up in St. John's Harbour for three weeks, by a squadron of equal number, but smaller ships with fewer guns and men, did Monsieur Ternay make his escape by night in a shameful flight." The fog was so thick that Lieutenant-Colonel Tulliken, posted on an eminence in the narrowest part of the harbour's mouth, could hear the noise and oarlocks but could not discern any of the ships.[24] The grenadiers had been ready for embarking, but De Ternay, anxious to grasp the opportunity to escape, left them behind in utter confusion. The small rowboats which towed his ships out the Narrows were cut adrift and also left behind.

A bomb battery was opened against the fort on the night of the 17th. The previous day Amherst had called upon D'Haussonville to surrender, saying:

> I know the miserable state your garrison is left in and am fully informed of your design of blowing up the fort on quitting it; but have a care, as I have taken measures to effectually cut off your retreat, and so sure as a match is put to the train, every man of the garrison shall be put to the sword. I must have immediate possession of the fort in the state it now is, or expect the consequences. I give you half an hour to think about it. I have the honour to be Sir, Your most obedient and humble servant.

To this the French commander replied, "Nothing shall determine me to surrender the fort unless you shall have totally destroyed it and I shall have no more powder to fire. I have the honour to be Sir, Your most humble and most obedient servant."[25]

On the 18th, after being fired on from land and sea, the French capitulated. The fort was surrendered in good condition. There was a considerable quantity of provisions and other goods, "collected promiscously [sic] into different storehouses of the enemy." It was stated that many of the Irish servants had been robbing and plundering their masters, and Governor Graves was to make restitution as far as possible and restore regularity to the country.

According to information supplied by seven French prisoners, examined separately by the governor at Placentia, De Ternay had sailed from Brest on May 8 with a badly manned squadron of sickly seamen. On the other hand the land forces were choice men composed of 6 companies of grenadiers of 45 men each, 6 piquets of 50 each, and 300 marines – 870 men in all. Following the fall of St. John's the grenadiers were to return to France leaving only the piquets to garrison the town under Lieutenant-Colonel Belcombe. It was a time of British persecution in Ireland and three hundred Irishmen enlisted in the French forces at Bay Bulls and St. John's. One of the French frigates was commanded by an Irishman named Sutton.

They had taken down all the old palisades and replaced them. They were surrounding the fort with a new ditch and were working on reducing the brow of a hill going down into the town(probably Hill o'Chips) behind which a body of men might have marched under cover and without molestation to within a pistol shot of the gate. Had the English not surrendered they intended to storm the fort the same night, for they felt they could march over the ditch and ramparts with ease and pull down the palisades with their hands.

On September 23 Captain Douglas, in the *Syren*, sailed for England with an account of the recovery of St. John's from the enemy. Captain Jervis of the *Gosport* took all nineteen of the wounded men and sailed for New York two days later. Colonel Amherst saw all his troops disposed of before he left St. John's. Two hundred and fifty remained in garrison under Captain Gualley of the 45th Regiment.

The six guns on the south battery (the old Castle) had been spiked by the enemy, and Captain Houlton of the *Enterprize* was directed to land six of his lower-deck guns in their place. However, the armourer of the *Superb* restored the guns so that they were as fit for service as ever. On October 7 Colville sailed from St. John's harbour with the *Northumberland, Shrewsbury, Bedford,*and *Superb* for Spithead, England, where he arrived on the 25th "without meeting anything remarkable on our passage."[26]

The Battle of Signal Hill, 16 September 1762, was the last battle of the Seven Years' War fought in North America, and the last engagement of any consequence between the English and French on this continent. In 1759 Wolfe's defeat of Montcalm at the Battle of the Plains of Abraham, in Quebec, had decided the fate of Canada. Three years later in St. John's, French dreams of regaining their territory in the New World were snuffed out forever.

On 20 November 1762, Mr. Pownall, Secretary to the Lords Commissioners of Trade and Plantations wrote to the Master of the Society of Merchant Venturers at Bristol requesting the sentiments of the merchants of the city touching on the expediency of erecting new forts on certain parts of the Island of Newfoundland. The Master acquainted the committee "that he waited on Mr. Nugent and Mr. Charles Townshend on the affair and received great assistance from these gentlemen who both promised him to use their utmost endeavours to have the Trade to Newfoundland taken particular care of."[27]

British refugees from the island were not given much sympathy in New England. On 22 October 1762 a memorial from Selectmen of the town of Boston, sent to the government of Massachusetts speaks of: "the several now in Boston who fled from Newfoundland during the invasion of St. John's by the French." It claims "if they remain here their want will be great, and it would be a saving to the province to send them back to Newfoundland on the best terms obtainable."[28]

No sooner had the French departed than the English embarked

on a rash of fort building. The following year saw Fort William rebuilt and work commenced on three other installations. Queen's Battery was erected on a plateau 420 feet above the Narrows. Begun in 1763 it was not completed until 1769. It was enlarged and made stronger in 1809. Crow's Nest Battery was built on the crest of Gibbet Hill at a site which had proved useful in the attack by the English on Fort William. Colonel William Amherst also ordered a new fort to be situated on the south side of the Narrows.

In 1623 earthworks had been erected in the area but these were not fortified until 1704. Fort Amherst turned the place into a full military establishment with defences, cannon, barracks, canteen, and supply buildings. It was named for the man who ordered its construction.

William Amherst, British commander in Halifax, ended his days as lieutenant-governor of Portsmouth, and aide-de-camp to George III. He married a celebrated court beauty and had his portrait painted by Sir Joshua Reynolds. His brother, Baron Jeffrey Amherst, who commanded the British forces in the French and Indian Wars, captured Louisburg in 1758 and Montreal in 1760. The town of Amherst, Massachusetts, is named for him. He died childless, and William Amherst's son succeeded his uncle as second baron. This son served as British ambassador to China and governor general of India.

A lighthouse was erected at Fort Amherst in 1811, immediately behind the fort. The military installation was abandoned when the British troops were withdrawn from Newfoundland, in 1870, and it soon fell into ruin. The last vestiges of the old fort and the original stone lighthouse were pulled down, and the lighthouse was rebuilt in 1954.

Fort Amherst was reactivated in World War II and today these fortifications are its main attraction. It is possible to drive to within a quarter of a mile of the lighthouse. A boardwalk winds along the sheer cliffs. There is a clearing on the right where the barracks were located for the World War II Canadian forces, at which time the fort was manned by ninety enlisted men and two officers.

Having reached the lighthouse it is necessary to brave some steep concrete steps, mounds of broken glass, rubble, and rude four-letter words on the walls to reach the concrete gun emplacements. Two twenty-foot cannon poke out from the crumbling concrete ruins. In the 1939-45 war St. John's was again threatened with invasion by the enemy. Many thought Hitler would attempt to take the island as a base for submarines for an attack on North America. On the afternoon of 3 March 1941, a German torpedo exploded just beneath the bunker of number-one gun sending a sheet of spray a hundred feet in the air. A few seconds later another torpedo streaked into the nets guarding the harbour mouth but did not explode. The U-boat was trying to sink an old sealing steamer, which was leaving port, so as to block the Narrows to shipping and convoys.

During a winter storm in World War II the surf pounding on the rocks of the Narrows did much damage to the Fort Amherst installations. Giant searchlights were knocked out, partitions were smashed and the gun emplacements were flooded. In another storm waves shifted stone blocks and knocked down concrete walls seventy feet above sea level.[29]

About 1770 a heavy chain was stretched across the Narrows from Chain Rock to Pancake Rock, and it was the duty of the troops to raise this chain each evening so that an enemy vessel or privateer could not sneak into the harbour under cover of darkness. During World War I a chain boom was again put in use. In World War II the Narrows were protected by a series of metal mesh anti-submarine nets.

Fort Townshend was begun in 1773 on the height of land which separated the harbour from Freshwater Valley. It was considered a safer location than Fort William, which was exposed to whoever commanded Signal Hill. An historic marker on the Fort Townshend site states it was "Constructed 1775-79 under Governor Lord Stuldham." That year Military Road was begun to link the two forts and was finished in 1776.

The chief engineer in charge of the construction of the fort was Colonel Pringle. He was actually in charge of all the new defences of the town, known as the "King's works," and this included building Military, King's, and Signal Hill Roads. As commander of the garrison, Pringle submitted a plan to enlist three hundred men who would work on the fortifications. Without waiting for a reply from London, which could take half a year, he enrolled 120 of the artificers and labourers to work on Fort Townshend. However, the government in London was not in sympathy with the idea and, to the embarrassment of Pringle, the men were rewarded with three pounds each for the artificers and forty shillings for the labourers.[30]

Fort Townshend was occupied in 1779 and the military was transferred there from Fort William. The fort was not completed until 1781. *The Times of London* described it in 1796:

> The harbour of St. John's is the completest in the island of Newfoundland, being situated in lat. 48.30 and long. 52.10. It is entirely landlocked, perfectly secure from all winds, and capable of containing 300 sail of shipping. The entrance is exceedingly narrow, and, being covered by very high surrounding lands, the wind always blows either directly in or out. This part is usually called the Narrows, and is well defended by Fort Amherst, mounting 17 guns, and Fort Frederick, mounting 9 guns; there are also two 24-pounders on a platform near the Chain Rock (called Chain Battery) admirably suited for

> raking an enemy coming in; but this no enemy would be rash
> enough to attempt, unless they had first secured the new Fort,
> or Fort Townshend. This fortification has been erected since
> the taking of the place by the French in the last war. It is
> named after Lord Townshend, who was Master-General of the
> Ordance [sic] at the time it was erected. Being seated on an
> eminence, it entirely commands every part of the harbour, on
> which side is a battery of twenty-two 24-pounders, which is
> impossible for any ship to elevate her guns high enough to
> incommode in the least. On the land side it is fortified as a
> Star-fort; but not sufficiently strong to sustain an attack in a
> regular way. This is the residence of the Governor of the
> island, who is usually a Naval Flag Officer, and who comes
> out in the spring, and returns before the frost sets in, for
> England. The garrison generally consists of two companies of
> regulars, one of artillery, and a provincial corps of fencibles.
> The old Fort is now in ruins, and only serves as a barracks for
> the soldiers and apartments for the military officers.

At the trial of a soldier of the fort accused of sodomy, testimony
showed that the men slept three to a bunk. Incidentally the defendant,
who claimed he was asleep and dreaming of a beautiful girl, was hanged a
few days later for his "unnatural crime."

In the winter of 1792-93 Capt. Thomas Skinner of the Royal
Engineers stationed in St. John's raised four companies of volunteers
at his own expense, known as the Royal Newfoundland Volunteers.
On 25 April 1795 the king granted Skinner, then a major and commanding officer of the Royal Engineers in Newfoundland, permission
to raise a regiment of fencible infantry, consisting of six hundred men.
Governor Waldegrave requested the Duke of Portland, secretary of
the Home Department, "to order provisions to be sent out to them as
soon as possible as . . . provisions are scarce and buying them at St.
John's might distress the inhabitants."[31]

Some of the officers of the garrison were granted captains' commissions in the Royal Newfoundland Regiment, as it was called, and
some of the prominent men of the town were appointed ensigns.

Skinner, who now held the rank of Colonel, completed work on
the fortifications and Queen's Own Battery was provided with guns
which were hauled up the cliff face from the sea. He also had furnaces
for heating shot built at Fort William, Chain Rock (Waldegrave)
Battery, and Fort Amherst.

Meanwhile, other defences had been erected around the town.
Twenty Mile Pond Battery, on the north side of Portugal Cove Road
almost at the eastern end of Windsor Lake, was a temporary earthen-
work battery of two 18-pounder carronades supported by a line of
trenches erected. Built in 1780, as part of the outer ring of defences of

St. John's, it was maintained until 1795. Cox Marsh Battery, on Torbay Road opposite the road leading to the airport, was an identical fortification, put up at the same time, with the addition of a barracks. It was abandoned in 1784. Nearby, just inside the present town limits of Torbay, a third identical battery was located from 1880 to 1885.

Quidi Vidi Battery, a temporary emplacement for two guns establishment by D'Haussonville in 1762, had fallen to Col. William Amherst's troops on September 17 of that year. The British decided to permanently block up the entrance to the village harbour by sinking an old ship. The scheme failed and when the American Revolution broke out in 1774 the battery was rebuilt and enlarged to contain four 18-pounder carronades and two 6-pounder cannon.

Abandoned in 1784, Quidi Vidi Battery was repaired again in 1791, and throughout the Napoleonic Wars mounted seven pieces of ordnance. It was then abandoned once more until the War of 1812 when it was rebuilt as a protection against attacks by American privateers. It mounted two 6-pounder cannon and was maintained until the middle of the nineteenth century. The battery was reconstructed in 1967 as a centennial project by the 56 FD Squadron of the Royal Canadian Engineers (M) and the Government of Newfoundland and Labrador.

Duke of York Battery was built on the southern shoulder of the crest of Signal Hill, just below today's Cabot Tower, in 1796. It mounted eight 24-pounder guns, four 18-pounder carronades, and two 10-inch mortars. Nothing of it remains today. On the opposite side of the Narrows, South Battery, or Fort Charles, was erected on the site of the Castle just above Pancake Rock.

Meanwhile, by the winter of 1795-96, the barracks at Fort Townshend and Fort William were not ready to receive Skinner's completed levy of recruits and the Royal Newfoundland Regiment spent its first winter in scattered billets around the town. A camp was provided on the parade ground, at Fort William, in June 1796, and the regiment began field training. By August it was ready for the defence of St. John's.

During the summer of 1796 the community was threatened with French invasion for the last time. The Directory of the French Republic gathered a military and naval force for the invasion of Newfoundland. Ten ships from Cadiz and ten ships from Brest were to be assembled off Cape Finistère, under Rear Admiral Richery. The ships at Brest were prevented from sailing by the blockade of the British Squadron. Unable to wait, Richery sailed for St. John's with ten ships. They were in very poor condition. The pumps of the flagship *La Jupitor* (74 guns) had to be worked every two hours and other ships were just as leaky. The inefficiency of the citizen officers and the

97

lack of discipline among the citizen sailors, who resented being pressed into service against their will, was another problem.

In the early light of the morning of 1 September 1796 a lookout on Signal Hill sighted the French ships about ten miles to the southeast of St. John's. They were hull down and just visible. The able-bodied men of the town were hastily assembled before Governor Wallace at Fort Townshend. All that morning and afternoon there was much activity. The tents of the Royal Newfoundland Regiment camp at Fort Townshend were struck and reassembled on the ridge of Signal Hill, as well as above Fort Amherst, to make the place look like an armed camp. Men dressed as soldiers paraded everywhere on the hillsides.[32] Wallace afterwards wrote to the governor of Nova Scotia, "We were very weak in numbers in the Royal Newfoundland Regiment, besides they were raw and undisciplined." Apart from a handful of marines, and the sailors of three warships and a sloop, the garrison consisted of 561 men of the Royal Artillery and Royal Newfoundland Regiment and 52 men of the Royal Newfoundland Volunteers.

For two days the enemy had tacked back and forth across the mouth of the Narrows only once coming within range of the guns of Fort Amherst. On September 4 they landed at the undefended community of Bay Bulls, eighteen miles south of St. John's.[33] They spent four days there looting houses and fishing property and on September 5 burned the community to the ground, with the supposed exception of two houses. In one, it is said, a pregnant woman had just given birth to a twin. The other was the house of Nicholas Coady, a world traveller who was abroad at the time. The French commander used his house as a land headquarters. It is claimed that a valuable crucifix, which the sea rover brought back with him from Europe, was taken from the house and carried into the hills for safekeeping by his neighbours when they saw the enemy approach. It was later donated to the parish priest and according to some, it is the one which can be seen today on the back wall of the Roman Catholic Church in Bay Bulls.

Richery was handicapped by having no intelligence of the defences of St. John's and no pilots for Newfoundland waters. He had to depend for information on John Morridge, master of a fishing ship to Governor Wallace who was one of the prisoners taken at Bay Bulls. If Morridge's tale is true then he saved St. John's single-handed, and is one of the unsung heroes of Newfoundland history.

Questioned by Richery about the advisability of attacking St. John's, and the strength of the garrison, Morridge told the admiral there were "5,000 at least and that had they attempted the Harbour they would not have succeeded as there was a boom and chain across it and 200 guns would play upon them at the same time." On hearing this information Richery and his officers "conversed together and from that time he thinks all thoughts of attacking St. John's were given up."

On September 8 the French sailed for St. Pierre and Miquelon, taking with them a reputed force of 1,500 regular forces who never saw action against the vastly inferior British garrison, and sixty-one prisoners from Bay Bulls. On September 28 the prisoners were given a schooner and released to make their way to Halifax. At night, when the French ships were out of sight, they changed course for Trepassey and St. John's.[34] The last French attempt to conquer Newfoundland had ended as a fiasco, thanks to the misinformation of John Morridge.

Early in August 1797 a military crisis of another sort threatened the peace of the town. On the morning of August 3 H.M.S. *Latona*, under command of Capt. Frank Sotheron, was preparing to sail from St. John's when her foretopmen, on being ordered aloft, refused to obey their officers. In a body they demanded to be put in irons. As Captain Sotheron moved to punish the ringleader, the men swore they would not be punished, the officers drew their swords, and the marines presented their bayonets. It was not until some blood was drawn that the mutineers retreated and the punishment was executed.

Governor Waldegrave boarded H.M.S. *Latona* and ordered the crew assembled on deck where he administered a literate, long, and severe tongue-lashing. He told the officers, "In case any further signs of mutiny should appear among you, not to think of confining the ringleaders but to put them to death instantly, and what is more, I have given orders to the officers commanding the Batteries to burn the *Latona* with redhot shot. . . . "[35] The sailors had mutinied in sympathy with Parker and his ill-fated mutiny of the *Nore* in England. Other ships in St. John's harbour were supposed to follow the *Latona*'s lead but that was the only incident, probably due to Waldegrave's prompt countermeasures.

It was reported that a soldier of the Royal Newfoundland Regiment had conversed with the seamen of the *Latona*, under a fish flake on August 8, and that he had promised the garrison would follow the navy in mutiny. Sgt. James Dailey revealed, on August 12, that he was the man but that he was drunk at the time, having taken ten glasses of brandy, and has no recollection of what was said. Skinner reduced him to serve in the ranks until he could be sent from the island. To quiet the minds of the inhabitants the Governor had them assembled at the Court House, where he had the late Sergeant take an oath of fidelity in front of the magistrates. He was then made a prisoner in the guardhouse until he was embarked on the frigate *Surprize*.

The Dailey incident angered the Governor because he did not

have the power to make an immediate example of the traitor. He complained to the authorities in England that the governor of Newfoundland did not have the power to order general courts-martial. He was obliged to send all offenders to Halifax for trial, as well as all witnesses, which sometimes included the commanding officers, leaving the town without an officer of rank. Because this was impracticable many escaped punishment.

The miserable life of a soldier of the garrison had not improved much since the days of Major Lloyd. Army life was a demoralizing existence and desertions were frequent, in spite of the most harsh punishments. Penalties were also severe for those caught befriending or sheltering a deserter. There was a reward of eighty shillings for anyone who apprehended one. The usual punishment was an inhuman lashing. Hanging was another deterrent that was not unusual.

The following are just two of the punishments meted out on board the *Shrewsbury* in St. John's harbour by Capt. Hugh Palliser on 30 September 1762, for desertion. Matthew Hay, seaman of the *Minerva*, "sentenced to receive six hundred lashes." Thomas Levin seaman of the *Superb*, "sentenced to be hanged until he be dead."[36]

A second gunner of the Royal Artillery, in Halifax, was sentenced to "receive one thousand lashes" for deserting his regiment, and then to be transferred "to the Savoy Prison in London to be sent from thence to such places beyond the seas as His Majesty shall think fit, there to serve as a soldier during his natural life."

This man, Thomas Hughes, reached St. John's in May 1796, on his way to England, and was placed in solitary confinement in the hole at Fort Townshend until July 1797, when Governor Waldegrave allowed him the "indulgence of walking about the interior part of the fort, till opportunity should offer to convey him to England as a prisoner." Hughes seized his own opportunity and escaped to Carbonear where he signed on as a seaman on a fishing boat going north. He was last seen that autumn in Trinity. The chase was given up and the man vanished from history. In 1797, in spite of such terrible punishments, twenty-two men deserted the Royal Newfoundland Regiment.[37]

On October 2 the first food supplies were drawn from the commissary stores and the salt pork issued was so putrid that a report on its condition was sent to Colonel Skinner, who reported that a man "peeled the skin of two pieces and thrust his fingers into the meat which I believe could not have been the case with sound meat; nearly all pieces were quite yellow."

A court of enquiry was held which found that out of 1,440 pounds of pork only 276 pounds were fit to eat, and 2,740 pounds of flour had to be thrown into the harbour. These rations were not replaced and, in near starvation, the soldiers struggled through the winter. By January 15 all available food in St. John's had been bought, or requisitioned, and there were only ten weeks' supplies left in the stores. To add to their troubles, on March 24, at 2:30 a.m., a fire broke out in Fort William. In less than half an hour the eastern front of the garrison was in a blaze which consumed the whole of the officers' barracks and six of the barrack rooms used by the soldiers. No lives were lost but all the medical supplies of Dr. Ogden, and much bedding, utensils, and stores were totally destroyed. The whole of Fort William would have gone except for the efforts of the officers and crew of H.M.S. *Shark* and the inhabitants of the town. Only a small quantity of lumber was available for repairs, and the weather was infinitely too cold to encamp the dispossessed soldiers because of snow and ice on the ground.

The Governor, wintering in London, seems to have received the news with apathy. His mind was more occupied with the rebellion that had broken out in Ireland under Lord Edward Fitzgerald. Fearing it would enkindle a similar event in Newfoundland, Waldegrave urged the Duke of Portland to order the Chief Justice of Newfoundland, D'Ewes Coke, to take up permanent residence in St. John's, because "nine tenths of the inhabitants of this Island are either natives of Ireland or immediate descendants from them, and that the whole of these are of the Roman Catholic persuasion." He felt that "it is therefore to the wise and vigilant administration of the civil power that we must look to preserve peace and good order (the present times considered) in this settlement." To ensure this he cultivated the friendship of the Roman Catholic Bishop, Dr. O'Donel.

To further guarantee tranquillity, His Excellency issued a number of orders to limit the pleasures of the garrison. He forbade unauthorized visits to grog shops and bawdy houses, and virtually forbade a favourite pastime of the soldiers, the keeping of pets. He ordered, "all dogs straggling about the Fort after Gun Fire to be bayonetted by the Centinals, or hanged by the Guard."[38] These repressive measures increased desertions and kept away volunteers.

During the winter of 1798-99 Brigadier-General William Skerret was appointed commanding officer of troops in Newfoundland, under direct supervision of the commander-in-chief in Nova Scotia. He arrived in St. John's in May, direct from Ireland, where as colonel of "Skerret's Horse," he had played an important role in helping put down the United Irishmen's Rebellion of Fitzgerald.

The first symptoms that perhaps the Governor had reason to be concerned about the Irish in St. John's appeared in the latter part of February 1800 when some anonymous papers were posted up at night threatening the persons and property of the magistrates, if they persisted in enforcing a proclamation they had published, respecting hogs going at large, contrary to a presentment of the grand jury. A one-

101

hundred guineas' reward was offered for the capture of those who posted the papers and the inhabitants offered two hundred more, but without effect. This was later seen as the beginning of the attempt at anarchy and the destruction of order which soon followed.

On April 20 the first signs of mutiny appeared in the garrison. It being Sunday, the troops were paraded to worship, the English to church and the Irish to chapel. It was a fine day but it was noted that some of the regiment went through their exercises in a careless manner. Dr. O'Donel, who had become Bishop in 1796, learned that there was reason to suspect that one of the two companies on Signal Hill was planning open rebellion. The information is said by some to have come from an Irishwoman's confession or more probably from her seeking advice of the cleric relative to her husband's participation. The French Revolution had filled the Bishop with revulsion for mob rule. He went to General Skerret with his information and the General kept the regiment at exercises all day Sunday, which prevented anything happening that day.

Captain Tremblett reported five or six of the soldiers to their commanding officer for being idle and dirty, and confined another for being drunk on the 23rd.[39] He told them that he would see justice done them. They concluded he knew of their scheme for an uprising in the colony and decided it must be on the following day. This information was passed to the General by the Bishop. It was probably assumed by his informant that, because he was Irish, he was in sympathy with the cause of the United Irishmen. In fact, he had a horror of all anarchy.

Between forty and fifty of the Royal Newfoundland Regiment were to desert with their arms on the night of April 25. They were to rendezvous about 11:00 p.m., at a powder shed behind Fort Townshend, on the east corner of present day Belvedere Street and Hayward Avenue. A party was held at Fort William for Colonel Skinner and it continued until a late hour preventing the men who planned to desert from leaving for their rendezvous unnoticed. For some reason, probably the vigilance of their officers, the troops at Fort Townshend also failed to join the mutineers.

About three minutes after the soldiers had left Signal Hill, Captain Tremblett noticed they were gone and gave the alarm. Only nineteen men were able to leave. The others had no time. Ten of the deserters were soon captured and the remainder fled immediately into the woods. Within a fortnight sixteen were taken. Several informed against others and implicated twenty more. Five of the mutineers were hanged on a scaffold erected near the powder shed and the rest were sent to Halifax for hanging.[40]

The mutiny sounded the death knell of the Royal Newfoundland

Regiment as an effective fighting force. David Webber, in his pamphlet, "Skinner's Fencibles," suggests that the poor living conditions of the troops, the near slavery of fishermen and labourers who were kept in debt by their employers year after year, the denial of religious and political freedoms, the laws which forbade the free movement of the inhabitants, and a host of other pieces of legislation that made any chance of betterment of the poor impossible, were contributing factors.[41] The regiment was disbanded in 1802, about two years after the aborted mutiny.

In 1803 Britain and France were again at war. England's forces were spread around the world with Napoleon's grand army of 100,000 preparing to cross the Channel. Britain called home all the units of its army scattered throughout its colonies to defend the British Isles. The garrison at St. John's was no exception.

Newfoundland now undertook her own defence, and within a few months of the departure of the garrison the Royal Newfoundland Fencibles were formed from veterans of the disbanded Royal Newfoundland Regiment. As soon as the force was ready to defend the colony it was embarked in five vessels for Halifax. Next day the Nova Scotia Fencibles disembarked to do garrison duty in St. John's. This ridiculous exchange robbed Major-General Skerret of 683 trained men acquainted with the area and its problems of defence. Obviously, armed Newfoundlanders were still not to be trusted in their own country.

Captain William Haley, who arrived with the Nova Scotia Fencibles, as Town Major of St. John's, saw the folly of trying to defend the town with men who were not acquainted with the place. On 20 July 1805 he recommended to Skerret that a volunteer force that could act as an auxiliary police, as well as a local militia, be raised for the defence of St. John's. The General readily agreed and the proposal was endorsed by Governor Gower. There was a long wait for a reply from London.[42]

Meanwhile, the citizens went ahead on their own and formed the Voluntary Armed Association in April 1804. By the autumn of 1805 a force of two hundred men had been raised to defend the town. General Skerret ordered "an allowance of four pounds per man for clothing, that rations be given them from the King's stores when they are called out for drill." They adopted the Rules and Regulations of the British Volunteers in order that they might become a truly organized defence force. They became the Loyal Volunteers of St. John's and were provided with a proper uniform when on duty. The Corps paraded for arms and foot drill twice a week and each man had to give twenty-six days to drill during the year. Officers were elected by popular vote within the Corps and, with the Governor's approval, were equal in rank to regular officers of the garrison. There was one great advantage. A member of the Volunteers could not be pressed into service in the Royal Navy.

The officers included such prominent men as Nathan Parker, a partner in the Bulley and Job firm, who came from New England, Henry Shea (father of Sir Ambrose), George Lilly (the famous judge), Simon Solomon (the postmaster), William Thomas (the prominent merchant), Robert Parsons (the newspaper editor), and several lesser-known personages.

On 22 October 1807 the whole Corps of 276 men paraded at Fort Townshend before the Private Secretary of Governor Holloway, who was ill, and received its regimental colours. Captain Parker, who had been in poor health for some time, resigned his commission on 12 October 1808, and James Macbraire (a merchant who left Newfoundland in 1821 with a reputed fortune of £80,000) was commissioned eight days later.

Macbraire's personality did not suit him for the leadership of a volunteer force. He was arrogant, high-handed, and considered a martinet by officers and ranks. Dr. William Carson, who was surgeon to the Corps, found him pompous and overbearing and they clashed several times. Because of the attitude of Macbraire the number of Volunteers dropped from 276 to 75. General Skerret departed Newfoundland and was replaced by Major-General Francis Moore who decided not to recruit any more fishermen into the Volunteers. In the summer of 1810 they were called on to act as Guards of Honour to the Governor and took part in sham battles in the woods near the town.

By the spring of 1811 the regular forces were at their peak of efficiency under General Moore who repaired old fortifications and erected new ones around St. John's. On the other hand, the Volunteers were in a sad state of decline. The General felt they were of "little or no use" due to their depleted ranks and inefficiency.[43] In September 1811 discipline was so poor that the Volunteers could not be trusted to service their own weapons, so that all rifles were called in to the Ordnance Depot at Fort William.

In 1798 a temporary battery of two 24-pounder cannon, a guardhouse, and travelling magazine, designed to support Chain Rock Battery had been erected on a height above the rock and named for Governor Waldegrave. In 1810 it was rebuilt with masonry parapets, magazine, and gun platforms mounting a traversing 24-pounder and four 24-pounders on garrison carriages. Waldegrave Battery was maintained until 1871.

Frederick Battery was erected on the south side of the Narrows in 1812, by Lt.-Col. Elias Durnford of the Royal Engineers. It was built on the site of the old Castle which had become Fort Charles. All that remains of it today is some of the red sandstone blocks which supported the bank above the shoreline. An historic marker on the spot tells the story of the installation.

A battery of two 24 pdr. and four 18 pdr. cannon named South Battery was erected on this site in 1744 to replace the South Castle destroyed in 1708. This fortification surrendered to the French under Comte D'Haussonville on the 27th of June 1762. The ordnance was re-vented but the battery, now called Fort Charles, was allowed to fall into disuse until 1776 when rebuilding of the battery began. Completed in 1777 as a battery on nine pdr. cannon with a magazine and barracks for nineteen men it was called after Captain T. L. Frederick, R.N., Commander of the winter squadron 1777-78. Enlarged to a battery of four 24 pdr. and five 9 pdr. cannon in 1782. It was again rebuilt in 1811 to contain two 36 pdr. traversing guns and five 24 pdr. cannon. This battery was allowed slowly to fall into ruins after 1815 and was abandoned in 1852.

Just inside the sparse remains of Fort Frederick an anchor and an upright cannon, imbedded in the rocks near the shore, mark the location of Pancake Rock. These rusting pieces of metal are all that is left of the log-and-chain boom that was once linked to Chain Rock and operated by soldiers from the nearby fortification.

On the afternoon of 20 April 1848 Dr. William Carson went to inspect the old barracks at Fort Frederick. A vessel had arrived from New York carrying on board a passenger sick with smallpox. The doctor looked over the disused barracks with a view to taking over the place as an isolation ward to prevent the spread of the disease. He noted a fire had been lit in one of the grates. This was later denied by the soldier in charge. In any case the building caught fire that evening and Fort Frederick burned to the ground.

The corporal who had been looking after the place claimed the building was given over to Dr. Carson about six o'clock. Carson claimed he was not in a position to assume the responsibility and that he had not the intention of doing so until the following day. Results of the inquiry into the fire were inconclusive.

A lighthouse had been established nearby at Fort Amherst. It was first lit on 15 March 1812. Much later, in 1885, a fog gun was fired every hour during daylight fog, and a horn was sounded between the intervals of firing the gun.

Isabella Durnford, the daughter of Lieutenant-General Durnford, kept a diary of her life in St. John's in the summer of 1809 when she arrived on board the transport brig *Brittania*. In her book, *Family Recollections*, she wrote of the various batteries:

> The fir-covered heights overlooking the entrance to the harbour of the chief town, St. John's, are planted with batteries romantically situated. The raging surf of the Atlantic's billows dashes against the embrasures of Amherst and Chain Rock batteries, and the line of battleship, as well as the red-sailed fishing skiff come almost within arms reach of the cannon. Midway, and crowning the eminence, guns commandingly point from Queen's Battery and the lines on Signal Hill; and other defensive positions are placed among wooded projections of Capes and bays, fragrant with spruce and juniper. . . .

Just as the Loyal Volunteers of St. John's were about to disintegrate and disappear they were suddenly given a new lease on life. On 9 July 1812 news was received that the United States had declared war on Great Britain and her colonies. St. John's once more faced invasion, this time from New England. Patriotic citizens, and those out to protect their own self-interests, flocked to the Volunteers. On the day war was proclaimed in the colony, the High Sheriff, John Bland, became chairman of a defence committee of seven persons who met at the Court House. They recommended that the Loyal Volunteers be completely re-established and that Captain Macbraire be given a field rank. On the recommendation of General Moore, the Governor refused the promotion, and a reluctant Macbraire accepted the command of the Corps once more, with the hope that the "Governor would reconsider his promotion to field rank at a later date."

There were some famous names among the officers of the reactivated Volunteers: James Stewart, William Grieve, James Clift, Patrick Morris, Donald McCalman, and George Niven. One name that was deliberately missing was William Carson. Macbraire and Governor Duckworth, who was not in sympathy with the doctor's anti-establishment pamphlets, conspired to appoint David Duggan as Surgeon to the Corps. Carson protested in vain.

According to the amended Rules and Regulations, fines of one to three shillings a day were imposed on the rank and file for a number of minor offences. These included being absent on parade, dirty clothing, or the wearing of any part of the uniform when not on duty. With a pay of one shilling a day this was a harsh discipline and the result was that by 14 September 1812 the strength of the Corps was down from 333 to 165 men. An infuriated Duckworth demanded that Macbraire bring it up to the intended strength of 500 men before His Excellency left the colony for retirement in England.

The Captain wasted no time in attempting to carry out the Governor's wishes. On one occasion he drilled the men for two and a half hours in heavy rain. By October 19 he was able to parade the Volunteers before Duckworth at Fort Townshend, in full uniforms, armed, and with twelve drummer boys. His Excellency was very pleased with the results. When Governor Keats arrived in June 1813 he commissioned Macbraire Major-Commandant of the St. John's Volunteer Rangers, which had a strength, on paper, of 414 men. Of these 247 were absent at the fisheries or other business. The recruiting of replacements became more and more difficult as the threat of American invasion faded.

By 30 June 1814 Governor Keats was writing to Macbraire:

> It is much and sincerely to be regretted that the laudable zeal which in the first instance appeared to animate the members of the Loyal St. John's Volunteer Rangers should so far have declined as to afford but little or no prospect of service becoming effective.... I have desired Major General Campbell to suspend the payment of the Volunteer Rangers from the 24th of July and I desire you will cause the accounts to be brought to conclusion on that day, and the Arms, Drums, and other Military Stores to be returned to proper officers authorized by Major General Commanding to receive them.[44]

On July 4, Macbraire wrote to Keats:

> The present weak state of the Corps is to be attributed to no other cause but the extraordinary and unprecedented encouragement in the fishery ... but Your Excellency may rest assured should the enemy attempt to land the Rangers will prove the patriotism and loyalty which is characteristic of His Majesty's subjects in this settlement ... at all times I shall be ready to step forward in discharge of the duty I owe by my Country and King.

With that exchange of correspondence it was all over for the Loyal Volunteers.

When Newfoundlanders refused to confederate with the other colonies of British North America in 1867 the Mother Country, in a fit of pique, decided to punish her unruly child by withdrawal of the garrison. In spite of strong protests by the Prime Minister and people of Newfoundland the soldiers were marched to the dock on the morning of 8 November 1870, loaded aboard H.M. Troopship *Tamer*, and transported to Halifax. The ramparts of the forts were levelled and the buildings fell into decay. Part of Fort Townshend was temporarily saved when it became a police barracks. Fort William ended its days as a railway station. It was eventually razed to make room for the aborted Avalon Hotel and finally the Newfoundland Hotel.

Waldegrave Battery sprang back to life during the Great War of 1914-18.[45] When the guns of August were heard in Europe there were several quasi-military outfits in St. John's, mostly teenage cadets. In

1901-02 a branch of the Royal Naval Reserve was formed with headquarters on board H.M.S. *Calypso*, then moored at a dock in the west end near the railway station. In addition, there were four boy cadet groups. The Church Lads Brigade of the Church of England was founded in London in 1891. The St. John's branch was formed the following year and an armoury was erected on Harvey Road, opposite the top of Long's Hill. Roman Catholics had the Catholic Cadet Corps, Presbyterians had the Newfoundland Highlanders, and Methodists had the Methodist Guards Brigade.

Another non-denominational group, for those over eighteen years of age, was the Legion of Frontiersmen, founded in London. In 1910 a branch was established at Battle Harbour, Labrador, by Dr. Arthur Wakefield. A second was begun at St. John's in 1912. To join, one had either to have seen active service in a war, had training at sea, or knocked about in the wilds. Those who did not possess one of the three qualifications could become members of the Auxiliary Force.

When war broke out Dr. Wakefield offered the services of the 150-member Legion for overseas duty on 11 August 1914 but the prime minister, Sir Edward Morris, declined. The doctor himself enlisted in the Newfoundland Regiment, as a lieutenant, and went overseas with the First Five Hundred, as did many other Frontiersmen.

On 8 July 1916 the Legion took over responsibility for manning Waldegrave Battery under government pay and a temporary attachment to the R.N.R. of H.M.S. *Briton* (formerly H.M.S. *Calypso*). Sgt. William Russell and William Dawe, William Avery, Cyril Daniels, Solomon Ivey, Arthur Lucas, William Norris, and Hayward Taylor, all with the rank of gunner, took over the ruined fort. Lt. Vere Holloway, son of Col. Vere Holloway, who at one time commanded the 13th Madras Native Infantry Regiment in India, was appointed Commanding Officer. This martinet, who wore a medal awarded his father, was a stand-in for George V or Nicholas II of Russia. His second-in-command was Sgt. E. Russell.

The Frontiersmen wore a uniform consisting of a dark blue flannel shirt, with patch pockets and brass buttons, a neckerchief, blue or khaki riding .breeches, and blue puttees. They wore R.N.R. seamen's caps instead of the Australian-type slouch hats normally a part of the uniform.

There was a small barracks at Waldegrave Battery where the gunners slept in hammocks. Their days were occupied building an extension to their living quarters and a stone wall around the fort. They were supplied with a 12-pounder gun marked "For Drill Only, 1900." Each gunner was given a .303 rifle and Holloway sported a revolver. When completed, the fort consisted of two powder magazines, living quarters for officers and men, a mess hall, and an office. The whole was surrounded by a stone wall with two wooden gates seven or eight feet high.

Starting in October 1916 a boom was placed across the Narrows from sunrise to sunset. A steam launch with a machine gun mounted in the bows was stationed outside the boom and the S.S. *Fiona* was moored in a position which enabled her searchlight to sweep the Narrows. Waldegrave Battery was ordered to hold its fire until an order came from the officer in charge of the launch.

The closest the Legion of Frontiersmen came to seeing battle was on the occasion when a coastal boat crashed through the boom. It was a hazy night with a storm brewing and Capt. Abram Kean was anxious to reach port before the storm broke in all its fury. Ignoring the war games of the Royal Naval Reserve and the Frontiersmen, the despotic officer crashed his ship through the boom defence and headed for a berth at the railway dock.

Lieutenant Holloway, a stickler for following the rules, was apoplectic. It is said he had to be physically restrained from taking over the gun and firing a pot shot at the railway vessel. The only other action the men saw was chasing the hooligans who, under cover of darkness, liked to throw stones at the barracks. During summer, tourists swarmed about the area taking pictures and the gunners were kept on their toes seizing cameras and confiscating the film.

In 1920 the main barracks building was sold and turned into a dance hall. It eventually fell into disrepair and was taken down. Nothing remains today of what was called Fort Waldegrave and the gun area has been turned into a parking lot. By the late 1920s the Frontiersmen themselves were only a memory.

World War II brought St. John's its next fort. In March 1941, without consulting the government or people of Newfoundland, the British government signed an agreement with the United States, which included the granting of bases in Newfoundland and Labrador, for ninety-nine years, to the Americans in exchange for fifty obsolete U.S.N. destroyers. The agreement was signed on 27 March 1941. Prime Minister Churchill wrote to the Newfoundland representative, Hon. L. E. Emerson: "I can readily appreciate the feelings . . . you told me might arise that Newfoundland was being asked in this agreement to give up much of what she holds of value. . . . Without this agreement it is impossible to say what would be the effect on the prosecution of the war and the whole future of the world. . . . " The Prime Minister seemed to be saying that Newfoundland was probably saving the world from Nazi Germany.

On 30 September 1940 Uncle Sam's representatives arrived to inspect the Argentia site. Two days later they came to St. John's and started looking over Pleasantville, on the north shore of Quidi Vidi Lake. In November a party went to Stephenville to survey for an airfield.

On 25 January 1941 the former German Liner S.S. *Amerika*, renamed the U.S. Army Transport *Edmund B. Alexander*, arrived off St. John's. Refitted as "the swankiest floating barracks afloat,"[46] the 21,000-ton vessel was carrying one thousand American troops to St. John's, under command of Col. Maurice Welty. These were the first Americans to serve on foreign soil in World War II.

For four days the transport waited outside the Narrows for favourable weather. She would be the largest ship ever to enter port, and great care and wisdom had to be exercised in getting her through the harbour entrance. Wind, snowstorms, and fog postponed the venture until about one hour after sunrise on January 29 when Master Pilot, Capt. George Ansty, aided by two tugs and two coastal steamers, nudged the former liner to her berth on the Southside. Ships in the harbour blew a welcome on their whistles and there was a display of flags and bunting. In spite of the early hour, crowds stood watching on the docks, as they had for days. Before the docking operation was over, the *Edmund B. Alexander*, vanished from sight when a thick fog suddenly reduced visibility to a few yards.

On deck, hundreds of G.I.s peered through the mist trying to glimpse the igloos and Eskimos they were sure inhabited the region. Cries of "Where's the town?" could be heard everywhere. What little they could see was not reassuring. Cold snow blew about the old dock and ramshackle sheds on the southside, and huge icicles hung from the bleak rock face. Now and then fishing shacks and stages were visible and the odd dilapidated fisherman's house. The ship's band tried to lift the spirits of those on board by rendering such airs as "Hail, Hail, the Gang's All Here."[47]

In February Colonel Welty established Headquarters Newfoundland Base Command in Sir Richard Squires' old home, 44 Rennie's Mill Road. Base construction began at Pleasantville on 5 May 1941. The installation was to be called Fort Pepperrell, after Sir William Pepperrell, a relation of the Outerbridge family of St. John's. Sir William led the land forces at the capture of Louisburg in 1745 and was the first native-born American to be created a baronet. His wife is now a brand name for sheets, pillow cases, and towels.

On 15 April 1941 a lease was signed with Carpasian Park Ltd. for fifteen acres of land at the southwest corner of Carpasian and Long Pond Roads, on which to erect Camp Alexander, a temporary land base for the men on board the troop transport. On 20 May 1941 the soldiers moved from the ship to their temporary tent community. Work pushed ahead on the building of Fort Pepperrell and the shot in the arm the economy of Newfoundland received from the construction of the American bases was a blessing for which Newfoundlanders must always be grateful. It put the country on the road to prosperity such as it had never known. The days of the Great Depression and seven cents a day dole money were soon forgotten.

The Fort Pepperrell barracks were of wood, framed with asbestos shingles. The two-storey, flat-roof structures are in use today as federal government offices and provincial government-operated apartment houses. On 24 November 1941 the move from Camp Alexander was begun. In February 1942 Headquarters moved from Rennie's Mill Road to the new base.

Following the war years Fort Pepperrell was switched from the Army to the Air Force. Then on 14 April 1958 it was announced that the Base would be phased out and all civilians would be dismissed from their jobs by the end of the year. There was great gloom throughout the city. On May 17 thousands of St. John's citizens attended the final Armed Forces Day celebrations at Pepperrell Air Force Base. The last Americans departed on 15 May 1960 when the United States Army Transportation Terminal Command Arctic, then in charge of Fort Pepperrell, closed headquarters. On 10 August 1961 the property was returned to Newfoundland when, in a brief ceremony, the American flag was lowered and the Union Jack of Great Britain and the Canadian Red Ensign were raised.

In addition to Fort Pepperrell, World War II brought other military installations to St. John's. The Newfoundland Home Defence erected a base camp at Shamrock Field, off Merrymeeting and New-town Roads. The Royal Canadian Navy built an installation on Water Street opposite Buchanan and Prince's Streets. Old buildings such as the West End Stores, were torn down, new ones put up, and the wharves repaired and lengthened for servicing destroyers and corvettes. A barracks for naval women (WRENS) was erected on the face of the Southside Hills above St. Mary's Church. One needed the agility of a mountain goat to reach these quonset-hut living quarters. Part of the circular roadway surrounding these huts can still be seen.

Buckmaster's Field, between Prince of Wales Street and Golf Avenue, was a popular playground where visiting circus troupes performed on summer nights and days before the war. The Canadian Army took over the field and built a sprawling headquarters on the site of what is now a housing development. Such names as Army Street and Navy Street commemorate the World War II tenants of the area. Buckmaster's Field was phased out after Fort Pepperrell closed and the Canadian military headquarters in Newfoundland was transferred to the old U.S. Headquarters building at Pepperrell. The Newfoundland government, in a petulant display of chauvinism, renamed the area Pleasantville, wiping out the memory of a twenty year relationship that had brought many millions of dollars into St. John's and saw over ten thousand Newfoundland girls marry United States servicemen.

Just before the turn of the century a cricket pitch was constructed on the north shore of Quidi Vidi Lake. To give the area a park-like aura the name Pleasantville came to be applied to the place. In September 1914 a military camp was established briefly on the site of the old cricket ground, just east of Virginia River, then Rutledge's Brook. Here the first volunteers for the Newfoundland Regiment of World War I were encamped. These soldiers, known as the First Five Hundred, or Blue Puttees after the colour of their leg wrappings, broke camp on October 3 and embarked for England on board S.S. *Florizel*.[48] The ostensible reason given by the government of the day for abandoning the historic Fort Pepperrell in favour of the innocuous Pleasantville was the fact that the locality was known by that name during the weeks of occupation by the Newfoundland Regiment. In the summer of 1915 the curling rink at Fort William became a barracks for the regiment.

It should also be mentioned that, from 1940 until after World War II, the Canadian services had a detention camp on the corner of Carpasian and Rennie's Mill Roads. Punishment was meted out here to servicemen guilty of crimes and breaches of military discipline. The barbed-wire-enclosed prison barracks stretched from the junction of the two roads as far south as Rendell Place. For some years after the war the buildings opposite Pine Bud Avenue were used as storage sheds by Atlantic Films. Eventually they were torn down and the site of the detention camp became a suburban housing development.

During Canada's Centennial year, 1967, a military tattoo was instituted on Signal Hill involving members of the Newfoundland Regiment and high school cadets, dressed in replicas of the colourful uniform of the Royal Newfoundland companies of the 1860s. The tattoo was dropped in 1969 when the Liberal government decided to practise the unfamiliar virtue of economy. It was restored by the Progressive Conservative administration in the summer of 1972.

3

They Bear the
Names of Governors

Sir Thomas Cochrane, the impractical visionary who did so many practical things as Governor of Newfoundland from 1825 to 1834. His influence on island life is felt to this day and ranks him as one of the great men of Newfoundland history.

Government House, St. John's, circa 1900. The building was erected by Sir Thomas Cochrane for a fantastic sum of money and was first occupied by him in 1828, three years after construction was begun.

Governor Sir Walter Davidson (child on lap) and Lady Davidson entertain a visiting VIP from England on the lawn at Government House. (Courtesy Newfoundland Public Archives)

LE MOYNE D'IBERVILLE.

From Winsor's N. & C. H. of America.

Le Moyne d'Iberville. He and his brother are renowned for their expeditions to Hudson's Bay and the Mississippi for France. With the help of Canadian Indians, he led an attack against Newfoundland in 1696.

118

LADY HAMILTON.

*From a portrait in the possession of
Sir E. A. Hamilton, Bart.*

Lady Hamilton. The wife of Sir Charles Hamilton, she was the
first wife of a governor to actually live on the island. She lived
in Fort Townshend for four years during her husband's
administration from 1818 through 1824.

119

ADMIRAL SIR C. M. POLE, BART.
From an engraving after Northcote.

Sir C. M. Pole. He was in command of the British fleet
that made an unsuccessful attack on the Spaniards at the
Isle of Aix in 1799. In 1800, he was appointed to the
Newfoundland station, only to hold the post for one
year, since he was called upon to succeed Nelson in the
Baltic.

ADMIRAL DE RUYTER.

Admiral de Ruyter. DeRuyter was the Admiral in
charge of the Dutch naval attack which captured St.
John's on June 6th, 1665.

GOVERNOR RICHARD EDWARDS.
From an engraving after Dance.

Governor Richard Edwards. Soon after his appointment as a Rear-Admiral in 1779, Edwards was sent to Newfoundland. Although his command was short (he resigned in 1782), he was known as an able administrator.

Lord Rodney. The accomplished naval officer became Commodore, Governor and Commander-in-Chief of Newfoundland in 1749, when he was only thirty-one years old. His remarkable naval genius is viewed as second only to Nelson.

The Hon. John Byng. Byng served as Governor from 1741 to 1743.

Sir J. T. Duckworth. After his appointment to the rank of Admiral in 1810, Duckworth served three years as Governor of Newfoundland until 1813.

DR. KIELLY.

Dr. Kielly. A charge of assault against him in 1838 sparked a legal controversy which eventually defined the role of colonial government in relationship to the English Parliament.

124

Sir Ambrose Shea. Born in St. John's in 1817, he became a Father of Confederation by his attendance as a delegate at the Quebec Conference. He was appointed Governor of Newfoundland in 1886, but could not serve because of his pro-Confederation views. He was transferred to the Governorship of the Bahamas, and died in London in 1905.

They Bear the Name of Governors

Men, steered by popular applause, though they bear the name of governors, are in reality the mere underlings of the multitude.
PLUTARCH, *Lives*

Plutarch notwithstanding, the history of Newfoundland shows that in many instances its governors, far from being mere underlings of the multitude, were in reality rulers of a multitude of mere underlings. For a long time there was no such thing as a governor in the colony. There was not even any law imposed by authority. Crime, violence, and public disorders were commonplace. St. John's was a lawless frontier where bawdy houses abounded, people reeled drunkenly from the numerous taverns, and robbery and murder were an ever-present menace.

In 1615 Richard Whitbourne was sent out to try to establish some sort of law and order. At Trinity he held the first court of justice in North America. When he reached St. John's, complaints awaited him from over 170 masters of vessels in addition to numerous others from fishermen and planters. For eight years Whitbourne struggled to sort out the mess and put an end to lawlessness. When he returned home at the end of that period nobody was sent to replace him and the situation soon reverted to what it had always been.

It was not until 1630 that the infamous Star Chamber of Charles I came up with a replacement which proved to be one of the worst and most brutal systems of governing devised in the history of British imperialism. The Chamber enacted a series of harsh laws for Newfoundland. For example any person accused of a theft of forty shillings (about ten dollars) was to be shipped to England for trial and, if convicted, hanged. Another forbade the setting up of taverns for the sale of tobacco or intoxicating beverages. The most inhuman of these laws was the one which provided for enforcement of the Star Chamber rules. It stated that the captain of the first ship to arrive in any harbour in the spring of the year would be admiral (ruler) of that harbour for the season. There was to be no overall governor for another hundred years. Meanwhile, every port had its own governor.

These fishing admirals were all the law there was and they

answered to nobody for their actions. A number of them were illiterate, sadistic, vengeful, and cruel despots who ruled always to their own advantage. Their punishments were often savage and the records show that it was not infrequent for a suspect to be condemned for some petty theft without a proper trial and then to be flogged so mercilessly that he died of the beating.

Tyranny always begets resistance and so it was with the rule of the fishing admirals. Settlers who hoped to survive were forced to defy them. As the fishermen knew that there was little justice to be found at the hands of these men, riots became commonplace and disorders were reported everywhere. Deserters increased greatly in number. Bitterness and bloodshed were the result.

In the English civil war Charles lost both his crown and his head. In 1635 Cromwell's Commonwealth sent a commission to St. John's charged with the government of Newfoundland. The fourteen commissioners were under the leadership of John Treworgie, a man of excellent character. About his leadership there seems to be some dispute. Judge Prowse maintains that under Treworgie's wise administration the island knew its first real government. Settlement increased and the colony began to flourish and prosper as never before. Prowse also maintains that there was extensive progress in the establishment of law and order. Other historians claim that the fact that he allowed himself to be imprisoned by Sir David Kirke at Ferryland, and was obliged to return to England for want of funds (his salary being six years in arrears), proves him ineffective and ignored by the Mother Country.

Treworgie seems to have had the best interests of the colony at heart and, with the backing of the navy, did manage to institute reforms.[1] He believed in the necessity for governmental regulation of Newfoundland and while in England sought a new commission and vessels to back up his authority. However, the Restoration was underway and Treworgie fell from whatever grace he was in. It might be said that his efforts eventually bore fruit in the years to follow.

After the coronation of Charles II Newfoundland planters, such as John Downing, went to England to plead the cause of proper government for the colony but the merry monarch paid them little heed, preferring to cavort with Mistress Nell of Old Drury. It has been suggested that the king was probably in the pay of the west country merchants who did not want to see a legal representative of the Crown settled snugly at St. John's.

Bad as were the fishing admirals in summer, there was no rule at all during those seasons of the year when the captains and their ships were at home in England. Following the destruction of the island capital by the French in 1696, a military garrison was sent out to winter in St. John's. The officer in charge of Fort William seems to have acted as a kind of governor during the winter months. Because of the alleged misconduct of one of these garrison commanders, Captain Lloyd and the subsequent investigation into his behaviour, the governing duties in winter seem to have passed to the senior naval officer, sometime around 1708. As time went by, these officers also began to assume the summer rights of the fishing admirals, and a form of legal control by the navy began to emerge.

In 1711 the citizens of St. John's met and drew up their own laws. For two years there was complete harmony, and a kind of local parliament started to evolve. This alarmed the vested interests among the west country merchants and their allies in the British government. An agitation was fomented against the local laws. Old disputes and personality clashes were encouraged and the venture came to an end. The people continued to send petition after petition to England and at last, in 1729, a governor was finally appointed to rule Newfoundland.

These representatives of kings and queens have been many. Some left mighty marks while others departed without a trace of their ever having been in Newfoundland. Here we can only deal with the more interesting of the long line of those who bear the name of governor, and with the three buildings in St. John's that served them as Government House.

For some years there was a lieutenant-governor at Placentia who fiddled the tune of the governor of Nova Scotia. In 1728 this man, Samuel Gledhell, found himself in conflict with Lord Vere Beauclerk, the naval commander of the Newfoundland station. Rather than submit to the authority of Lord Vere, Gledhell claimed he was responsible only to the governor of Nova Scotia. Beauclerk sent a detailed report to England in which he once more pointed out the desperate need for civil government in the colony. This time the Duke of Newcastle took a personal interest in the matter and, in May 1729, succeeded in having Lord Vere appointed as first Royal Governor of Newfoundland.

Unfortunately for the colony, Lord Vere Beauclerk, who was born in 1699, as third son of the first Duke of St. Albans and a mother who was sole heir to the Earl of Oxford, was forced to give up the post and his place in Newfoundland history. Acceptance would mean his having to vacate his Parliamentary seat and the Crown wanted his vote in the House of Lords. Thus a new order in council, dated 22 May 1729, appointed Capt. Henry Osborne, of H.M.S. *Squirrel*, as first Governor of Newfoundland and Placentia. Beauclerk remained the commodore of the convoy and Osborne as his naval subordinate.

Captain Henry has been described by a contemporary as a man of cold, saturnine disposition, who scarcely ever made a friend. In command he was said to be austere, not always able to distinguish between tyranny and the exaction of due obedience. He was also little attentive to the merits of others. This third son of Sir John Osborne of Chicksands, Bedfordshire, was considered a good officer. At the age of thirty-one, he found himself in St. John's entrusted with the governorship of the island.

Though he was a conscientious and honest young man, Henry Osborne had neither the authority, experience, nor political abilities of his commanding officer on the station. The result of this was a split in authority that led to confusion and contention among the settlers and fishermen. The governor looked after civic duties and formal functions, while the commodore administered the law and ran things behind the scenes. Though Osborne was dedicated to the fulfilment of his task it was, in fact, Lord Vere who established civil government in Newfoundland. The great drawback was that he was unable to play in public the role that was his in private. After witnessing the difficulties faced by Governor Osborne in trying to assert his authority against the will of the fishing admirals and west country merchants, Beauclerk urged the government in England to give its representative in the colony clear and positive authority and the means to back it up. His recommendations were completely ignored.

In 1731 Capt. George Clinton was appointed as both commodore and governor. So haphazard seems to have been this appointment, that when Clinton arrived in St. John's on 30 June 1731 he found Osborne with the convoy, still under the impression that he was governor. With the arrival of George Clinton, Captain Henry disappears from our island story except as a street name in a St. John's subdivision. He subsequently became Commander-in-Chief in the Mediterranean in 1757 and Vice-Admiral of England in 1763. He died in 1771.[2]

Of George Clinton much could be written. Newfoundland's second governor was born in 1686 to the sixth Earl of Lincoln. He seems to have realized the frustration of trying to govern without authority and contented himself with the enjoyment of his position and sending a single report home. A least that is all the record we have of his administration.

On his return to England Clinton led the life of a wastrel and, by his own confession, became so fearful of his creditors that he left home each day at dawn and stayed away until after dark. He began to agitate for the position of governor of New York as a means of escaping his debts. Though he secured the post in 1741 there was a long delay and he did not reach New York until 1743. During the next ten years his weakness of character and total dependence on the advice and support of others diminished the authority and independence of the governorship of the colony of New York which Clinton's more worthy successors were never able to completely regain. He retired to a country estate, up the Hudson, with a bottle and a trifling circle whose main amusement was to play billiards with his wife. Following his return to England, Clinton was made a governor of Greenwich Hospital and served as a Member of Parliament until, debt-ridden, he expired in 1761. His son, Sir Henry Clinton, was supreme British commander in America from 1778 to 1781, following which General Washington gave the entire British forces the boot.[3]

Robert McCarty finds himself numbered among the select because he was not only the first Irishman to reside in St. John's as governor of Newfoundland, but also a very colourful character. As Viscount Muskerry of Cork and titular Earl of Cancarty, he arrived off the island shores in 1733. Following his term as governor, this charming rogue, who had lost an eye in a drunken brawl, attempted to recover his family estates which had been lost in Ireland. In this he was frustrated because of having made an enemy of the powerful duchess of Marlborough.

With little to forfeit he fought for the Stuart cause in France. When Bonnie Prince Charlie's bubble burst, Viscount Muskerry found he was not in the company of those pardoned. Granted an annual pension of a thousand pounds by Louis XV, he went off to Boulogne where he kept open house and regaled his drinking associates with tales of such close friends as Bolingbroke, who helped plan the Jacobite rising in 1715, and Dean Swift, who agonized over feces and wrote of Stella and Gulliver's travels.[4]

Admiral John Byng had been born in 1704 and became his sovereign's representative in Newfoundland thirty-eight years later. He has the distinction of being the only governor of the island to have ended his life in front of a firing squad. The *Newgate Calendar* says of Admiral Byng, " . . . whatever his errors and indiscretions might have been, [he] was at least rashly condemned, meanly given up, and cruelly sacrificed to vile political intrigues."

Byng's father, a brilliant naval commander, was rewarded for distinguished service by the titles Baron Byng and Viscount Torrington. His son John was also an esteemed naval officer and one of Newfoundland's better governors. That his career ended in disgrace may be due, for the most part, to his exceedingly fine character.

The unfortunate story began in the closing years of the inept reign of the weakling king, George II. His government was now hopelessly locked in a war with France, and French encroachments on English territory were increasing at an alarming rate. The citizens of England had vainly petitioned the king for the removal of his ministers.

It was in this atmosphere of despondency that Admiral Byng, the former governor of Newfoundland, was appointed commander of a fleet of ten ships that was to reinforce the garrison at Gibraltar, and then pursue a French fleet, which had sailed from Toulon with thirteen ships and a large number of transports containing 15,000 troops.

Instead of heading for America, as was believed, the French descended on the British possession of Minorca in the Balearic Islands, off Spain. Minorca fell, with the exception of the fortress of St. Philip which was besieged.

In reporting on these events from Gibraltar, Admiral Byng had some harsh observations and censorious comments. He also brought to the attention of the authorities at home the neglected state of the Gibraltar garrison and the inadequacies of his fleet. He pointed out that there were artillery men at Gibraltar who had been to Minorca, and he concluded with the opinion that no effective assistance could be given the besieged garrison. This intemperate communication made him implacable enemies in the government, who subsequently sealed his fate.

On approaching Minorca, after having failed to open a communication with the fortress, Byng's fleet met the French ships and the two formed a line of battle. For reasons of his own the Admiral did not follow this up and the French, unsure of the outcome, sailed away to fight another day. The British gave chase but the enemy fleet was soon out of sight. Admiral Byng called a council of war in which it was decided to abandon the defenders on Minorca, already heavily bombarded by French shore positions, and return to Gibraltar.

Byng's letter home, with news of the engagement, was carefully expurgated by those in authority so that any casting of blame on the ministers was removed. When the edited version was released, hired agitators whipped the crowds into a fury of indignation and the Admiral was brought back to England a prisoner. All the way from his landing at Greenwich to Portsmouth, where he was court-martialled on board the *St. George*, he had to be protected from howling mobs which demonstrated against him and burned him in effigy.

So sure was the Admiral that he had done the correct thing, and that he would receive true justice at the hands of the court, that he ordered his carriage to stand in readiness to hurry him home to London following the hearing. When he was found guilty and the sentence of his judges was pronounced, Byng was dumbfounded. The court-martial and the Lords of the Admiralty forwarded a strong recommendation of mercy to the king but it did not succeed. The defamed incompetents of the ministry made it clear to His Imperial Majesty that only the death of the unruly admiral could possibly appease the fury of the people, a fury they had themselves fomented. Even so, one of the Lords Commissioners refused to sign the death warrant because his conscience objected to its legality.

Abandoned by British justice, John Byng faced death in front of two files of marines on the quarterdeck of H.M.S. *Monarque* in Spithead Harbour on 28 February 1757. He stood with composure and a resolute conviction of the rightness of what he had done. Against his wishes a blindfold was applied because it was feared that his calm unflinching stare might intimidate the marines and spoil their aim. Moments after kneeling on a cushion placed on the deck, five musket balls ended the life of the former governor. Europe heard of his fate with shock and astonishment.[5]

The president of Admiral Byng's court-martial, and the admiral who pronounced the sentence of death over him, was the same man who had succeeded him in the governorship of the Newfoundland colony. If anyone were to call Thomas Smith a bastard he would be on very safe ground, for the gentleman was reputedly the illigitimate son of Sir Thomas Lyttleton. If Smith was the only governor to be so designated by fact, he was not the only governor to be so designated, as we shall see.

In 1749 Capt. George Brydges Rodney arrived in St. John's on board the forty-gun ship H.M.S. *Rainbow* to assume his duties as governor. Later historians were to rank Baron Rodney as second only to Nelson in the annals of Britain's great pre-twentieth-century admirals. By the time of his appointment, the role of Governor, Commodore, and Commander-in-Chief of Newfoundland was a much coveted position. Rodney, who was thirty-one years old, had already distinguished himself in the great victory of Ushant when Hawke defeated the French fleet. [6]

Cardigan is immortalized in a sweater, Sandwich in a snack, and Raglan in a raincoat. Rodney's name lives on in a small rowboat, still called a rodney, in many of the outports of Newfoundland. The crowning glory of his Lordship's career came on 9 April 1782 when, in a formidable battle off Dominica in the West Indies, he gained a brilliant victory by breaking the French line under De Grasse. This victory led to England's obtaining advantageous peace terms with France following the American Revolution.

Rodney's successor in the role of governor was Sir Francis Drake who deserves a footnote by being a direct descendant of the brother of the great Sir Francis Drake of bowling balls and Armada fame. The first Sir Francis died without issue and the line passed to his brother.

Enter John, second son of the fourth Lord Byron. The first son was the notorious "Wicked Lord" who set London tongues wagging by his wild deportment in the crumbling ruins of the family seat, Newstead Abbey. His brother John, known as "Foul Weather Jack," circumnavigated the world in 1764, while dedicating himself to the same debauched merrymaking as the Wicked Lord. "Foul Weather" scandalized British society by an open liaison with an amorous servant girl whom he transferred to a London flat, after his wife failed to appreciate finding her in their bed.[7]

In 1769 Jack Byron was governor of Newfoundland. We have no record of his escapades in the small capital but we can be sure that the honourable gentleman was not above being slightly dishonourable where a St. John's wench with a well-turned ankle, or an ample bosom, was concerned. He later became a rear admiral and died a vice-admiral of the White in 1786. The Governor's son, Mad Jack Byron, inherited his father's zest for riotous living. As an officer of the guards he served for a time in America during the Revolution. However, he was soon back in England devoting himself to his more accustomed role as a dandy in the salons of London. At twenty-two the scalawag youth ran off with Lady Carmarthan. This would not have been so bad had she not had a husband and three children. A divorce was promptly obtained by the cuckold. The lady bore Mad Jack three children during the five years of their relationship, but only one, Augusta, survived. Following the death of Lady Carmarthan, John Byron married Catherine Gordon, a twenty-year-old who was among the wealthiest young women in Bath.

The marriage of Mad Jack and Catherine gave the world one of the greatest poets ever known to literature. They named him Charles Gordon. Unable to constrain her profligate husband, Catherine paid off his debts and sent him to live with his sister in France. The degradation continued and, after sinking even deeper into debt, he died within a year. Little Charlie was ten years old when his grandfather's brother, the colourful old Wicked Lord, finally succumbed to his unrestrained adventures and passed on without an heir. The title and ruins of Newstead Abbey went to the fledgeling poet who was to keep up the family tradition by earning himself the appellation, the Bad Lord Byron.

The poet's connection with Newfoundland did not end with Grandfather Foul Weather. The libertine lord, in trying to escape the recriminations and hysteria of a frenetic affair with Caroline Lamb, sought the refuge of Caroline's mother-in-law. The understanding Lady Melbourne consoled the poet and arranged an introduction that led to his marriage on 2 January 1814 with her niece, Annabella, daughter of her brother, Sir Ralph Milbanke. The father of Lady Melbourne and Sir Ralph was the brother of Admiral Mark Milbanke, who made quite an excellent Newfoundland governor from 1789 to 1792. Being unmarried, His Excellency died without admittable issue. The Milbanke connection with St. John's is maintained in the name of a city street.

Besides his grandfather and Annabella, Byron was linked to the island colony by his dog, Boatswain. There is a popular misconception that this animal was a Newfoundland dog. It was not, but that he was a dog from Newfoundland, his tomb at Newstead Abbey shows quite clearly. In a burst of pagan defiance the young poet buried the dog on the site of the abbey altar. With him was interred Joe Murray, a manservant. Byron intended that he himself, and another manservant, William Fletcher, would also be laid to rest in the same tomb. These plans were, however, shattered when a whispered scandal, involving the poet in incest with his half-sister Augusta, forced him to flee into exile, where he died at thirty-six years of age.

The inscription on the dog's tomb reads:

> Near this spot
> are deposited the remains of one
> who possessed beauty
> without vanity
> strength without insolence
> courage without ferocity
> and all the virtues of man
> without his vices.
> This praise which would be
> unmeaning flattery
> if inscribed over human ashes
> is but a just tribute to
> the memory of Boatswain, a dog
> who was born at Newfoundland
> May 1803
> and died at Newstead Abbey
> November 18, 1808.

The myth of Boatswain being a Newfoundland dog obviously emanated from a misreading of the inscription. It claims only that he was born in Newfoundland. Upstairs in the abbey there is an oil painting of the dog done from life. It shows an animal, knee high, with a pointed snout, bushy tail and white ruff on his chest. What he appears to have been is a sheep dog, or border collie. There were a lot of sheep in the colony in the early 1800s and sheep dogs were not uncommon. How one found his way from Newfoundland to Newstead Abbey is not known. The animal could have been a gift from one of the naval officers who was a friend of Foul Weather Jack, though the old man died two years before the birth of the poet. Byron was not to meet Annabella Milbanke until two years after the death of Boatswain, so the dog could have had no connection with Governor Milbanke.

Boatswain died prematurely after having been bitten by the rabid dog of the postmaster from Mansfield. His passing was greatly mourned by the poet who wrote a moving poem to his memory. The Bad Lord Byron had one other indirect connection with Newfoundland. During his student days at Marischal College, Aberdeen, a classmate of his was a young Scot, named Sandy Bannerman, who was to become a popular nineteenth-century governor of the island.

The Newfoundland dog, once thought to have been praised by Byron, is generally believed to have sprung from a native Indian dog. With the coming of Leif Ericsson to Newfoundland around 1000 A.D., the Viking dogs are thought to have been crossed with the native breed. The two strains developed into one, while undisturbed, during the next five hundred years. Following the rediscovery of the island by John Cabot, the fishermen of Europe brought with them the beautiful Great Pyrenees dog of the Basques. These played a large part in the further development of the Newfoundland breed. A particoloured dog was evolved in England after 1550 and when the artist, Sir Edwin Landseer, immortalized the breed in his painting, "A Distinguished Member of the Humane Society," they became known as the Landseer Newfoundland.

There are many tales connected with the exploits of the huge black, web-footed animal. It is one of the friendliest, most devoted and loyal pets in the world. It has an uncanny natural instinct to retrieve people from the water. Until recent times it was harnessed to snowsleds to haul firewood from the forests, or to wheeled carts to haul provisions and produce. The Newfoundland also pulled mail and passengers over trails impossible for a pony in the days before highroads were built.

There have been many distinguished owners. Richard Wagner, the composer, had two, and he introduced them at a dinner party by saying, "We shall now be entertained by Nature's Gentlemen." Robert Burns wrote of Caesar, his Newfoundland dog, that he was a gentleman and scholar and came from a place where sailors went to fish for cod. . . .

"But though he was o' high degree..

The fient a pride—nae pride had he."

In recent times Senator Robert Kennedy was the owner of a much-admired member of the breed.

A close relation is the Labrador retriever, a dog which is also native to Newfoundland, where it was always called the St. John's dog. The name Labrador was later applied to it in England. The animal had little, if anything, to do with Labrador. The St. John's dog is known to us today as the flat-coated retriever. The Golden Labrador was evolved from it.

Between the governorships of Byron and Milbanke, St. John's welcomed John Campbell, a Scot and the son of a minister of the church. Campbell was over sixty at the time he became governor. He is of interest to us because of his wife's first cousin, Capt. William Bligh. This thirty-year old naval officer sought a commission in the Newfoundland squadron at the time of his in-law's appointment, but instead of obtaining a cushy job with his cousin's husband, Bligh found himself sent with his ship to the West Indies. Had Captain William been able to secure the assignment he sought in the Newfoundland squadron, Nordhoff and Hall, Metro-Goldwyn-Mayer, and generations of moviegoers might well have been robbed of riches, and Charles Laughton of one of his most famous screen portrayals as captain of H.M.S. *Bounty*.

Bligh's ship is said to have called in at St. John's on the way to the West Indies and the arrogant young captain spent a few days visiting with Governor Campbell. This was half a dozen years before the incident in the Pacific which was to give him immortality. Some years after the mutiny on the *Bounty*, Bligh was himself a despotic governor of New South Wales.

Sir Hugh Palliser, who ended his days as a baronet, was a Yorkshireman from the West Riding, having been born at Kirk Deighton in 1723. He entered the navy at the age of twelve and received steady promotions. In 1762 he was sent, with a small squadron, to recapture St. John's from the French but arrived too late. It had already been retaken by Colonel Amherst. Two years later Palliser became governor of Newfoundland.

A dictatorial and overly paternalistic man, he was a humanitarian who has been highly praised for his work in the colony. Prowse says of him,

> The Governor had only one great fault—beyond his own circumscribed vision he could see no horizon; he had no faith, no hope, no future for the colony; the one narrow insular idea of the age pervaded his official mind, that it should be a fishing colony, used for one great purpose only in his eyes, supplying men for the Navy.... On all who opposed his views he poured out the vials of his wrath.... No ruler since the days of Charles II hated the country he was set over more bitterly than Sir Hugh Palliser.[8]

The Governor is remembered for the Fishery Act, called Palliser's Act, and the introduction of the Moravian missionaries to Labrador. He concluded a treaty with the Labrador Indians and was instrumental in sending Cartwright to that territory. It was during his four-year reign that Wesleyanism was introduced into the island but, at the same time, he forbade any two Roman Catholic Irishmen to live in one dwelling and they were not allowed to keep public houses.

In 1759, while in command of H.M.S. *Shrewsbury* operating in the St. Lawrence, a young man named James Cook, who was on board learning to survey, came to Palliser's attention. They became lifelong friends, and it was during Palliser's administration that Cook spent several years in Newfoundland charting the shores of the island.

The famous surveyor was in and out of St. John's on survey expeditions from 1764 to 1767. That final summer he surveyed the Bay of Islands and discovered the site of the city of Corner Brook. A monument to him was erected there by the federal government in 1972.

Cook's work in Newfoundland completed his apprenticeship as a surveyor. He had shown himself extremely competent and in 1768 was given command of H.M.S. *Endeavour* and sent to look for new lands in the Pacific. He proclaimed British sovereignty over Australia in 1770, after having rediscovered Abel Tasman's New Zealand the previous year. In 1778 he discovered the Hawaiian Islands, formerly called the Sandwich Islands, and it was there that he was killed by natives. Palliser erected a monument to him on the grounds of his home in Vache, Buckinghamshire, with an inscription by Admiral Forbes, the one man who had stood out against the condemnation of Admiral Byng. Palliser Bay in New Zealand was named by Cook for his friend, the former governor of Newfoundland.

In 1779 Admiral Richard Edwards was appointed to the vice-regal post in Newfoundland. By then St. John's was a busy centre of trade for an island population of over twelve thousand. Fort Townshend had been under construction since 1773 and the older military installations were being strengthened. The governor's office was becoming a busy place.

Admiral Edwards appears to have decided it would be more convenient for all concerned to have his headquarters on land rather than on his flagship. He wrote to London, "I find it necessary from the situation of this island to reside on shore for the more inspection of the works which I have given directions to be erected against the approaches of the enemy from the outharbours." This decision gave St. John's its first Government House.[9]

In the summer of 1779 Governor Edwards took up residence in a house on Duke of York Street, sometimes also called Kenny's Lane. The thoroughfare no longer exists but it is not difficult to place. It started at Duckworth Street, about fifty yards east of Cochrane Street, and ran northwest to a pathway that is now Gower Street. The angle of Duke of York brought it out on Gower about fifteen yards east of Cochrane Street. The lane disappeared after the 1892 fire, but the name is preserved in York Street, a new street created to intersect the old.

The first official residence of the governors was on the estate of John Stripling, a leading publican who came from the English west country. The house which Governor Edwards occupied was probably the Stripling family home. Unfortunately, no sketch or photograph of it exists and we do not even know its location on the street.

The building is described in derogatory terms in official correspondence but it must have been one of the better houses of its day.

Archbishop Howley, who visited the dwelling before it was destroyed in the Great Fire of 1892, says that it had a gable roof and was "not of any very elaborate architectural pretentions but it was of a somewhat more durable and expensive character than ordinary wooden dwellings of the time as the Oak beams can testify. . . ." The house was over a hundred years old at the time of its visitation by the cleric, who writes that he was unable to find the date of its erection but by 1880 it "was of very remote antiquity." Howley goes on to say, "In 1795 it was rented by Doctor O'Donel (consecrated Bishop the following year) and Dr. Ogden M.D. for Mr. Brine. Known as Mary Stripling's Plantation it consisted of a house and garden. Mary Stripling of Ashburton, County of Devon, Kingdom of Great Britain, spinster. The rent was £5.15s per year."

A search of the parish records in Ashburton reveals no Striplings having lived in the town. A similar search of the County of Devon baptism, marriage, and burial records, as well as the Land Tax Assessments, shows no mention of Mary Stripling. She seems to have collected her rents and disappeared from history.

In the spring of 1780 great alarm was felt when it was learned that a French fleet, with one hundred soldier-laden transports, had sailed from Brest in May. Governor Edwards returned from wintering in England to find the colony in a state of vigilance with an invasion expected at any moment. He must have decided it would be safer living in a fort than in an exposed part of the town, for we find him writing to Colonel Pringle, the chief engineer, asking him to give immediate directions for the repair of the artillery barracks at Fort William for his use until Fort Townshend should be in a condition to receive him. For some reason this was not done and the governor went on living in the residence on Duke of York Street. Possibly the Colonel was so busy trying to rush the new fort to completion that he had little time for the Governor's request. The invasion threat evaporated when it was found that the fleet from Brest was bound for the French territory of Louisiana.

With the completion of Fort Townshend in 1781, the Governor took possession of a summer residence there, after having spent two seasons in the first official abode. As time went on little care seems to have been taken of the new quarters. Few improvements were made and the building was allowed to fall into disrepair. By 1815 we find the sadly neglected domicile at Fort Townshend described, in dispatches to the secretary of state, as "a very old building in a very exposed situation, the rooms are small and it is by no means a comfortable dwelling." It was then only thirty-four years old.

Different governors tacked rooms and corridors onto the place until it was completely disjointed, having long passages with borrowed light. The weight of the slate roofs had injured the structure so that all efforts to render it watertight were in vain. The house formed the east side of the barracks square. When the fort was abandoned, in favour of Signal Hill, and the ramparts were levelled, the building was enlarged. It was of wood, two storeys high, with cellars and offices attached. There was also a stable, cowhouse, and outdoor privies. It contained a living room twenty by forty feet, a dining room twenty by thirty-five feet, a parlour, an office for the governor, four bedrooms, and three servants' bedrooms. Adjoining was an office for the secretary and one for the clerks. Each room and office had a fireplace. In spite of the considerable sums eventually spent to try to put it in shape the uncomfortable dwelling was at the mercy of every gale.

A plaque on the wall of the Central Fire Station, which now occupies the site of the house, bears the legend OLD GOVERNMENT HOUSE. This tablet, erected by the provincial government in recent years, reads:

> A two-storey wooden dwelling house designed by Lt. John Caddy, R.E. as the summer residence of the Governor of Newfoundland was erected on this site in 1779. Repaired and enlarged in 1812 it was found to be unfit for year-round occupation after the appointment of Vice Admiral Sir Francis Pickmore as the first resident governor in 1817 but continued to be the official home of the governor until the present Government House was completed in 1829.

This plaque is in error for Pickmore was never knighted.

In 1812 ill health forced Vice-Admiral Richard Keats to retire from an active role in the war with America and he was appointed governor of Newfoundland. Two years later he was writing to the Earl of Bathurst that his private affairs required his presence in England and he wished to be allowed to bring his business as governor to a conclusion. In May of that year His Royal Highness, the Prince Regent, acting for his father, George III, who was utterly insane and incapable of rule, was pleased to appoint a friend of Keats, Vice-Admiral Francis Pickmore, to be governor of the island. He finally arrived in September on board H.M.S. *Hydra*. Pickmore stayed in his new domain two months and then took off for London to enjoy what was left of the "season."

During his absence the most awful winter conditions were experienced by the settlers at the beginning of one of the bleakest periods St. John's was ever to know. Actual famine threatened, for inadequate provisions had been imported. Were it not for Capt. David Buchan, who was in control in the capital, things would have been far worse. With courage, skill, and deep concern this officer was able to feed hundreds who would otherwise have starved.

For this, and other reasons, it was decided in February 1817 to direct future governors to reside on the island during the winter months instead of returning to England with the end of the fishing season. On being informed of this, Francis Pickmore wrote His Majesty's government regarding the condition of the house appropriated for his dwelling. He stated that it was

> . . . situated on an eminence; built slightly of fir weather boarding, exposed to the North-east or coldest winds—and though a sufficiently good one as a summer habitation, is in no way suited for a winter residence in that climate, which I had the opportunity of experiencing the truth of, even in the month of November last. The snow having in the course of a very short snowstorm, accompanied with a gale of wind, penetrated into the bedrooms—Nor is it capable of being rendered a fit winter residence, unless by taking down entirely and rebuilding it on a different plan; and even in that case the site is so circumscribed that I should, in the event of the measure I allude to being adopted, be disposed to recommend in preference, the erection of a new house in some more eligible situation than that which the present one occupied.[10]

The Earl of Bathurst sent a reply to his correspondent with, what one might call, post haste. He advised His Excellency that, under existing circumstances in England, it had been necessary to pull tight the purse strings. It was most important to avoid any expense of so considerable an amount as must be incurred by erecting an adequate residence. Then the Vice-Admiral was recommended to hire, for a term, any house in St. John's, or its neighbourhood, which might afford him a temporary residence. And so in the early autumn of 1817 Francis Pickmore was sent back to Newfoundland, as a lamb to the slaughter. He arrived on September 30 to become the first governor to take up permanent year-round residence.

The hard winter of 1817, generally called the "Winter of the Rals," was a terrible season. A severe frost sealed off the coast from shipping in early November and continued without let-up until spring. Added to the misery of this cold there was a continuation of the previous year's starvation, and then the awful scourge of fire. Nearly a thousand persons had been left homeless by fire in February 1816. Then in 1817, on November 7 and 21, the first Great Fire destroyed the whole of the downtown area including most of the warehouses containing the island's food supplies. Over two thousand were without shelter, and winter was coming on. The suffering of the dispossessed populace increased when roaming gangs of half-starved, lawless men, call rowdies or "rals" everywhere threatened life and property. Vigilance committees were formed for the protection of the law abiding.

Three days before the most miserable Christmas of his life,

Admiral Pickmore hovered over his desk in the drafts of Fort Townshend and wrote the secretary of state that he, had been unable to procure a suitable winter residence in or near St. John's. The homeless thousands filled every foot of available space. He added that the recent calamities had convinced him that Government House should be unconnected with the town and so he was endeavouring to make the present one tenable. That he failed in this is evidenced by the following entry in the Colonial Records for Thursday 24 February 1818. "His Excellency Francis Pickmore, Esquire, Vice Admiral of the White, Commander and Chief in and over the Island of Newfoundland and its Dependencies, departed this life at 6.00 o'clock this evening."

The sixty-two-year-old gentleman, who was already ailing, caught a chill in the official wind trap. This developed into a bronchial congestion and earned him an extra notch in Newfoundland history by becoming the first of two governors to die in office, at St. John's. The *Naval Chronicle of 1818* tells us: "The lamented event took place . . . after an indisposition of a fortnight's continuance, which did not portend dissolution until a few hours previously."

His body was removed from the fort in public procession to a temporary vault, in the wooden Anglican church, attended by all officers of the naval, military, and civil detachments. The Roman Catholic bishop was among the chief mourners. Rev. Thomas Grantham performed the service to the accompaniment of minute guns from the ships-of-war and the forts.

Great exertions were made to cut a channel through the ice, which was several feet thick in the harbour, so that H.M.S. *Fly* might convey the earthly remains to England. Captain Browker of H.M.S. *Sir Francis Drake*, the senior naval officer of the station, succeeded in government and ordered nearly three hundred shoremen and forty sailors from the *Drake* and the *Egeria*, as well as the whole crew of the *Fly*, to work daily at cutting a channel large enough to let the *Fly* reach open water. It took three weeks to cut the necessary 2,856 yards. Governor Pickmore departed St. John's, for the last time, preserved in a puncheon of rum.

In July 1818 Captain Browker was relieved of his pro-tem governorship by Charles Hamilton, though we read in the "Naval Chronicle" of the appointment of one, Amelius Beauclerk, who certainly never served. Hamilton was no stranger to North America. He had been created a baronet in 1776 for the important part he took in the defence of Quebec in the preceding year.

Governor Hamilton arrived, to borrow a phrase from George Eliot, "with a sweet face by his side." Henrietta, only daughter of a well-known Charing Cross banker, was a widow with a four-year-old son when she married the baronet. She is the first governor's wife to have set foot in the colony. It is fortunate for us that she did, for Lady Henrietta was not only a pretty and charming woman of intellect; she was also an accomplished painter. It is she who visited Mary March, and later Shanadithit, and painted the watercolour miniatures which are the only true visual records we have of these famous Indian women, indeed of any of the vanished Beothuck tribe.

The Hamiltons must have succeeded in making the drafts welcome at Government House for they survived the winters and returned to England in 1825, still sound in limb and body, having spent seven years in their tumbledown quarters. Sir Charles, a stern, unbending conservative, gave it as his opinion to the secretary of state in 1823: "There can be no doubt the unfit state of the Government House and the total want of all the usual comforts which the inhabitants of St. John's find necessary in the winter was in great measure the cause of Admiral Pickmore's death."[11]

The British government finally took the hint and Hamilton's successor, Sir Thomas Cochrane, the most far-sighted and progressive of all our governors, was "furnished with liberal means for the task of making provision to meet the want of a new residence." Sir Thomas's interpretation of "liberal means" was to prove beyond the wildest imaginings of their august Lordships. The original estimate for Government House presented to Parliament, was £8,700 (over $40,000). By the time Governor Cochrane had finished his dream house the final cost was close to a quarter of a million dollars, a fantastic sum for any colonial dwelling in those days. Had the result been a thing of beauty it might be understandable. From the outside, Cochrane's Government House still looks more like a prison than a viceregal dwelling. Prowse was compelled to say that "Government House is a huge pile of unredeemed ugliness." Time has mellowed the features of the building somewhat, and like the harsh face of an ugly sister that one becomes accustomed to, it seems to soften and improve with age.

The final plans appear to have been drawn by Cochrane himself, before coming to Newfoundland. They are roughly based on those of Admiralty House in Plymouth, England. Somewhere along the line, a planner confused the island of Newfoundland with the islands of the West Indies and, according to one provincial government historian, a moat was added so the water would keep snakes out of the building. When it was discovered there were no reptiles of any sort in Newfoundland, the wall of the moat was cut into basement windows for the house. The moat exists to this day.

The skyrocketing costs and personality conflicts marred the entire construction period. On 6 August 1827 Lieutenant-Colonel Lewis, commanding officer of Engineers, wrote the Governor to complain: "The plans furnished by His Excellency are very defective in detail and if they had been made by a professional man the errors in question would not have happened." The Colonel was told, in a curt reply, he had no business judging the conveniences of a plan made by His Excellency.

When Lord Bathurst complained that plans for the house were on too extensive a scale His Excellency replied to the Secretary of State: " . . . in a climate where so large a portion of time must be passed indoors, the indulgence of rooms a little larger than might be requisite in a temperate climate might be admissible in a building intended to be permanent and durable." Bathurst resigned himself to allowing the work to proceed.

A site off Military Road, on the barrens between Fort William and Fort Townshend, was chosen. Being on the outskirts of the town it was thought to be safe from the plague of fire. The wisdom of this was twice proved in the Great Fires of 1846 and 1892. A new roadway was made from the waterfront to the site, and today this street bears the Governor's name. The building was constructed of rough, red sandstone quarried from behind Waldegrave's Battery, on Signal Hill, with some rubble stone quarried from the Southside Hills. The timber came from Halifax.

Construction did not begin until 1827. Workmen's wages in Newfoundland being considered too high, the engineers brought out twenty-eight masons, twenty-five carpenters, and one slater from Scotland to work for 4s. 4d. a day, a little less than one dollar. The Governor began changing the plans long before the house was finished. Three succeeding commanding officers of engineers registered bitter complaints regarding his interference with their work.

Cochrane altered things here and there according to whim, adding extensively to the wings. After the chimneys had already been erected in the partitions, he decided to have double doors between the dining room and drawing room, and between the drawing room and ballroom. The chimneys had to come down, at considerable expense, to allow this. Against all advice he ordered the dining-room fireplace to be put in a position where some of the guests at table would be roasted and the result was that the fireplace could almost never be used. In despair, the first commanding officer sought and obtained permission to return to England. His replacement was not so fortunate, for he collapsed and died on the job in 1830. The third officer persevered in spite of difficulties and saw the work completed. The outside gutters and drains of the building are decorated with the royal cipher of George IV in whose reign construction was begun. The new Government House, built under the supervision of William Haddon (who died in New York 10 June 1876), was occupied in 1829 but was not completed until 1831. Soon afterwards part of the roof blew off and the unexplainable north entrance proved so cold that a series of porches were added to further detract from the undistinguished architecture. In the year of its completion a court of inquiry was ordered to investigate the phenomenal cost. Somehow, Sir Thomas managed to survive the investigation. At the same time, he was renovating a country estate, Virginia Waters, which he purchased on Logy Bay Road.

The ceilings in the downstairs rooms of Government House were later decorated with elaborate frescoes by a painter named Pendikowsky, who had been to jail in St. John's in 1880 for forgery. In exchange for a remission of sentence, the Polish citizen, who vanished as readily as he had appeared, painted the rooms at Government House and the ceilings of the chambers in the Colonial Building.

In 1835 Sir Thomas obtained a new commission, with very extensive powers, and was constituted in point of fact and law the first civil governor. Although he had been a naval officer, the military establishment resented its loss of civic control. A man of tremendous energy, Cochrane threw himself into the task of reform and fair administration. Prowse says "Sir Thomas Cochrane is now universally admitted to have been the best Governor ever sent to Newfoundland." The great Patrick Morris wrote in 1828, "I maintain that he has done more real good to the colony, since his appointment, than all his predecessors put together." Sir Thomas certainly advanced the country to a more civilized state. He inaugurated a Supreme Court; encouraged the cultivation of land for farming; pushed the island's first roads to Topsail, Bay Bulls, Torbay, and Portugal Cove; recommended the establishment of a university; fostered schools for the poor, as well as the rich; and recommended the establishment of a municipal council for St. John's. He advanced the social life of the town by supporting himself in splendour, mostly at his own expense. He lavishly entertained at table, both local residents and visiting strangers. If he had a weakness, it was his fawning over Capt. David Buchan, who was the apple of his eye and undisguised favourite. In England the family was known as "the mad Cochranes," but the Governor's vision does not reflect the epithet; his official residence makes one wonder.

Over the years assorted royalties and VIP's have found a night's lodging under the roof of Cochrane's mansion. Besides a glittering array of dukes, duchesses, consorts, princes and princesses of the blood, the house has hosted King Edward VII, King George V, King Edward VIII, King George VI, and Queen Elizabeth II.

The papers of Sir Thomas Cochrane, in the Scottish National Library in Edinburgh, reveal a man of culture who enjoyed living up to the image of a nineteenth-century governor. Married in 1812, he had two sons and two daughters. Every ten days or so, he would have a formal dinner party at Government House for ten to a dozen people. His list frequently included the Chief Justice, or the Roman Catholic Bishop. Sir Thomas visited the theatre almost every week and on 1 May 1827 took Bishop Scallan along as his guest. He tells us the population of the town that year was 10,214·Roman Catholics and 4,951 Protestants, for a total of 15,165.

The governor had eight servants who were paid a total of £56 per month. His expenses were as lavish as his style of living. In one month in 1834 they came to £445.8.6 sterling or £513.19.1 in Newfoundland currency. The property value of the items in Government House that he left to Governor Prescott when he departed was £871.11.3. His wine cellar was auctioned by Clift's for £316.16.6, and might have brought more at another time, but His Excellency was anxious to have the cash. [13]

In 1836 Cochrane did Newfoundland history a service by asking Rev. John Chapman, Church of England Minister at Twillingate, to investigate the story of a child named Ann Simms, of Fogo, who was suspected of having become Pamela, wife of Lord Edward Fitzgerald, the great Irish leader. Mr. Chapman held a hearing at Fogo and the results are in the Cochrane papers. Unfortunately, some of the documents are missing. The testimony came from people who had known the child and her mother, and their sworn statements reveal a fact long denied by the Fitzgerald family. Mr. Chapman sums up his investigation by stating: "On my mind there is no doubt but Mary Symms child Ann was the very person who was taken with her mother to Christ Church, this far the history is quite clear, and I have no doubt but if the history of that child can be traced from that point it will then appear quite evident that the same child afterwards became Lady Fitzgerald." [14]

So great a man as Sir Thomas Cochrane did not depart St. John's with the approbation of the crowds ringing in his ears, but took his leave amidst the jeers of an unruly mob of Irishmen. Cochrane's greatest failure was his inability to submerge his white, Anglo-Saxon, Protestant feelings, or fears, and this unfortunate flaw brought his enlightened rule to a bitter end.

Sir Thomas was made a rear admiral in 1841, and returned to active duty with the navy. On 5 February 1842 David Buchan, who appears to have disposed of his property in St. John's, transferred to Cochrane's flagship in the East Indies. That same year Buchan became a Member of Parliament in England.

A man known in the army as "The handsome Colonel Harvey" was the next to take up residence at Government House. Sir John Harvey, an ex-inspector general of constabulary in Ireland, had been a governor of New Brunswick, but was dismissed because of a squabble with the Governor General of Canada over a boundary dispute he had attempted to settle by himself with the Governor of Maine. Finding his services terminated after forty-seven years in public service, and almost devoid of private means, Harvey set about enlisting the aid of powerful friends who could help him get reinstated. On 16 September 1841, he arrived in St. John's and began a rule marked by tact and diplomacy which helped to heal the wounds of religious tumult left by Cochrane and Prescott, and restore harmony to the colony. He showed great skill in patching up the differences between Governor Prescott and the Roman Catholic clergy, and even placated Bishop Fleming.

In 1842 the new governor was called upon to put all his conciliatory powers to the test when it was decided to restore self-government, which had been suspended because of the violent political and religious quarrels that were threatening to tear the country apart. Harvey was able to convince Dr. Fleming and his priests to stay out of the election and representative government was restored with amazing calm. The only incident was when a Protestant judge tried to arrest John V. Nugent, a Roman Catholic candidate, for non-payment of libel damages. The judge was given a reprimand by the Governor for his timing of the arrest.

Sir John was a cultured man of refinement and equanimity. He was in great need of the latter virtue, for his son Frank was probably the blackest sheep in any family to occupy the governor's mansion.

Frank Harvey had not been long in the colony when he earned the distinction of being shot at while committing a theft. A butcher named Mitchell, of Circular Road, shot at young Harvey while the lad was robbing his garden. On 12 November 1851 a reward of ten pounds was offered for the apprehension of parties having wrecked and stolen knockers from the hall doors of many of the houses on Water Street. Officials said no information was given, but the leader of the gang was thought to be Frank Harvey. If so, then he must have stayed behind when his father left Newfoundland, or else returned on a visit. The following year his sudden death was announced in Dublin.

In August 1846, a month after the Great Fire, Sir John was given a transfer to Nova Scotia. Another son of his, presumably more circumspect than the raffish Frank, married a daughter of Dr. Spencer, the Bishop of Newfoundland.

The newspaper *Pilot* had this to say of Harvey's successor, Sir Gaspard LeMarchant on 31 July 1852:

> His Excellency the Governor made his public embarkation on board H.M.S. *Cumberland* on Tuesday evening at four o'clock. His departure from the island is hailed with deep satisfaction. It is like the removal of a plague spot from the victim of disease. Few regret his absence, save the few official parasites who accompanied him to his place of embarkation. For the good of the country, we trust we shall never see his like again.

146

Sir Gaspard's honest appraisal of what was going on in Newfoundland at the time earned him the emnity of three of the most powerful factions in the colony. First, he felt the curse of the island was the fortune-hunting merchant from England who stayed only long enough to amass wealth and then took his departure. This view was not appreciated by the financial establishment, who educated their children abroad and looked forward to passing their twilight years enjoying the comforts of the Old Country.

Next, he alienated himself from the masses by his belief that the aim of the people was to depend on welfare and that they should be roused to more self-reliance. Toward this end he encouraged agriculture and discouraged dole handouts.

His suspicions of the power of the bishop and clergy of the Roman Catholic Church, to influence the electorate of the colony, gave him more enemies. Had Bishop Fleming not been a dying man, trying to complete his great cathedral before the grave welcomed him, the display of fireworks between the two would probably have been more impressive.

On 16 June 1852 a scant six weeks before his final departure, Governor LeMarchant was hanged in effigy. The *Pilot* reported:

> On last Wednesday great excitement was created in the vicinity of the Police office by an unlawful seizure on the part of the Senior Stipendiary Magistrate of the effigy of His Excellency Sir J. G. LeMarchant, Governor of Newfoundland and its dependencies. It appears that a concourse of people who took this way of exhibiting their dislike to his policy was carrying his effigy, suspended by the neck, through the streets followed by a drummer and fifer, playing the Dead March, when the Magistrate seized the corpse and insisted on taking it to the Police Office. The crown remonstrated with him on the impropriety of making a prisoner of His Excellency, but for the purpose of shewing an example of obedience to the *prototype*, they complied. But after arriving at the Police office, they relented and denied the Magistrate's right to *their Governor*. As they could not, however, then try the question of *Habeas Corpus*, they offered bail for the good conduct of His Excellency, if his worship would not let him out for the night. But no go, for it is not every day that such an officer is caught in the grasp of the law. He was a portly person, well filled — had apparently fed well on Smithfield beef and pudding. Wore a full dress coat of a Colonel—two stars on the tail, trousers with red stripes down the sides....

His Excellency, seems not to have been unduly upset by this demonstration. When the procession reached the mall, opposite the top of

Cochrane Street, where the burning was to take place, LeMarchant came out of Government House to take a look at the effigy to make sure his aquiline nose had been properly reproduced.

Sir Charles Henry Darling, who inaugurated responsible government in 1855, has a place in this procession of notables by being the first and only Canadian to become governor of Newfoundland. The son of a former lieutenant-governor of Tobago, and a mother whose father was a some time governor of the Bahamas, Darling was born at Annapolis Royal, Nova Scotia. Prowse calls him a remarkably able man of vast experience. Australian history refers to him as so inept and unsuccessful a governor of Victoria in 1863 that he had to be recalled to England.[16]

Alexander Bannerman, the classmate of Byron, was a Scot who came to rule Newfoundland in the King's name in 1857. Knighted in 1851, when Governor of Prince Edward Island, he also served in that capacity in Bermuda before his appointment to Newfoundland. However, our interest here is not with Sir Sandy but with his wife, Margaret Gordon. Her place in history was assured, not by marrying Sandy Bannerman and becoming first Lady of Newfoundland and other places, but by being the beloved of Thomas Carlyle, the famous English man of letters.

Born in Prince Edward Island in 1798 Margaret Gordon was reared as an orphan by a widowed aunt in Aberdeenshire. In later life, she was an intimate friend of General "Chinese" Gordon, who died in the Sudan at the hands of the Mahadi's forces in the fall of Khartoum. Judge Prowse believed Lady Bannerman claimed him as a relative but it is certain the two knew of no such relationship, though her father and Lord Gordon's great-grandfather served with the British forces in Nova Scotia.

Margaret was nineteen at the time of her first meeting with the twenty-three-year-old Carlyle. The year was 1816. Two years later they were formally introduced at her aunt's home and the young writer fell very much in love. She is the Blumine of his autobiography, *Sartor Resartus*, and in writing of her he says, "The first love which is infinite can be followed by no second like unto it." Their affair lasted two years and seems to have been a very one-sided passion.

Margaret Gordon broke with Carlyle in 1820. Informing him of this by letter, she begged him, "When you think of me be it as a kind sister.... I give you not my address because I dare not promise to see you." Not one person ever heard her mention her acquaintance with the brilliant man of letters and it was not until after her death that she was revealed in Carlyle's *Reminiscences*, as his first love, and the inspiration for Blumine. He tells us that he never did or could speak of her again after her good-bye to him in Scotland.[17]

We now come to a man who has been called the Beau Brummel

of our colonial governors, Sir Anthony Musgrave, who received his appointment in 1864 and had an American wife. He was given immortality of a sort when the community of Muddy Hole had its name changed to Musgrave Harbour. It was a place of uncertain reputation for, in 1835, Archdeacon Wix reported from there that he found a floating grog shop that kept all hands in a state of intoxication during the length of its stay. Sir Anthony himself is represented as being somewhat more than naughty. The cloak of infamy is also extended to the shoulders of his private secretary, Captain Mesham. Both, we are told, were supposed "to have been exceedingly partial to the ladies whose smiles and other attractions they evidently adequately appreciated." Alex A. Parsons adds to the gossip in *Governors I have Known*, by saying of Musgrave, "He had no steady purpose in life save that of amusing himself . . . a man without scruples, without a due sense of moral rectitude, without principles . . . he was an evil element in our society."[18] A generation bred to the attraction of movie idols would probably find the bushy-faced, aging Sir Anthony not quite its idea of Casanova. The staid corridors of Government House were never again to echo with the licentious revels they knew in the time of Governor Musgrave and Captain Mesham.

Sir Henry Fitz-Hardinge Maxse did the residence the honour of expiring within its walls, the only governor to take such a way out and the first to die in office since poor Pickmore. Sir Henry departed this life from agitated wounds he received in charging half-a-league-onward with the ill-fated Light Brigade in the Battle of Balaclava. He had served throughout the Crimean War on the staff of Lord Cardigan. In 1864 he was governor of Heligoland. Very fond of acting and theatricals, Sir Henry preferred the more cultured European climate of Germany to either England or Newfoundland. Married to a German, he won literary distinction by publishing a translation of Bismarck's *Letters to His Wife and Sisters: 1844-1870* and made many trips to visit her and his favourite theatres. Having never really settled in the island, Fitz-Hardinge Maxse had the misfortune to be in St. John's when death overtook him in 1883, the second year of his term. His body was forwarded to England and Governor Glover, who was then governor of the Leeward Islands, having previously served in that capacity in Newfoundland from 1876 to 1881, was called back for a second time to complete the term of Maxse which was not due to end until 1885.[19]

The year 1886 saw the German influence at Government House continue when our only German-born governor was appointed to the colony. Sir G. W. des Voeux was born at Baden in 1834 and did not settle in England until he was five years old. Before coming to St. John's he had previously served as governor of St. Lucia, Fiji, and the Bahamas. Afterwards he was governor of Hong Kong.

Described as being "more Irish than the Irish," the whimsical and sentimental Cavendish Boyle, Knight Commander of the British Empire, arrived to take up his duties in Newfoundland a year after the turn of the century. He was looked upon as a man of fervid imagination, flowery rhetoric, and poetic genius. Though much of what he wrote would now be considered doggerel he has gained immortality by a piece of verse in which he raptured about sun rays crowning the island's pine-clad hills. One must allow poetic licence, for few pine-clad hills exist in Newfoundland. Be that as it may, Sir Cavendish chorused "We love thee, we love thee, we love thee, Newfoundland," and the refrain has been repeated thousands of times yearly ever since.

The first performance, in public, of this Ode took place on the night of Tuesday, 21 January 1902, at the Casino Theatre in the Total Abstinence Hall. The play performed that evening was *Mamzelle* with Jessie Bonstelle in the lead. The *Evening Herald* described the event in these words:

> At the theatre last night Miss Foster rendered with exquisite feeling a new song entitled 'Newfoundland'. It proved a pleasant surprise and the general appreciation of it was marked by an unstinted applause and by the audience joining spontaneously in the chorus. It now transpires that the song was composed by our popular and esteemed governor, Sir Cavendish Boyle . . . . The Governor's poem may be destined to become our colonial anthem, for we sadly lack one.

Frances Daisy Foster had no subsequent theatrical career.

The McAuliffe Stock Company was still playing at the same theatre on May 2, with *Kathleen Mavourneen* to a practically full house. Again the *Evening Herald* is the source of our information that

> Mr. Chapman sang 'The Holy City' and followed it with Sir Cavendish Boyle's Ode to Newfoundland. At the conclusion of which a pretty tableau was shown. Miss Carroll, robed in pink, white and green, stood on a pedestal representing Terra Nova, and was supported on the one side by a fisherman bearing the 'Native' colours and on the other by a Naval Reservist supporting the Royal Standard. It was a fitting ending to the Ode, and the audience took up the last refrain which was sung with vim. His Excellency and suite occupied the boxes and were greatly pleased.

The next day the song was given general distribution. The *Evening Herald* reports:

> We have to hand to-day a copy of our future Colonial
> Anthem 'Newfoundland' for which we thank the publisher,
> Herr Krippner. The cover of this edition is certainly very
> appropriate and immediately attracts the eye of every New-
> foundlander. In the foreground a fisherman and one of our
> Naval Reserve holding entwined the pink, white and green
> and the Union Jack, while in the background is one of our
> sealing fleet, and H.M.S. *Charybdis*, the whole forming a
> picture which must please the most artistic eye. Of the music
> we need say little as it and its talented composer are too well
> known to admit comment and it will be a valuable addition to
> the repertoire of every musical Newfoundlander.

The chaplain of H.M.S. *Charybdis*, Rev. James Black, attracted attention on October 25 of the previous year, when he shot himself dead,
with his own revolver, in a copse of shrubs on the Southside Hills.

Professor Krippner, a German music teacher in St. John's, composed the first musical accompaniment for Sir Cavendish Boyle's
poem. On 20 May 1904 an Englishman, Sir C. Hubert Parry, provided a new setting. It is generally admitted, apart from his genius as
a composer, that Sir Hubert rendered great services to his art by his
work as a teacher and historian. He was director of the Royal College
of Music in London.[20] Strangely, the "Ode to Newfoundland" which
is, beyond all doubt, his most-performed work, is not listed among his
compositions in Grove's *Dictionary of Music and Musicians*, and
present staff at the Royal College of Music are most reluctant to
admit to his composing the tune. In 1908 the "Ode" was published
with new music by Alfred H. Allen, organist and choirmaster at the
Anglican cathedral. However, the version adopted as the national
anthem for Newfoundland was the one by Parry.

Governor Boyle is remembered, not only by the "Ode to Newfoundland" but also by a hockey cup. The Boyle Trophy, which he
presented to the community, has become as important to St. John's
sport as the trophy of Governor Stanley is to the sport of Canada and
the United States.

Sir Ralph Williams, a parson's son from Carnarvonshire, became
in 1909 the first Welshman appointed to the governorship of Newfoundland. After leaving, he wrote a book, *How I Became a Governor*, which was, to say the least, unflattering to his island domain. Nor
was he the last viceregal Welshman to disturb the sensibilities of
Newfoundlanders. A native of Gwaenysgor, Sir Gordon MacDonald
brought to an end the line of British governors stretching back to
Henry Osborne. A Labour peer who had gone down into the coal
mines as a lad of thirteen, Sir Gordon arrived in the colony in 1946.
It was to be his role to act as midwife in the difficult delivery of a new

Canadian infant in 1949. The natural desire of peoples everywhere for independence almost caused an abortion of the Whitehall scheme, but through tender care, and the injection of a wonder drug named Joseph Smallwood, the fetus of confederation was brought through a difficult gestation, and Newfoundlanders became possibly the only people in history to voluntarily vote their nation out of existence. The Latvians of the U.S.S.R., the Moslems of Bangladesh, or even the Dervishes of the Sudan, might find this difficult to understand. No such problem exists for the average Newfoundlander who, blind to nearly five hundred years of neglect and maltreatment by Britain, is so saturated with a colonial mentality that he can still rally "round the Imperialist flag" as the sun sets on a vanishing empire.

Sir Gordon, a dour teetotaller with an almost unintelligible Welsh accent, sailed home to Britain on 6 March 1949 to receive his certificate of pedigree, an elevation to the peerage. At the time of his departure, the *Evening Telegram* editorial was a hymn of praise to His Excellency. In the "Letters to the Editor," two days later, someone signing himself E.A. was moved to the following outburst of poesy:

> The prayers of countless thousands sent
> Heavenwards to speed thy safe return
> Ennobled as thou art with duty well performed
> Bringing peace, security and joy
> Among the peoples of this New Found Land
> So saddened and depressed until your presence
> Taught us all discern and help decide what's best for
> All on whom fortune had not smiled
> Remember if you will the kindness and the love
> Devotion and the rest that we the people have for thee.
> —Farewell!

There was unbounded excitement when the papers hit the street that afternoon, and red-faced embarrassment in the editorial offices of the *Evening Telegram*. The poem was an acrostic, and citizens were reading down the capital letters at the beginning of each line to discover that the last British governor was not so highly thought of as appeared at first sight. The mortified daily, gulled by one of the trade's oldest tricks, watched helplessly as the edition quickly sold out. Lord MacDonald, full of age and earthly honours, set off in pursuit of his eternal rewards on 21 January 1966. If he passed away unsung it was because Newfoundlanders generally were unaware of his true role in their past and future. Many feel he should be numbered among the Fathers of Confederation.

And so the insubstantial pageant faded, and the little lives of our

Colonial governors are rounded with a sleep. Sir Bulwer Lytton, in one of his sketches, has characterized their Excellencies as belonging to that class of men "who are less valued for any precise thing they have done than according to a vague notion of what they are capable of doing." Lord MacDonald could be the exception to prove Lytton's rule. Long ago in England the question was asked of a governorship: "Is it worth while for a strong man of position to take it?" Perhaps the answer might be found in Colonel McCallum. He came out to the viceregal post in Newfoundland in 1898. It has been said of him, "The British government spoiled an excellent military officer to make an indifferent governor."[21]

Following Confederation with Canada in 1949 the post was changed to Lieutenant-Governor, and a series of distinguished Newfoundlanders have been called on to fulfill the ceremonial duties required, in an age when cutaways, striped pants, Anglophile accents, and garden parties are being pressed in memory. These ceremonial gentlemen reside in the Government House of Sir Thomas Cochrane where any transient or resident of the town may drop in and sign the visitor's book. The door is always off the latch. The book is kept in a porch at the rear of the residence, an entrance Judge Prowse characterized as being "as cold as Siberia."

4

The Trade of Using Words

John Kent, a native of Waterford, Ireland, who came to Newfoundland as a young man to work with his brother, Robert Kent. A third brother was Mayor of Waterford. Kent married the sister of Bishop Fleming and in 1859 became the country's second Prime Minister. He died in 1872 and is buried at Belvedere Cemetery, St. John's. His feud with Dr. Edward Kielley, in 1838, was settled by the Privy Council and resulted in a change in British Colonial Law.

U.S.S. *Niagara*, H.M.S. *Gorgon* and H.M. Brig *Atlanta* in St. John's harbour following the laying of the first Atlantic cable August, 1858. (Courtesy Public Archives of Canada)

Water Street looking west towards Williams Lane and Adelaide Street. S. H. Parsons studio is at the right and Cullen's stone building juts out into the street on the left. (Circa 1885)

George Crosbie's Central Hotel where the founding father of the Crosbie Empire (which now includes Eastern Provincial Airlines) began in business. The first St. John's telephone exchange was located above Lindberg's jewellery store. (Circa 1885)

The controversial and opinionated John Valentine Nugent who came to Newfoundland from Ireland and was Principal of Castle Rennie, the first inter-denominational school in St. John's from 1844 to 1850. Appointed High Sheriff in 1859, he died in 1877. His sister-in-law, Mary Ann Creedon, established the Sisters of Mercy in Newfoundland and his daughter became the first Mercy nun professed outside the British Isles.

Bishop Michael Anthony Fleming from a painting done by a foreign artist and presented by the Bishop to the Sisters of Mercy. Born at Carrick-on-suir, Ireland, in 1792, he was Bishop of Newfoundland from 1829 to 1850. He built the Roman Catholic Basilica and was influential and controversial in Newfoundland religious and political life. He died at Belvedere Monastery in 1850.

Guglielmo Marconi seated in front of his history making wireless receiver in the downstairs front room of the Old Hospital. Note the paint peeling walls and battered cupboards. (Courtesy St. John's City Hall)

Marconi and his assistants on the steps of Cabot Tower during the time of his historic experiments with wireless in December, 1901. This was not the building in which he received the first transatlantic wireless message. (Courtesy St. John's City Hall)

Drawing of the Old Hospital Signal Hill showing Marconi's mast. The first wireless message transmitted across the Atlantic was received in the downstairs room at the right of the building. Note the wires leading into the room. The old hospital was destroyed by fire in 1918. (Courtesy Newfoundland Provincial Archives)

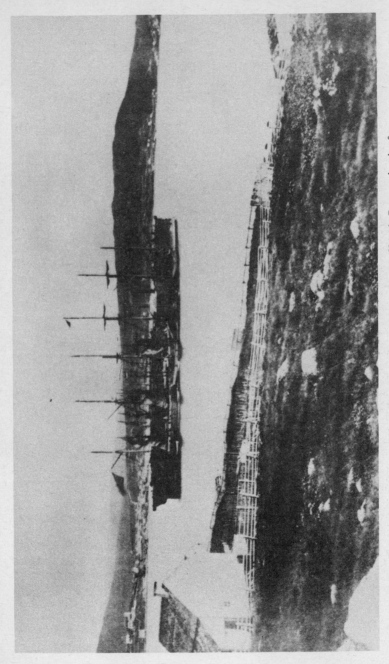

The s.s. *Great Eastern*, the greatest ship in the world at the time, is shown in the harbour at Heart's Content shortly after landing the Atlantic cable 27 July 1866. (Courtesy Newfoundland Historical Society)

The landing of the first Atlantic cable at Bay Bulls Arm, Trinity Bay, 5 August 1858. Over it the first submarine messages were exchanged between Europe and North America but the cable went dead after only a few weeks. (Courtesy Newfoundland Provincial Archives)

167

The trophy presented to Frederic Gisborne at the time he left Newfoundland in 1856. The inscription reads "As a testimonial of the high esteem entertained for him by the community of Newfoundland and for the indomitable energy he displayed in traversing the hitherto unexplored regions of the island preparatory to the introduction of the electric telegraph, as well as to mark the universal admiration of his successful endeavours and scientific ability in carrying out that enterprise, which he himself projected. '*Labor omnia vincit*'."

Frederic Newton Gisborne, a native of Manchester who worked on some of the earliest telegraph lines in Canada. In 1851 he outlined to the Newfoundland Legislature a plan for a telegraph line across Newfoundland. The line which he began eventually grew into the transatlantic telegraph.

Sir Patrick McGrath the brilliant and volatile editor of the Evening Herald who was paid $4,000 and given a knighthood for successfully documenting Newfoundland's claims to Labrador in a protracted dispute with Canada that was settled in Newfoundland's favour by the Privy Council in 1927. He died in 1929.

The old General Post Office on Water Street which housed the Newfoundland Museum on the second floor. The building which opened in 1886 was torn down in the early 1950s. Note the cab standing in the cab rank while the enemy which doomed it, the automobile, goes by on the right. (Courtesy St. John's City Hall)

The Trade of Using Words

*If I have at all learned the trade of using words to convey truth and
to arouse emotion you have at last furnished me with a subject.*
ROBERT LOUIS STEVENSON *Letter to Father Damien*

The ability to think and transfer thought is a unique attribute of man.
With the development of what we call the media (newspapers, magazines, radio, television, movies) men began to draw less and less on
their own inward selves and came to rely more and more on outside
stimuli that subjected them to common influences. Perhaps it is the
growth of media in a community that helps change it from a village,
where private life dominates, into a town or city, where the flow of
communication leads to a communal existence. If this is true, then St.
John's probably turned from being a provincial settlement into a
cosmopolitan society with the advent of the first newspaper in 1807.

Before the newspaper, people depended on the town crier for
what news was available. We do not know when the first of these
gentlemen appeared on the streets of St. John's. We are certain that
around the turn of the nineteenth century men were employed to cry
government proclamations and new laws so that the illiterate, then the
majority of the population, would be aware of the regulations governing their conduct. On 24 February 1824 a notice was sent to the
merchants and inhabitants of the town from the magistrates, announcing the appointment of John Freeman to the office of Public Crier for
the Government.

As late as 1860 the merchants and shopowners appointed Paddy
FitzGerald to act as a night watch and cry the news of fires or other
calamities within the growing city. Paddy spent many years on duty on
Water Street, pulling doors and shutters, and his cry of "Twelve
o'clock, fine night, and all is well," was a familiar one in all parts of
the town. We are told that even when wind storms shook the shutters,
and rain drenched the earth, the stentorian gentleman never forgot to
cry out, from force of habit, that it was a fine night and all was well.

The first letter sent from North America was written in St. John's
harbour on 3 August 1527 by John Rut, on board *Mary of Guildford*.
The voyage was set up by Cardinal Wolsey to discover the northwest

172

passage, at the urging of the Bristol merchant, Robert Thorne. The fleet consisted of "two fayre Shippes . . . well manned, vitailed, having in them divers connyng men."[1] They were the *Samson*, commanded by Master Grube, and the *Mary of Guildford*, commanded by Master Rut. The *Mary*, built in 1524, was a 160-ton vessel used by Henry VIII to convey wine from Bordeaux to the royal cellars. The voyage appears to have had a certain appeal, for Lord Edward Howard, son of the Duke of Norfolk, beseeched the worldly Cardinal to get him a berth "for the bittyr passion of Krist."[2] He did not have enough pull with His Eminence, but Albert de Prato, Canon of St. Paul's, "went therein himselfe in person."[3]

The expedition sailed from Plymouth on June 10 and separated on July 1. The *Sampson* was never seen, or heard of, again. After encountering "many great Islands of Ice and deepe water . . . ," Master Rut lost his taste for northern adventure, and headed south, on a summer cruise to the Caribbean. He entered the harbour of St. John's on August 3 and, a contemporary tells us, "writ this letter to King Henrie in bad English and worse writing. . . . "

The communication begins, "Pleasing your Honourable Grace to heare of your servant John Rut with all his company here in good health thanks be to God. . . . " The rough old seadog, a man of imposing stature, goes on to tell of the parting of his ship with the *Sampson*, of the great islands of ice, of "divers great beasts," of a "marvellous great storme," and of the voyage southward along the coast to seek his "fellowe." The letter concludes,

> . . . the third day of August we entered into a good harbour called St. John and there we found Eleuen Saile of Normans and one Brittaine and two Portugal barks all a fishing and so we are ready to depart towards Cap de Bas that is 25 leagues as shortly as we have fished and so along the Coast until we may meete with our fellowe and so with all diligence that lyes in me toward parts to that Ilands that we are commanded at our departing and thus Jesu save and keepe you Honourable Grace and all your Honourable Reuer. In the Haven of St. John the third day of August written in hast 1527, by your servant John Rut to his uttermost of his power.[4]

The means used to dispatch this historic communication to King Henry is unknown. Perhaps one of the Norman ships, or the Breton, had a full load of fish and was about to sail for home. It is possible that one of their captains carried the letter that assured Rut of a place in North American postal history.

The first post office in the United States was established in 1789. The Newfoundland census for 1796, seven years after the American venture, lists John Mundy as a St. John's postal clerk. Exactly what

Mr. Mundy did we cannot be certain because there was no post office in the community until the following century.

On 10 May 1803 Christopher Towill of Teignmouth-in-Devon, and seasonally a resident of St. John's, wrote to the Lords Commissioners of the Treasury in London seeking the establishment of a postal system and packet service between England and Newfoundland, touching at Kinsale, Ireland, and including a packet service in the colony from St. John's to Catalina, in the north, and to Trepassey, in the south.

In the year 1792, according to Towill, the merchants of St. John's petitioned William Pitt for the establishment of a packet, but without success. Towill offered to send two packets a year from England to Newfoundland with letters, to be delivered and received, at and from all the harbours between Catalina and Trepassey, for the sum of £1,200 per annum. He pointed out that, as there were no boats in Newfoundland, the letters must be carried from harbour to harbour in small vessels hired by him for that purpose.[5] Their Lordships, "by a great and admirable condescension," did not think proper to communicate their approval on Towill's application.

However, things must have been happening, for two years later, 18 April 1805, Francis Freeling, Esq., secretary to the General Post Office in England, informed the governor of the island, Sir Erasmus Gower, that his appointment of Simon Solomon to the office of Postmaster, had been sanctioned by the postmaster general, but no regular scale of payment to masters of vessels, or for the services of the postmaster appears to have been agreed upon until 1809. That year, in order to give encouragement to the bringing and delivering of letters to the island, and in conformity to the Act of Parliament, Governor Holloway authorized Mr. Solomon to pay at the rate of one penny per letter to the master, or other person of any vessel, who might bring letters to the island and deliver them to him at the Post Office of St. John's. He was allowed to demand twopence on every letter he might deliver from his office.

Prior to 1805, a correspondent had to be continually on the watch for an opportunity to send letters by whatever vessel happened to be sailing, and then had to take a chance on whether or not they ever reached their destination. Letters were forwarded to Newfoundland by Halifax mail and sent to St. John's by any accidental opportunity, either on ships of war or traders. With the appointment of Mr. Solomon, the English postmaster general made up mail for Newfoundland whenever a ship happened to be leaving London or Liverpool for St. John's. Twopence was paid each vessel for every letter so conveyed. The postage rate for the sender in England was one shilling.

Solomon was a watchmaker with a little store on Water Street. At first he merely received letters from correspondents for transmission overseas, on any available ship, or received the letters ship's officers brought to St. John's, from Europe. Governor Holloway's authorization for him to make a penny profit on every letter caused him to devote as much time to the post as he did to jewellery. By 1814 he was so busy handling mail that he had to advise the people of the town that letters addressed to them from abroad would no longer be delivered. Instead, a list of mail being held would be affixed to the outside of the office door.

Solomon's establishment was a couple of doors east of Scanlan's Lane. The little building was right in the path of the Great Fire of 1817. The postmaster took an ad in the *Royal Gazette*, December 26 of that year, to tell the sad tale of his plight, and how "after a residence of upwards of twenty-five years in this town, [he] had the misfortune of being burnt out on the eventful 7th of November last by which accident he lost the fruits of his industry since first coming here." He begged leave to inform the public that he had taken the shop lately occupied by Mr. Thomas Phippard, watchmaker, where all matters relative to the post office would, for the present, be transacted. He also intended carrying on his own business of clock and watchmaker.

In 1820 he seems to have added to his professions. On April 27 he opened the Free-Mason's Tavern in which the coffee room was fitted up with boxes. There was also board and lodging for outport visitors, and an apartment taken by gentlemen of the town for a reading room.

A regular Colonial Post Office was opened on Duckworth Street in 1826, opposite the Bank of British North America. It was on the west corner of what is now called Gregory's Lane, then known as Solomon's Lane. In 1839 Governor Prescott increased Mr. Solomon's remuneration to sixpence on all incoming letters and twopence on all newspapers received. Twopence was the permitted profit on all letters sent.

The postmaster was put on the vague salary of £30 or £40 per annum ($150 or $200). He took his son to work with him, as an assistant, and the volume of mail they handled was quite considerable for there was a large military garrison and naval force at the time. Unfortunately, no statistics are available.

Simon passed away on 8 December 1839, and early in the new year his son, William Lemon Solomon, was appointed to succeed him. He lived in a house on the west side of Monkstown Road, a short distance north of Catherine Street. The property was afterwards that of the Lemon family (owners of Dicks & Co.) and, in recent years, has been in the possession of James Greene, who was leader of the Progressive Conservative opposition at the time the legislature moved from the Colonial Building to the Confederation Building.

The first regular postal connections with the outside world were begun with Nova Scotia in 1840. Four years later a regular mail steamer, S.S. *North American*, commenced operating between Halifax and St. John's. She arrived in Newfoundland, for the first time, on the morning of April 22 and tied up at Stewart & Co.'s wharf. A newspaper of the day stated: "A new and improved style of communication opened up between the Mother Country and with the North American provinces and the United States." In December the ship was feared lost, when she was ten days overdue, on the return voyage to Halifax. She eventually reached port after having been battered severely by wind and sea. The turnaround period in St. John's, for the Royal Mail Ship, S.S. *North American*, was seventy-two hours. The average passage was three days. By 1845 the post between England and St. John's, via Halifax, was taking between forty and forty-two days.

In 1840, also, the first postage stamps were issued in England. It was 3 October 1856, however, before the first stamps to be issued in the island arrived on board a vessel from England belonging to Baine, Johnston & Co. Ltd. They were placed on sale the first day of January the following year. These stamps were almost identical in design to those used by the other colonies of Eastern Canada. They incorporated the thistle, rose, shamrock, and crown with the inscription, ST. JOHN'S, NEWFOUNDLAND.[6] But it was 1852 before W. L. Solomon succeeded in urging the Legislature to pass an amendment to the Post Office Act, authorizing the local use of the stamps.

In 1846, the year these first stamps arrived, the Great Fire wiped out the Duckworth Street Post Office. Mr. Solomon reopened in a house, spared by the flames, on the west side of Garrison Hill. In the late thirties and early forties the place had been operated as a tavern by Thomas and William Parker. It was a favourite pub for the military at Fort Townshend. The land on the west side of Garrison Hill, from Queen's Road to Harvey Road, was granted to the Parker brothers in 1832, for twenty shillings (about $5.00). The Post Office stayed on Garrison Hill for four years, until a new building opened on Water Street. Parker's Tavern was torn down 25 May 1861 to make room for a family house. This was destroyed in the Great Fire of 1892 and the present structure erected. The house, at the foot of the hill, was occupied until 1973 by the Sisters of Service as a hostel for working girls.

Construction of the Market House, on the site of the present Court House, was begun in 1849. The ground floor was occupied by a provisions market, and the top floor, off Duckworth Street, by the Court House. The middle floor, which was entered by a door on the side of the hill, was mostly given over to the Post Office.

In both the old post office, on Duckworth Street, and the new one, on Market House Hill, the system of mail delivery was much the same. From 1814, mail was not delivered but "called," by the postmaster or his assistant. This system was in operation until recent years in many outports of Newfoundland. Whenever a ship with mail arrived in St. John's, word spread rapidly through the town and people from everywhere converged on the Post Office. A surging mass of humanity (most of whom had no possibility of ever receiving a letter) and dogs would gather about the building and spill over into the roadway. Whenever the name of somebody in the crowd was called he would valiantly elbow his way to the wicket. It often happened that just as the letter would touch his fingertips, there would be a heave and a surge by the mob, and amidst shouts and laughter the frustrated individual would be swept helplessly down Solomon's Lane or Market House Hill. Sometimes it took the addled postal clerks up to three hours to disperse the mob. Commercial firms owned boxes, but there was no public access to them. Their mail had to be delivered over the counter.

On 26 April 1850 the Assembly appointed a committee to inquire into the subject of the establishment of a postal system within Newfoundland. This committee reported favourably and on 31 May 1851 an act was passed by the Legislature providing £1,000 currency for the establishment and maintenance of an island post office. The appointment of postmasters was vested in the governor, and their management was placed in the hands of William Lemon Solomon, who became postmaster General. His salary was fixed at £75, in addition to which his imperial appointment gave him £100. In all, this gave him an income of about $900 per year.

A scheme to carry postal facilities to the principal settlements as far north as Twillingate, and as far as Gaultois on the South Coast, was inaugurated by the Postmaster General on 15 October 1851. Nine years later, on 21 November 1860, a regular mail service between St. John's and the outports came into operation. A few months previously ill health forced the retirement of William Solomon, who was only forty-nine years of age, ending a fifty-five-year family control of postal affairs. He died on December 10 the following year.

Advances in the postal system continued in the city. On 1 February 1864 money orders were introduced, and on 29 September 1886 the first pillar box appeared on the streets. It was erected inside the railing at the entrance gate to the Colonial Building on Military Road. The tall red boxes were soon familiar sights throughout the town.

What was called Penny Postage was introduced into the country on Christmas Day 1898. The rate was three cents for delivery of a letter within Newfoundland.

As the demands of crime and punishment increased, the Court House wanted to take over the other floors of the Market House. It was decided to build a proper general post office on Water Street, on a vacant lot that had once been a shipyard east of Queen Street. On 21 May 1886 the builder, C. H. Jost, wrote to the Acting Colonial Secretary, on Atlantic Hotel stationery, to say he was ready to turn over the keys of the new Post Office, but before doing so, he wanted the balance of the contract paid immediately, so he could go home on the *Portia*. A warrant was issued for $15,000 and the keys handed over.[7]

This massive red brick structure resembled a church rather than a public building. It had a saddle roof flanked by a large square tower that jutted out toward the street, in the west, and a sort of belfry-like spire above the eastern corner, with a glass-enclosed observatory and cupola at the top. In front, a wide flight of steps led to the main entrances which were flanked by six marble Ionic pillars. These later made their way to Premier Smallwood's Russwood Ranch, on Roches's Line, where they are incongruously used as gate posts.

The edifice was no thing of beauty, but in time it became one of the most treasured Victorian façades in a city robbed by numerous fires of interesting old buildings. It was threatened in the 1892 fire but survived when the flames were halted, in their westward sweep, at Beck's Cove. Early in the 1950's the Canadian government, which had taken over the postal services at the time of Confederation, announced the old Post Office would be torn down to make way for a modern glory. Citizens' groups and newspapers agitated to have the shell of the G.P.O. saved. Ottawa officials were unmoved by the pleas of distant Newfoundlanders anxious to preserve some of the character and flavour of Victorian St. John's for future generations, and wrecking crews went to work with a will. Some old stone buildings between Post Office Square and Queen Street were also levelled, and the Argo Construction Company of Montreal erected a featureless, black granite block designed by the Halifax architects, D. A. Webber and C. A. Fowler. This eighty thousand square feet of functional, reinforced concrete was completed and occupied in 1958 at a cost of approximately $2,450,000. During its years of construction the Star Hall, a former movie house on Henry Street, at Dick's Square, served as a temporary general post office.

The year following the one in which St. John's obtained the advantage of a postmaster, the frontiers of civilization were moved even closer by another innovation. This was the work of John Ryan, a United Empire Loyalist born in Newport, Rhode Island, who had moved to Canada where he learned the newspaper trade under John Howe, father of Nova Scotia's great prime Minister, Joseph Howe.[8]

Eventually Ryan became King's Printer in the town of Saint John, New Brunswick, where he also published a newspaper. When the seat of government was moved to Fredericton in 1788, the young Loyalist refused to make the move and lost his official job. Nearly twenty years later he was in St. John's attempting to get into the newspaper business in a community where no press existed. With a view to providing a remedy for this want, he set about making a favourable impression on the merchants and principal inhabitants. In 1806 he submitted proposals for the establishment of a newspaper to Governor Gower. His plea was accompanied by two hundred signatures including that of Bishop O'Donel, who signed for his successor, Bishop Lambert; the Reverend Mr. Harries of the Church of England; Chief Justice Tremlett; Generals Skinner and Murray; and Captain Tonge, first president of the Benevolent Irish Society.

The demand of such celebrities was not to be ignored, but His Excellency felt the project fraught with hazard. A newspaper could be a menace to the good order of the community, and even to the peace of the world. The venture was not lightly assented to. It was hedged in with restrictions to protect the public, and especially His Majesty's government, from its sinister implications and perfidious influence. A formidable document was issued by Sir Erasmus Gower, Knight, Vice-Admiral of the Red, Governor and Commander-in-Chief of the Island of Newfoundland, which read:

> Whereas the Magistrates, Merchants and other principal Inhabitants of St. John's have represented to me that the establishment of a printing office and the publication of a newspaper in this town would be beneficial to the trade of the Island in general ... by circulating mercantile advertisements and communicating much useful information to the outports; and whereas the said Magistrates, Merchants, and other principal Inhabitants have requested that I will allow Mr. John Ryan (whom they recommended as a person of good and respectable character) to settle in this town for that purpose. I do hereby grant permission to the said John Ryan to establish a printing office in St. John's and publish a weekly paper to be called The Royal Gazette And Newfoundland Advertiser, provided that he shall give bond in the Court of Sessions for two hundred pounds sterling, with good securities, that previous to the printing of each number of the said paper he shall submit the perusal of the proposed contents thereof to the Magistrates in the said Court of Sessions and not insert in the said paper any matter which in the opinion of the Governor for the time being may tend to disturb the peace of His Majesty's subjects. But in order to avoid as much as possible

the crowding of the lower path with persons not immediately concerned with the fishery or trade I cannot allow him to occupy any house below the Upper Path for his intended purposes. Given under my hand and Seal, at Fort Townshend, St. John's, Newfoundland, the 22nd of September, 1806. E. GOWER.[9]

On September 5 he had given a Walter Charles Davids permission to open a printing office, on the same terms, but Davids vanished immediately without ever starting his paper. He was probably unable to raise the necessary funds.

Poor Erasmus! Yelping at the heels of the Post Office had come those rogues known as actors, seeking permission to bring their notorious profession to the town. It was haltingly given, on condition they not become destitute, and now this. Would the strict censorship, and heavy bond, prove enough? At least the thing had been kept out of the Lower Path where crowds were apt to congregate and cause a disturbance.

Ryan went at once to New Brunswick where he acquired a press, type, and materials. On 27 August 1807 a newsboy named Billy Barnes appeared on the streets of St. John's and, as the apprehensive authorities looked on, walked up and down the Lower Path selling the first issue of the *Royal Gazette*. The printing office was located on the south side of Duckworth Street a few doors east of Prescott Street.

John Ryan left Newfoundland in the spring of 1814, for New Brunswick where he died that same year. Of his seven children, three sons were printers and it was to one of them, Lewis Kelly Ryan, that he left the newspaper, with the proviso that he pay his widow, Amelia, the sum of £300 for twelve years. All printing materials belonging to him in New Brunswick went to a nephew.

The will of the deceased editor shows that, besides the newspaper, he brought Negro slaves to Newfoundland. The will, witnessed by George Lilly, Notary Public, contains the following bequest: "I will and bequeath my female slave Dinah her freedom immediately after my decease, and that her two children Cornelius and Rachel, be retained in the service of my family, or bound out to some creditable person until they come to the age of twenty-one years, then to enjoy their freedom."[10]

Posterity does not record what became of Dinah or if her children ever secured their freedom. One other case of black slavery in Newfoundland is known to history. Back in 1675 Thomas Oxford, one of the first merchants to settle in St. John's, "had his covenant Negro servant valued worth £60 taken from him last fishing season, all which he is ready to make out by bill of sale and oath."[11] The west country men who had plundered the place carried off Mr. Oxford's slave.

In 1832 Lewis Ryan took John Collier Withers into partnership with him and soon afterwards retired from the business. The Withers family continued as editors for over half a century. The *Royal Gazette* is still published every Tuesday, as the *Newfoundland Gazette*, and is a government paper for proclamations and official notices.

During the many fires that swept through St. John's numerous volumes of old newspapers were destroyed so that the earliest issues of the *Gazette* known to exist today date back only to 1810. The first three years have all been lost. There are gaps in all newspapers up to 1892.

Capt. Sir William Eliot has described in his *Naval Sketch Book* how the early St. John's papers were printed. Writing of the period from 1817 to 1819, he does not name the editor but it is most probable he was referring to Lewis Kelly Ryan. Here is what the Captain had to say:

> Notwithstanding that newspapers in this colony are saleable without being subject to any duty, it would appear that the profits arising from that of even the most extensive circulation, are no more than competent to the maintenance of a family. In the instance alluded to, the various departments of exertion left no individual, young or old, male or female, unoccupied. The father took the literary lead, and wrote the leading article; the son-in-law (a half-pay purser in the navy) sometimes sported a quiet quill on a little quackery in political economy; the mother, not having much pretensions to letters except in type (for she could assist as compositor at a pinch), collected and arranged little recipes for preserves, pickling and pretty progeny; whilst the daughters, who were spinsters, professing total ignorance of the mystery of the latter composition, confined their talents to aiding in the composition of type, and correcting the press, which usually went on during the hour of tea, when every avowed contributor considered himself a privileged guest. . . .
>
> Maugre all the bustle of the scene, the blunders to be corrected, and brogues of the ladies (for all residents speak almost equally discordant in either an Irish or Devonshire accent), the scene was interesting enough to collect many of their contributors, to dissipate the *ennui* particular to a place so circumscribed as to society, by correcting the errors of the press in their own contributions. . . . [12]

The Captain tells us that the several contributors determined on "an extraordinary selection of literary *aliases*, or *nommes de guerre*. The most ordinary were Mercator, Piscator, Viator, Benbow, Bobstay and even Boreas, which were indifferently affixed to epigrams, elegies, political squibs, tales of love and satirical poetry."[13]

Some years before the visit of Eliot to Newfoundland, one man got a subscription to the newspaper by fiddling, not the accounts, but with a bow on a violin. An old list of subscribers to the *Gazette* carries the entry, "Augustin Macnamara, commenced Nov. 1, 1810. To be paid for in fiddling." The mind boggles to think of John Ryan at his desk composing a stinging editorial with Macnamara standing nearby scraping out a tune suited to the editor's mood.

These nineteenth-century newspapers were a combination of advertisements, shipping news, rewards for deserted sailors and servants, countless insolvency notices, patent medicine claims, bits and pieces from British and North American newspapers, and articles on affairs of the day. Local news was almost invariably ignored. The obituary, now so valuable to researchers, had not come into fashion, and only the passing of persons of quality was noted. Pungent wit and scathing satire were the order of the day, and editors seemed to take a pride in scarifying each other. The pomposity of officials and politicians was lampooned, and those prominent in public life were mercilessly exposed to the jibes, barbs, and humour of such ageless critics as Pro Bono Publico and Fair Play.

If flowery rhetoric was in fashion, so also was high literary merit, not only among editors but contributors as well. There would be long, passionate dissertations on the abominations of the Mussulman (Moslem), the fall of Sebastapol, or a sure cure for the discomforts of diarrhoea, while a major fire in the town, a public hanging, or a fever that swept away a large part of the population, almost escaped notice. Editors probably figured everyone already knew the facts by word of mouth, so there was little point wasting space in the four tightly packed pages of their papers, by repeating the story. Local news rarely filled more than a single column. Frequently there was none at all. The print was often small and uneven. Reading it by candlelight, or even by lamplight, must have been a challenge to the eyesight and an invitation to blindness.

The muse of poesy was always a welcome visitor to the local scribes and the results of her inspiration found a ready market in the press. Back in 1819 one could be stirred by "Invocation," extracted from a poem entitled "Newfoundland," written in two parts by B. Hannagan:

> The land I sing, where fish and oil abound,
> And od'rous flakes the public streets surround;
> Where five long months the driving snows assail,
> And ice keeps off the packet and the mail . . .

D.I.O.'s poem. "A Raking Broadside at Parting," published 21 December 1819, shows a similar interest in fish and oil. He writes:

> Farewell to the stench of each stage,
> The odours of oil in the 'vat';
> Adieu to the radical rage,
> And the system of plundering Pat . . .

In "Verbum Stultis," an anonymous poet tried to put his fellows in their place by writing,

> Ye manglers of rhyme,
> and ye murd'rers of prose,
> If you had your deserts
> You'd get pulled by the nose . . .

In writing of the early nineteenth-century press of St. John's, Captain Eliot says; " . . . above five if not six months of the year, the editorial tribe must draw entirely from their own necessarily circumscribed and stinted wells of information, being frequently altogether excluded from intercourse with Europe from November to April." [14] This was not only true of Europe. A letter in the Massachusetts State Library in Boston complains that because of winter conditions in 1772 there was no communication for many months between New England and Newfoundland.

According to A. B. Perlin, one of the most eminent journalistic figures in Newfoundland newspaper history, this isolation did not much improve until well into the present century. In his book, *The Story of Newfoundland*, Perlin says our present daily newspapers did not have an immediate news-gathering service until after Confederation in 1949 when they were linked by teletype to Canadian Press. He says:

> Before that time news was received by telegraph from the C.P. and by wireless from Reuter's and other news services. For many years, the only foreign news service available to the daily press of Newfoundland was a brief daily telegraphic summary; and in most of the island's settlements, a local and foreign news summary, relayed by telegraph and written by hand in a book which was passed out to all who displayed interest, was the only means of keeping up with current events. [15]

Eliot tells us there were four newspapers established in St. John's, a town of less than eight thousand people, prior to 1820. The *Royal Gazette* was followed in July 1815 by the *Newfoundland Mercantile Journal*, a paper of a very high order, published every Thursday by Donald McPhee Lee, in a building on the north side of Water Street, east of Holloway Street. Another important paper was *The Times*, published by John and Richard McCoubrey every Wednesday and Saturday, on the north side of Duckworth Street opposite the present War Memorial. The *Newfoundlander* was brought to life by Edward Dalton Shea, 29 October 1836. It became an institution among the newspapers of St. John's and was available every Monday and Thursday. After the 1846 fire it was located on Duckworth Street, west of Telegram Lane and next to the Post Office.

Certainly the most controversial editor of any newspaper ever published in St. John's was Henry David Winton. The motto of his publication, the *Public Ledger*, was "Open to all parties—influenced by none." Whether or not the columns of his paper were open to all parties is doubtful. That it was influenced by none is certain. Winton was an arrogant, opinionated man of intellect who defied politicians, fearlessly faced mobs, survived sadistic mulilation, and bitterly pushed forward ceaseless attacks, especially against the Roman Catholic clergy, who were making their influence felt in the political life of the day.

Born in Exmouth, Devon, in 1793, the fifth son of a clergyman, Henry Winton was induced by friends to emigrate to Newfoundland in 1818, at the age of twenty-five, and opened a stationery, bookbinding, and printing shop on the north side of Water Street, just west of Prescott Street. He brought with him a son of the same name who was born in Dartmouth, England, in 1817, and has often been confused with the father. Henry, Sr., lived to be sixty-two and died 5 January 1855, while Henry, Jr., died in 1866, at the age of forty-nine years.

This stormy petrel of Newfoundland newspapermen was a printer before coming to the island, and in 1820 he founded the *Public Ledger*. He soon became involved with William Carson, Patrick Morris, Sir James Pearl, and others in the struggle for self-rule but, after representative government was introduced, he had a change of heart and according to his obituary in the *Public Ledger*, was

> often heard to regret the part which he took in the matter, after experience convinced him that this country was not prepared for the reception of what was called in those days the "great boon"—a local legislature. It took no long period after the concession of this "boon" to convince him of his error, and to show him the great evils which it was doomed to inflict upon the community by the rending of those social ties which had hitherto so closely existed between all classes and creeds.

Winton's first real notoriety was the result of a disturbance brought about by his attacks on the Roman Catholic clergy for their political interference. Strangely enough, his arch-enemy, Bishop Fleming, was an early ally of Winton in opposing self-government. The Prelate writes:

> At the period of the election of 1833, my opinion remained unchanged as to the evil effects likely to be produced on the peace of the Colony and harmony of private life, by the establishment of the House of Assembly. I have made no secret of that opinion for a long time previous, and advised those who consulted me not to make any effort to be elected. With this opinion, I had determined to confine myself and my clergy to instructing those entrusted with the franchise on the nature of the duties which had devolved upon them, and exhorting them to exercise the trust for the benefit of their fellow citizens without reference to the interests of any particular candidate or party.

In spite of his lofty intentions the Bishop found himself in the midst of a sectarian squabble and his priests began to side with the Roman Catholic and Dissenter candidates against those of the Church of England persuasion. Dr. Fleming charged that in Winton's paper

> articles were directed against us as citizens and Christian Ministers; our sermons were burlesqued in the most ribald terms; the most abominable doctrine was attributed to us; the utmost Christian humility could hardly endure the insults heaped on our characters; and even the characters and conduct of some religious ladies living in St. John's, and whose time is devoted to instruction of the poor, were assailed and vilified.

On Christmas night, 1833, Winton's attacks on the Roman Catholic clergy brought a mob howling to his door on Water Street, opposite Hunter's Cove. The holiday crowd was incited to violence by mob orators. As the gathering began to get out of hand, stones flew and windows were smashed. A cry went up to burn the premises and lynch Winton. The *Newfoundlander* tells the rest of the story in its issue of the following day:

> The peaceable inhabitants were thrown into a state of great confusion and alarm last evening, at seeing a detachment of about 80 men from the Royal Veteran Companies, with fixed bayonets, parading Water Street, in consequence we found on inquiry, of another threatened attack on Mr. Winton's house. The magistrates and constables were also in attendance, and, altogether, the scene was one which we hoped never to have witnessed in St. John's. . . . Some few individuals, who showed a disposition to be disorderly, were taken up and conveyed to

gaol.—about 8:00 the Rev. Mr. Troy came into the street and earnestly entreated the crowd to disperse—a request which was almost immediately complied with.[16]

On Boxing Day the Bishop went to Government House where he remonstrated with Governor Cochrane for his foolhardiness in calling out the insufficient troops. He claimed a tragic riot had been narrowly averted by Father Troy's action. Fleming appeared satisfied with the goodness of the Governor's intentions and following the interview announced to his congregation: "I have the pleasure to inform you that the most lively scene of regard for your peace, happiness and liberty is the object of his deepest solicitude. . . . Avoid for his sake, for my sake, for God's sake every appearance of insubordination and riot. . . . Suffer not yourselves to be drawn into any excesses. . . . "

That was not the end of the affair for the Governor. He found himself in hot water with the Colonial Office for not reporting the depleted state of the garrison.[17]

The Christmas disturbance had its beginnings in 1832 when a youthful Irish immigrant to the country, and colonial reformer, John Kent, offered himself for election to the island's first representative government. One who objected to Kent, as a newcomer and political opportunist, was Henry Winton, in the September 18 issue of the *Public Ledger*. What really upset Winton was that Kent's advocacy was at the urging of his brother-in-law, Bishop Fleming. Kent replied to the *Public Ledger* article by justifying the right of the Bishop to influence his flock on behalf of any candidate. Winton retorted, on September 21, that such clerical interference in the political life of the colony was intolerable. He advised the Bishop not to overrate his strength as he was not, as he might assume, beyond the reach of the press.

This placed the editor and the cleric on a collision course. The new Legislative Assembly which was elected, proved a henhouse to the British Colonial administration, and the chickens of centuries came home to roost within hours of its opening. The bitter years of English oppression, the denial of human rights to settlers, the inequalities faced by servile Irishmen, the harsh penal laws against Roman Catholics, the restrictive interdicts against religious dissenters, the gross illiteracy of the electorate, and the political inexperience of the elected manifested themselves in a pettiness and fickleness that was to be a cause of violent party strife for three decades. To offset the influence of Catholics and Dissenters in the reform-minded assembly, the Governor packed the Legislative Council, a kind of mini-House of Lords, with Church of England reactionaries. The two houses were immediately at loggerheads, and the country was seriously split along religious lines, for the first time. Bigotry and animosities, unknown before the granting of self-government, emerged to plague Newfoundland for the next 130 years. It was not until the election of 1972 that religious differences seemed not to matter in most electoral districts.

The election of Patrick Keough, a Wexford-born, Roman Catholic in favour with the Governor, over the father of self-goverment, Dr. William Carson, upset Bishop Fleming and he was behind an attempt to have Keough disqualified in favour of the doctor. Discontent grew among Roman Catholics and Dissenters. Cochrane had always termed the former the "lower orders." Religious bigotry and social prejudice appear to have been his Achilles heel, and they eventually brought about the downfall of this greatest of colonial governors.

A major blunder seems to have been the appointment of the recently dismissed attorney general of Upper Canada, Henry John Boulton, as Chief Justice of Newfoundland. It is odd that a man so full of vision and dreams as Cochrane would concur in the appointment of this arrogant, stubborn, and inflexible conservative who was still licking the wounds he had received from the great reform agitator, William Lyon Mackenzie.[18] As Chief Justice, Boulton headed up the Legislative Council with powers to undermine, and even squash, decisions of the Assembly.

Before the Assembly could meet for a second time, in 1833, it was necessary to hold an election to fill vacancies left by two members removed to the Council. William Thomas and Timothy Hogan, a Roman Catholic not amenable to clerical pressures, presented themselves as candidates. The Bishop took to the pulpit to advocate the election of Dr. Carson while Hogan, denied the sacraments for three months, faced financial ruin when his business was boycotted by the faithful. The unfortunate man recanted his heresy and withdrew from the contest, making a public apology to the Bishop. This injustice was too much for Henry Winton to bear. Into the charged atmosphere he plunged, taking up Hogan's cause in the December 10 issue of the *Public Ledger*. His well-founded charges of clerical interference were interpreted as anti-Catholic outbursts, and he was denounced from the pulpit by the priests. The Bishop afterwards claimed he had to resort to this means of defence as all newspapers were closed to him. This is an odd claim in view of the fact that he was much admired in the pages of Carson's newspaper, *Patriot*.

The night after the Christmas disturbance outside Winton's house, Carson, Kent, Patrick Morris, and other reformers held a public meeting which produced four resolutions. They expressed the determination of the meeting to counter a despotic attack on the liberty of the people, to ask of the Governor the reasons for outrages committed by the troops, to thank Bishop Fleming for having exerted a calming influence, and to send aid or sympathy to those injured or in jail. Governor Cochrane and Bishop Fleming immediately became involved in a public exchange of accusations and denials.

A series of letters in the columns of the *Patriot* accused His Excellency of bigotry, injustice, and despotism. When a lawsuit was about to be instituted by the Governor against Robert John Parsons, the proprietor and printer, the writer revealed himself to be Father Troy, the Bishop's Vicar General. But many thought Troy had only signed and submitted the letters which had actually been composed by John V. Nugent, a schoolmaster who had also come out to Newfoundland from Waterford. He was prominent in the ouster of Judge Boulton and accompanied Dr. Carson to England in the cause.

Cochrane now got mixed up in an exchange with Carson whom he suspected of attempting to achieve his recall. He retaliated by abolishing Carson's position as district surgeon, altering it, and then offering it to Dr. Edward Kielly. The newspapers had come a long way in the twenty-seven years since Governor Gower had hesitatingly granted John Ryan permission to print his much circumscribed journal.

By 1895 the *Evening Telegram* was openly castigating Governor Sir Terence O'Brien for "an inordinate fondness for pomp and glory" and claiming that his alleged misdeeds could "only be obliterated by the departure from our shores of the most incompetent and unpopular governor that ever ruled here." On the other hand the *Evening Herald* vindicated him as "Every inch an Irish gentleman. . . . "

Meanwhile the press of 1833-1834 continued to sting those in office and the pulpit. Governor Cochrane was recalled and received a derisive farewell, demanded by Father Troy, from the Irish element. However, Bishop Fleming was afterwards to say of him, if it were in his power he would make any sacrifice to bring back Governor Cochrane, "the best governor that had ever been in Newfoundland." His successor, Capt. Henry Prescott, arrived in St. John's, 3 November 1834, just in time to witness two of the most sensational incidents in the history of Newfoundland journalism.

On 11 May 1835 the following letter was anonymously published in the pages of the *Patriot* under a nom de plume, Stick a Pin Here!

BENEFICIAL EFFECTS OF HANGING ILLUS-TRATED.—We understand that a lecture was delivered yesterday in the Court House to the Grand and Petit Juries, on the opening of the Central Circuit Court, by the President of the Council in his capacity of Chief Judge, on the very great benefits which hanging the people confers on society, arising, no doubt, from its sedative effects on the human system, which, to the uninitiated are truly astonishing. The same excellent plan is to be followed up, in order to quell the fiery spirits which at this moment keep up a truly wholesome ripple upon the surface of society, which it would appear fearfully disturbs the repose of the honourable lecturer, and all other despots who shall dare to subvert the Charters of the land, and plant

in their stead the unalloyed principles of arbitrary sway! Go it,
ye Cripples!

Mr. Justice Boulton, the "honourable lecturer" did not take kindly
to this brief epistle reflecting on his judicial honesty, and cited the editor,
R. J. Parsons, a remorseless fighter for responsible government, to appear before the Central Circuit Court to show cause why attachment
should not be issued against him for a contempt alleged to be contained
in the letter. Parsons filed an affidavit in court, denying authorship, but
admitting he was the printer of the paper. He refused to acknowledge
who the author was. When finally brought before Judge Boulton, who
certainly had a prejudiced interest in the outcome of the case, the editor
made a lengthy defence and protested, in strong terms, against the whole
proceedings which he characterized as unconstitutional and illegal.

The Chief Justice was unimpressed by the defence and before
delivering judgement said that Parsons, by refusing to acknowledge the
real author of the article in question, assumed for himself all the
responsibility which attached to it. He then quoted a great number of
cases and opinions of the highest legal authorities in support of the
course he was pursuing, and concluded by sentencing the editor of the
Patriot to three months' confinement in the common jail of the town,
and to pay a fine of fifty pounds to the king. He was to remain in
confinement until the same was paid, and on release to find security
for his good behaviour for twelve months.

A great hue and cry arose. Boulton had driven a decisive nail in
his coffin, for Dr. Carson, one of the paper's owners, became his
implacable enemy. The editor's admirers paid his fine and the bewhis-
kered gentleman was released within days to avoid unrest and demonstrations by the volatile people of St. John's.[19] Carson headed for the
Colonial Office in London and Boulton was soon back in Canada in
search of a job.

The same month in which Robert Parsons had made newspaper
history in 1835, his fellow editor, the notorious Henry Winton,
achieved immortality by becoming the subject of a sadistic attack.
Winton had been unimpressed by the mob violence of Christmas
night, 1833, or by the placards later posted on the walls of his house
by night threatening him with death. He did take to carrying a gun on
his person, but would have been wise to take more elaborate precautions, as he continued his undeterred opposition to the political activities of the Roman Catholic clergy and their shepherd.

Shortly after four o'clock on the afternoon of Tuesday, 19 May
1835, Henry Winton left Carbonear on horseback for Harbour Grace,
three miles distant. He was joined by Captain Churchward of the brig
Hazard, who was proceeding on foot. They had gone up the hill out
of Carbonear and were on their way down the slope leading toward

189

Bristol's Hope when a gang of ruffians, hideously disguised with painted faces, suddenly issued from the woods on the right of the road. Instantly one of them felled him from the horse by a heavy blow on the side of the head with a stone. Captain Churchward was seized and rendered helpless. As the fiery editor lay on the ground he was pounded by blows. The Captain tried to cry out, but was taken into the wood, to the left of the road, and threatened with death if he made a noise.

The attackers filled Winton's ears with mud and gravel. When he asked, "Do you intend to murder me?" one of them replied, "Hold your tongue, you bastard," and opening a clasp knife, cut two pieces out of the unfortunate man's right ear.[20] After a further scuffle they cut off the other ear and left him insensible. As he regained consciousness he saw the shadowy figures of his attackers vanish into the nearby woods. A few moments later Captain Churchward was able to free himself and go to the aid of his battered and bleeding companion. He helped Winton over the hill to Harbour Grace where he was taken to the surgery of Dr. Stirling, grandfather of the famous singer, Toulinguet Stirling. The doctor carefully and skilfully stopped the haemorrhaging and dressed the wounds. The *Ledger* claimed: "The immense effusion of blood was so copious as to be traceable along the road even to the precincts of the town."[21]

As might be imagined, the attack caused great indignation. The outraged government sent a constable to Harbour Grace and Carbonear to investigate and obtain leads, but nothing came to light. The gang had run away to live and attack another day. The reward for the capture of the culprits was increased from £200 to £500 without success. It was alleged at the time that the deed was committed by Irishmen, but in more recent years researchers have come to believe the thing was far better organized than an emotional outburst by a group of Paddies. Suspicion has fallen on Winton's political opponents of several persuasions. It was noted that the mutilation of his ears was done with surgical precision, so that he would not bleed to death, and Dr. Molloy, whose tombstone can still be seen in the old cemetery at the back of Godden's property in Harbour Grace, has been named as the perpetrator of the deed. Some people foolishly observed that Dr. Stirling did not seem at all alarmed when the semi-conscious editor was brought to his door. No arrests were ever made and the mystery goes unsolved. Winton felt he was under "deepest obligation to Doctor Stirling for unceasing acts of kindness under circumstances the most painfully distressing." By June 2 he was restored "to a degree of comparative health and strength and resumes his intercourse with his readers."[22]

Five years after the attack on the editor, the foreman of the *Ledger*, Herman Lott, was subjected to one of the most peculiar experiences of any newspaperman who ever worked in St. John's. After dark, on an evening in February 1835 as he was walking between the office and his home, Lott was hailed by someone calling his name. The person came up and persuaded him to go to the assistance of his master's son, at a spot mentioned. On their way there they were joined by a third party who entered into conversation with them. Suddenly, Lott felt his arms tightly pinioned behind, rendering him helpless. He was blindfolded and hurried along a series of streets to a house somewhere in the town. A door was opened at their knock and they were led upstairs, where the handkerchief was removed. Lott discovered he was in a small room almost totally devoid of furniture. Some kind of white sheeting or calico covered the walls and ceiling, except for the fireplace area where some burning coals drove the chill from the February air. In front of the fireplace there was a small table and two chairs on which were seated two men clad all in black. There were openings for the eyes and mouth cut in the hoods of their long robes. On the table were pens, ink, and paper. These ominous figures began a severe interrogation of the young man in disguised voices. They wanted to know who wrote for the *Public Ledger*, who visited Winton's house, whether he kept arms in his house and carried them about his person. They got as little information from Lott as he could give. When the interview was over the newspaperman was advised that it would be dangerous for him to tell anyone of his experience. Should he divulge a word of it "an unseen and unknowing hand would be in his way." His eyes were bound once more and a bell sounded. He was led out of the house into the blackness of the unlit streets. After about a quarter of an hour's walking, the rope which bound his arms was suddenly cut, and he was spun around violently three or four times so that he staggered and fell against a fence. He tore the bandages from his eyes, but there was nothing but the sound of retreating footsteps in the night.[23]

In view of what transpired three months later, Lott would have been wise to heed the warning and keep his mouth shut. Either at the urging of Winton, or because of his own sense of outrage, next day he made a deposition on oath as to what had happened. On May 15 Herman Lott was on business for Winton in Conception Bay. As he journeyed on foot, between Carbonear and Harbour Grace, he reached the spot where the assault had been made on his editor, in 1835. It was between noon and one o'clock in the afternoon. Suddenly four men disguised with black crepe over their faces, rushed from the wood on the side of the road and began to attack him. One of them cried out "Long looked for is come at last." Lott made some resistance with his sword-stick but was thrown down, overcome, and beaten unconscious with a stone. When he recovered his senses he found himself alone, his face and hands were covered with blood, and his ears had been mutilated in much the same manner as Winton's. A considerable reward was offered for information, but nobody came forward to claim it and, as in the case of his boss, the incident went unsolved.

PROCLAMATION.

By His Excellency HENRY PRESCOTT, *Esquire, Companion of the Most Honorable Military Order of the Bath,*

(*L. S.*)

H . PRESCOTT. *Governor and Commader-in-Chief in and over the Island of Newfoundland and its Dependencies, &c.*

WHEREAS on FRIDAY the 15th of this Instant May, a most atrocious and diabolical outrage was committed by Four MEN, at present unknown, on the Person of Mr.

HERMAN LOTT,

of St. John's, who was then on his way from Carbonear to Harbor Grace in this Island. And Whereas it is no less especially necessary to the ends of Justice than essential to the protection and safety of the lives of all Her Majesty's subjects, that the perpetrators of this daring outrage should be detected and brought to punishment : I do therefore call upon all Her Majesty's faithful subjects to aid and assist Her Majesty's Officers in discovering and apprehending the Persons concerned in perpetrating the aforesaid crime ; and for the speedy detection of whom

I do hereby offer a REWARD of

THREE HUNDRED POUNDS, STG.

to any Person or Persons (except the Person or Persons who actually committed the said outrage,) who shall give such information as will lead to the Apprehension and Conviction of the Offenders. AND I DO ALSO PROMISE A

FREE PARDON

to the Person or Persons who (being an accomplice or accomplices, but not the actual perpetrators of the said crime) shall give such information as aforesaid.

Given under my hand and seal at the Government-House at St. John's in the aforesaid Island, the 18th day of May in the third year of Her Majesty's Reign, and in the year of our Lord, 1840. By His EXCELLENCY'S Command,

JAMES CROWDY, *Sec'y.*

Printed by J. T. BURTON, Harbor Grace.

The animosities between Henry Winton and Bishop Fleming did not carry over to the grave. When the great exertions on behalf of his cathedral broke his health and the cleric was facing death he began to "make his soul." He longed for a return to the unity and peace in which Newfoundlanders of all faiths had lived prior to the coming of representative government and the introduction of political and religious strife. His overtures seem to have met with a sympathetic response and we are told that toward the end of his life the people of the city wondered at seeing the two men walking together through the streets on the most friendly terms. Charles Pedley, the Newfoundland historian, tells us there are a number of rather touching instances of this happening. One he received from the lips of Mrs. Winton after the death of the two men.

The Widow Winton told Pedley she was sitting alone in her parlour one day when a knock came on the door. A servant went to open it and she turned to see who was calling. She was startled and thrown into a tremor to see Bishop Fleming entering the room. He came and sat down in a chair opposite hers and began to talk. To Mrs. Winton's amazement, the Prelate told her that his days were numbered and that he wished to die at peace with all his neighbours. As they took tea he lamented the bitterness which had prevailed in the community. Revealing the unsuspected virtue of humility he said that if he had given offence, or done any wrong to Mr. Winton, he wished to be forgiven and reconciled to him. There were other parties with whom Bishop Fleming had been in a state of hostility who received and accepted a like reconciliation.

Henry David Winton is not only confused with his son, who carried on his father's profession, but also with Francis and Robert Winton. In 1860 Robert Winton founded a newspaper, said to be the city's first daily paper, called the *Daily News* which he issued every morning at 169 Duckworth Street. This was not the present *Daily News* but an earlier journal of the same name. The fate of Robert Winton is a puzzle. He disappears from history with the failure of his paper. Francis Winton first issued his newspaper, the *Day Book*, 31 December 1861. It was also a daily and was published in a small building on the east corner of Duckworth and Cathedral Streets. It did not long survive and on 31 August 1865 he began the publication of a somewhat more successful paper called the *Chronicle*. Francis Winton was elected to the House in 1882 and he too vanishes.

A. B. Perlin in his *Story of Newfoundland* likens St. John's newspapers of the last century to Sir Joseph Porter's sisters and his cousins and his aunts, in that they can be reckoned up by dozens. The two surviving newspaper publications in the city are a legacy of the last century. The *Evening Telegram* was launched 2 April 1897, as a daily journal by William J. Herder. A small paper of only four sheets, it was first printed on Duckworth Street, at the east corner of Prescott Street. The press was run by hand, but the paper was attractive and became popular. It was blessed with a very capable editor in Alexander A. Parsons, a man of appealing personality who contributed greatly to the paper's success.

In 1898 Parsons was to become involved in a legal battle over letters to the editor, much as his namesake had earlier. In the issue of the *Evening Telegram* for Friday, August 19, there appeared a letter signed "Sub Judice" under the heading "That Fresh Outrage." The writer complained about putting the steamer *Fiona* to use on Circuit Court Service to the outports of the island. He wrote:

> That vessel [Fiona] has been little better than a floating brothel ever since she was purchased. I have heard people in the outharbours say ... the legal gentlemen would be found drunk in their berths and unable to land ... gentlemen of the long robe come to dispense justice, and unable to stagger ashore when court opened ... this obsolete mode of holding court cannot be defended except on the score of a useless picnic.

Both editor and proprietor found themselves before Chief Justice Emerson and Judge Morison, charged with contempt of court. The defendants claimed that taxpayers had a perfect right, as citizens, to offer an opinion in the press, or elsewhere, on the use to which the vessel was, or ought to be, employed. They saw in the letter no imputation of misconduct on the part of the court, since the proceedings referred to in the communication related to transactions that were past, and there was no intention, obvious or implied, to throw contempt upon the Supreme Court on Circuit, or any other court. The justices did not see it quite that way and at six-thirty on the evening of October 8, held the letter to be a libel upon the Supreme Court and sentenced both gentlemen to thirty days.

As soon as Judge Emerson had delivered sentence, the sheriff was called and the prisoners were hurried off directly to the penitentiary. By four-thirty on the afternoon of the 10th, there was a petition for their release on Water Street East, and another in the west end. One thousand signatures were affixed the first day praying His Excellency, Governor Murray, "may be graciously pleased to exercise the Royal Prerogative of mercy and remit the sentences of the prisoners."

Not everyone looked upon the two gentlemen as martyrs in the cause of journalism. The *Daily News*, and especially the *Evening Herald*, a bitter political rival of the *Telegram*, applauded the verdict. The *Herald* went so far as to crow: "Justice has at last overtaken the

194

guilty and the public should rejoice." The *Telegram* described this statement as "journalistic brutality."

At seven o'clock on the evening of 17 October 1898 Governor Murray was "graciously pleased" to order the culprits released to their admirers, feeling that the imprisonment already undergone was sufficient atonement. The *Telegram*'s circulation jump of 35 per cent was another kind of atonement. It must not be imagined that the editor and his boss languished in their cells like petty criminals. They were given v.i.p. treatment in comfortably appointed quarters, where meals were brought to them from the outside, and even their barber came to give them tonsorial relief.

The front page of the *Evening Telegram* carried a mass of advertisements for nearly half a century. This page was changed over to news coverage 1 October 1941. The paper was also published on pink newsprint from 16 September 1882 until 27 February 1942—over sixty years. There was one issue published on white paper during that period. When the new paper mill opened at Grand Falls a complimentary roll of its first run of newsprint was sent to the local press. The *Evening Telegram* for 27 January 1910 was published on this white paper. When World War II made it impossible to obtain pink newsprint any longer the *Telegram* was switched permanently to white. In 1956 the printing presses were moved from Water Street to the basement of the Newfoundland Clothing Company factory on the west corner of Duckworth Street and Telegram Lane. In 1961 the editorial and commercial offices of the paper took over the rest of the building. Lord Thompson of Fleet added the *Evening Telegram* to his international newspaper chain in 1970.

As we have seen in the *Fiona* case the *Telegram*'s great rival in politics and invective was the *Evening Herald*, a paper of distinction, which might well have survived to the present day had it not been dealt two fatal blows. The *Herald* began life in a building on the east side of Prescott Street, just above Duckworth Street, as the *Evening Mercury* in 1882. Its motto was "This Land of Ours." In 1889 it became the *Evening Herald*. The paper was blessed with a highly literate and capable editor, John E. Furneaux, who, before founding the *Mercury*, was in the drapery business. In 1888 Furneaux was on the Municipal Council Board. He aspired to the House of Assembly in 1899, as member for Fortune Bay, but was defeated. The first fatal blow was given the *Herald* on 3 June 1907, when Furneaux died unexpectedly at the age of fifty-three years. An assistant, Sir Patrick McGrath, took over as editor. The second fatal blow fell between 6:45 and 8:45 a.m. on 12 December 1918 when a $40,000 to $50,000 fire destroyed the offices and plant. Two years later Sir Patrick gave up the struggle to keep the journal alive and left Newfoundland.

The other surviving St. John's newspaper, the *Daily News*, was first issued by J. Alex Robinson, as a four-page journal, from a building on the west corner of Duckworth and Bell Streets, 15 February 1894. Ownership of the *News* changed hands in 1898, but Dr. Robinson again assumed control in 1906. He was succeeded in this by his brother-in-law, Hon. J. S. Currie, who was with the paper from the day it began publishing. In recent years the *Daily News* has changed owners and editors several times in a grim act of survival. Following the Great Fire of 1892 it moved into a modern building on Duckworth Street opposite City Terrace. Dr. Rendell's fashionable brick house next door, to the west, became its editorial offices. On 21 August 1972 the advertising, circulation, and administrative offices moved to 206 Water Street, a building which had been occupied since the Great Fire by Grey & Goodland Ltd., a stationery and printing supply firm which published the famous magazine *Christmas Bells*, on its small printing press in the last century. The booksellers' retail business moved to a location on the south side of Water Street, two or three doors east of Hunter's Cove, and the printing press to the basement of the Board of Trade Building. On 1 March 1971 the printing of the *Daily News* moved from Duckworth Street to the plant of Robinson-Blackmore on O'Leary Avenue.

One innovation which the *Daily News* introduced was a weekly paper called the *Free Press*. This was a regular size newspaper, paid for by advertisers and delivered free to householders in St. John's and Mount Pearl. The venture lasted from 28 April 1971 to 4 May 1972. A *Daily News* supplement, *Newsmagazine*, published in the late 1960s, was a valuable outlet for local writers and historians. Unfortunately, it did not long survive.

The man whose agitation was a decisive factor in forcing the government into establishing the coastal boats system and the railway line around Conception Bay was Bishop J. T. Mullock, who must also get credit for being the first to suggest, in print, that the colony should have a telegraph system. For years the Roman Catholic bishop preached that the prosperity of Newfoundland depended on the development of modern means of communication. His pen was seldom idle, and his letters to the press, frequently verging on libel, were dogmatic, no-nonsense missives that were avidly devoured.

In a letter to the editor of the New York *Courier*, 8 November 1850, His Lordship wrote:

> I regret to find that in every plan for Transatlantic Communication, Halifax is always mentioned, and the natural capabilities of Newfoundland are overlooked. . . . Now would it not be well to call the attention of England and America to the extraordinary capabilities of St. John's as the nearest tele-

graphic point?.... From St. John's to Cape Ray there is no difficulty in establishing a line passing near Holy-Rood along the neck of land connecting Placentia and Trinity Bays and thence in a direction due west to the Cape.... Thus it is not only practicable to bring America two days nearer to Europe by this route, but should the telegraphic communication between England and Ireland, 62 miles, be realized, it presents not the least difficulty.... I hope the day is not far distant when St. John's will be the first link in the electric chain which will unite the Old World and the New.

A year later Frederic Gisborne, a native of Manchester working at the time as an engineer with the Nova Scotia Telegraph Company, arrived in Newfoundland to build the St. John's and Carbonear Electric Telegraph Company line around Conception Bay. Gisborne soon appeared before the Legislature with a plan he had prepared in the manner suggested by Bishop Mullock. His telegraph line from St. John's to Cape Ray would be connected to Cape Breton, by carrier pigeon, or steamer, and eventually by submarine cable. The politicians were impressed enough to vote him £500 for a survey. This was completed in three months, between September 4 and December 4, through 350 miles of rugged wilderness. The party were often near starvation, and one member actually died, before the route was laid out.

An act was passed in the spring of 1852 incorporating the Newfoundland Electric Telegraph Company. It was given exclusive rights to all telegraphy in the island for the next thirty years, as well as a land grant on completion of the line. Gisborne sailed for New York to raise the £100,000 authorized capital. Backers were not easily found and those that were proved troublesome and unreliable. It was not until the following summer that work on the line was begun westward from Brigus with 350 men. Only forty miles had been laid when Gisborne ran out of cash for the payroll and his bills were dishonoured by his New York agents. The pioneering engineer lost all he had and the Newfoundland Electric Telegraphic Company was insolvent.

Frederic Gisborne returned to New York in search of new backers and it was there, in January 1854, that Matthew Field introduced him to his brother Cyrus, a thirty-three-year-old who was already retired from business as a millionaire, after having begun work in a mercantile office at the age of fifteen for a dollar a week. Field saw beyond Gisborne's plan and dreamed of a cable communication with Europe.

As a result of this meeting, the New York, Newfoundland and London Telegraph Company was incorporated, by an Act of the Legislature, and it took over the charter of the Newfoundland Electric

Telegraph Company. The colonial government also offered £ 50,000 in bonds toward the completion of the project. The new company was granted the sole right to land cables and receive telegraphic messages in the island for fifty years. This was to cause much ill will and many complications in the future, but at the time nobody foresaw the coming era of wireless telegraphy. [25]

The new company paid off the debts of the old. Work was resumed in 1854 and the line to Carbonear completed in 1856. With that Frederic Gisborne vanished from the story. Before leaving he was presented with a tall silver trophy, "a very beautiful, valuable and appropriate piece of plate by the inhabitants of the city of St. John's, Newfoundland, as marking their sense of the energy and perseverance he has displayed in traversing the previously unexplored parts of the island in anticipation of the introduction of the telegraph." [26]

Gisborne was not averse to giving credit where it was due, and in accepting the plate he acknowledged, "I may be pardoned for making honourable mention of His Lordship, Bishop Mullock, whose high order of talent is universally acknowledged. To him is due the credit of an expressed belief of connecting Newfoundland with the continent of America with the electric telegraph shortly before I had myself publicly announced my intentions." The Bishop did not express a belief. He had asserted a certainty.

The story of Cyrus Field's great venture in laying the Atlantic cable is one of setbacks, disappointment, and even heartbreak. After many trials the first Atlantic cable was landed at Bay Bulls Arm, Trinity Bay, 5 August 1858. The directors in England sent a message to their fellows in America in a transmission that took thirty-five minutes. After that, Queen Victoria cabled James Buchanan, and the President of the United States sent a cordial reply. Four hundred messages later the cable parted under the ocean and, in 1865, another attempt was made by Cyrus Field to lay a cable. This one was brought ashore at Heart's Content at two o'clock on the afternoon of 27 July 1866. At five o'clock the shore end was placed in the cable office and the first signals were heard from Valencia, Ireland. The success of this venture placed Newfoundland in the eye of the world as a centre of international communication, and made Cyrus Field one of the immortals of his century.

In choosing a subordinate for Newfoundland manager of his company, soon to be known as Anglo-American Telegraph, Field picked twenty-two-year-old Alexander Mackay, chief electrician of the Nova Scotia Telegraph Company. Mackay landed at Port aux Basques on 22 June 1857 and with a gang of men walked the length of the land line to St. John's, repairing as they went. Winter storms, theft, and vandalism had left the line in a dilapidated condition. The young manager soon had an efficient system working between the

198

island capital and Canada, but Gisborne's submarine cable to Cape Breton was in poor shape and, in 1867, Anglo laid a submarine line from Heart's Content to the Canadian mainland. The old land line fell into disuse.

In 1919 some fishermen, jigging for cod in waters near Cape Ray, hauled up a short length of the 1866 cable. This is now on display in the Newfoundland Museum. Composed of a seven-strand copper core, it is covered with three eighths of an inch of gutta-percha rubber.

Other submarine cable outfits followed hot on the heels of the successful Heart's Content venture, and the agreement signed by the Newfoundland government with Field's cable company soon came back to haunt it. The Direct United States Cable Company laid a line across the ocean into Conception Bay in 1875, but was enjoined from landing there by the Newfoundland Supreme Court when Anglo claimed its monopoly. The injunction was sustained by the Imperial Privy Council. The only exception to the exclusive rights was the Newfoundland government which might establish land lines itself in parts of the island where Anglo did not choose to do so.

When the monopoly expired in 1905 the island was invaded by cable companies. Besides Anglo-American there was Western Union, Commercial Cables, and the previously mentioned Direct United States Cable Company. The government established a department of posts and telegraphs that united its telegraph and postal services.

In 1901 the Anglo monopoly became involved in a much more celebrated case than that of 1875. In November, a twenty-seven-year-old, well-to-do Italian inventor from Bologna, sailed from Liverpool for St. John's, on board S.S. *Sardinian*. His name was Guglielmo Marconi and he was accompanied by two assistants, G. S. Kemp and P. W. Paget. Except for their rather unusual luggage, which consisted of hampers of wireless equipment, containers of hydrogen, and kites and balloons, their arrival in St. John's went unnoticed.

A reporter from the *Evening Telegram* sniffed something in the wind and went to interview the new arrivals at the Cochrane Hotel where they were staying. Marconi disarmed him by saying he was in Newfoundland in response to a request from the Minister of Marine and Fisheries to investigate setting up a wireless station to help reduce the number of shipwrecks. Nothing was said about the real purpose of his visit, the transmission of a wireless signal across the Atlantic.

Wireless telegraphy was first demonstrated in St. John's on 12 September 1899 by a Mr. Bowden. The editor of *Trade Review*, M. A. Devine, was asked to write the first message. He was inspired to pen "God Save the Queen."

On 7 December 1901, the day following his arrival, Marconi

called on Governor Boyle and Prime Minister Bond, who offered him what resources they could for his secret experiments. Accompanied by the Minister of Marine and the Inspector of Lighthouses, he set out to find a suitable site for a wireless station. Of this search Marconi writes:

> After taking a look at various sites which might prove suitable, I considered the best one on Signal Hill, a lofty eminence overlooking the port and forming a natural bulwark which protects it from the fury of the Atlantic winds. On top of the hill is a small plateau some two acres in extent which seemed very suitable for the manipulation of the balloons and kites.[27]

On a crag on this plateau rose the new Cabot Tower, erected in commemoration of the famous Italian explorer John Cabot and designed as a signal station. Close to it was the old military barracks, then used as a hospital.

> On Monday, December 9th, we began to work. On Tuesday we flew a kite with 600 feet of aerial as a preliminary test and on Wednesday we inflated one of the balloons which made its first ascent in the morning. It was about 14 feet in diameter and contained about 1,000 cubic feet of hydrogen gas, quite sufficient to hold up the aerial which consisted of a wire weighing about ten pounds. After a short while however the blustery wind ripped the balloon away from the wire. The balloon sailed out over the sea. We concluded, perhaps the kites would be better, and on Thursday morning in spite of a gusty gale we managed to fly a kite up to 400 feet.
>
> The critical moment had come, for which the way had been prepared by six years of hard and unremitting work, despite the usual criticism levelled at anything new. I was about to test the truth of my belief.
>
> In view of the importance of all that was at stake, I decided not to trust entirely to the usual arrangement of having the coherer signals record automatically on a paper tape through a relay and Morse instrument, but to use instead a telephone connected to a self-restoring coherer. The human ear being much more sensitive than the recorder, it would be more likely to hear the signal.
>
> Before leaving England I had given detailed instructions for transmission of a certain signal, the Morse telegraph "S"— three dots—at a fixed time each day, beginning as soon as word was received that everything at St. John's was in readiness. If the invention would receive on the kite-wire in Newfoundland, some of the electric waves produced, I knew that the solution of the problem of transoceanic wireless telegraphy was at hand.

I cabled Poldhu [a station in Cornwall where the transmitter was set up] to begin sending [on December 12th] at 3 p.m. in the afternoon English time, continuing until 6 o'clock, that is from 11:30 a.m. to 2:30 p.m. at St. John's."[28]

It is often erroneously believed that Marconi set up his equipment on the ground floor of the newly opened Cabot Tower. He did not. What he used was the downstairs front room, on the northwest side of the old hospital building. A photograph shows him at his wireless in front of the dilapidated walls. His reason for choosing this place was probably to give himself greater secrecy, since Cabot Tower was very busy. Men from the town were always on duty there signalling to ships or mercantile firms, and there were many visitors.

The atmosphere in the small room was strained that morning as Marconi awaited the signal from Cornwall, two thousand miles over the ocean. Suddenly at 12:30 p.m. he heard three little clicks. He stiffened with excitement as they sounded several times in his ears. Though he listened intently he was not satisfied without corroboration.

"Can you hear anything, Kemp?" he said, handing his assistant the receiver. This is how he describes that moment of history:

> Kemp heard the same thing that I did, and I knew then that I was absolutely right in my anticipation. Electric waves which had been sent out from Poldhu had traversed the Atlantic, serenely ignoring the curvature of the earth which so many doubters considered would be a fatal obstacle. I knew then that the day would come on which I should be able to send full messages without wires or cables across the Atlantic was not very far away. Distance had been overcome, and further developments of the sending and receiving apparatus were all that was required.[29]

They heard the three dots repeated over and over again. Paget, who was outside, was called in, but because he was somewhat deaf, he was unable to hear the signals. Around two o'clock the wind fell off and the kite dropped. The signals disappeared. About twenty minutes later a fresh wind caused the kite to rise again and the signals came back loud and clear until transmission ceased at two-thirty that afternoon.

Marconi and his assistants returned in silence to their hotel, keeping their secret to themselves for two days, during which they constantly checked the results. On Saturday, December 14, the inventor announced his news to the world that transoceanic wireless had become a reality. On Tuesday, a distinguished party of citizens assembled on Signal Hill where Governor Boyle, Prime Minister Bond, and others heard for themselves the Morse signals flashing from Cornwall.

News of the sensation was greeted with skepticism by another great inventor, Thomas Edison. He refused to believe the event possible and declared it a "newspaper fake." The reporter from the *Evening Telegram*, who returned to the Cochrane Hotel for a far more rewarding interview, was less restrained. He rhapsodized:

> The very thought of it sets one aghast. The humble genius who received the Telegram reporter at the Cochrane Hotel makes no vain-glorious boast about what he has achieved. He is as modest as a schoolboy and one would not think that he is the wizard who wrought this awe-inspiring wonder of science, that realizes the tales of the Arabian Nights and the stories of Jules Verne. It is no wonder that New York stood astounded and refused to believe the news when it was flashed over the wires on Saturday night. Newspapers were skeptical and before sending the report to their printers, wired for confirmation of the news.
>
> The citizens of St. John's even doubted the truth of it on Saturday night. They had cast an occasional glance up at Signal Hill the past few days while the experiments were going on. They had seen electrically-charged kites whirling in the storm-tossed air over Signal Hill, but did not attach much importance to the matter . . . .
>
> Nowise the less Wednesday the 11th December, 1901, will be put down as a memorable day in the history of the world—a day on which one of the greatest achievements of science was accomplished. It will be a proud boast for the people of Newfoundland to say in the words of the poet, when looking back on it, 'Magna pars quorum fuimus'. We heartily congratulate Signor Marconi on his success! There is a fascination in imagining him sitting at his table in the building on Signal Hill, with watch in hand, waiting for the hand to point to the moment agreed upon with his friend on the other side of the Atlantic. The hand moves slowly around, the scientist's mind is strung to powerful attention.
>
> Will the dreams of his life—his soul's ambition—be realized? A quiver like an angel's breath breathes over the receiving instruments, and the delicate recorder begins to move, low as the whisper of a dying child at first, but in half a minute gaining strength. The secret of the age was being yielded grudingly, as it were, to the ear of the high priest of electoral [sic] Science—Signor Marconi. The sounds were now distant, and what ravishing music they made when the three dots of the letter S (. . . . .) were repeated growing stronger each time.
>
> A new spirit was born to science with a tip of its wing on each side of the ocean. The old Atlantic cable heard the news, quivered and groaned. Telegraph cable stocks slumped on the market on Saturday evening, and there was fever-heat excitement among business men.

The old Atlantic cable did not quiver and groan alone. Its owner, the Anglo-American Telegraph Company, quivered and groaned much more loudly and Alexander Mackay conjured the spectre of the monopoly rights, which still had three years to run, to haunt the government and people of Newfoundland, as well as put to flight the celebrated Italian inventor.

On Wednesday Marconi was invited to a public luncheon at Government House, where he was guest of honour. After toasts and congratulations he departed with some government officials for Cape Spear, a few miles from St. John's. The Cape is the easternmost point in North America, the closest land to Europe. Here Marconi looked over a possible site for a permanent wireless station. Bad news was waiting when he returned to the Cochrane Hotel. A gentleman in the lobby introduced himself as a solicitor acting on behalf of the Anglo-American Telegraph Company, and he handed the inventor a letter threatening a court injunction, restraining him from receiving any more telegraph messages from outside Newfoundland. The company intended to enforce the terms of the 1854 Act in the courts.

Anglo had reason to be worried at the time. Subsequent history proved otherwise. The first Atlantic Cable had cost nearly $14,-000,000, whereas Marconi had spanned the Atlantic, by wireless, for about $250,000. Stock exchanges reflected a sharp drop in the price of Anglo-American shares. Rival companies, such as Commercial and Western Union, shared the alarm and concern.

Indignation against Anglo ran high in Newfoundland as the banished Marconi boarded the train at St. John's, at five o'clock on the afternoon of December 22, and took his departure for Nova Scotia. The largest crowd ever witnessed at Fort William Station gathered to wave the young Italian farewell. There were newspaper reporters there from all over the world. They had flocked to the city on hearing of the successful experiment. That afternoon resentment against Anglo flared almost to the point of riot. Families came from miles around to glimpse and cheer the new idol of a world changed forever by his fourteen days in St. John's.

Peering out from under the pile of abuse heaped upon him, Hon. Alexander Mackay defended himself by stating that he would do anything to help scientific progress in telegraphy, but that his first duty was to safeguard the interests and rights of his company.

When the monopoly expired in 1904 the whole of the island telegraph system was consolidated under the name of the Newfoundland Postal Telegraphs, and became a sub-department of the General Post Office to which it was subordinated. The memory of Marconi's expulsion was short lived and Mackay was invited to head up the new government system, as General Superintendent of Telegraphs. However, his days were numbered. He died at his residence, 3 Musgrave

Terrace (now 23 Gower Street), in 1905, having made an invaluable contribution to the development of his adopted land, both in the field of the telegraph and the telephone.

The first electrical telephone was described by P. Reis in 1861, but the first one of practical use was that invented by Alexander Graham Bell in 1876. It was made possible by Michael Farraday's discovery of electromagnetism.

Two years after Bell's voice was carried electrically to an assistant in an adjoining room, the invention reached St. John's when Alexander Mackay installed one for the private use of the General Post Office. It was operated between the residence of John Delany, the postmaster general, 2 Monkstown Road, and John Higgins, the meteorological recorder, 48 Southwest. It must have been considered more a novelty than a useful means of communication, for it was six years before the next telephones were installed. In 1884 Mackay linked the office of Archibald's Furniture Factory, at the corner of Duckworth Street and St. John's Lane, by telephone to the manager's residence in Devon Row, nearly half a mile away to the east. This obviously proved the worth of the instrument. The following year a public telephone service was begun.

The Anglo-American Telegraph Company, set up an exchange over John Lindberg's jewellery store at 171 Water Street, next door to George Crosbie's Central Hotel. When the 1892 fire destroyed the building, the exchange reopened four months later, above the dry-goods store of James Black, at 276 New Gower Street. There it remained for the next seven years.

The system was acquired by the Western Union Telegraph Company in 1899 and moved into the Exchange Building, just east of the steps leading up to City Terrace, where part of the equipment is still located. When the Avalon Telephone Company was incorporated in 1919, it took over the franchises of Western Union as well as the telephones of the United Towns Electric Company in Conception Bay. The following year a long-distance line was built to Carbonear. The first toll call was made from St. John's on 27 November 1920. A submarine cable was used to connect the city to Bell Island in 1925.

When Avalon took over from Western Union, there were 800 telephones in use. By 1930 their number had grown to 6,000, and in 1950 it passed 14,000. The 100,000th telephone in Newfoundland was installed in Grand Falls in 1971. Along with this domestic growth the company moved to link the country to the outside world, and in 1939 a radio link was realized with the Bell Telephone in Montreal. Following Confederation, land lines were leased from Canadian National Telegraphs. In 1962 the system was taken over by Bell Canada.

Until just before Confederation, to place a call it was necessary to lift the receiver and wait for the voice of Central to inquire "Number please?" She then rang the number she was given, such as 73J or 462R. If the line was busy the caller was so informed. It was not unusual for a line to be busy because as many as three houses often shared the one line, and neighbours in the same, or adjoining streets, were able to eavesdrop on each others' gossip. This arrangement, which had given rise to such tear-jerking, popular ballads as, "Hello, Central, Give Me Heaven" ('cause my mommy's there), was made impersonal in 1948 by the introduction of the dial system to St. John's. At the same time a five-storey office building was erected by the telephone company, on the corner of Duckworth Street and McBride's Hill. A short time later new exchanges were built on Anderson Avenue, at Wishing Well Road, and on Allandale Road, just south of Elizabeth Avenue.

During the late 1960s and early 1970s international surveys showed, on a per capita basis, that Canadians did more telephoning every day than citizens of any other nation. Within Canada, also on a per capita basis, the St. John's public used the telephone more than people in any other Canadian community. The instrument is not a convenience to subscribers in the province's capital; it is a way of life.

The media outlet the world was to know as radio had its birth on Signal Hill in that moment when Signor Marconi received the first wireless signal from England. On 25 July 1920 the hill was again used for radio experiments. This time it was for the transmission of the human voice. A communication was kept up with S.S. *Victorian* during the whole of her trans-Atlantic voyage. A second receiver in the Canadian Marconi office in the Board of Trade Building, St. John's, operated by the office assistant, Daisy Myrick, also picked up the S.S. *Victorian* broadcast.

Early in 1921, J. J. Collins, the manager of the Marconi office received two radio transmitters. One was intended for sale to Sir William Coaker, for installation at Port Union. With the other, Mr. Collins assembled VOS, an infant radio station, the first in St. John's. The test program featured H. Gordon Christian, a local musician, and B. Morris. Reception on the half-dozen receiving sets in the city was reported clear and distinct. The St. John's Radio Club was formed in the autumn of that year by interested amateurs. On 9 July 1922 VOS gave its first official broadcast. Taking part were W. J. "Billy" Wallace, a star of Hutton operettas; Sandy Lawrence, a noted singer; Jack Canning, another well-known voice; Professor Hutton himself; and some businessmen of the town.

VOS was in the Pope Building at the lower end of McBride's Hill, on the west side, where VOCM was afterwards located. Mr. Collins presented twice-weekly concerts that were full of thrills and excitement. Catwhisker crystal sets picked up the broadcasts as far as twenty-five miles away. In 1923 the call letters were changed to 8AK

205

and listeners were beginning to hear transmissions through loudspeakers rather than headphones. The station moved to Collins's house at 9 Parade Street and became 8JJC. It was from this station that the first remote radio broadcast in Newfoundland took place 25 January 1925. A hockey game in the Prince's Rink was relayed to the station by telephone and sent out over the air.

On 20 July 1924 a station went on the air in Wesley United Church on Patrick Street. It was the brain child of Rev. J. G. Joyce, the minister of Wesley. The call letters were 8LR, the initials standing for Loyal Reid, of the Reid family who were to operate the station. It went on the air 4 November 1924 with a gramophone production of Gilbert and Sullivan's *The Gondoliers* and broadcast twice weekly. It later became VOWR, the oldest continuing broadcasting service in Newfoundland.

By 1925 radio was becoming an industry. The Marconi wireless transmitting station at Mount Pearl, a ship-to-shore service, was up for auction with no buyers. It was suggested that the government take it over, and that a broadcasting studio be installed in the Newfoundland Hotel, which was under construction. Nothing came of either idea.

At the International Radio Conference in Washington in 1927 Newfoundland was assigned the call letters VO. Various commercial stations were launched by individuals and business houses. The most important of these was opened in 1931 by Ayre & Sons Ltd., as VOAS. The following year VONF and VOGY made their advent to the air waves. VOGY, Newfoundland's first full-time commercial station, had its studios in the Crosbie Hotel. It began broadcasting on 12 September 1932. On 5 March 1934 it moved to new studios on the top floor of the Newfoundland Hotel.

VONF, with W. F. Galgay as studio director, was a subsidiary of the Avalon Telephone Company and made its debut 14 November 1932 from the Dominion Broadcasting Company studios, McBride's Hill. It had the sole rights to rebroadcast programs from NBC in the United States. In September 1934, VOGY and VONF were amalgamated and from October of that year they operated from the VOGY studios in the Newfoundland Hotel, as radio station VONF. On 1 April 1949 the studios began broadcasting as CBN. Confederation brought to the province the Canadian Broadcasting Corporation. Evicted from the hotel by its new owners, Canadian National, the CBC moved to the rat-infested Minard's Linament Building on Water Street, just west of Cochrane Street, until its new studios were ready in the T.A. Building, Duckworth Street.

In 1936 Joseph Butler and Walter Williams incorporated VOCM as a commercial broadcasting station with a 250-watt transmitter. Today it is the key station of the Colonial Broadcasting System, with studios in St. John's, Grand Falls, Gander, and Marystown. VOCM's original studios were in the Tabernacle School, near the southeast corner of Parade Street at Harvey Road. They later moved to the Pope Building, on the west corner of McBride's Hill and Water Street. From there VOCM transferred to modern studios on Kenmount Road late in the fall of 1967.

In 1939 the Dominion Broadcasting Company became the Broadcasting Corporation of Newfoundland. It was on VONF that an ex-newspaperman, Joey Smallwood, started his "Barrelman" program for F. M. O'Leary Ltd. O. L. Vardy and Alan Fraser were news commentators. The redoubtable Aubrey Mack had made his first appearance in 1936, using the name Ted Baker.

With the coming of the Americans to St. John's in 1941, the city got another station in the base-operated VOUS, located at Fort Pepperrell. This carried all the best U.S. radio network shows and Armed Forces Radio Service broadcasts, without commercials, and its demise, after the war, was greatly lamented.

In October 1951 Geoff Stirling and Don Jamieson combined forces and, with a staff of fifteen, put radio station CJON on the air. Their Newfoundland Broadcasting Company and the CBC both sought television licences from the Board of Broadcast Governors. The CBC application was turned down and, in September 1955, CJON-TV began the province's first television transmissions of Channel 6 in St. John's. Because of government regulations CJON-TV became an affiliate of the CBC network and all network programming was carried on CJON-TV by kine (film) until 1959, when microwave facilities became available. In October 1964 the public corporation's own television outlet in St. John's, CBNT, went on the air and CJON reverted to kines of the CTV commercial broadcasting on a one- or two-day-delay basis, the only live regular network broadcast being the Wednesday night hockey game. In 1973 Mr. Stirling's original radio investment was reported by the newspapers to have developed into a $20,000,000 fortune.

With the advent of CBC television the performers union, the Association of Canadian Television and Radio Artists, was organized in St. John's and opened an office at 203 Water Street, 16 February 1965. As with CBC radio, CBC television brought about much employment for local entertainers at professional fees. The new media created such local stars as Joan Morrissey and John White. Membership in ACTRA meant that the distinction between amateur and professional in acting, singing, and writing became very blurred.

Before leaving the story of radio and television in St. John's, the following item from a local newspaper, 17 February 1911, is worth attention.

Messrs. A. H. Rau, R. Crane and D. Sarnoff, three members

of the American branch of the Marconi Company, arrived by the *Florizel* last evening from New York bringing along the wireless apparatus to be placed on Job Brothers and Company's ships, Beothic and Neptune. The work of installing it will be commenced at once.

D. Sarnoff was David Sarnoff, a young man born in Russia and brought up in New York, who was to become General Sarnoff, head of RCA and NBC, and the most powerful man in radio and television in the United States. On 13 March 1911 he was on board the *Beothic* at six o'clock when she sailed through the Narrows with the rest of the sealing fleet. The young American wireless operator sent his first message back to Job's on March 18 from a position 118 miles northeast of the Wadhams.

Sarnoff kept a diary of his spring on the ice and his adventures included helping the ship's doctor pull some abscessed teeth belonging to the assistant wireless operator on Belle Isle. Another time he was chased over the ice by an old dog hood seal. Somebody on board the ship fired a shot that finished off the animal just before it caught up with the young American. For many years General Sarnoff kept a mounted, stillborn, Whitecoat seal as a souvenir of his spring in Newfoundland.

Television is the reproduction of images by electronic means. In the last century there were various inventions and devices for the reproduction of images. It all began in 1839, when a French landscape painter named Louis Daguerre gave the world a new medium. Daguerreotype was a process which made possible the development of the art of photography.

The word photographer was not coined until 1847. The members of the profession were first known as Daguerrean artists. Probably the first of the breed in St. John's were Messrs. Valentine & Doane, who announced in *The Times*, 15 March 1843, that they "have completed an apartment fitted for the purpose of Daguerreotype Portraiture... they are confident of producing pictures of exquisite beauty."

Their daguerreotype rooms at the Golden Lion Inn were open daily from one to four o'clock. Persons acquainted with the art were respectfully invited to call at the rooms and examine specimens. Portraits were taken in any state of weather.

The more conventionally minded could have a portrait completed in oil. Mr. Valentine would be happy to take on a few commissions if early application was made. The Golden Lion was near the east corner of Holloway and Water Streets, afterwards the site of the Temperance Hotel.

The fate of Valentine & Doane's enterprise is unknown. The gentlemen probably moved on when customers became scarce. We have no known example of the work of these pioneer photographers.

Dr. J. J. Dearin, truly a man for all seasons, added daguerreotype portraiture to his professions of politician, chemist, and dentist, as can be seen in the chapter dealing with the medical history of the city. Another early photographer was M. H. Grant, Daguerrean artist of Saint John, N.B., who appeared on the local scene in June 1855. He took rooms over the store of Elmsly & Shaw, grocers, 305 Water Street, next to Lash's Railway Hotel, "for the purpose of taking Daguerreotype likenesses."

Next came an American invention, ambrotype, whereby photographs could be reproduced on glass. In 1858, if not earlier, a man named D. Adams opened ambrotype rooms over his American Oyster House and Coffee Saloon, two doors east of McMurdo's Lane. This site was to be used by several photographic firms. If examples of Mr. Adams's work exist, they are not identified.

In 1858 J. Forbes Chisholm moved from Nova Scotia to St. John's and opened a bookstore. Six years later the firm of Smith & Chisholm took over new and extensive premises on the east side of Beck's Cove, two doors north of Water Street. That year the partners advised the public that the ambrotype rooms in their new establishment possessed every facility for producing likenesses with accuracy and dispatch. Smith died, or was bought out, and Chisholm became a leading bookseller of the town for half a century.

A business rival, McKenny & Dicks, had a stationery shop and photographic studios in the building where Adams had been located. Around 1870 F. Page Wood opened a photography shop at 178 Water Street, a few doors east of Clift's-Baird's Cove.

The tintype, invented in 1875, made picture taking much easier. A number of tintype parlours sprang up in St. John's to satisfy the Victorian urge to capture the essence of the age in stiff composure, standing against a painted backdrop, or seated with a carefully arranged hand resting on a desk or table. The tintype was a photograph taken as a positive on a thin tin plate. It was replaced by George Eastman's invention of a continuous roll of sensitized negative film which came ten years later. Eastman put a camera in everybody's hands.

The Matthew Brady of Newfoundland photographers was S. H. Parsons. His legacy to us is a priceless record of many outstanding photographs of St. John's taken before and after the 1892 fire. His Photographic Studio and Fine Art Emporium was located at 310 Water Street. The building still stands three doors east of Williams Lane and is now a Chinese restaurant. Sleater's store was on the ground floor and Parsons occupied the upper two storeys. Fortunately the Great Fire was stopped at the beginning of the block where the studio was located, else a heritage in photographs might have been lost. Unfortunately, the photographer was out of town that day and no actual photographs of the fire are known to have been taken. On his return Parsons took some classic pictures of the smouldering ruins.

S. H. Parsons was born at Harbour Grace, where he began his work in photography. He eventually moved to St. John's and died there in 1908, at the age of sixty-four, leaving a son to carry on the business. When the east end of the city was rebuilt, after the Great Fire, he relocated on the upper floor of a building on the west corner of Prescott and Water Streets, with the entrance on Prescott Street. The slanting window of his studio could be seen, in the side of the building, until recent years, when it was removed. Parsons was given international recognition in 1888 when he won a silver medal and was awarded a certificate of merit at a photography exhibition in Barcelona.

Two of S. H. Parsons's assistants, E. W. Lyon and James Vey, eventually became the master's leading competitors. Lyon & Vey operated from the same address as did McKenny and Dicks. The partnership did not survive. Lyon moved to 68 Victoria Street, following the 1892 holocaust, while Vey's studios were located in the imposing new Gazette Building, at the east corner of McBride's Hill. When the newspaper ceased publication, this tall red-brick edifice was taken over by the Bank of Montreal and finally torn down. James Vey occupied a printing and finishing room in the copper-roofed, octagonal tower of the building. His fame as a Newfoundland photographer is shared only by S. H. Parsons and Elsie Holloway.

Holloway is, beyond doubt, the greatest name in local photography in this century. Robert E. Holloway was born in England in 1850. At the age of twenty-two he came to St. John's as principal of the Methodist College and retained the position for thirty-two years, giving his name to Holloway School. An amateur photographer of some distinction, he travelled about the island taking pictures. Two of his photographs appeared on Newfoundland stamps and one was copied on a Canadian banknote.

He was preparing to publish a book of his photographs when death overtook him in 1904. The text was completed by his family and the book printed in England in 1910. His daughter Elsie, with her brother, opened a studio on the north side of Henry Street, at Bates Hill, with an entrance angled between the two streets. The brother soon took off for points west and the sister was forced to carry on alone. The building was gutted in a fire, 27 January 1975.

Over the years this tyrannical spinster photographed generations of Newfoundland citizens. Besides the high and the mighty, she also snapped numerous family groups. Each spring, thousands of boys and girls, laughing and shouting like pilgrims on their way to Canterbury, were marched down Henry Street or Bates Hill, along with masters, mistresses, brothers, and nuns to face the eye of the camera, and the equally stern eye of Elsie Holloway. Knickered legions of scholars stifled evil grins as they stared indolently at the birdie Miss Holloway actually held in her hand.

Hockey teams, football teams, basketball teams, dramatic troupes, operatic casts, and all who sought immortality on celluloid assembled in the second-floor studio on Henry Street. There were few in St. John's who escaped the lens of Miss Holloway's camera during the first half of the twentieth century. Yet when the aging recluse died, ill and lonely, in 1971, her passing was ignored by radio, television, and the newspapers.

In October 1898 the U.S. Picture & Portrait Company opened a very up-to-date studio in the Dyer Building at the southwest corner of Water Street and Beck's Cove. The newspapers of the day made much of the fact that the whole building was fitted with electric light, employed in the taking of the photographs.

Anthony Tooton, a native of Syria, arrived in St. John's in late 1903 or early 1904. After failing to find suitable employment he entered the photographic business for himself and soon dominated the field of processing the work of amateur photographers. His firm still dominates the field after more than seventy years. In 1905 Tooton opened the Parisian Photographic Studio, opposite Knowling's West End Stores on Water Street, upstairs over the Green Lantern Cafe. In the late 1920s he moved to the present downtown building, opposite Williams Lane and had as an upstairs tenant a commission merchant who sold chocolates, named Chesley Pippy, who was to become one of the two or three wealthiest men in Newfoundland.

In 1911 Tooton was appointed as sole distributor for Kodak products in the island by George Eastman, founder of the Eastman Kodak Company. Tooton's Ltd., in answer to the demands of expanding business, eventually erected a large film-processing plant on Cabot Street, and later a branch office was opened in the Avalon Mall.

5

These Our Actors

Duckworth Street in winter before the Great Fire of 1892. A gas lamp hangs over the Court House door. The next building is the Union Bank and behind it the Athenaeum. The Presbyterian Kirk stands in front of the Bank of British North America, later the Commercial Bank. All the buildings shown in this photo with the exception of the two banks were destroyed in the Great Fire of 1892. (Courtesy St. John's City Hall)

215

The famous Octagon Castle of the celebrated Professor Danielle. Opened at Octagon Pond by Prime Minister Whiteway, in 1896, the building was destroyed by fire in 1915. Note the Caribou horns over every window. The professor, who stands in front of the horses, displayed his coffin to the public in one of the tower rooms. (Courtesy Newfoundland Public Archives)

216

London Tavern, from a sketch by W. Eagar

The famous old London Tavern. The centre of St. John's social life from 1800 to 1820 this inn, near the junction of York and Wood Streets, catered to governors, admirals and bishops. The Benevolent Irish Society was founded here in 1807.

217

Theatre had become fashionable by 1914 when these society belles performed a pastoral play on the lawn of what is thought to be Virginia Waters in aid of the World War I cot fund. Reading from left to right, back row — Miss Agnes Hayward, Miss Bradshaw, Mrs. Colvile, Mrs. Chater, Miss Rendell. Front row — Miss Doyle, Miss Ayre (Cupid), Mrs. Herbert Outerbridge, Miss Jessie Job, Miss Flora Clift (reclining). (Courtesy Provincial Reference Library - Newfoundland Section)

218

Miss Emily Mare (later married to Hon. R. B. Job) who was principal soprano at the Roman Catholic Cathedral and also a popular local star of concerts and operettas. (Courtesy Provincial Reference Library - Newfoundland Section)

The St. John's-born Broadway star Donald Brian as Prince Danilo in the first American production of "The Merry Widow" which ran for 416 performances in 1907-8. (Courtesy Library & Museum of the Performing Arts)

The cast of a traditional St. Patrick's Day play "Molly Bawn", 17 March 1919. The performers are Capt. J. J. O'Grady, Jack Pippy, Ida Howlett, Phil Moore, Paddy Grace, Mary McCarthy (afterwards Madam Gomez of Cuba), Minnie Viguers and Billy Comerford. (Courtesy Provincial Reference Library—Newfoundland section)

221

Arts & Culture Centre at St. John's which was built by the Federal and Provincial Governments to mark Canada's Centennial. The building houses a library, theatre, art gallery, museum, restaurant and other facilities. (Ben Hansen)

The silver cup presented by the leading citizens of St. John's to Bishop O'Donel at a farewell dinner held in his honour at the London Tavern at the time of his retirement to Ireland in 1807.

Georgina Stirling (known professionally as Marie Toulinguet). The Twillingate lark studied opera in Paris, debuted at La Scala in Milan and was on the verge of an operatic career in America when diphtheria ruined her voice and caused her to return to St. John's.

224

Professor Charles Hutton was born at St. John's 20 August 1861 and died 1 February 1949. The greatest impresario the city was ever to know, he produced memorable operettas and was given a papal knighthood for his work with the Roman Catholic church and schools.

225

These Our Actors

These our actors as I foretold you were all spirits and are melted into air . . .

WILLIAM SHAKESPEARE, *The Tempest*

If ye olde St. John's was as squalid and sordid a place as some eyewitness accounts would have us believe, then it was no worse than most North American towns of the time. As for amusements and diversions, it was better served than the majority of frontier communities. Until the beginning of the nineteenth century the most readily available entertainments seem to have been women, drink, and cards.

As far back as 1541, one of Cartier's captains mentions the presence of females in the port. Whether or not these women were sin sisters of the wild plantation, or hard-working pioneer wives, is now a matter of conjecture. However, there can be no doubt at all that the oldest profession was entrenched in the life of the town by the eighteenth century. One observer writing of St. John's around 1775 noted, " . . . the number of licenced houses in the said harbour are amounted to more than eighty in number, many of which are houses of ill-fame where the fishermen and seamen resort, and get drunk." Thirty years later, in 1805, we find Governor Gambier urgently enjoining his magistrates to enforce with the utmost rigour laws against such abuses as adultery, fornication, polygamy, and immorality then rampant in the community.

The Jezebels of the West Atlantic appear to have suffered little from the more legitimate sources of merriment, until the early 1800s. St. John's was a place in which no painted lips parted in an aria at the opera house, no polished bosom shimmered temptingly from behind the limelight of the music hall, and no tigress of the stage tore a passion to tatters at the theatre. Devoid of such frivolities as music, dance, and drama the town was wide open to the ways of the wicked.

It is not difficult to imagine what it must have been like in the 1700s as damsels of flawed virtue, their eyes flaring like St. Elmo's fire, sought out the large numbers of soldiers, sailors, and fishermen who, drink-inflamed, staggered about the paths anxious to share what Lord Byron was later to call, "a love for beauty and sin." Throughout

226

the hours of darkness the endless ripple of coarse laughter permeated the lanes and byways that ran beneath the flakes and fish stores of the ships' rooms. As wantons kissed and cuddled wayward lads, little heed was paid to the lesson to be learned from their fallen kindred of earlier days who, fouled by disease, lurched through the shadowy mists to miserable hovels, where they drowned in drink until they mercifully perished.

The only real competition known to these frolicsome wenches came from cards and demon rum. And strong competition the rum was. For example, in 1775 when the population of St. John's was around 1,500 (including infants in arms) the import of rum for that year was 250,000 gallons—to say nothing of whiskey, gin, brandy, wine, and cider.[1] The demon's appeal would appear to have been unconfined by age for there are shocked accounts, by visitors of the day, regarding the numbers of drunken children seen staggering about the roadways. As late as the 1830s Bishop Fleming complained of employers giving a portion of rum three times a day to boys working for them.

The Colonial Records were begun in August 1749 and almost the first two entries deal with those eternal companions, fisticuffs and booze. That month the governor forbade the repetition of a riot that had lately happened in the town between His Majesty's troops and servants employed in the fishery. For good measure he also gave notice that "Persons shall not presume to sell any strong liquors without a licence."[2]

Attempts to regulate the sale of liquor in the town go far back in history. The Merchants of Exeter wrote to the government in March 1675 complaining of the governor of Newfoundland who "hath pleased to Licence to keep Tippling Houses for the selling of Wine, Beare, Brandy and tobacco . . . ." The merchants also observed: "Such is the barrenness of that island and the inhabitants for the most part poore and debauched, and that their poverty and debauchery putts them upon committing all vices and mischiefe, by debauching seamen . . . . " That same year the Merchants of Plymouth claimed the inhabitants were "Debauching our men, Tempting them by wine and women not only to unfaithfulness but to common Drunkenness . . . not regarding the good old lawes . . . in the yeare 1633 forbidding any Taverns and Tippling houses . . . ." This would seem to indicate that St. John's had become such a wild place by 1633 that liquor-serving establishments had been forbidden by law.

In the town of 250 years ago taverns abounded. The number reached forty-six by the year 1726.[3] In 1775, as we have seen, 250,000 gallons of rum flowed into waiting throats and eighty taverns helped dispense these spirits. By 1785 the Grand Jury was recommending that they be reduced to twenty-four but the principal inhabitants recommended sixty-four. The governor granted permission for forty. Aaron Thomas, in his journal of a visit in 1794, states: "Grog shops are very numerous in St. John's. Rum here is very cheap, it being brought from the West Indies and only pays 1/ a Gallon Duty. A person who is fond of malt liquors will find them very dear. One Shilling a bottle of London Porter is the price."[4]

At the beginning of the nineteenth century, when the town had about 3,500 of the island's 20,000 people, the import of rum had fallen to 220,000 gallons.[5] If only half of it was consumed in St. John's, it works out at more than thirty gallons per head for every man, woman, and child. A century later, consumption was down to a paltry one-third of a gallon per head for all liquors. The ultimate indignity was heaped on the memory of our besotted ancestors in 1915, when a majority of 20,000 voted for prohibition in a plebiscite that saw just over 40 per cent of those eligible to vote bother to do so. The Act was enforced 1 January 1917 and not repealed until 1924. The measure had earlier been defeated, on 18 April 1887, when the speaker cast the deciding vote in a seventeen-to-seventeen tie in the House of Assembly.

In the old days a tavern keeper was obliged to perform police duties in order to obtain a licence. Robert Parsons, the proprietor of the West India Coffee House was High Constable in 1807, and thirty-four other owners, including two women, doubled as police. Their duties as lawkeepers were taken seriously. This is attested to by the fact that the firm of James Macbraire was forcibly entered on Saturday night, 1 March 1817 and "by the vigilance of the town patrol one man was arrested and part of the plunder recovered."[6]

The seemingly endless quantities of liquor consumed in old St. John's were generally quaffed from the tankard of a colonial tavern. Of the hundreds that existed before 1800, the earliest we can locate is the Ship. There exists a painting of it done around 1770. The Ship was located on Water Street, east of the War Memorial, and its story is told in the chapter dealing with transportation.

Each of these taverns had its own gaily painted signboard, and these beckoned customers to such centres of social intercourse as W. Best's Bunch of Grapes, located at Bulley's Farm, south of what is now LeMarchant Road. At the turn of the eighteenth century, the west end could boast of John Widdicombe's Rose and Crown, Edward Angell's Britannia near the west corner of Water and Springdale Streets, John Cahill's Tavern For All Weathers, Patrick Murine's Flower Pot, and Mary Hennessey's Royal Standard. The central division of the town had Richard Perchard's Royal Oak, facing Hunter's Cove. West of it there was Patrick Redmond's Ship Assistance, Robert Dooling's Red Cow, John Fitzgerald's Jolly Fisherman, Michael Hanlen's Shoulder of Mutton, Margaret Walsh's Sailor, and others. East of Hunter's Cove there was Dennis Murphy's Wheatsheaf, Daniel Driscoll's Bird-in-Hand, and Michael Mara's Sun. John Murphy's Duke of York was on Duckworth Street, just east of Cochrane Street. This tavern gave its name to Duke of York Street. The Plymouth Tavern, advertised for sale in 1818 "on the road from Fort William to Signal Hill," seems also to have given its name to Plymouth Road.

At the top of Temperance Street, Charles Power's Plough was located near Brine's Bridge, also called Pour's (Power's) Bridge. This is believed to be the old building, with massive stone walls, torn down on Council orders when damaged by fire in recent years. Robert Brine's Butchery was some distance from Brine's Bridge, at the foot of Robinson's Hill, now called Pringle Place.

A favourite drinking spot for officers at Fort William was the Crown, near the top of Pilot's Hill. At the foot of the hill was the Rising Sun which later became a convent. The Globe lived up to its illustrious name by offering theatrical performances. Mr. Doyle, and later Mr. Douglas, were the proprietors. B. Hannagan, the owner of the Crown and Anchor, was another who dabbled in the arts. In addition to a glass of your favourite, he would sell you, for three shillings, a copy of his poem "Newfoundland—in 2 parts with added songs, epigrams, etc." At the foot of Holloway Street Mrs. Matthews pulled the taps in the Golden Lion from 1818 onwards.

What Maxim's was to early nineteenth-century Paris, the London Tavern was to early eighteenth-century St. John's. The rooms of this handsome, colonial-style building witnessed much of the social history of the age. Around the blazing fire, in glorious uniforms and tankard in hand, stood the officers of the garrison. Merchants, the whisper of whose names could terrify, bent their curled and oiled beards over the billiard table. In the dining room, secure in the softness of candlelight, the Roman Catholic bishop, the garrison commander, or even His Excellency the governor might be spied sampling the excellent liquors and "sumptuous meals."

The man who brought this touch of elegance into the life of the town was Cornelius Quirk. Where he came from we do not know, but the London Tavern was already in business when on 26 April 1804 he purchased it for a hundred pounds from Michael Little who had acquired the land from the estate of absentee landlord William Ellis of Woodbury, Devon.

For some reason all historians have placed the London Tavern at King's Beach, on Duckworth Street. It was on Duckworth Street, but much further east, standing in a garden near the junction of what were later to be York and Wood Streets. The lane leading to the tavern eventually became known as Hill o' Chips (an extension of the road of the same name, below Duckworth Street), and later, Wood Street. When Quirk took over the inn from Little, the grant included two gardens in front, a garden and potato ground in back. A sketch of the place by William Eager shows a fence and two trees in front of the building. Eager did not arrive in Newfoundland until 1830. If his sketch was drawn from life, then the inn appears to have been divided into two private homes in 1830. On 23 August 1806 governor Gower gave Quirk permission to lengthen his large public room, to widen his kitchen, and to enlarge his store, in consideration of the new road passing through his premises. This new road was Gower Street which cut across the back garden.

In 1811 Cornelius Quirk was advertising his services for hire as a "public accomptant," his occupation when he purchased the tavern "at his house near the Ordanance [sic] Yard." The Ordnance property was along the west side of what is now Ordnance Street.

Cornelius Quirk is first mentioned in October 1803, when he registered a claim to four acres of land extending from the old entrenchment to the road linking Vinnicomb's Hill to Quidi Vidi. The old entrenchment refers to Old Fort Waldegrave, and Vinnicomb's Hill is now Signal Hill Road. In 1796 Joan Vinnicomb was given a grant of land by the governor, to compensate her for opening the road from Fort William to Signal Hill through her property which was in the possession of her family "beyond memory."

The London Tavern was the scene of many memorable events. On 5 February 1806 a group of Irishmen, mainly Protestant, founded the Benevolent Irish Society over dinner at the inn. This club is now one of the oldest indigenous, fraternal organizations in North America. The Society for Improving the Conditions of the Poor held an annual breakfast at the tavern, attended by the governor, at which collections were made on behalf of charity. There were forty-seven business and government leaders at table for the farewell dinner tendered the retiring Roman Catholic bishop, James O'Donel, before his departure for his homeland in 1807. The company presented him with an elaborate silver cup. His Lordship reported, " . . . the fete was, as usual, uncommonly expensive and splendid." General Skerret, the garrison commander, was also given a send-off at the London. Freemasonry was introduced to Newfoundland in 1774 and the London Tavern became the home of the principal lodge. We are told of the famous old inn, that "nothing could exceed the friendship and conviviality of the evening . . . as Barbara Allan, Hearts of Oak, and Bonnie Dundee, were rapturously encored."[7]

Lieutenant Chappell, in a rather supercilious account of a visit to the colony in 1813, speaks of the London Tavern as being the best in St. John's. Quirk's ownership of this refuge of gastronomic delights lasted a scant ten years. On 9 June 1814 William Firth announced that he had taken over the London Tavern and its billiard table from

Cornelius Quirk. Its prestige seems to have diminished but little under Firth.

The last mention we have of the inn is a newspaper advertisement which appeared in May 1818. This shows the tavern survived the Great Fire of 1817, which wiped out the whole of the central part of the town. After that it simply vanishes from history. It probably became a private home when the lease expired in 1820. There is a reference to it in a newspaper for 25 July 1833 when Mrs. Michael Mara announced she was taking boarders at her house on Duckworth Street, two doors west of the old London Tavern. At the same time John Crute advertised that he had a "daily conveyance from St. John's to Portugal Cove," leaving from two doors east of the old London Tavern, premises he had taken over from Thomas Morton. Mr. Morton lived at 88 Duckworth Street, near the foot of Ordnance Street, but the number disappeared after the 1892 fire.

By 1812, the year of the war between Canada and the United States, the number of grog shops had increased from thirty-six to fifty-one, but the opposition was becoming organized. It found its champion in Michael Anthony Fleming, the Roman Catholic bishop. Aware of the tragedy liquor had brought into so many homes, His Lordship rose in the pulpit of the Old Chapel, on the morning of Sunday, 2 October 1841, and denounced the evils of drink. He proclaimed a grand temperance movement that was open to people of all faiths. By November 13 over three thousand had been enrolled.

The crusade received a boost on Sunday, November 20, when Father Murphy of Ferryland took the pledge at the foot of the altar, then rose and spoke in such glowing terms that six hundred signed it then and there. The group of zealots held their first annual parade on 6 January 1843, which was known as the "Tee-Total Procession." It included one hundred farmers on horseback, two by two, the garrison band, two amateur bands, and a portrait of Queen Victoria. At Government House the procession was greeted by His Excellency. By the end of 1844 over ten thousand had signed the pledge.

While the Catholics were taking the pledge, in aid of temperance, their Protestant brothers were taking tea. *The Times* of 8 February 1843 announced a Temperance Festival under the auspices of the Church of England Total Abstinence Society and the patronage of His Excellency the Governor. According to the newspaper, "The members and other friends of the above society will DRINK TEA TOGETHER in the upper room of the factory [behind the present Synod Hall on Queen's Road] on the eve of Tuesday the 14th, at 6 o'clock. The Band of the Royal Newfoundland Companies will . . . be in attendance." There is no record of how the soldiers enjoyed their tea but there was another gathering in July on the lawn of Cherry

Gardens, Waterford Bridge Road. By 1850 the Congregational Meetinghouse, at the foot of Victoria Street, had become Temperance Hall.

Caught up among the converts to the cause was a man named William McGrath who had a blacksmith's shop on Water Street, at the west corner of Hill o' Chips. Early in 1858 he consulted with a few friends and, as a result, a meeting was held in the open field west of his forge, a large flat stone, projecting from the embankment serving as a table. This meeting led to the founding of the Total Abstinence and Benefit Society, 16 May 1858. Temperance Street, then under construction, was so named to commemorate the first parade of the society. During its first four years, meetings were held in the Factory, but by 1862 the condition of this building rendered it necessary to move to St. Patrick's schoolroom, River Head, and later to the Cathedral Fire Brigade Hall.

In 1866 the society purchased the site it was to occupy for nearly a century. This was on Duckworth Street, just west of Bell Street. In 1871 it was decided to construct a suitable hall, but until 1873, the two semi-detached, colonial-style dwelling houses were used as headquarters. In May of that year the dwellings were sold and removed and on July 11 the cornerstone for the new hall was laid. The gable-roof building was of two floors with the gable facing Duckworth Street. The front consisted of a long row of small windowpanes, with a door at each side, and there was an auditorium upstairs. The T. A. Hall, as a sign on it proclaimed, was formally opened with a soiree on Boxing Night 1873. Some four hundred persons attended and enjoyed themselves as the band "discoursed sweet music." That same year a literary and dramatic club was founded and the new hall began to attract theatrical entertainments.

The Great Fire of 1892 reduced the edifice to ashes. The cornerstone for a new structure was laid 29 June 1893 by Bishop Power, and a splendid building arose. Of wooden construction it was 106 feet long and 65 feet high. The lower floor was leased. The second floor was used for the society's clubrooms and the upper floor was occupied by a fully equipped theatre that was to become the most famous in Newfoundland entertainment history.

Playing cards were a gift of the ancient world. The small, oblong pieces of pasteboard became known to Europeans in the fourteenth century. Hearts, diamonds, spades, and clubs appeared in France shortly before 1550. We can be sure that by the time of Gilbert's visit to St. John's in 1583 they were already a popular pastime with his crews. The invention of whist in 1663 meant that cards were here to stay, for out of it developed bridge in 1886. Whist was a favourite of the gentle sex. There is a story of a well-known St. John's matron of the long ago who woke from a comfortable snooze in the middle of an Anglican parson's sermon and, suddenly hearing his voice, which had been much in evidence the night before at her own house, cried out loudly, "Hearts are trumps!"

Whenever a deck of cards appeared, the spirit of gambling walked abroad. In 1734 a game known as "brag" was devised. The Americans later refined it as poker. Whether it was whist, brag, or any other variation, the lamps of nineteenth-century St. John's burned far into the night as stakes grew on tables.

Frequently this amusement led to violence and sometimes even to death. The last fatal duel fought in the town was triggered by a game of cards.

One snowy evening, at the end of March 1826, the officers at Fort Townshend were in their quarters sipping toddy and gambling at cards. As the playing and drinking continued, a young ensign named Philpot made a number of foolish moves, which resulted in his becoming unpleasant and quarrelsome. His losses, combined with the effects of the toddy, made his behaviour towards one Captain Rudkin especially nasty. The underlying motivation for this unpleasantness was said to have been the fact that they were rivals for the charms of the same young Irish girl who lived in a cottage near Quidi Vidi.

Late in the evening the pot contained £2.8.6 (around $12.00). Philpot faced a showdown with the dealer who was Captain Rudkin. The other players had thrown in their hands. Rudkin won the pot with a card he dealt himself from the pack. The naval ensign cried out that the army officer had cheated and seized the stakes which were on the table.

The Captain rose, took them from him, and started to withdraw from the room. Philpot pursued him into the passageway, threw a mug of hot toddy into Rudkin's face and kicked him in the rear. Only a duel would now satisfy the army man's honour. On the morning of March 30, he met Philpot in a clearing near Brine's tavern at Robinson's Hill. Pringle Place now marks the site of the confrontation.

Ensign Philpot, with the commander of a small man-of-war yacht in the harbour as his second, stood facing the sun. He was still quite agitated because of his losses the previous night and angrily refused all efforts by the Captain to resolve the quarrel. Mark Rudkin, with Dr. Strachan as his second, and George Morrice as an assistant, stood facing the irascible sailor.

Finally pistols were loaded, handed to the two men, and the command to fire was given. Philpot sprang into the air firing wildly. Rudkin's gun fired and the naval ensign fell backwards to the ground, a red hole in his chest, above the heart.

As soon as word of the fatal duel spread through the town, popular feeling was immediately on the side of the victim. Duelling had been forbidden by law so an order was issued at once for the arrest of the victor and his companions. When word reached Rudkin, in his place of hiding, that Dr. Strachan was taken and in jail, having been charged with murder, the Captain surrendered himself without delay.

Ensign Philpot was buried in the Anglican churchyard close to the site of the present cathedral. Hordes of the curious accompanied the corpse from Fort Townshend to the grave. However, the fickleness of the mob soon manifested itself in the Court House. The small building on Duckworth Street echoed to the angry mutterings of the spectators as soon as it became apparent that Rudkin and his companions were being tried by an extremely hostile judge. They had been committed to trial by Newfoundland's first Grand Jury, sworn in on April 12. It consisted of the foreman, T. H. Brooking, and such well-known men as Benjamin Bowring, Nicholas Gill, and James Clift. In charging the jury, Justice Tucker ordered the members to find all three guilty of murder. To everyone's amazement, especially the judge's, the verdict returned was "Guilty but without malice."

His Honour was furious. He angrily denounced the finding as not possible and refused to accept it. The jury, just as angrily, refused to reconsider. At this point counsel for the accused pointed out that a verdict of guilty showed malice aforethought. If there was no malice the verdict must be one of innocence. At the urging of the judge the jury finally withdrew to bring in a proper finding. The court was tense with excitement when the gentlemen returned, after ten minutes, to render their verdict of "Not guilty."[8]

A chorus of lusty cheers filled the room. They drowned out Tucker's indignant shouts for order. The accused men were hustled from the building on the shoulders of their fellows and carried up Garrison Hill to the fort accompanied all the way by singing and cries of acclaim from the townspeople.

That, however, was not the end of the story. Soon it was whispered about that a very restless spirit was being seen near Rennie's Bridge, then called Pringle's Bridge, at a spot where Captain Rudkin's horse was said to have shied three times the morning he rode to the duel. The ghost had a red spot on the breast of a military uniform. Many generations of courting couples were to huddle close to each other as they walked along Rennie's banks, before urban sprawl drove the phantom from memory. The pistols used in this historic, fatal encounter are displayed today in the Military Museum at the top of the Confederation Building.

The last duel fought in St. John's took place 25 September 1873. Again the choice of weapons was pistols. A young fellow named Din Dooley had come to town from Heart's Content and was soon attempting to win the heart of a prominent city lass who was already spoken for by one Augustus Healey. The matter could only be settled by a duel.

Satisfaction was to be obtained in Fort Townshend hollow, a small glen located behind the former USO building on Merrymeeting Road. At the exchange of shots Dooley fainted while Healey stood firm. Unknown to the lovesick protagonists, their seconds, Fred Burnham and Thomas Allan, had loaded the pistols with blanks, turning the tragedy into farce.

A short time later the duel was resumed with fists behind John Casey's barn on the higher levels, an area above the old town. Though Healey won the fisticuffs, neither swain won fair lady. It is reported that she married a man far less belligerent, and certainly less romantic.[9]

As for the third of the readily available entertainments in old St. John's the first authenticated glimmer of a red light is seen in the letter of Rev. John Jackson, complaining of Captain Lloyd to the Lords Commissioners of Trade and Plantations, mentioned in Chapter 2. This letter from the distressed clergyman read:

> He was a great promoter of whoring and Adultery amongst the people, he took one Short's lawful wife into his own bed, without the fort and within, and within building apartments for that purpose with the Queen's timber, boards, etc.
>
> This woman was known to be a notorious thief and whore before he took her, to whom he gave such absolute power over the soldiers that he [who] shewed the least dislike of serving her, she caused to be whift [whipped] and abused, at her pleasure by his example and encouragement of this sin, he made another Sodom of that place.
>
> As to religion he had none, but a meer debauched libertine . . . for he was a constant breaker of the Sabbath . . . he hath often gone about the harbour on the Lord's Day with his fiddle on purpose to divest people from coming to church, the rest of the day he revell's away with his companions in dancing and rioting with their whores. Nay, which is worst than a beast, he hath chosen such companions who have been so audaciously imperdent [sic] as to dance all stark naked together to the shame of all modest persons.[10]

The tradition established by the nude dancing ladies would appear to have been an enduring one for in 1971, nearly 270 years later, the manager of a surburban club appeared in court at St. John's charged with having permitted some professional females from outside the province to dance in their buff in front of the customers.

At one time Mistress Short appears to have been on very friendly terms with the Reverend Mr. Jackson. What happened to sour the relationship we do not know. Bampfylde-Moore Carew, who has been called the king of the beggars, visited St. John's several times early in the 1700s and in his biography has left us a priceless piece of information.

On one of his travels Carew went from Bath to Bristol where he passed himself off as Aaron Cock, a planter of St. John's, Newfoundland, to whom he bore some resemblance. He said he was in want of means due to having been shipwrecked off Ireland. A number of the Newfoundland captains in Bristol who knew his pretended father, mother, and sister, who was remarkable on account of her deformity and crookedness, questioned him to establish his identity.

Writing of this experience in the third person Carew says:

> Among other Things they asked him if he remembered how the Quarrell happened at his [Aaron Cock's] Father's, which was of such unhappy consequence to Governor Collins, when himself was a Boy; and our counterfeit Aaron said, that the Governor, the Parson and his wife, Madam Short, Madam Bengy, Madam Brown, and several other Women of St. John's, being met together and drinking at his Father's, in the Height of Liquor there happened a warm Dispute among them concerning the Chastity and Virtue of Women, the Governor obstinately averring (having no wife himself) that there was not one honest Woman in all Newfoundland: What think you than of my wife? Says the Parson; Nay, the same I do of all other Women, all whores alike, answered the Governor roughly. Hereupon, the women all enraged fell upon him, disfigure his face with their Nails, and tear his cloaths; the Parson's wife cut the Ham-String of his Leg with a large Case-Knife, which made the poor Governor a Cripple for his whole life thereafter.[11]

Captain Lloyd was called home to England to answer Mr. Jackson's charges. His replacement was Captain Moody, a conscientious but enigmatic officer who reorganized the fort and imposed discipline on the garrison. Moody seems to have allied himself with the anti-Lloyd forces and this brought about his temporary downfall. As we saw in Chapter 2, on his return from England the reinstated and promoted Major Lloyd used the whipping and death of one of the Jackson's servant girls as a substantial plank in his platform of counter-charges that led to the recall of Moody and Jackson.

Unfortunately, for those with an appetite for the more sensational aspects of colonial life, Madam Short and the nude dancing ladies of Fort William disappear from history with the parson's complaint.

By 1794 more sophisticated amusements than whores and naked dancing were being offered the growing town. The census for that year reveals the presence of one M. Dawson who had as his occupation, fiddler. All the knowledge we have of him is that he came to the island in 1776, was Roman Catholic, married, had no children, and

236

lived in a house near King's Beach. We also know that a Mrs. Doyle, wife of one Dicky Doyle, a fiddler, was buried on 16 October 1775, but no further information is available. Her husband predates Dawson by a year or two as the first professional entertainer in St. John's.

The year 1867 saw the deadly sins back in competition. That year a petition was sent to Governor Musgrave for a gas lamp to be put in front of some houses of ill fame on Duckworth Street between Fort William and Maggoty Cove Bridge (top of Temperance Street), where "Scenes of the most disgusting immorality are constantly occurring in the day time as well as at night and it is not very unusual to witness an exhibition on Sunday of drunkenness and obscenity on the part of females." [12] Musgrave, who had a notoriously unmanageable roving eye above his mutton chops, rejected the petition.

That same year, one of these bordellos caused a Monsignor of the Roman Catholic Cathedral to be fined for advocating morality. On 16 July Rt. Rev. Scott attempted to rescue a young and innocent girl from one of the town's dens of sin. The victory for virtue was not achieved without violence. When the madam attacked the Monsignor, in the process of his saving the maiden, he resorted to the use of his walking stick to defend himself, was arrested, charged in court with assault, and fined by Magistrate Carter.

The first mention of professional theatre in St. John's is contained in the Colonial Records. On 29 July 1806 Governor Gower wrote: "Gentlemen—The four persons named in the margin, who are arrived here from Quebec, being players, have requested I will allow them to exhibit their Theatrical Representations in St. John's. You are to do so, so long as they shall continue to conduct themselves in an orderly and decent manner." [13] It would appear the governor subscribed to the old axiom, relating to actors, "Lock up your wives and daughters when the rogues approach."

One of these particular rogues was a female, the first actress ever to perform in St. John's, just as her male companions are the first actors. The names of the quartet were Walter C. Davids, Michael Henry, James Ormsby, and Mary Ormsby. What their "Theatrical Representations" consisted of we do not know. The first newspaper did not come into print until the following year. The four would appear to have been the kind of strolling players, popular at the time, who presented various scenes from favourite plays, usually at an inn or tavern. The presentation of any of the multi-character, full-length dramas of the time would have been impossible with such a small cast. It is likely the four were English players on their way back by ship from Quebec to England, when a stopover enabled them to perform in St. John's.

For want of earlier proofs we must accept 29 July 1806 as the birthdate of the legitimate theatre in Newfoundland. In this, the island was not far behind the continent. The first regular professional theatre had been established in Charleston in 1763. The Puritan population of New England did not suppress "painted vanities" by laws and fines until much later.

In May 1816 William B. Row, an estate agent and fisheries supply merchant, who lived on the road to Pringle's Bridge, moved his business to new premises. Ten months later, 14 March 1817, the *Mercantile Journal* carried the following advertisement: "For the benefit of the poor there will be performed on Tuesday evening the 18th inst., at the store lately occupied by Mr. Wm. B. Row, the celebrated tragedy of 'The Fair Penitent' . . . Doors to be opened at half-past six and commence at half-past seven." Admittance tickets were available at five shillings each at the offices of the *Mercantile Journal* and *Royal Gazette*.

As far as can be ascertained, "the celebrated tragedy" was the first full-length play ever performed in St. John's, and 18 March 1817 must go down in history as the natal day for local stage drama. In spite of a most exhaustive search the exact location of Mr. Row's store remains uncertain.

Hot on the heels of their first success, "The gentlemen associated for the purpose of performing dramatic representations in and for the charities of this town" were presenting, 8 April 1817, "the much admired melo-drama 'Point of Honour' the whole to conclude with 'Bon Ton or High Life Above Stairs.' " Tickets were available at the counting houses of Thomas Williams and William Thomas. The venture, now called Theatre St. John's, was under the patronage of the worshipful magistrates. The papers prove the attraction was a hit, for we read, "In consequence of the Theatre not affording sufficient accommodation for more than a limited number a repeat performance was staged the following evening." That concluded the first theatrical season in the island capital.

Capt. Sir William Eliot, who was in St. John's in 1818-19, has left us an invaluable description of these early productions in his *Naval Sketch Book*. He writes:

> The metropolis not being able to boast of even a barn, which from time immemorial has been conceded, by even saintly magistrates, as the privileged tenement of heroes of the sock and buskin, it became necessary that a "regular-built" (for so they termed it) theatre should be erected on shore by the sons of the sea, the expenses of which, including decorations, scenery, stoves, property, puffing, wigs, wardrobe, lights, scene-shifters, theatrical-tailors, and midshipmen's millibers, were entirely defrayed out of the profits of the first month's performances.
>
> The discipline observed by the manager, though perhaps

savouring less of that adopted on the boards of a stage than on those of a deck, was nevertheless essentially calculated to support the dignity of the drama. . . . It was not unusual to hear a young middy at rehearsal, who perhaps had to personate the part of the tender "Ophelia", complain that his "catheads" were clumsily fitted to his bows.

The deputy stage-manager, who formerly had been a votary of the sock, presumed no little upon his Thespian experience; although, be it known, he had never had the honour of belonging to a *Royal* company, until in the marines (having been a private in that corps). He proved, however, an acquisition to the stage, as he . . . would, on the shortest notice, in the event of any performer disappointing the management, jump with more self-satisfaction into another man's socks, than ever did heir into testator's shoes.

. . . Hamlet's advice to the players was nothing compared with *his* to his pupils. . . . In his opinion, the perfection of the art, as he used to term it, entirely depended upon the rapidity of the utterance.[14]

Captain Eliot leaves us the following actual dialogue from one of those far-off St. John's rehearsals. A tragedian is complaining to the deputy stage manager of the length of his part.

"Here's a hell of a soliloquy, as long as a main-to-bowline— ran it clean off the reel before breakfast—can't remember a word of it now."

"A trifle that, sir. Mere desertion of the mind—trust to Providence and the prompter."

"Damn the prompter, he's always ahead of his reck'ning."

"Well, sir, say something o' your own—audience never the wiser. Tell 'em 'there's a tide in the affairs of men, taken at the flood, leads on to fortune,' and so on. Fishermen, you know, sir, like you all the better for that. Remember once, sir, dreadul dilemma in *Octavian*—crowded audience—forgot my part; when with a little presence of mind (by-the-by gentlemen, presence of mind is everything on the boards) called to my mind a few lines out of *Lear*, and instead of being, as another might, mute as a mackerel, I began, as *Hamlet* says, to spout like a whale, catching a clap from every hand in the house by the trap."[15]

Before opening night free admissions to the dress rehearsal were granted to seamen of the squadron and soldiers of the garrison. The fun was reciprocal as sailors watched their fellows and officers, in oakum wigs, impersonate the parts of maids and ladies. It was doubted whether the actors more amused the audience, or the audience the actors, as the jacks called out, piped, and hooted.

Captain Eliot ends his description of naval theatricals in the community by observing: "There were not wanting objectors on the score of the pregnant immorality of theatrical representations, who thundered evangelical anathemas, through the medium of the press of St. John's, against the promoters of rational amusement ... many of these very individuals formed part of an attentive and highly-gratified audience."[16]

The gentleman amateurs were organized by the Society for Improving Conditions of the Poor in St. John's. The Chief officers were William Thomas, Thomas Williams, and James Blaikie. In the spring of 1817 they took over the store of William B. Row, to stage some plays and raise money for charity. The venture was a success but, in November, the Great Fire wiped out much of St. John's. There were no plays in 1818. Either Row's store was destroyed, or put to other uses. Indications are it was in the one block that was saved and probably served as a temporary shop or warehouse.

A newspaper ad, 4 February 1819, under the bold heading, PRIVATE THEATRICALS, announced a pre-season sale of tickets. We must assume Row's store was renovated as a proper theatre, as there is no mention or indication, anywhere, of a change of site. The town's second theatrical season swung into high gear, 18 February 1819, with the much-admired comedy, *John Bull*. This time the enterprise was under the distinguished patronage of His Excellency the Governor, Sir Charles Hamilton. The reason for thinking a proper theatre had come into being is an item in the *Mercantile Journal*, March 11, to the effect that "The gallery of the St. John's Theatre is to be improved before the next performance so as to enable those in the back seats to have a full view of the performance." Some defect in the construction of the gallery must have gone unnoticed until the patrons complained.

There were no women on the stage, and the soldiers, sailors, and local lads who essayed the various characters assumed theatrical names. One of them, Mr. Marcus, found the season extremely hazardous when, during the second performance, Wednesday, February 23, a patron rose in his seat and decried his acting in the afterpiece, *A Miss in Her Teens*. The argument was carried to the stage where the critic physically attacked the actor. Crito wrote of the incident in the press:

> What very rough treatment poor Mr. Marcus met with, nothing but knock down blows and the most abusive language, in the place of argument; poor man, if he had not fortunately had on his coat of armour, I fear he would have been nearly crushed to death—however, I am happy to say he received no material injury and your readers may soon expect him to appear in public again.

The incident brought a spate of letters to the editor. Some denounced the immorality of the theatre, while others praised its charity and defended its moral good. B___ wrote to bewail the rudeness of the patron to a man trying, "not only to please but to be useful to others." Word soon got out that George Niven, a prominent young merchant, was the culprit who started the altercation, by going to the theatre with the avowed purpose of causing a fuss. Niven denied in the newspapers that he was one of the young men accused, since he was not at the theatre that evening. He named A.Z. who, he said, was "very deservedly kicked out of the theatre on Monday evening . . . that self same ear-cropper [was] one of the very lads who fought at 50 paces!!! upon the Barrens the night of the tremendous row." This statement leads to the speculation that Marcus and his critic fought a duel near Military Road, the night of the fuss at the theatre. In the midst of all this uproar another actor, Mr. Bounteous, passed away. A young lady wrote to the press, lamenting the death of so great a man. She wondered if St. John's would ever see his like again. She also took the occasion to condemn the repeat performance of *John Bull*, and called for a production of *The Rivals*.

By April of that tormented year, 1819, calmer waters had been reached and the management delighted in the fact that all expenses had been met and the monies from future productions would go immediately and wholly to the society, for the relief of the wretched. Two performances of *Honey Moon* brought in receipts of £48.5s. There was to be one more tribulation before the season ended. Following the final performance of the beautiful comedy, *Speed the Plough*, an unpaid debt of twenty pounds was discovered and the company was forced to repeat the play on June 4, to wipe out the deficit. All's well that ends well, as the deputy stage manager might well have cried and, after paying off the debt, the management was able to dispose of the effects and take its leave while thanking a public who "so kindly nurtured the Drama in the capital of Terra Nova in its infant stage." It was a remarkable season and shows either a large company, or players who were quick studies, for a new play was presented every week throughout the winter and spring, with two performances, usually on Tuesday and Saturday.

For some reason it was decided not to continue the venture and to dispose of the effects. On 19 August 1819 the property was up for sale. It was advertised as "A valuable lot on Water Street going back to Duckworth Street, next door to Coleman's, formerly the Amateur Theatre." This notice makes it possible to pinpoint the place with some accuracy. An advertisement in the *Mercantile Journal* on June 3, ten weeks before the property went on sale, contains the information that D. H. McCalman "Has on hand a general supply of goods, also bread and butter. Pearl Barley, Oat Meal, Split Peas, Hyson, Sourchong and green tea, soap, etc., at his shop in the stone building next door to the Amateur Theatre."

Known locally as McCallum and Coleman, McCalman was an important merchant with outport holdings. His "shop in the stone building" was at the east side of the foot of McMurdo's Lane, which was, in the early part of the nineteenth century, known as McCallum's Lane, McCallum being one of the corruptions of the name McCalman. The position of his shop is verified by another ad in the *Mercantile Journal*, 3 June 1824, by which time the merchant was deceased and his wife had taken over the business. On that day, Alexander McCourby, a hairdresser, who had the distinction of having been publicly denounced by Dr. Kielly for dabbling in medicine, gave notice that he had removed "to the house nearly opposite Mrs. M'Calman's" and adjoining Bainte, Johnston & Co.'s stone buildings. Johnston's buildings were opposite McMurdo's Lane. Tickets for the plays were "available at Mrs. M'Calman's."

There can be little doubt that the first theatre in St. John's was on a site occupied for much of this century by Grey & Goodland's bookstore, and in the 1970s by the *Daily News*. Its performances were well patronized. The fifteen which were given in 1819, resulted in the fantastic sum of £549.14.10. Based on a suggested government ratio of comparative money values, today this was the equivalent of more than $20,000.

For some reason, the theatre itself continued in existence. The 1820 season gave birth to a competitor when the Globe Tavern presented, of all things, a Juvenile Theatre. On Monday, January 31, weather permitting, Mr. Graham's pupils were to present the much-admired comedy, *The Poor Gentleman*. Obviously, the weather did not permit and the debut of the Graham moppets was postponed to February 7.

The first local actor whose real name has come down to us is Edward Kennedy, mentioned in the press, 9 March 1820. The newspaper comments: "The town reaped a considerable degree of amusement last winter from the excellence of Mr. Kennedy in those broad Irish characters . . . ." Other comments indicate he might have been a professional actor in Ireland, before settling in Newfoundland. Kennedy was a favourite performer for some years.

In spite of the rival presentations at the Globe, hit followed hit at the Amateur Theatre, and much-admired comedies, popular farces, and celebrated tragedies filled the season. A newspaper critic at one of the entertainments reported that "the gentlemen performers acquitted themselves admirably." He added that their director, Chief Justice Forbes, "is always solicitous for the rational entertainment of those among whom fortune may cast him."

The packed houses continued into 1821 and 1822. On 17 January 1822 the *Mercantile Journal* said it understood the old theatre was refitted in an elegant style, and that the characters were already cast for "the celebrated comedy, *John Bull*," which was to commence that portion of the winter amusements. There is little doubt about patrons obtaining their money's worth. An ad for the March 18 production of *The Man of the World*, together with *The Irishman in London*, advises that the performance will commence sharp at 6:30 p.m. and that the final curtain will fall at precisely 11:00 p.m., four and a half hours later.

By May 1822 it had become obvious that the theatre building was too small for the demands of both actors and audience. It was decided to construct a new playhouse. Newman Hoyles, the father of Prime Minister Sir Hugh Hoyles, wrote Governor Hamilton on October 7, requesting "a piece of ground for the purpose of erecting an amateur theatre."

The Colonial Records for 1822 contain the following proclamation signed by Governor Hamilton.

> *Whereas* application has been made to me for a piece of ground whereon it is proposed to erect a building to be used as a Theatre for the benefit of the Poor of St. John's by subscriptions in shares... I do hereby grant and appropriate the piece of ground herein described situate in the said Town, being part of the ancient Fishing Ships Room called "Gallows Hill" to be held for the purpose above mentioned, and for no other purpose whatever. Given under my hand and seal at Fort Townshend, St. John's, Newfoundland, the 10th October 1822.

There is added a notation, by the Crown surveyor, which reads:

> Situated on the Ancient Fishing Ships Room called Gallows Hill and extending along Duckworth Street (40 feet wide) from the S.W. Corner of the Widow Cahill's garden sixty one feet, then westward forty six feet to the road (20 feet wide) leading from the Barrens to Duckworth Street, from thence N. Eastwards sixty one feet to the Widow Cahill's ground and along that ground forty six feet to the point first mentioned forming an oblong square as described in the plan.[17]

Translated into today's nomenclature the plot of land was at the corner of Duckworth Street and Queen's Road, formerly called the road leading to the Barrens. This road later became Playhouse Hill and, during the first half of the twentieth century, Theatre Hill. Gallows Hill, so named because it was the site of public hangings during the 1700s, embraced today's Carter's and Bates Hills. In actual fact, Bates Hill was a river that emptied into Beck's Cove.

An elaborate ceremonial accompanied the laying of the foundation stone for the theatre on 8 November 1822. The procession left Hannagan's Crown and Anchor Tavern at one o'clock, headed by two constables, magistrates, clergy, guard of the military, members of the theatrical committee, and numerous masonic officers. In the parade that moved west on Water Street and up Williams Lane, the architect carried a mallet, the superintendent carried the plan, and the secretary carried the constitutions on a cushion. A platform stood at the east end of the site and while the masonic anthem was played the treasurer placed a sealed bottle containing an inscription on parchment in a cavity of the stone, so that the gallows gave way to amusement of another sort.

The inscription on the parchment read: "This Foundation stone of a Theatre for Dramatic Representations, was laid in solemn form, with Masonic honours, in full procession, on the 8th day of November, 1822, in the presence of the civil and military authorities and by a large body of the inhabitants by Thomas Shanks, master of the Benevolent Lodge of Free and Accepted Masons No. 312." The morning had been cloudy but the sun shone out just as the procession reached the spot and gave additional lustre to the various jewels and appointments of the fraternity. The band played music from *The Beggar Girl*, and the company retired to the Crown and Anchor, where "Success to the theatre" and other healths "were drunk with three times three."

Besides granting the piece of land, the governor had loaned the Amateurs fifty pounds, with the understanding that "if the plan should hereafter fail the building might be converted to some other purpose of greater utility to the poorer classes generally." In all, the theatre cost three hundred pounds. This is not much when one considers that Mr. Stewart's stone house, built a little earlier, had cost three thousand pounds. The only sketch we have of this theatre in St. John's is in a view of the town painted from Signal Hill in 1831. It appears to be an elongated salt-box building with four windows and no doors facing on Duckworth Street. The entrance was probably on the west side. J. J. Broomfield of the Phoenix Fire Office sent the following description of the place to London, 8 November 1845, by which time its days of glory were almost over: "The Theatre, which forms the angle of these two streets is a small timber and shingled building, not 30 ft. high—is used occasionally during the winter season, but never in the summer—and it is nearly insulated, little danger to be apprehended to the surrounding buildings in the event of the theatre being burnt."[18] We also know that on the inside there was a gallery and boxes.

The new Amateur Theatre was opened to the public Monday evening, 17 February 1823, "with the celebrated melo-drama of The Castle Spectre when an address written by Rev. Mr. Blackman was spoken by Mr. Harvey." Blackman was a twenty-five-year-old clergyman at St. Thomas' Church where his memorial plaque may still be seen. His poetic work began:

> Friends of the Cause, which Charity sustains
> To soothe pale Hanger and Afflictious pains!
> I come to bid you welcome to a stage—
> The pride and credit of a gen'rous age—
> . Here quarrels cease and here the private feud
> bends to a nobler cause, the public good.

In spite of the parson's protestations quarrels did not cease. The event became full of risk when it was whispered about that a "native poet," whose poem for the opening had been discarded at the last minute in favour of that by the Englishman, Mr. Blackman, had employed a number of gentlemen to call out for his rejected address. The local bard was heard to say, "He understood there was to be a row in the theatre."

Precautions were taken and the production went ahead with "entirely new and appropriate music, scenery, dress and decorations." There was no demonstration and after the play several comic songs were performed, including one composed and sung by a Scotsman, Aaron Hogsett, the Clerk of the Court, who lived at the foot of Signal Hill Road. The battle over the opening speech was conducted in the newspapers, which were filled with letters of accusation and denial for weeks to come.

Rules governing the behaviour of patrons were published at the start of the 1824 season. Any person cheering or calling out names would cause the performance to stop for the evening. No calls on the band for particular tunes would be attended to, and no children would be admitted without being paid for. An appeal went out for "such gentlemen of the army, navy and the town as may be inclined to assist in getting up plays" to come to the aid of the theatre.

In May a list of the names and addresses of paupers, aided by the proceeds from the plays, was published in the press, under first-class and second-class headings. Between February 22 and May 15 a total of £105.5.1 had been expended on the poor.

Each year the dramatic offerings at the new theatre continued without let-up. Two shillings got you into the pit for the 1826 season opener on January 26 of *The Road to Ruin* and *Matrimony*. In 1827 it cost three shillings for a box seat to the season openers, *Rob Roy* and *A Cure for Heart-Ache*. The laughable farce, *Where Shall I Dine*, was the popular offering for 1834. A constant patron was Governor Cochrane, who frequently had Bishop Scallan or the Chief Justice in his theatre party.

In 1839 patrons were urged to attend the plays because the

proceeds were needed to repair the building, which would otherwise shortly become unfit for its purpose. In order to boost funds, the laughable piece, *P.S. Come To Dinner*, was presented.

J. B. Jukes, writing of Newfoundland in 1839-40, says: "There was an Amateur Theatre, the profits of which were devoted to charitable purposes, and a performance took place once a fortnight in which their several parts were well sustained both by the actors and by the audience." Another writer speaks of hot wax from candles in the theatre chandelier dripping on the heads of uncomfortable patrons sitting underneath.

For some reason no woman ever appeared on a local stage. Most likely it had something to do with the general belief that professional acting was for men of low morals and women of no virtue. Actresses were the nadir of female decadence. The atmosphere surrounding the stage apparently precluded participation by even amateur ladies of decency. As for attending a theatre, reputable women of society dared not show themselves in such low surroundings.

In the 1830s and '40s such females as Fanny Kemble, Louisa Lane (Mrs. John Drew), Clara Fisher, and Ellen Tree began to establish the respectability of actresses in the United States. The floodgates were opened in St. John's on a pleasant Monday evening, during the summer of 1841, when a person billed as "the celebrated Miss Davenport," made an appearance before a crowded house, at the Amateur Theatre, and "More than realized the expectations formed of her." The *Newfoundlander* said, "When the curtain fell for the night the deafening cheers and waving of handkerchiefs continued for several minutes." The newspaper pronounced her "Nothing short of a miracle."

Strange as it may seem, this critical euphoria was the result of her having created, not some wilting female of charm and grace, but the title role in Shakespeare's *Richard III*. We read that a more delighted audience was never seen as she produced "that whirlwind of passion so excellently illustrated in the dying scene." The fact that the actress was ably supported by Mr. and Mrs. Davenport reveals an even more astonishing truth. The "celebrated" creature was Jean M. Davenport, a child of eleven or twelve years of age.

Born in 1829, in England, she was a female Master Betty, and probably equally odious. Her debut took place in a theatre on the spot where the Pest House of the Great Plague stood, near Tothill Fields, Westminster, when her father and she played Vincent Crummles and the Infant Phenomenon, two of the characters in *Nicholas Nickleby*. At the age of eight the new sensation of the boards was playing Richard III to crowded London houses. She soon made the role her own. As a child prodigy, in 1838 she went with her parents to America, where she continued to astound audiences in such unsuitable parts as Shylock and Sir Peter Teazle. It was while returning to England from this tour, in 1841, that she made St. John's history by becoming the first female to appear on a theatre stage in Newfoundland. It was thirty-five years since the visit of Mary Ormsby, with the strolling players from Quebec.

Appalling as it may seem to us now, "the celebrated Miss Davenport" was a great success wherever she appeared. Some historians write of her with scorn. It is said of her mature years that "She was an actress of great talent and intellectual judgment but she lacked fire." After settling in America, as an adult, she translated *La dame aux camelias* into English in 1853, and was the first to call it *Camille*. Following her creation of the role, all the great ladies of the American stage subsequently appeared as the unhappy courtesan.

Tickets for Jean Davenport's opening night in St. John's, 2 August 1841, were quickly snapped up at five shillings each, or 2s.6d in the pit. The box office sold out within one hour and angry patrons, who could not gain admission, became a threatening mob. The little lady calmed them by sending assurances that she would repeat each play on Wednesday and Friday. Everyone from the governor down attended, and the newspapers "Never heard an audience more gratified . . . never was applause more merited."

On September 14, she offered a "Monopologue—comprising a complete history of her life and public career." She had also performed in *Honeymoon*, *Wallace*, *Rob Roy*, and *Romeo and Juliet*, a role in which she was to make her adult debut in London three years later. Her performance as Miss Capulet "elicited from the audience unbounded applause." Her closing production, *School for Scandal* on September 14, in which she was to play Sir Peter, caused such an outbreak of hysteria that she launched into a series of farewell performances that could only be rivalled by Nellie Melba.

School for Scandal was postponed when the children of Thomas Cleary, the keeper of the theatre, who lived in the building, came down with some disease which caused the house to be closed. Miss Davenport and company took advantage of the postponement to go by stagecoach and packet steamer, from Portugal Cove to Harbour Grace, where she electrified audiences for two nights, at the Court House, in *Richard III*.

After completing her last farewell performance, the "fair child of Genius" agreed to stay on and do several more for the newly arrived governor, Sir John Harvey. St. John's audiences were the last to see the Infant Phenomenon. She left on board the *Commodore*, around November 10, for Leghorn, wintered in Italy, and in the spring of 1852 went to Paris, where she finished her education, before returning to the stage as an adult actress. She had been three and a half months in Newfoundland.

On 22 November 1841, less than two weeks after the departure of Miss Davenport, the St. John's Theatre, as it was known from then on, opened under the professional management of H. W. Preston who had lately arrived from Halifax with "a very respectable Corps Dramatique." This first resident stock company gave performances every evening before "a crowded and fashionable assemblage." Governor and Lady Harvey, who had lately arrived on the scene, attended two productions, but after that chose to stay away from the theatre. Their absence was noticed and criticized in the local press. One letter writer stated: "It is a matter of regret that the governor's box should be so long vacated by the representative of Our Most Gracious Queen . . . the 'box' which is an ornament to the theatre has been tastefully fitted up by the talented ladies of the Corps Dramatique." Other letters complimented Mr. Preston for being astonishingly persevering in trying to induce His Excellency to come to the theatre, especially following Lady Harvey's recovery from her indisposition. However, he was not to be successful that year.

The Corps included four actresses. They were Miss Hildreth, Mrs. Preston, Mrs. Chapman, and Mrs. Wilson. Among the actors a great favourite was Mr. Grierson, who was a brilliant Romeo. He also essayed Richard III and Henry IV. These performers worked for little or no salary. Each was given a benefit during the season and allowed to keep the proceeds. In April 1842 they made history by touring their plays to Harbour Grace and Carbonear in an effort to spread culture about the island.

In October of the following year *The Times* announced: "Mr. Preston has just arrived from the States with a 'perfect star' to complete the corps dramatique who are now busily engaged in making preparations to commence hostilities." Many people think the word "star" a Hollywood invention. Actually, it came into theatrical use in the English provinces in 1824. On the night of November 8, the "perfect star" was unveiled in the season opener, Shields' tragedy of *Damon and Pythias*. He turned out to be Mr. Rodney who took the role of Damon "as played by him with great success in all the principal theatres in the United States." The remainder of the company was unchanged except for Mrs. Wilson who was replaced by Miss Oakley. Mr. Cunningham was an addition to the male players. Casts were completed by local performers who were each listed in the playbills as "an amateur actor." The professionals appear to have all been from the United States.

Sir Richard Bonnycastle wrote of St. John's drama in 1842: "A theatre has been long established by amateurs in which a company of players from the United States have been performing this winter; but the taste for this amusement is not very great amongst the wealthy classes who do not mingle very frequently in public. . . . "

Such snobbery may account for the empty seats in Governor Harvey's box. He was finally prevailed upon to return to the theatre on the night of 28 April 1843 when the town was treated to the première of the first locally written play of which we have sure knowledge. From his office in the St. John's Theatre, H. W. Preston issued assurances that His Excellency and Lady Harvey would honour the theatre with their presence for the tragedy (no longer "celebrated") of *Gentleman Grey; or The British Soldier* by Thomas Watson of the Royal Newfoundland companies. After undergoing attentive revision the play would be fortunate to have "the part of Gentleman Grey by Mr. Chapman who, having recovered from a severe indisposition, has kindly consented to give all possible effect to this representation." The author played the old grave digger and, in the character, performed a new comic song. It was promised that "After the tragedy Mrs. C. will dance the Cachucha." The evening was to conclude after a variety of incidental amusements with the Comedietta of *Perfection* in which Mrs. Preston and Mrs. Chapman would appear.

One of the last notices we have for the famous playhouse is that of December 1845. On the 24th, for three nights only, a collection of wax figures from Madame Tussaud's Museum, London, was on stage. Among the personages to be viewed were Queen Victoria, Prince Albert, and the entire Royal Family. The Ethiopian Serenaders performed in fancy costume and the band of the Royal Navy Company played some appropriate tunes.

In June, the following year, the Great Fire of 1846 levelled all of downtown St. John's and the Amateur Theatre passed into legend. It was to be sixty years before another theatre would be built on the site.

Out of the crucible of fire there emerged the Golden Age of professional theatricals in St. John's. Dozens of travelling companies took ship in New York, Boston, Halifax, and English ports to display their talents and mine the gold in the island's theatrical hills. Following the catastrophe of 1846 Garrison Theatricals revived the drama at the new British Hall, on Prescott Street, in the centre of what is today the Bond Street intersection. Officers and Subalterns of the Royal Newfoundland companies acquitted themselves well in such plays as *Don Caesar de Bazan* and *King O'Neill*.

The year 1852 saw the "celebrated Hearn Family" giving vocal and dramatic performances in the old Court House "with entrance from Duckworth Street." Strangely enough a number of visiting singing troupes and soloists performed in the Court House. The Factory, west of Garrison Hill, also served as a theatre. The Juvenile Minstrels (the Hughes Family) gave a farewell concert there 23 October 1844. In September 1856 the Factory displayed the "Grand Dioramas and Panoramas of the Russian War," with Professor Baldwin, "The great American magician who has astonished the world for the last ten

249

years." The *Patriot* tells us: "Professor Baldwin's magic performances give great satisfaction to those who have witnessed them. . . ."

In September 1860 the Tyrell & Landigan Company was at the Mechanic's Hall, with *Jessie Brown; or The Relief of Lucknow, Hamlet, Macbeth*, and other attractions. Tyrell painted the scenes, in addition to his acting and managerial chores and Mrs. Landigan was the leading lady.

Armstrong's Sail Loft, on Duckworth Street, was the scene of dances and theatricals. Fitted up with a stage, the place was entered from Mahon's Lane.

The oldest theatre still standing in the capital was erected in 1861, on the northeast corner of Queen and George Streets. It is also the city's second oldest Roman Catholic Church. We can only regret there is at present no law of any kind to protect this historic structure and guarantee its preservation for posterity.

Known as Fishermen's Hall, its cornerstone was laid 23 May 1861, on a piece of property owned by John Broom and leased to James Cullen, father of Maurice Cullen. Jonas Bartar, who died tragically in the Apple Tree Well Fire, owned the adjoining land to the north. The site was originally known as Lady's Ships' Room. The harbour waters in those days came to the north side of Water Street. The "Lady" who owned the ships' room could have been Mrs. Fursey, the only female landowner shown on Thornton's plan in 1689. A man named Stephen Knight took possession of Lady's Ships' Room for £150 in 1811. This was probably the Stephen Knight of Parker & Knight.

Built of square-cut whinstone, with a slate-covered gable roof, the building was opened 28 October 1861, five months after construction started. On the night before the official opening, a visiting trapese artist by the name of Trenear thrilled admiring crowds in the theatre with an exhibition of tight-rope walking.

On 27 August 1862 the first St. John's Flower Show was held in the building. That same year John Healy from Boston used it for his "completely balanced company" of actors. That season the Healy players gave the town its first production of that glorious cliché *East Lynn. The Two Orphans, The Streets of New York*, and *Octoroon* were among their other offerings.

According to one newspaper, on 6 October 1863 "Fisherman's Hall [was] crowded almost to suffocation to witness a mechanical representation of the war in America." This box-office hit was *La Rue's War Show*, which was the sensation of the continent. In St. John's it was hailed as "truly 'ne plus extra' of the age." Still, sorrow was expressed, because "sufficient justice was not shown to the noble Confederates in the paintings."

On the night of 20 February 1867, at Fishermen's Hall, the

curtain was rung up on *How to Rule Your Wife*. This comedy, consisting of seven actors, five actresses, a variety duo, and a harpist, launched the second St. John's season of the Wilson & Clark Company. The musicians performed during the intermissions and scene changes. The Wilson & Clark season was the first in which a professional dramatic troupe brought with it, not only a complete repertoire of plays, but also complete props, costumes, and scenery. The same players were here again in June 1869, opening with *Gypsy Queen*. Following that, there was a summer visit to New York and a return to Fishermen's Hall once more in the autumn.

In June 1872 George E. Wilson opened a four-month season at the Victoria Rink, which he renamed Wilson's New Theatre, in Bannerman Park. His star was Nellie Boyd, supported by a company of eight men, three women and "a wonderful child star." Wilson advertised for six musicians for one year to tour with the company from St. John's to Halifax and the West Indies.

By September Wilson's New Theatre found a competitor in Signor Rubini who was appearing at the Drill Hall with marvels of magic. Rubini called his act "Cagliostromantheum of Prestidigitation."

In Fishermen's Hall the Star of the Sea Society was founded and formally instituted on 28 February 1871. In 1873 it was taken over by Bishop Power and reconstructed internally so that it became a two-storey building, of which the upstairs was consecrated as St. Peter's Chapel. The ground floor was given over to a convent school, operated by the Sisters of Mercy. St. Peter's continued in service until the opening of St. Patrick's Church in 1883, at which time the school took over the whole of the building. In 1903 it was sold to Frank McNamara and turned into a commercial office and warehouse. Following the closing of the McNamara business it was idle for a time. Its present occupant is a scrap-metal dealer.

In 1873 a new Total Abstinence Society Hall was erected on Duckworth Street opposite the top of McBride's Hill. The Healy Company came to play there that first year with *Ticket of Leave Man*, opening on November 1 and considered the finest comedy that ever came to the town. On 17 September 1879 Nannery's Company was pulling up the T.A. curtain on its season opener, *Led Astray*. In October the Josie Loane Dramatic Company used the theatre to give the city its first H.M.S. *Pinafore*. The soprano lead, Clara Fisher, stayed behind and reigned as St. John's queen of song for many years. In 1882 the Harkins Theatrical Company opened a season in the T.A. Hall with a November 27 presentation of *The Banker's Daughter*.

While all these professional companies were playing to packed houses local amateur groups were also turning customers away from the doors. By the late seventies the appearance of professional actresses on the stage had broken down the reserve of the local ladies and early in the eighties they began taking over the female parts from their men folk. Miss Bounds and Miss Costello are believed to have been the first local actresses.

St. John's witnessed its first opera only three years after it saw its first play. This was *The Duenna; or The Double Elopement*, an opera in three acts by Thomas Linley with libretto by R. B. Sheridan, first produced at Covent Garden in 1775, and in New York in 1786. It opened in St. John's 20 May 1820 and ran to the end of the month. The soprano roles were probably taken by boys.

In February 1814 B. Foley had announced the commencement of a school "for the instruction of those who may wish to attain the polite accomplishment in music." It was located on Holloway Street, "nearly opposite Hart & Robinson's." The size of the student body is unknown. The musical development of the town appears not to have been hastened much by this early venture.

There was a Handel & Haydn society in the late 1830s. The newspapers tell us that on 5 April 1838 Lady Prescott was "at home to a very numerous assemblage of ladies and gentlemen who were entertained with a variety of vocal sacred music by the Handel & Haydn Society of the town who performed with infinite taste and judgement."

In 1834 Miss Stacey was teaching pianoforte. A. Deuchar was giving a course of lessons in dancing at Mr. Beck's Coffee House in 1842, under the patronage of His Excellency the Governor and Lady Harvey. The first local composition seems to be "The Newfoundland Camp Gallopade" which was printed in manuscript form in 1852 and dedicated to Colonel Law.

The wreck of a ship of the Galway Line, near Trepassey, enriched the musical life of the community in 1859. On Tuesday, July 5, according to the *Newfoundland Express*, "Miss Agnes Heywood—the eminent vocalist . . . Having been thrown upon our shore by the unfortunate wreck of the *Argo* has been numerously solicited and has consented to give a musical entertainment . . . ." Miss Heywood, who had a reputation as a concert artist in both London and New York, sang at the British Hall, in the Colonial Building, and at the Roman Catholic cathedral.

Local singers came into their own in February 1861, when the Masonic Hall was lent for a Grand Concert by a group conducted by Mr. Stacey, possibly a relative of the pianoforte teacher. There was a performance of *Messiah, Elijah and Eli*, and "selections from oratorios." That same year, according to Louise Whiteway, in her well-researched paper, "History of the Arts in Newfoundland," the Athenaeum was including music in certain of its programs.[19] This was a literary institute and library that began on Water Street and, during the prime ministership of Sir Hugh Hoyles, became a handsome Victorian building on Duckworth Street. The Athenaeum lectures were interspersed with readings and music, even as the dramas at the theatre in those days had singing between the acts and scenes.

In 1881 a new genius in the field of musical parody appeared, when a young fellow named Johnny Burke was inspired to write an operetta about the attempts of residents of a Conception Bay community to prevent the railway from going through in June 1880. The dispute turned to violence and was finally settled by the diplomatic manoeuvring of Judge Prowse. The resulting operetta, *The Battle of Foxtrap*, opened February 2, in the T.A. Hall, and was an immediate success. Burke followed it with other hits such as *The Runaway Girl from Fogo*, *The Topsail Geisha*, and *Cotton's Patch*.

The Academia was organized in September 1882 by Sir Edward Morris. Its twenty members met in a building on the west corner of Prescott and Water Streets, which contained a lecturing, debating and reading room, concert, smoking and gym. Earlier that year, on April 12, the Benevolent Irish Society had opened its new club on Queen's Road with a Grand Dinner attended by Bishop Power and three hundred guests. With an entrance from Military Road the building, called St. Patrick's Hall, included the most up-to-date theatre in St. John's. However, this year of shining achievement was not without its cloud. On Wednesday, 27 December 1882, the *Evening Mercury*, in "A plea for music," lamented "the intended departure of Miss Fisher from our shores" and that "the only professional vocalist in Newfoundland should be obliged to leave us for want of patronage." However, she did not leave for several more years.

On 2 August 1867 Maggie Mitchell, a St. John's native who became prominent in the United States, was giving a farewell concert at the T.A. Hall. She was to die in Brooklyn, 29 June 1888. In 1876 the same hall was playing host to a Scottish vocal group known as The Kennedy Family. The Mendelssohn Club of Boston, a chamber concert group consisting of a quintet, was performing at the Athenaeum on 21 August 1878.

The Athenaeum seems to have been admirably suited to concert programs. Blair's Minstrels were the visiting attraction there in June 1883, and in July it was taken over by the Corinne Opera Company in performances of such undoubted hits as *H.M.S. Pinafore*.

The St. John's School of Music was instituted on 2 October 1887 at 31 Victoria Street. Its four teachers offered instruction in pianoforte, organ, singing, violin, viola, and violoncello.

On the afternoon of 11 May 1891 crowds followed Governor O'Brien and his Lady to the Old Factory on Queen's Road where a new invention, the phonograph, was to be exhibited for the first time by A. A. Urquhart.

Actors, singers, and musicians were not the only entertainers available to St. John's audiences in Victorian times. As far back as 22 September 1847 the townspeople were flocking to Brown's Field, on Monkstown Road, for the opening of the New York Circus Company. On 25 June 1877, at the T.A. Hall, the Bohemian Troupe of Fancy Glass Blowers gave an "unrivalled exhibition in glass blowing .... The handsomest lady in the hall was given an elegant case of glass work."

The Great Fire, in the summer of 1892, took with it almost every theatre and concert hall in the city including the T.A. Hall, B.I.S. Hall, Synod Hall, Old Factory, British Hall, Academia, and the Athenaeum. As so often happens with fires in old towns, in some ways it proved a blessing in disguise. The Total Abstinence Society rebuilt a magnificent wooden T.A. Hall, for $31,000 on their Duckworth Street site. The top floor of this three-storey building contained a completely modern theatre with three entrances from Henry Street by an inclined ramp forty feet deep. Known at first as the T.A. Hall, the theatre opened in 1894 with a performance by the Mercantile Investment Club's Dramatic Society which raised $2,600. This theatre, which eventually became famed as the Casino, contained 5 dressing rooms, 2 private boxes, 400 opera chairs, 300 gallery seats, and room for 600 in the pit, for a total capacity of 1,350. The stage measured 26 feet high by 25 feet deep by 56 feet wide. In 1908 the Casino became the Metropolis and, in 1910, the People's Theatre. It then returned to the Casino and finally became the Capitol Movie Theatre.

When the gutted shell of the Benevolent Irish Society building on Queen's Road was rebuilt after 1892 it also contained a modern theatre on the upper floor, with an entrance from Military Road. The new B.I.S. Hall became known as the Nickel Theatre and it is still in existence, though no longer in use as a theatre. Its stage appliances cost a thousand dollars and a Mr. Hollis, of New Jersey, was hired as scenic artist in charge of decor. The B.I.S Dramatic Company, a group of local amateurs under the inspired direction of T. M. White, opened the theatre with three performances but after that had to move out because of a previous booking by a professional company. The excellence of Mr. White's B.I.S. players is attested to by the fact that their 1892 production of *East Lynn* was held by the press to be just as good as the professional production by the Josie Mills Company in the Star Hall.

While theatre companies and concert singlers came and went, the town had advanced to a point where, in 1894, it was ready to establish a musical tradition of its own. That year a gaunt music teacher, Prof. Charles Hutton, staged four Gilbert & Sullivan operettas, *H.M.S. Pinafore, Patience, The Sorcerer*, and an unforgettable *Mikado*. Under the direction of the Professor, sometimes called Sir Charles because of a papal knighthood, local stars emerged and year after year the town turned out to see Louise Orr and Joan Rendell in *The Quaker Girl*, Cabot Fitzgerald and Mary Egan in *The Prince of Pilsen*, and Billy Wallace in *The Belles of Cornville*. Probably the last operetta staged in St. John's was *The Belle of Barcelona*, seen at the Casino shortly before Famous Players took over the theatre.

Mr. Hutton, who while studying music in England had fallen under the D'Oyly Carte spell, was the organist and choir director at the Roman Catholic cathedral. He was intimately associated with Mt. Cashel orphanage where he fostered among the boys a love of music that survived until the middle of the present century. It was at Mt. Cashel that Hutton found his protégé, Ignatius Rumbolt, who was eventually to shine as brightly as his mentor and become one of the great names on the St. John's musical scene. Rumbolt inherited the cathedral choir from the professor and was also in charge of the glee clubs of several important schools throughout the city. He guided the careers of some of the important singers of the day and reorganized the Memorial University Glee Club. He later founded the University Extension Choir. Eleanor Mews, who studied voice in Europe, initiated the Memorial University Glee Club in 1933, building on a group which had been organized in 1929-30 by Mr. Bevan and his successor, Mr. Morgan. In 1951 Miss Mews, by then Mrs. Eric Jerrett, formed a city-wide Glee Club of eighty voices.

In 1968 Rumbolt staged a monumental revival of a 1900 Hutton success, *The Geisha*. Time had not been kind to the Edwardian sentiments of the musical piece and, in spite of Rumbolt's excellent musical supervision, stage direction by Michael Cook, and fine singing by Wynn Ann Wadden in the title role, the excitement was just not there. The taste of patrons had changed to Broadway musicals. The first of these was Sylvia Wigh's production of *The Boy Friend*, staged at the Memorial University Little Theatre in 1962. The first lavish presentation of a musical, using an orchestra, was her 1964 production of *My Fair Lady*, which opened November 16 at Holy Heart Auditorium, starring Roma Butler as Eliza, Geoff Seymour as Higgins, and Paul O'Neill as Pickering. In spite of its faults that production set a trend for the annual sponsorship of a musical comedy by the Kinsmen's Club that continued unbroken into the 1970s.

Meanwhile, back in July 1894, to the delight of music lovers, the famous Fisk Jubilee Singers were appearing at the new T.A. Hall. It was known as the Casino in January 1898 when it welcomed Jessie Harcourt and the American Repertoire Company from Portland, Maine, with fourteen members and "a number of coon singers." The opening of *My Geraldine* for Monday, January 2, had to be postponed because of the non-arrival of the express.

Ardis Allworth's Company played in the same theatre that year

255

for fifty, forty, thirty, and twenty cents, and in October the attraction on stage was the Boston Criterion Comedy Company in *Everything Bright, Happy and Up-to-Date*. The sensation of the season had taken place in the spring. On April 21, in the T.A. Hall, the great expert on hypnotism and catalepsy, Professor Lawrence, as part of his performance, put to sleep a young man named Michael Cullen, promising to awaken him the following evening. Cullen was taken downstairs and put on display in a room of the T.A. Hall on Duckworth Street. Crowds gathered about the window that night and all the next day to look at the sleeping man who appeared to be suspended, like a stiff board, between two stools.

The next evening a full house watched breathlessly as the sleeping form was carried on stage in the presence of Dr. Shea and Dr. Harvey. The newspapers tell us the professor counted three and slapped his hands, and "the young man arose from his bed and calmly walked across the stage to the room amid such a storm of applause as was never known in the city before."

The Newfoundland Choral & Orchestral Society, a project of Charles Hutton and W. Moncrieff Mawer, appeared at the Methodist College Hall on 3 February 1910 with a performance of *The Erl King's Daughter*, which included 170 singers and an orchestra of sixteen members. Admission was sixty and twenty cents. Some competition existed for this group from the Church of England Men's Bible Class Orchestra, of five strings and four winds, under the direction of Rev. J. Bell.

Georgina Ann Sterling was born at Twillingate in 1867. She was to know the heights and depths of human experience. Her life was as tragic as any opera in which she sang. Her studies took her to Paris where she was accepted as a pupil by Matilde Marchesi, teacher of Nellie Melba, Frances, Alda, and others. It was Marchesi who suggested that Nellie Armstrong call herself Melba, after her home town of Melbourne, and it seems it was she also who suggested that Georgina Sterling call herself Marie Toulinguet, after her home town of Twillingate.

The Newfoundland girl made her debut most auspiciously in a La Scale production of *Norma* in Milan, where she was acclaimed by the Italians and stayed on in Italy to acquire more experience.

During the winter of 1896-97 she was in St. John's on her way to America. On October 4 she sang at Gower Street Church. Two days later she was at St. Andrew's. Then on the 9th she began a series of concerts with tenor Joseph O'Shaughnessy, at the Methodist College Hall. Charles Hutton accompanied them at the piano and all three were acclaimed as accomplished artists.

In 1897 the lady was prima donna with Colonel Mapleson's Imperial Opera Company in America. At one time, Mapleson had been considered for the general managership of the Metropolitan, but the job went to Leopold Damrosch. Mapleson's stars, such as Adelina Patti, Etelka Gerster, Sofia Scalchi, and Christine Nilsson, almost bankrupted the Metropolitan's tours with their fierce competition.

In 1898 Toulinguet was back in Italy when the irresistible Sofia Scalchi cabled her the offer of a New York season. The local diva turned it down to gain the experience offered by a contract to sing in Venice where she made a great hit.

The leading Venice newspaper reported:

> We have come to the last representation of "Marco Viconte" and the public has never withdrawn its patronage, crowding the theatre nightly, the favourite of the public is without doubt the Prima Donna Marie Toulinguet who ... sings with grand passion and sentiment, and her voice shows to great advantage in the high notes.

Another paper reads: "A most brilliant appearance and surprise was Miss Mary Twillingate in 'Marco Viconte'. She is destined to receive the greatest honours in her Italian course." A new Mass was composed and Maestro Tacheo insisted she sing the leading part. When she hesitated she received a telegram which said, "Orchestra and Chorus refuse to practice without you, everything in confusion, utterly ruined unless you come, don't refuse us."

Soon after her return to North America she contracted a throat ailment that utterly ruined her voice. Her career wrecked, the hapless girl returned to St. John's where she took to the bottle. Few realized that the tragic figure of a fallen woman tottering into an alcoholic sunset with her gentleman callers, on Duckworth and New gower Streets, had sung in Bellini's *Norma* on the stage of La Scala, the greatest opera house in the world. Friends and relatives finally convinced her to return to her old home in Twillingate, where she tried to retrieve her self-respect and was beloved by many in the community. She died on Easter Sunday in 1935. A story was spread about that because of her dissolute ways she was buried outside the Twillingate cemetery fence, but this was malicious gossip. In a snowstorm her grave was mistakenly dug outside the family plot but this was not discovered until the spring. A monument marks the grave today and the one recording we have of her voice "Lo, The Gentle Lark" shows it to be powerful, sympathetic, and of rare beauty.

American critics had written of Toulinguet in her Mapleson days: "The astonishing voice ... came as a revelation"; "Mlle Toulinguet is an artist such as we have not had in this country in many a year ... "; and "Such a voice one hears only once in a lifetime . . . ."[20]

On 14 April 1899, at the T.A. Hall, the New York Stock Company presented a new play that was to become a St. Patrick's

Day standard in Newfoundland, *The Bells of Shandon*. In any history of St. John's theatre mention must be made of these St. Patrick's Day dramatic presentations. For nearly three-quarters of a century the tradition of attending amateur theatricals on the great Irish holiday was a feature of the life of the town. Some years there were as many as three or four competing productions, and these invariably included a revival of *The Bells of Shandon*, or of *The Shaughraun*. Between the acts stiff Irish tenors and intrepid sopranos warbled "Danny Boy," or "The vale in whose bosom the bright waters meet." Foremost among the directors of these diversions was Kathleen Hayes, whose work in the west end stretched from the 1970s back through half a century.

In recent years the locally written play has begun to achieve prominence. The first modern success in this field is attributed to Grace Butt with *The Road Through Melton*. Her most ambitious work was probably *New Lands*, a costumed cavalcade of Newfoundland history, produced in 1947, to celebrate the Cabot discovery. Other plays followed and, in 1949, Mrs. Butt brought honour to St. John's when her play, *Part of the Main*, won the O.Z. Whitehead Award as the best one-act play in Ireland's Dublin Theatre Festival International Play-writing Competition, where the author had the pleasure of seeing the work produced.

Ted Russell's radio drama, *The Holdin' Ground*, became a popular stage play of the 1960s when the Northcliff Drama Club of Grand Falls presented it in a drama festival. Cassie Brown's *The Wreckers* was also seen on the St. John's stage. Tom Cahill's theatre version of Harold Horwood's novel, *Tomorrow Will Be Sunday*, was the winner of the 1967 provincial Drama Festival and was seen that summer, with its local cast, at Expo in Montreal. Mr. Cahill's own play, *Jody*, was a 1972 Drama Festival winner at St. John's. It was later repeated as a Summer Festival production at the Arts & Culture Centre for two seasons. Rewritten by the dramatist, it was called *Starrigan*. Paul O'Neill's three-act tragi-comedy of the time of the troubles in Ireland, *The Hush of the Starling*, was chosen by CBC drama network supervisor, Esse W. Ljung, as the first full-length play to win the province's Arts & Letters Competition. In 1971 Michael Cook's original play, *Colour the Flesh the Colour of Dust*, set in colonial St. John's, won that year's Drama Festival. It was subsequently heard on the CBC national radio network and given an Eastern Canadian tour by the Neptune Theatre of Halifax with St. John's actress, Flo Patterson. In 1973 another Cook play, *Head, Guts and Sound Bone Dance* won the Newfoundland Drama Festival.

The coming of the twentieth century saw the professional theatre continue to flourish in St. John's. It is impossible to mention all the players and companies performing in the city. The century began with the opening of the Woodward-Whitman Dramatic Company on New

258

Year's night, in the Casino, with the five-act drama *California*. Receipts that night were not much below five hundred dollars and "the people were packed like sardines in a box." On January 16 the troupe became the Metropolitan Dramatic Company, and the Casino became the Metropolitan.

The first decade also brought to the community a lady who was to become known in the United States as "The maker of stars." She was the beloved actress, Jessie Bonstelle. It was on 21 January 1902, when Miss Bonstelle was playing the lead in *Mamzelle*, at the Casino, that one of the company, Frances Foster, gave the first public performance of the "Ode to Newfoundland," with the McAuliffe Stock Company. Miss Bonstelle returned a number of times after that with her own company. Her last visit was in 1909 when she had competition from the Klark-Urban Company that opened on September 18 with *The College Girl*. Jessie Bonstelle scored in New York with the Schuberts and, in 1910, went to Detroit where she took over the management of the Garrick Theatre. By 1925 she had her own Bonstelle Playhouse. Today, Jessie Bonstelle is honoured as the founder of America's Community Theatre Movement and as the discoverer of such stars as Katherine Cornell, Melvyn Douglas, and Ann Harding. She had enormous popularity in St. John's.

Soon after the turn of the century, flesh-and-blood performers began giving way to flickering shadows on a silver screen. The first local portents of disaster to the live theatre almost passed unnoticed. Only one newspaper commented on the Magic Lantern Exhibition held in Carew Street School (a forerunner of Bishop Field College) on 11 December 1898. It said that "The different pictures thrown on the screen were loudly applauded." The next ominous happening occurred 13 February 1901. Few could see how such an unpromising event would eventually change the entertainment history of the world.

Originally scheduled to open January 29, for one week only, the Cineograph promised moving pictures of the Queen, the Pope, and the South African and Chinese wars. However, the death of Queen Victoria caused it to be postponed until after her funeral. It was postponed again "in consequence of an accident to a portion of the apparatus." It finally got off to an unfortunate start on February 13.

This abortive happening appears to mark the first showing of a motion picture in Newfoundland and is the birth date of the movies on the local scene. Here is what the *Evening Herald* had to say about the Lubin Cineograph.

> The T.A. Hall held a large audience last night to see the Cineograph, but a more disgusted gathering never left any place of amusement. The pictures first shown were excellent slides for lantern views made by artist Vey, and consisted of

259

views of local celebrities. They were the best part of the program, for the moving-picture exhibition was a complete failure. Some films were put on wrong side up, and all were indistinct, the proper focus was not obtained and the operator did not know how to work the machine. The views are of the best and put in the shade those of the biograph, but it requires a man that understands this machine to work it. After fifteen minutes of agony the audience started to leave. Mr. Wilson sang three times but was so disappointed at the failure of the pictures that he had no chance to show his ability. He apologized to the audience for the failure and even went to assist the operator personally, but to no purpose, and he finally gave up in despair.[21]

Norris Wilson was billed as one of the finest baritone singers of Philadelphia.

How the reporter knew the views were superior to those of the Biograph is a bit of a mystery, for they were exhibited for the first time six nights later, February 19, at the British Hall. The press might have had a private preview. The *Herald* reported:

About 500 persons saw the Biograph in the British Hall last night. The scenes were excellent and applause was general . . . . The final scene in which Lord Roberts is shown, was excellent and the audience became enthusiastic as he stood in the carriage preparatory to moving away. The band played at intervals and some of our best-known vocalists sang . . . [22]

Admission was thirty and twenty cents with tickets on sale at Grey & Goodland's.

On 25 January 1904 the *Evening Herald* announced that "6,500 feet of the latest and most up-to-date motion pictures, embracing all the latest subjects in war, train and fire scenes with thrilling effects, also acrobatic, comic and miscellaneous, will be shown the holiday evening, Next Thursday, January 28th, in the T.A. Hall."

In 1907 the flicker came permanently to St. John's when the B.I.S. Hall was leased and converted to the use of the moving picture. The first conventional movie was shown in the newly named Nickel Theatre, 1 July 1907 at 1:00 p.m. with about twenty-five people present. The age of the cinema, as we know it, had begun. Next day the *Evening Telegram* reported:

The Nickle Moving Picture Exhibition opened in St. Patrick's Hall yesterday and attracted a large crowd. The number of spectators was rather small at the opening but increased in the evening and at night the hall was filled. The audience for the day was about 2,000 persons . . . . The pictures shown were very distinct and suit all tastes "from grave to gay, from lively to severe". Miss Amy Hickey was the soloist and she sang with much acceptance . . . . Ladies are asked to remove their hats.

The *Daily News* report castigated the ladies for the importunity of their millinery: "Ladies will be conferring a benefit on all if in future they will remove their hats." The *Daily News* also noted that Miss Hickey was presented with a handsome bouquet by some admirers. Her opening program is not given but in subsequent weeks, aided by lantern slides, she intoned "Cheer Up, Mary," "We Parted When the Sun Went Down," and "The Bird in Nellie's Hat." By September Amy was replaced by Miss Bride Murphy in the afternoon, and Miss Patty Ring in the evening. Professor McCarthy was at the piano, a place where he stayed firmly entrenched until dislodged by the coming of sound.

Two months after these momentous days at the Nickel, the T.A. Hall was also opened as a cinema for motion pictures on 3 September 1907. The press tells us that "the ushers (gentlemen all) looked after the patrons in fine style." While the Nickel never looked back, the Casino reverted to the legitimate stage. The W. S. Harkins Company opened there on 24 January 1911 with *For Her Sake*. It was playing at the Casino again in 1914, on the night that the great sealing disaster overtook the steamer, *Newfoundland*, at the ice fields.

At the Nickel, the presentation of motion pictures and illustrated songs was continuous from twelve noon, and there was "Nothing cheap but the price," which was "5¢ to all parts of the house." On 19 September 1907 a person called Critics, wrote to the *Evening Telegram* to acclaim the whole operation. This correspondent said, the theatre "is held in the highest esteem by the people of St. John's and it holds a unique position which it has won by reason of its own merits." The writer showered congratulations on Mr. Trites, the "courteous manager," Mr. R. D. McKay, the "skilled operator," and Thomas Dalton, his assistant. That Christmas there was the Great Nickel Limerick Contest with a season ticket "and two other substantial prizes."

The 1907 Nickel movie theatre was not long behind the times. In 1903 Edison made the first American narrative film, *The Great Train Robbery*, and it was not until 1908 that the first "movie star" was born when Florence Lawrence was lured from her fifteen-dollar-a-week job with Vitagraph to a twenty-five-dollar-a-week job as the "Biograph Girl."

When Patrick Laracy opened the Crescent Theatre on Water Street, opposite Holdsworth Street, the Nickel Theatre faced permanent competition. The Crescent was parallel to the street, at the back of what is now the east end of the Arcade Stores. It advertised "the latest and best in music—drums and effects."

On Saturday, 23 February 1918, the 600-seat Nickel was showing Irene Castle in *Patria*, and the 500-seat Crescent, lovely Marin Sais in *The Vanishing Linesman*. That night the Nickel's owner, J. P. Kiely, and the Crescent's owner, Patrick Laracy, boarded the S.S. *Florizel* to sail to New York for meetings with their distributors. Early next morning the ship struck the reefs off Cappahayden and Laracy was one of the nearly one hundred passengers lost in the disaster. The Crescent then passed into the hands of J. P. Kiely. When his lease expired the theatre was taken by Edward Boulos who operated it until it closed in 1947. For a number of years the building collected dust and rats. In the mid-1950s several groups investigated the possibility of turning it into a legitimate theatre but costs proved prohibitive as no grants were available. It was finally purchased by the Arcade Stores and added to the floor space of that concern.

The Nickel was not to close until 26 June 1960, after nearly fifty-three years of bringing movies to the people of St. John's. The sign, still preserved over the entrance, announces, "The Nickel— Photo Plays." The old house has since been used for bingo games. In the early spring of 1973 an attempt was made to reopen the Nickel as a cinema, but the City Council refused permission on the grounds that St. Patrick's Hall was not a first-class building.

In 1883 the old site of the New Amateur Theatre, on Duckworth Street at Queen's Road, was sold to Callahan, Glass & Co. for $1.20 per foot. This was used as an illustration of the high advance in value of city building sites. Callahan, Glass & Co.'s Furniture Factory, a four-storey building that was the largest retail store in St. John's, arose on the land. The firm was ruined when gutted by fire in a spectacular blaze at 5:30 p.m., Monday, 17 June 1895. Heat from Callahan's fire was so intense it broke the window glass and ignited curtains in City Hall, directly across the street. With the advent of movies the land was acquired by Tom O'Neill and Tom Cody, who again erected a theatre on the site, nearly one hundred years after the laying of the cornerstone for the New Amateur Theatre. But what a difference! Where the 1822 play-house looked very much like a converted barn, the 1918 movie palace lived up to all that its name indicated. One newspaper reported: "It will be known as 'The Majestic' and those who have seen the interior agree that a more appropriate name could not have been chosen." The proscenium arch for the stage, intricately hand carved by Dan Carrol, was constructed and erected by the Shipbuilding Company of Harbour Grace. The upper part of the proscenium is still preserved in the building.

This beautiful ramped theatre, in which no seat obscured another, was a miniature masterpiece. After many delays and much inconvenience it opened on Monday evening, 3 March 1919, under the patronage of

His Excellency the Governor, with the CCC Band in attendance. The movie was *Trilby*, starring Wilton Lackaye as Svengali and Clara Kimball Young in the title role. Admission was ten cents, floor; twenty cents, balcony.

The original owners were forced to sell out and the Majestic was taken over by Stan Condon, and from then on its character was sadly changed. Besides being the scene of some of the last of Professor Hutton's operatic triumphs, the theatre played a part in some of the political upheavals of the day. It was the birthplace of the famous political riot of April 1932, which then moved to the Colonial Building. There, in the excitement that followed, the Legislature was wrecked and the Prime Minister barely escaped lynching.

The theatre was also the scene of the workers' meetings in such troubled times as the bakers' strike in the thirties, and the railway and carpenters' strikes of the forties. Responsible government rallies were staged in the Majestic, and it was Confederate Party headquarters during the stormy days of political turmoil in 1948-49.

In October 1927 Al Jolson went down on one knee and sang "Mammy." When he got up again the history of the movies had changed forever. By the fall of 1929 some five thousand theatres were equipped for sound. In St. John's the Nickel and Majestic were two of them. That summer technicians from Western Electric came to the city and converted the equipment of both movie houses. The first talkies were shown on 26 August 1929. At the Nickel all seats were fifty cents to see John Boles, Myrna Loy, and Carlotta King in *The Desert Song*. At the more lowly Majestic, patrons spent thirty cents for the pleasure of hearing Patsy Ruth Miller talk on *The Fall of Eve*.

The downhill slide of the Majestic Theatre ended in the early 1950s. On 14 May 1953, to the heartbreak of those who wanted to see it restored as a legitimate playhouse, plans were submitted to Council to turn the theatre into an appliance store and warehouse, known as Majestic Sales, which was later changed to Heap & Partners (Newfoundland) Ltd.

There were other movie theatres in the city before the advent of sound. The British Hall became known as the "British Theatre—Paramount photo play picture palace." The owner, Mr. Rossley, had as his motto, "All that the name implies." On stage it offered Arthur Priestman Cameron from Yorkshire, the entertaining singer who had settled in St. John's and was a great favourite on stage and radio. The Crescent was "Exclusive for Fox pictures." The Queen, on Water Street, almost opposite Steer's Cove, charged five cents in 1915 for admittance to its "Universal Picture Palace."

The proprietor of the British Theatre had earlier operated two smaller theatres, Rossley's East and Rossley's West, which combined slightly vulgar vaudeville with movies. The motto for both theatres was the eye-catching phrase, "They are not forbidden by the church."

263

Rossley's East, in the Mechanics' Hall on Water Street at Haymarket Square, was closed in the summer of 1915 for renovations and had a Grand Reopening on Monday, 16 August, under the distinguished patronage of Lady Davidson and the Misses Davidson. The bill included the Australian Merry Makers; Don, the greatest performing dog in the world; Jack Russell, a Canadian entertainer; and Olive Russell, who had the distinction of being a lady baritone. The following Saturday, Her Ladyship and the Misses again extended their patronage to the opening of the Royal Punch & Judy show as performed before Royalty in London with Don, the wonder dog. The theatre is now a night club of sorts.

Rossley's West, a building on the west side of Hutching's Street, was known also as OUR'S. In June of 1915 the daughter of the owner, Miss Bonnie Rossley, appeared there in the great pantomime *Bo-peep*. Rossley's West has now completely disappeared.

The Star of the Sea Association, founded in 1871 in Fishermen's Hall, was looking for a site on which to build when the Roman Catholic Old Chapel on Henry Street was destroyed by fire on 23 July 1874. On this site the first Star Hall was built, to be destroyed by fire in 1892. It was rebuilt the following year and the government hired it immediately for Supreme and District Court quarters while awaiting construction of the present Court House. That took ten years. When the court moved out the theatre was rented to travelling companies and local amateurs.

On 23 December 1920 the edifice was again visited by fire, this time with fatal results. One reserve fireman was killed when a wall of the building fell into the street. Four others were injured. The Star Hall had cost twenty-seven thousand dollars in 1893. Its value at loss was estimated at about fifty thousand. The society set to work and cleared away the rubble, and the present structure opened 8 January 1922. The top floor was leased by Stan Condon and contained a very up-to-date movie theatre named the Star, in honour, not of Hollywood, but of the Virgin Mary. In 1951 the theatre closed for about a month. It reopened October 15 under the management of Famous Players and on 27 May 1957 it closed its doors as a cinema for the last time. In June of that year the old General Post Office on Water Street was torn down and the building served as Post Office for two years until the new one was built. After that the Star became a Bingo palace.

There was also a movie house on the north side of New Gower Street, a few doors east of Casey Street. Managed by the Star owners during the thirties and early forties, it was known to the public as the Little Star, though its actual name was the Regal. It later became the Belmont Tavern.

The Casino Theatre continued to attract visiting artists. In 1935, however, Famous Players took a lease on the building and on Monday, June 14, it opened as the Capitol Theatre. The picture chosen for the gala opening at eight-thirty that night was the Gainsborough version of the stage hit, *Chu Chin Chow*, starring Oscar Ashe and Lily Brayton. It was billed as "The mightiest of all musical spectacles produced on the most lavish scale in the history of the screen." In attendance were the Governor and Lady Anderson, Mayor Carnell, who performed the opening formalities, members of the bench, the church, the government, and the council.

During the night of 26 October 1946 the wooden frame building was gutted by fire. The Total Abstinence Society rebuilt it in steel and concrete but the venture bankrupted the organization. Expected to cost less than a quarter of a million dollars, it cost over six hundred thousand, and it became necessary to rent the planned clubrooms on the third floor to the CBC for a radio studio. Eventually the entire building had to be sold to Famous Players. Ironically, Famous Players offered to replace the whole structure after the fire, at no cost to the society, provided the company be given ownership of the theatre. This was turned down because some members feared immoral films might be shown and there would be no way to evict. The fear may not have been unfounded, for today the theatre is noted as the city's leading outlet for "skin flicks." The rebuilt Capitol was opened at 8:00 p.m., 20 November 1950, by the lieutenant-governor, Sir Leonard Outerbridge. The film was Somerset Maugham's *Trio*.

In 1927, J. J. Duff erected the Duff Building on Water Street, opposite Steer's Cove. The lobby of the building led to the Queen movie house, at the back, on George Street. This theatre had a striking proscenium stage and was a vast cinema. During World War II the Queen came under the management of the Nickel. It was renovated, reopened as the York Theatre, and became a second-run house for features that had played the Nickel the previous week. When it finally closed its doors the Queen, or York, was taken over by Steer's and is now used as a warehouse.

On the night of 1 September 1944 George Murphy and Ginny Simms sang and danced their way through the movie, *Broadway Rhythm*, to mark the opening of the "Showplace of Newfoundland," the Paramount Theatre on Harvey Road, built on the site of the old Parade Rink. The Paramount had the island's first Cinemascope screen. 3D had made its local bow at the Capitol.

On a Sunday evening in February 1973, during a showing of *Mary, Queen of Scots*, the concrete roof of the Paramount Theatre collapsed with a loud crack. The wooden beams held, keeping the tons of broken concrete from spilling on the patrons, but a day or two later it fell in. The Paramount was closed for much of 1973 while the roof was supposedly rebuilt. It never reopened.

The Cornwall Theatre on LeMarchant Road, opposite the West End Fire Hall, was a fine cinema but it had a brief career. It opened

8 October 1948 with Sonja Henie and John Payne in *Sun Valley Serenade*: adults, forty cents; children, twenty cents. It then came under the management of Famous Players. The advent of television in 1955 sounded the death knell for the Cornwall, as well as most of its sister houses and this theatre also ended up as a warehouse.

The Avalon Mall Theatre was built at the time the Mall was constructed and opened 25 April 1967, with a very commonplace film, *In Like Flint*.

The city's first drive-in theatre was constructed on Topsail Road, less than half a mile west of the Trans-Canada Highway overpass. It was named the Clearview and opened in the summer of 1972. A drive-in had been attempted some years earlier, in a meadow opposite the Old Mill night club, on Brookfield Road, but this operation, consisting only of a screen and loudspeaker nailed to the side of a barn, failed.

The Community Concert movement was begun in St. John's by Darroch Macgillivray, with the aid of the Rotary Club, in 1946. Over the years it brought some of the outstanding concert artists of the world to the city including Jesu Maria Sanroma, Dorothy Maynor, George London, William Primrose, and Jennie Tourel. These performers played in such unsuitable places as school gymnatoriums where overheating, wooden chairs, and the lack of a back-stage powder room presented annoying obstacles.

Some of the leading professional actors of stage and screen "trod the boards" in St. John's in days gone by. The Florence Glossop-Harris Company was at the Casino in 1926 and again in 1929. The first season's offerings of this "capable and well balanced" troupe included *The Ghost Train, Charley's Aunt,* and *Twelfth Night*, and in the 1929 season there was *French Leave, The Silver Cord,* and seven of Shakespeare's plays. A leading actor with this talented group was Roger Livesey, who was to become a highly respected star in England. Ernest Jay was another of these distinguished thespians.

Francis Compton, a brother of Fay Compton and Sir Compton Mackenzie, brought his small company to the Casino and filled the smaller parts with local actors. The noted stage and screen comedy performer, Edward Everett Horton, played stock in St. John's as did William Farnum, who became a Fox star in such pictures as *Du Barry Was a Woman* with Norma Talmadge. Ian Keith made his acting debut in the city and this led to screen roles such as John Wilkes Booth in Walter Huston's *Abraham Lincoln*. William Duncan, who played St. John's for several seasons, was a silent star with Selig in 1913. He moved to Vitagraph in 1919 and became a popular hero in westerns.[23]

The Alexandra Players, a theatre group formed from the Alexandra Repertory Theatre in Birmingham, England, arrived in St. John's

266

on board ship in December 1947 and played from January to March of the following year at the Pitts Memorial Hall. The juvenile lead with these players was a personable young actor named Alex McCowan who was to become one of the great stage actors of the 1960s when he created the role of *Hadrian VII* in London and New York, to spectacular reviews. He then starred in movies. John Gabriel, the company director, was married to a Bowring from St. John's and it was through this connection that Bowring's firm sponsored the Alexandra season. Gabriel afterwards became a respected teacher at the Royal Academy of Dramatic Art in London and a familiar face on British television and in films.

In 1951 Leslie Yeo and Hilary Vernon, an actor and the leading lady with the Alexandra troupe, formed the London Theatre Company with Oliver Gordon and George Paddon Foster. Their first season opened in St. John's in October and ran until the following April. For the next five years the company continued to play to delighted audiences in Bishop Field College auditorium on Bond Street. The advent of television in 1955 is credited with killing the city's last and most permanent professional repertory theatre just as it killed most of the movie theatres. Many distinguished actors found their way to Canada with the London Theatre Company, including Joseph Shaw, Norman Walsh, Moya Fenwick, and the incomparable performer, Gillie Fenwick. Others returned to England to find fame in the West End and in films. Valerie Hermanni was a lead in Agatha Christie's record-breaking *The Mousetrap*. Ronald Fraser became a star in *The Long, the Short and the Tall*, and a host of other pictures. Charles Jarrott became the director of such outstanding films as *Anne of the Thousand Days*, and *Mary, Queen of Scots*.

Some well-known personalities got their theatrical feet wet in the St. John's amateur theatre movement. Ludovic Kennedy, who was to write such books as *10 Rillington Place* and marry prima ballerina Moira Shearer, took roles with the St. John's Players when he was in Newfoundland as secretary to Governor Walwyn. Hal Holbrook, who won fame in the U.S.A. with his theatrical portrayal of Mark Twain, was an American G.I. when he began his acting career with the Players. Edward Bishop, who emerged as a top British television star, in the role of the Commander in the series *U.F.O.*, was an American G.I. named George Bishop when he appeared on stage for the first time in the Theatre Guild production of *Rope* at Holy Cross auditorium on Patrick Street.

Reference is made elsewhere to John Murray Anderson, Donald Brian, and Frank Knight, three St. John's citizens who were to have highly successful careers in Hollywood and New York. Others were to follow them into the profession. Gladys Richards studied at the Royal Academy of Dramatic Art in London and became a leading actress with Lord Longford's Dublin Gate Theatre in Ireland before returning to Canada. She returned home to St. John's for a season with the London Theatre Company. Paul O'Neill, a pupil at the National Academy of Theatre Arts in New York, played in touring companies and summer stock in the U.S.A. and in repertory, touring, films, and a London play, *Double Bend*, in England. He returned to Newfoundland and a career as drama supervisor with the CBC. Ruby Johnston studied dramatics at Denison University in Ohio and toured America with her husband, Hal Holbrook, in their own show *Theatre of Great Personalities*. After divorcing Holbrook she continued to pursue her theatrical interests in the United States and Canada, where she played a lead in *Volpone* at Stratford. Roma Butler's lovely operatic voice earned her a successful singing career, which included the leads in such national CBC television presentations as *H.M.S. Pinafore* and the première production of *Darling Cory*. On her marriage she went to live and teach in Detroit. Mary Lou Farrell was a St. John's beauty queen who became Miss Dominion of Canada. Her voice got her into professional community musical theatres in the U.S.A. where she met and married Peter Palmer, who had won acclaim in the title role of the Broadway production and movie version of Al Capp's *Lil Abner*. Mary Lou Collins left St. John's in the mid-1960s and became a singing sensation in Toronto where she was featured on several of her own CBC-TV specials. She toured with Bob Hope and became a popular nightclub performer, as well as a recording artist. Lynn Channing of St. John's went to England to study voice in the late 1960s and made her operatic debut, to enthusiastic reviews, as the Queen of the Night in a Sadler's Wells London production of Mozart's *The Magic Flute*, in 1971. She then sang at Glyndebourne until 1974. That same year saw the first two St. John's high-school pupils, Brenda Devine and David Ferry, accepted as students by Canada's National Theatre School in Montreal, after the school held nationwide auditions. In 1973 several St. John's performers were in Toronto appearing on stage and in CBC-TV dramas as professional actors.

The St. John's Players, mentioned above, grew out of Grace Butt's dream of establishing the Community Little Theatre movement in Newfoundland. One evening in October 1937 she called a meeting at her home which resulted in the formation of the group. They were offered the use of the small stage in Memorial University College, on Parade Street, and it was there that their first production, *The Admirable Crichton*, was staged.

The Players got their constitution, 29 April 1939, and during the early years they took part in radio dramas on station VONF. With the advent of CJON-TV the St. John's Players' stage production *Gayden*, starring Flo Patterson, became the first full-length locally produced play to be presented on Newfoundland television.

They were invited to present *Ladies in Retirement* at the Dominion Drama Festival in Saint John, N.B., in the spring of 1952. Adjudicator Michel St. Denis, of London's Old Vic, awarded the trophy for Best Actress to Carmel Kemp of St. John's.

Other groups came and went in the years that followed. The Theatre Guild was organized by Sylvia Wigh in the early 1950s and it produced some quality plays. The Theatre Arts Club was organized in 1956 by John Puddester, John Holmes, John Perlin, and Paul O'Neill. It gave the town a memorable production of *The Hasty Heart*. After winning the Regional Drama Festival this play went to the Dominion Drama Festival in Edmonton.

The Theatre Arts Club was the first St. John's theatre group formed especially to tour plays to outport communities. It was also the only amateur theatre group in St. John's to have its own clubrooms, a well-appointed suite on the top floor of a building on Duckworth Street, two doors east of Cathedral Street.

West of the Theatre Arts Club, the corner building was occupied by the Arts Centre of E. Fredd Davis. A blonde, juvenile actor and assistant stage manager with the London Theatre Company, Davis decided to stay behind in St. John's when the players returned to England at the end of their last season. His Arts Centre operation included a theatre school, speech studio, painting and sculpture studio, and a theatre company of amateurs called The Wayfarers. On the top floor were the living quarters of Davis and some of his workers. The building had a small bistro-type restaurant which later became a kind of speakeasy membership club, which was the undoing of the operation. Because of it, the founder was haled into court where he was fined for selling liquor without a licence. Soon afterwards the Arts Centre folded and Davis left St. John's. He surfaced briefly in Toronto, New York, and Hollywood before returning to London and establishing himself as an international astrologer and Tarot Card reader of international repute, with movie stars as clients and a column in the London Evening News.

The story of the stage in St. John's took an upward turn in 1961 when Memorial University's fully equipped Little Theatre gave local players their first proper stage on which to work. This was augmented by the Holy Heart of Mary auditorium, on Bonaventure Avenue, 21 September 1962. The Holy Heart structure gave St. John's its first modern theatre capable of handling visiting opera and ballet companies, as well as concert artists and local productions. It was the most important step forward since the opening of the Casino, and Holy Heart served the town well until the coming of the Arts & Culture Centre theatre.

Prior to 1967 the federal government gave each province a sum of money for the erection of a memorial to Confederation in each provincial capitol. The grant was to be matched dollar for dollar by the province. Newfoundland's share was two and a half million dollars. Ground was broken in April 1965 for a five-million-dollar project, to be known as the Arts & Culture Centre. By the time it was finished, two years later, it had cost eight million. The complex was opened 22 May 1967 by Premier Smallwood and that night the first performance of the Dominion Drama Festival was held on the stage of the 1017-seat theatre with the presentation of the St. John's Players' production of Tom Cahill's adaptation of Harold Horwood's novel *Tomorrow Will Be Sunday*.

The most recent cultural development in the city of St. John's has been the evolution of the St. John's Symphony Orchestra. In 1957 the CBC asked Eric Abbott to form a symphonette which the broadcasting corporation hoped might grow into a symphony orchestra. Its major weakness was strings and when Mr. Abbott left for Boston in 1960, to obtain a doctorate in music, the group disbanded. Several unsuccessful attempts were made to keep it going.

In 1962 some interested members of the former symphonette approached Memorial University, and Prof. Nigel Wilkins rounded up the survivors to form another orchestra. It was taken over by the Extension Division. With the departure of Wilkins from the scene the membership dropped off until the venture was revived by Zdanek (Stan) Navratil, a native of Czechoslovakia, who was teaching at the university. Under his leadership the group played for various musicals and operettas, and even attempted a few concert performances.

The St. John's Symphony Orchestra was incorporated in January 1970 as a non-profit organization existing on several small grants from various levels of government.[24] It also moved from the control of the Extension Department to the Arts and Culture Centre. With the departure of Navratil from Newfoundland the conductor's baton passed into the hands of Ian Mennie, a native of Scotland, and a Memorial University professor. Under Mennie's leadership the forty-seven-member group expanded its activities and began to give symphony concerts on a regular basis.

The Calos Youth Orchestra, a kind of junior symphony, began during the 1969 Christmas vacation when a group of young people in St. John's got together on their own. They jumbled the initials of each others names and came up with the word Calos which they afterwards found out was the Greek word for an experience.

In the summer of 1970 the group asked Gordon Bartlett, a bandmaster, to become its conductor. He accepted, and under his leadership the organization flourished.

6

To Live by Medicine

Dr. William Carson, the most famous figure in Newfoundland life, was born in Scotland and came to the island from England in 1808. He wrote pamphlets, organized demonstrations and agitated constantly for reforms in justice, administration, health, and politics. Carson led the fight for self government all the way to Whitehall. He is one of a trio of giants (with Governor Cochrane and Bishop Fleming) who dominated early 19th century Newfoundland life with their dreams, ideals, vigour and determination. He died at St. John's in 1843.

Hon. Lawrence O'Brien, a native of Ireland who resided in St. John's for nearly 60 years. Head of the firm of L. O'Brien & Co. he was Member of the House of Assembly for St. John's 1842 - 1852 and resided at Rostellan, formerly Dr. William Carson's home "The Billies". Appointed to the Legislative Council in 1853 he was president from 1855 to his death, 28 June 1870, age 77 years.

Hon. James Tobin was born in Ireland. He established the shipping firm of J. Tobin & Co. at St. John's and was appointed by the Crown to the Amalgamated House in 1843. He became a member of the Legislative Council when Responsible Government was granted in 1855. He offered his property off Military Road, "Monkstown", named after his birthplace near Dublin, for a Poor Asylum but the offer was refused.

Private Phil Jensen, a returned veteran who helped collect the funds which established the TB treatment centre known as Jensen's Camp. (Courtesy Provincial Reference Library - Newfoundland Section)

Miss Mary Walsh who later married James Howley, son of James P. Howley who wrote the great source book "The Beothucks of Newfoundland" sits atop Signal Hill in front of the old Hospital where Marconi received the famous wireless message from Cornwall. Circa 1900. (Courtesy Newfoundland Provincial Archives)

Ethel Dickinson, the Newfoundland nurse who gave her life nursing 'flu victims in the emergency hospital set up in the King George the Fifth Institute during the Spanish 'Flu Epidemic of 1918. (Courtesy Provincial Reference Library - Newfoundland Section)

278

To Live By Medicine

To live by medicine is to live horribly.
                    CARL LINNAEUS *Diaeta Naturalis*

It has been generally accepted that the first mention we have of a doctor, other than ship's surgeons, in St. John's is one found in an affidavit by a person named Minshew supporting charges made by Rev. John Jackson against Captain Lloyd during the tumultuous days of the Captain's command of Fort William in 1703. Mr. Minshew testified to the officer's "barbarity to the surgeon."[1]

There are earlier mentions of doctors to be found. The surgeon James Yonge says he found a doctor in port when he reached St. John's in 1669. In a list of planters' rooms in the community compiled on orders of the governor, 25 August 1701, and found in the Colonial Records, there is a notation that the plantation of William Hanbury, in the marsh, was obtained from Dr. Medhurst. The marsh was in Maggotty Cove at the foot of Temperance Street, then a river. In all likelihood Dr. Medhurst was a garrison surgeon who took a lease of land which he later sold. Again it is probable that he was here for several years, so that he would be practising medicine at St. John's in the 1690s.

In the ensuing years the medical needs of the fishermen and settlers were cared for by surgeons of the garrison or by those on naval vessels frequenting the port. A Dr. Delaney is mentioned as possibly the first non-military doctor resident in St. John's. He was practising there in 1777. The first medical men whom we can be sure were permanent residents, would seem to be three who are spoken of in a survey for altering the roads in the town in 1780. Their names are King Brown, Rowe, and Dodd. The latter was also appointed a magistrate that year by Governor Edwards. Dr. Gardiner, who founded the town of Gardiner, Maine, was a resident in 1783.[2]

The appointment of a doctor to the courts was not unusual. Educated men were not easily found and doctors and clergy frequently doubled as justices of the peace. Around 1790 D'Ewes Coke, a doctor who had settled at Trinity, moved to St. John's where he was

279

appointed as one of two assessors of the court in 1791. The following year he replaced John Reeves, as Lord Chief Justice, at a salary of three hundred pounds per annum. Coke presided in the Supreme Court until 1797.

In May 1802 another surgeon, Jonathan Ogden, who occupied a room and surgery at Fort William, became Acting Chief Justice. He had come from Nova Scotia in 1784 where he was employed at Halifax as a surgeon's mate. By 1794 he was a magistrate at St. John's and, no doubt, caught the eye of the Governor when he prepared a report on the mutiny of the garrison, which his friend Bishop O'Donel helped put down in the winter of 1799-1800. Ogden literally disappeared from history a few years later. He took a leave of absence because of ill health and was going to England on a rest cure when the vessel on which he was sailing was lost with all hands.

There were at least two other resident doctors in the town by 1797. David Duggan, acting surgeon to the Royal Newfoundland Regiment, and John McCurdy were medical men who petitioned the governor that year for permission to enclose "pieces of ground."[3]

In connection with Dr. John McCurdy it is necessary to mention Dr. John Clinch, who came to Bonavista, from England, in 1775. He later moved to Trinity and returned home in 1787 to be ordained a clergyman by the Bishop of London. He returned to Trinity where he served as doctor and parson for the next thirty years.

While studying medicine in London, Clinch had as a classmate his boyhood friend, Edward Jenner, and the two kept up a regular correspondence all their lives. In May 1796 Jenner discovered vaccination when he tried innoculation with cowpox. Clinch wrote for details which were sent with a sample of the vaccine. The first innoculation in the New World is said to have been performed by John Clinch at Trinity in 1798. He was so delighted with the results that the following year he travelled to St. John's to try to fight an outbreak of smallpox. He probably arrived late in the fall of 1799.

When Governor Pole reached St. John's in the summer of 1800 he found the disease had broken out at Portugal Cove. The Governor and his infant daughter had been successfully vaccinated just before they sailed from England and with the conviction of a convert he was determined to spread Jenner's gospel of salvation. When Dr. McCurdy was asked to vaccinate the people of Portugal Cove and St. John's early in October 1800 he found that many people in the town had already been vaccinated by Clinch, probably late in 1799 or early in 1800. The material which McCurdy and Clinch used was brought from Jenner by his nephew, George, who was a parson at Harbour Grace before his recall to England to help his uncle defend his discovery. Upwards of seven hundred persons of all ages were vaccinated that year in St. John's. Thus the city has the honour of being

280

the first in the New World where vaccination was used against an epidemic of smallpox. Soon afterwards it was in use at Halifax, and in 1801 the practice spread to the United States.[4]

On 23 October 1811 Drs. John Pennell and Henry H. Tullidge announced in the local papers that, having met to take into consideration the very low and inadequate terms under which the medical practice had been theretofore conducted, they were determined to adopt the following regulations:

> 1st: That each fisherman, shoreman, or single man shall be charged in future 20 shillings ($5.00) per annum instead of 10. 2dly: That families be charged according to their different circumstances; but that no medical man shall make any agreement to take from any family a sum no less than what was paid to the medical gentleman before employed. And we do hereby bind ourselves in the forfeiture of fifty pounds, if either should deviate from the above regulation.

Three years later, 16 June 1814, a Dr. Donergan, who had a surgery and rooms near the Old Chapel that stood on the site of the Star Hall on Henry Street, lost everything in a fire that destroyed some houses in the area. He may have taken over the establishment of Dr. Allan, and is said to have given his name to the Square on which he lived at the back of the Old Chapel before he moved to Harbour Grace.

The newspaper ads of the early nineteenth century tell us much about medical life at the time. Who can imagine a newspaper of today carrying this notice, which appeared in the *Mercantile Journal* for 29 July 1819, and was signed by Drs. Kielley, Proctor, Bunting, Stanilan, Warner, and Bradshaw:

> We the undersigned members of the medical profession have carefully investigated the symptoms under which Mrs. Kenny has laboured as far as it was in our power to do so, and are decidedly of opinion, that she has not laboured under a Gonarrheal affection nor been infected with Lues Veneria [Syphilis]. Her complaint we have no hesitation in pronouncing to have been Fluoralbus [a white discharge from the urethera] of long standing.

This examination took place on July 26. Immediately beneath it there is an ad taken on July 22 by John Kenny to the effect that, "The subscriber will not be accountable for any debts contracted in his name after this date without written order from himself." It is interesting to speculate what domestic storm might have caused Mrs. Kenny to advertise to the town that she did not have venereal disease.

The Dr. Kielley mentioned in the ad was the celebrated Edward

Kielley whose 1838 feud with the local legislature affected the whole of the British Empire. In 1820 Dr. Kielley was again using the local press to reach his fellow surgeons. On December 20 he appealed "To the several regular medical practitioners of the town of St. John's" in these words:

> Gentlemen—For the sake of humanity, I think it my duty to call the attention of every regular medical practitioner in this community, to the case of a man, who about a month ago was under my care for a FUNGOID TUBERCULATED TOE and at that period I recommended amputation in consequence of which he employed____McCoubrey, a barber of this town, who promised to cure it without an operation; but being again called upon this morning, to examine the state of the tumor I found it so much extended that it is my opinion it will be necessary to amputate Three Toes instead of one, and I therefore request your presence to decide, at 12 o'clock tomorrow, at my house. I give this publicity in the hope that it will be the means of putting a stop to the presuming ignorance of this, or any other man endangering the lives of our fellow creatures. I am, gentlemen, your obdt. servant, Edward Kielley, Surgeon.[5]

The doctor's name appeared in the Letters to the Editor of the *Mercantile Journal*, 15 July 1824, when a jury foreman felt compelled to write:

> Gentlemen—A relative of the medical defendant in a later trial requests you will insert in your paper the verdict of the jury which was as follows:—"The jury unanimous in a quitting the Defendant of the charges brought against him in this disgusting action." For self and fellow jurors, John Burke, foreman.

The veil of mystery surrounding this declaration is lifted by a letter which appeared beneath Burke's. Signed by Dr. Warner, a Royal Navy surgeon who had settled in the town, it disavows that he had persuaded Mr. and Mrs. Shea of Twillingate to prosecute Dr. Kielley. He threatens libel action against anyone repeating the story. Warner, who was, by then, in charge of the Riverhead Hospital, ends his letter by speaking of the injury of the accusation to his professional practice.

Dr. Kielley's interesting career reached a momentous climax in 1838 when he was summoned before the House of Assembly on the complaint of John Kent, who was to become the second Prime Minister of the island nation. On Tuesday, August 7, around noon, Patrick Byrne was on his way east along Water Street, to attend to a matter at the Court House for Dr. Kielley. As he passed Kent's (Beck's) Cove the doctor called to him and told him to show Mr.

Kent, who was standing in his doorway, the paper he was carrying. As Kent stood speaking to Byrne, Dr. Kielley came up to them, waved a clenched fist in Kent's face, called him a lying puppy, and said he would pull his nose, and that his privileges would not protect him. This reference was to the privileges of the House where Kent, a Member, had made some statements on the subject of the St. John's Hospital, to which the doctor took exception.

What should have been a case of common assault in the law courts, became something much more than that when Kent had Kielley summoned to the Bar of the Assembly, where he was charged with having violated the privileges of the House by making an attack on one of its Members. The medical man was refused permission to be a witness on his own behalf. Instead he was told his only recourse was to throw himself on the clemency of the Assembly.

Far from being apologetic, Kielley pointed an accusing finger at John Kent and called him a liar and a coward. He was found guilty of a gross breach of the privileges of the House. He replied that he was not aware that his conduct would be considered a breach of the privileges, or he should have been sorry to have acted as he did, and stated that theirs had been a private quarrel between him and Mr. Kent. The upshot was that the doctor was directed to withdraw, and it was resolved that he should remain in the custody of the Serjeant-at-Arms.

The Irish born, ex-naval surgeon, immediately became the centre of Conservative adulation. A rhyme of the time asked,

Oh, did you see Dr. Kielley O,
his boots all polished so highly O,
with his three cocked hats and his double bow knot
and his fiddle to coax the ladies O.[6]

In charge of the Serjeant-at-Arms, complete with mace in hand, Edward Kielley was marched from the Assembly to the prison, in the old Court House opposite Cathedral Street. In the days which followed his arrest the House became involved in a comic opera of irrational absurdities. When, on appeal, Judge Lilly released the doctor on grounds that his commitment was not legal, the Serjeant-at-Arms, still with mace in hand, was seen dragging the respected justice and the High Sheriff, who allowed the appeal, off to house arrest with a cheering mob of their supporters howling along behind. In a meeting at the Mechanics' Hall another faction demanded a commission of inquiry into the state of the administration of justice, claiming that the people of the country never had any confidence in Mr. Lilly, as a judge, and that they never considered him fit by habit or education to preside at the bench.

The Governor finally stepped in and ended the farce. Dr. Kielley's case was heard again in the autumn and two out of three justices gave an opinion in favour of the House. The surgeon appealed this decision to the Privy Council in England and their findings, in his favour, set a precedent by limiting the powers of colonial legislatures throughout the whole of the British Empire.

Kielley's adversary in most of these proceedings, was another physician who, as Speaker of the House, was one of the truly great men of Newfoundland history. William Carson was born in Scotland. He obtained the highest honours in his classes from the College of Edinburgh. Domestic circumstances connected with his wife's family caused him to leave England and he was induced by a number of influential merchants trading in Newfoundland to settle in St. John's.

Dr. Carson is said to have arrived on 23 April 1808, bringing with him letters of the highest commendation, yet was nominated surgeon to the St. John's Volunteers in January that same year. In 1812 Governor Duckworth "peremptorily refused" to allow him to continue in the post. Carson attributed the Governor's attitude to the fact that he had published a brochure of reasons for colonizing Newfoundland. In it he said that the British government should "Give small plots to faithful fishing servants; and keep the Irish here, instead of making the place a stepping stone to the U.S." The agitation begun by Carson in such pamphlets was eventually to lead to the right to settle permanently, independence for the courts, representative government and, finally, responsible government as a free and independent colony.

The Scottish doctor so rankled the bureaucracy that Governor Pickmore wrote of him in 1817: "The invaluable Dr. Carson has been again striving to stir up the common people on account of their wants. He is a rank person, and if possible ought to be removed."[7] It was Pickmore himself who was removed, in a puncheon of rum, the following spring, when a draught ended all his earthly cares.

In a letter to the colonial secretary, Earl Bathurst, in 1817 Carson castigated the British government for the fact that there had been no judge appointed to the Supreme Court for sixteen months. He also claimed people were scared of the Courts of Oyez and Terminer. In the same letter he demanded for dissenting clergy the right to perform marriages. His friend, Bishop Fleming, wrote a letter in support of this appeal.

In 1819 we find Governor Hamilton lamenting "the growth of a strong democratic spirit" and "Subscription of an annual stipend to Dr. Carson for his systematic opposition to the governor." With the departure of Hamilton, and the arrival of Governor Cochrane, Carson's fortunes took a change. Cochrane favoured local government for Newfoundland and supported Carson and others in trying to organize a town council for St. John's. In 1829 the Governor forwarded to London a memorial from William Carson and a Committee of Inhabitants pointing out that "The population and trade of the Island merits a legislature, like other colonies."

These appeals resulted in the granting of representative government in 1833. Ironic as it may seem the doctor was defeated in the first general election for the government that he, more than any other man, had helped to secure. He later won a St. John's seat in a by-election and became Speaker of the House. This brought about the circumstance of his confrontation with his fellow medical practitioner, Edward Kielley.

In 1828 Governor Cochrane asked Carson to be his doctor, but the relationship soon soured when Carson found that some of the governmental medical plums were going into the basket of Dr. Warner, and there were angry exchanges between himself and His Excellency. These unpleasantries increased to a point where the whole community became involved. Meetings, brochures, editorials, and an especially overwrought cleric, Fr. Troy, so worked on the mob that the able and visionary Thomas Cochrane was pelted with mud and insults by the citizenry as he drove to the dock with his daughter on their day of final departure, rather like one of the disgraced nobility of France going in a tumbril to the guillotine.

Cochrane's last official act, in his role of governor, was to renew the leave of absence of Captain Buchan, the naval officer who was his undisguised favourite. One can only speculate, from existing proofs, if the bad blood which developed between the governor and the doctor was not injected with a little poison by a waspish Buchan. In 1899 Buchan and Rev. John Leigh, a Church of England parson, had a brutal whipping inflicted on two men, Butler and Landrigan, for contempt of a surrogate court at Harbour Grace. Carson made much use of this incident in an argument that eventually led to the abolition of the surrogate courts. Buchan was tried on board ship at St. John's. He was found to have acted within his rights but was castigated by the navy for the severity of the punishment.

When the free constitution of Newfoundland was subverted in 1841 by Lord Stanley, more or less as a result of the incidents which grew out of the Kielley case, it was Carson who led the fight for the restoration of the people's right to govern themselves. In 1842 the Amalgamated Legislature was instituted, but it was too late. The island was no longer content. Carson, Morris, and others now demanded full responsible government. In 1848 the original constitution was briefly restored, but by this time William Carson was dead.

The great man passed away on Sunday, 26 February 1843, at the residence of his son on Water Street. The funeral took place the following Friday at three in the afternoon, and he was laid to rest in the Anglican Cathedral churchyard, about a dozen feet from the wall opposite the Court House steps leading to Water Street. The uncared-for plot is marked only by a plaque supplied by the Job family, who were relatives, for attachment to the original tombstone in 1950. The inscription reads: "In memory of Wm. Carson, M.D. who died February 26th, 1843, 73 years. Son of Samuel and Margaret (MacGlacherty) Carson of the Billies, Kirkcudbright, Scotland, who for 35 years strove for the welfare of Newfoundland."

His residence, too, has all but vanished. A modish house named "Billies," it stood at the top of Rostellan Street. The Honourable Laurence O'Brien later bought the property and redesigned the place as an imposing mansion, which he called "Rostellan," a name from his native Ireland. This house still stands, although much changed in character. The Carson-estate cottage, a quiet retreat where the doctor wrote many of his pamphlets and letters demanding self-government, was torn down in 1967 and St. Pius X Boys' School built on the site. Only a few of the trees remain on Elizabeth Avenue.

With Dr. Dobie we have the beginnings of the drugstore business in St. John's. The first of the pharmacy profession was probably William Newman, who announced in the press, 28 July 1814, that he had recently opened a druggist shop in the town near Mr. Stabb's house. Dobie's Chemical Establishment appears to have opened around 1821. It is first mentioned in the papers in January 1822 when the doctor announced he was giving "his advice gratis to all such as may apply from the hours of 10 to 12 each day." He appears to have been taken advantage of by at least one client, Elizabeth Fleming. On December 23, about seven o'clock in the evening, the lady in question went into the shop of Dr. Dobie. While he was occupied in treating a patient behind a partition, she got over the counter and took a trunk containing a hundred pounds in cash and articles to the value of twenty pounds. The doctor instantly missed his money and at once suspected Elizabeth Fleming, who perhaps was next for an appointment. Justice of the Peace, James Blaikie, instituted a search of her house, in the upper part of the harbour, and the loot was found in the chimney bar, where it had been stuffed into three stockings. At first the lady denied everything, but when the trunk was located outside, buried in the snow of her meadow, she confessed.

The Chemical Establishment, located in Baine Johnston's Stone Buildings, opposite McMurdo's Lane of today, was doing so well by 1824 that Dr. Dobie took on as assistant John Walsh, a medical graduate of the University of Edinburgh. Dr. Walsh announced in the press, "Payment for his visit will be expected the moment he has delivered his opinion." His office hours were from eight in the morning to eight o'clock at night.

Thomas McMurdo arrived in St. John's in 1823 and opened a chemist shop on Water Street. In 1838 he appears to have moved across the street, possibly taking over Dr. Dobie's shop. On May 8

McMurdo, surgeon apothecary, took leave in the newspaper to "inform his friends and the public that he may be consulted in the various branches of the profession at his residence, No. 2 Stone Buildings." When burned out in the 1846 fire he found temporary quarters in a shed erected on Gower Street, opposite the foot of Long's Hill. In August 1834 he was living at Mount Ken, on the banks of Stream Ken, now Leary's Brook. McMurdo died in 1880 and the business passed to his son-in-law.

In 1839 the Royal Dispensary opened to the public on April 1, in a building on King's Beach. Intended as a self-supporting institution, it promised to be "attended by a physician and surgeon and to maintain a resident assistant professionally qualified." Donations were sought from the wealthier classes. Fees were five shillings single and ten shillings for a family.

Dr. Dearin, an original character, if ever there was one, was an apothecary and a Member of the House of Assembly for St. John's East, but he was not a doctor. His pharmacy was on the west side of Funny Lane on Water Street, a site occupied during the middle of this century by the Colonial Bookstore. His brother, George, worked with him in the store. His wife was a sister of Hon. Laurence O'Brien Furlong. In November 1853 at Medical Hall, opposite W. & H. Thomas & Co., he was ready to take likenesses by the daguerrotype process that would be a true image of the subject and also to perform all operations in every department of dentistry, fitting with pure mineral teeth either by pivot or spring. He was also selling Pulvermacher's portable hydro-electric medical chain constantly to be worn on the body under the garments supplying electricity or vital energy to the whole body.

The volatile Dr. Dearin was not the first person to perform operations in every department of dentistry in St. John's. In November 1841, A. Plimpton, Dentist, etc., was in residence at Mrs. Gushue's near the Wesleyan Chapel. In an article in the *Journal* of the Canadian Dental Association, Dr. J. P. Millar of Charlottetown, P.E.I., says that the first dentist to announce his arrival in Charlottetown was a Mr. Plimpton in July 1850. He claimed to have been in St. John's, Newfoundland, for ten years previously.

On 15 June 1852, W. L. McKay, repeated an ad he had first placed in the *Newfoundland Express* on May 25 in which he intimated to the ladies and gentlemen of St. John's and the outports that he was prepared to perform all operations on the TEETH in a manner that would ensure satisfaction. Having practised five years in the colony he could give the highest testimonials. Invalids would be attended at their own residences. Others could visit him on Scotland Row. This range of fine homes on Church Hill was where most dentists could be found.

In July 1859, Dr. Macallastar was fully prepared to treat any case of surgical or mechanical dentistry at No. 1 Scotland Row. And so the profession multiplied. It was not until 1893 that the government passed the first Dental Act. It set up a Dental Board of three dentists and four medical men but was inactive until 1900.

Medical doctors got their profession organized much earlier. On 2 May 1867 a Medical Society was begun at St. John's with Dr. H. H. Stabb, who was born at Torquay, Devon, in 1812 and came to Newfoundland in 1832, as first president. This group held a convention at Whitbourne in 1896. During their 1926 convention a public meeting was held in the Casino Theatre to show laymen how medical men kept abreast of the times.[8]

The first hospital we know of in St. John's was one built in 1725 by the navy on the southside about a quarter of a mile east of Long Bridge. An historic marker, which stood on the spot in the early 1970s, told the story in some detail. The following is the inscription:

> A small hospital for the treatment of sick and infirm seamen from the ships of the Royal Navy serving in the Newfoundland squadron was built near this site about 1725. Originally designed for use during the summer when the squadron was on station this building was found inadequate for the increased number of patients from the large squadrons stationed here throughout the American Revolutionary War and was replaced by a larger building erected nearby in 1779. The old hospital was used as a naval storehouse until 1786 when it was pulled down. The new hospital was maintained until Newfoundland ceased to be a separate naval command in 1825. A brewhouse for the brewing of spruce beer to combat scurvy amongst the ships crews was maintained near this site during much of the eighteenth century.

Sickbay Room No. 6 in the gatehouse of the artillery barracks at Fort Townshend served the military as a hospital from November 1780 until some time in 1783. The following year Jonathan Ogden was posted to St. John's from Halifax and on 20 September 1795 we find him writing his colonel requesting "that some place should be provided for a hospital because of the overcrowding of the sick and healthy in the barrack-room." The colonel sent the letter to the governor who directed that a convenient house should be found immediately for the purpose.

Dr. R. W. Harper, who prepared notes for a lecture on the General Hospital in 1934, seems to suggest that the former Government House on Duke of York Street, not far from Fort William, was adapted to Ogden's purposes.[9] He certainly had something to do with the building for Bishop Howley records that Dr. Ogden and Bishop

O'Donel took a lease on the place. Wherever it was, the hospital lasted for ten years.

In 1805 the military opened a new hospital near the present Colonial Building on Military Road. It stood in a garden somewhere near the rear entrance to the Colonial Building. An historic marker not far away, on the east side of Bannerman Road, bears the title, "Old Garrison Hospital," and contains this inscription:

> A single storey wooden building to house 41 patients was erected near this site about 1805 to replace the garrison hospital at Fort William. Condemned, in 1841, it was occupied until 1852 when a new and larger brick building was erected on the site of the General Hospital for the use of the garrison of Newfoundland.

The story as told on this plaque is at variance with the facts contained on maps and in certain records. First, it did not replace the garrison hospital at Fort William but near Fort William. As we have seen, there was no hospital at Fort William for ten years. Second, the maps and records indicate that the hospital could look after thirty-one patients in ten beds. How this was done is a bit of a puzzle. Possibly there were chairs or stretchers to accommodate twenty-one out-patients. The new hospital on Forest Road did have room for the treatment of forty-one patients and this may be the cause of the misinformation. At one o'clock on Friday, 11 July 1852, shortly after it was abandoned, the building was sold by auction on condition that the successful bidder take it down, remove it, and clear the ground.

Meanwhile, Dr. Carson gave a preview of what his adopted country could expect from him by immediately demanding of the authorities a civilian hospital. In July a grand jury observed that "The establishment of a public hospital near the town for the reception of sick and hurt fishermen, seamen and others, is an object truly desired." The success of the Scottish firebrand in this regard is borne out in his letter to Earl Bathurst in 1817, in which he claims, "the Hospital owes its existence to my exertions."

It was not until 1811 that Governor Duckworth acted on the proposals. In a proclamation issued on September 30 he ordered the merchants and masters of servants to stop one penny in the pound of wages for the hospital fund as they would be the principal beneficiaries when the place came into being.

The foundation stone for this hospital was laid by Governor Keats on 4 June 1813, in the grounds of what is now Victoria Park on Water Street West. At that time it was considerably outside the town. The public subscribed the £2,135 it cost to erect the institution.

Of this, the sum of nineteen pounds went "to cover rum for the men who hauled the frame."[10] Though it opened in 1814, under the auspices of a board of directors, there was to be no resident doctor until 1874.

The first medical report is dated from 10 June to 30 August 1814. In that period forty persons were admitted. Of these, twenty-one were discharged as cured, two died, and seventeen remained as patients. Operating costs were £210 (about $2,000). The fee at the hospital was fifteen shillings per week. Drs. Carson, Kielley, and Warner were tolerated as visiting physicians only. In 1820 Warner, who had arrived in St. John's three years earlier and had a practice on Duckworth Street at the foot of King's Road, was appointed as first house surgeon. It was a non-resident post.

That same year the building was eighty pounds in debt and an effort was made to encourage subscriptions by offering anyone who could hand over the sum of six pounds the privilege of sending in one patient a month free of charge. In spite of this encouragement the better off shunned the institution, much preferring to have their operations at home. From what we read they were wise, for the place sounds more like a house of horrors than a house of healing. The insane occupied the basement cells, chained to benches and walls, with straw for bedding. Their food was passed to them by means of tin cans tied to long poles. Food was bad and scanty. There were no fires and the open state of the building was such that it was a wonder the poor patients were not frozen to their beds.[11]

In 1835 Chief Justice Boulton said of the establishment: "I Fear the general condition of the hospital is anything but creditable and that in a proper examination into the conduct of it, a scene of wretchedness and misery will be brought to light which must be heart-rending to anyone whose minds are imbued with the smallest tinge of humanity."[12] By then there were so many poor and destitute being boarded there that there was hardly any room for the sick.

Lunatics were also kept in the jails at St. John's and Harbour Grace. In 1835 Governor Prescott wrote to the Colonial Office asking if they couldn't be taken from the jails and sent to England. The reply was not encouraging.

Things grew worse before they got better. Imagine the scene at the hospital in winter during the 1830s. Those with injuries or operations were crowded next to fever patients who moaned and wept in their contagion. The aged paupers babbled in the corridors. In the unheated building it was so cold that the moisture formed frost on the walls and floors. Snow blew in where windows could not be closed in their frames. In the icy basement the rheumatic insane cried out in agony while those too demented to realize their condition rattled their chains and fouled their bedding.[13]

290

The *Morning Courier* cried loudly for a radical reform of the institution. An editorial on 18 July 1845 summed up conditions at the hospital in these words:

> It is truly heart-rending to behold the accumulation of human misery which is there to be seen. If, gentle reader, you take your stand in the lobby leading to the wards, you will see to your left hand those poor afflicted mortals whom the Almighty has been pleased to deprive of their reason, and then turning to your right hand you will behold those who He has afflicted with disease and sickness. This should no longer be permitted to exist. The lunatics should not be under the same roof as the sick and the dying. We have been told that the nourishment given to the patients is very indifferent, and that the attendance is also very bad, there being only TWO men (and one of thes ∙ only occasionally) a woman and a girl to attend on upwards of 60 persons who, we are informed, have now the misfortune to be placed there.

Later that year, as a result of the *Courier's* editorial and other pressures, there was some relief for the sick when the insane were unshackled and transported to a house recently acquired at Palk's Farm on Waterford Bridge Road. Dr. Stabb was put in charge of the farmhouse he had induced the government to purchase.

Three years later, in his report dated October 1848, the thirty-six-year-old doctor claimed:

> The house at Palk's Farm affords means of cleanliness and some comfort for the insane but little else beside. The means required for classification do not exist, not even to allow of the separation of the noisy from the quiet. No securely enclosed airing ground exists for excited patients—nor the fields necessary for farming operations to employ the able-bodied who pass the greatest part of their time in listlessness, idleness and apathy.

It took eight more years to convince the authorities to provide a proper mental hospital.

The cornerstone for the new institution for the confinement of lunatics, to be known as the Lunatic Asylum, was laid at four o'clock on the afternoon of Wednesday, 27 July 1853, by Governor Hamilton and his Lady. It was put in place by three strokes of a mallet while the band burst forth in a rendition of "The Banks of Newfoundland." The ceremony was followed by "fête" dancing in the open air, "to the spirited music of the band until the shades of evening." Dr. Stabb became superintendent of the asylum, and over the years did much to better the lot of the unfortunates in his charge. The hospital has grown with time until today it is probably the largest institution of its kind in eastern Canada. After well over a hundred years the place was finally given the dignity of a name in the spring of 1973. Lunatic Asylum had given way to Mental Hospital and this in turn became Waterford Hospital, an attractive name, but one that did nothing to honour the great work of Dr. Stabb.

In 1847 Dr. Bunting was appointed to the supervisory post at St. John's Hospital, Riverhead, at a salary of a hundred pounds per year. With the departure of the insane patients things improved, but only slightly. The sick were transported to the hospital by the same springless longcart that carried the dead to the grave. George Garrett performed this chore without assistance.

There was no public morgue in those days, and during the 1840s the government gave a certain standing salary to Nancy Coyle, who lived in Carter's Meadow on Playhouse Hill, opposite Yellow Belly Hill. In terms of today's nomenclature this would be on the corner of Carter's Hill, at Queen's Road, opposite Bates Hill. A man named McNamara afterwards had a cooperage in Mrs. Coyle's corner house. It was Nancy's purpose in life to care for the unidentified dead, especially those bodies found in the harbour. This was no small contract in a badly lit seaport town, thronged with foreign vessels from one end of the year to the other, with rum at a penny a glass, and wharves well greased with seal fat and cod oil. When an unknown or unclaimed body was fished out and examined by the coroner it was taken immediately to Mrs. Coyle's where it was washed decently and laid out. From there it was taken and buried.

Nancy Coyle was as skilful as she was kindhearted and she was said to have brought many a "corpse" back to life in her time. There was a story of a Dutch sailor who was being nailed up in his coffin at Mrs. Coyle's, when he suddenly revived, and after a horn or two of rum, was soon his own man again. Mrs. Coyle's was also a *refugium peccatorum* for all the locked-out young tradesmen who used to board above the shops of their masters in those days. A light in the window, at the top of Yellow Belly Hill, always proclaimed that Mrs. Coyle was engaged in her usual work of mercy, and that there was a sure shelter for all that night.[14]

On 29 June 1849, H.M.S. *Trincomalee* arrived in St. John's from the Southern Shore with some severe cases of smallpox on board. Without asking the permission of the civil authorities, the captain had the stricken sailors transferred from his ship to the hospital, after which he and the boat's crew came ashore. When a howl of protest was heard from the citizenry, the governor censured the captain and ordered the ship to the quarantine ground. The *Patriot* claimed in its pages, "After all the mischief that could possibly be apprehended had been done—His Excellency the Governor ordered her into quarantine." Another such incident later involved H.M.S. *Diamond*.

There was a triumph of sorts recorded at the hospital a day or two before 7 July 1849 when Dr. Samuel Carson, son of Dr. William Carson and a beloved physician, used chloroform, inhaled through a handkerchief, for the first time in Newfoundland and painlessly removed the mortified finger of a woman. The heroine's name is lost to history. Soon afterwards Carson was arrested and charged with "interfering with nature" when he used chloroform on a woman giving birth.

The long-demanded official inquiry into the hospital was finally begun in 1851. Dr. Carson had complained to the tribunal, "the diet of the hospital is defective, inasmuch as necessary changes cannot be effected by private medical men for their own patients, and no wine is allowed." This was certainly a turnabout in official attitude from the early days when one of the rights of the surgeons was that they could finish a bottle of port before proceeding with an operation.

Dr. McKen wanted a General Hospital with four physicians and a surgeon whose duties would be "to enter in a journal a brief history of every case, to prepare and dispense medicines, to visit patients morning and evening, in addition to the visits of the medical officers, and to receive and attend to cases of accidents and emergency." How proud this foresighted man would be of the General Hospital of our day.

The most revealing testimony was that of Dr. Stabb who said in his evidence:

> The building is unfit . . . all the wards are exceedingly cold and the water in one of them was frozen hard on the floor within a few feet of the fire in winter where two [of his] patients lay. They were obliged to have their beds removed during the night in consequence of the snow having beaten in on them. Despite plenty of clothes they could not sleep from excessive cold.[15]

He thought the rambling gable-roof structure too large for a general hospital, which also lacked waiting rooms, indoor bathrooms, hospital apparatus, and even a proper operating room.

Dr. Bunting would have testified except for the fact that he was dead. The first keeper of the institution died the year of his appointment, 1847, when he contracted typhus, while treating an outbreak at the hospital. Plagues of various sorts were no stranger to most towns and cities of the nineteenth century, and St. John's was no exception. Besides the constant threat of smallpox from visiting ships there was

293

typhus, cholera, and diphtheria as well as perpetual outbreaks of measles, typhoid, and scarlet fever.

An item in the *Royal Gazette*, a few days after the Great Fire of 1846, probably passed unnoticed. It said: "Considerable alarm seemed to be experienced in England by the nearer approach of the much dreaded Asiatic Cholera, which, after lurking about Persia for some years, has made its appearance in the Russian territory in Europe." It took eight years for the lurking menace to travel from Russia to Newfoundland.

The first mention of cholera in the newspapers of the plague year, 1854, is on Saturday, May 6, when the brig *Edward* arrived in St. John's from Liverpool, with forty-two passengers on board, taken off a wreck in the Atlantic. The ship docked at Brookings in the east end. A number of the rescued were discovered to be suffering from something more than seasickness. On investigation it was found to be cholera.

Where the shipwrecked vessel sailed from is not clear. The *Edward*, her passengers, and crew were ordered immediately away from the dock to the quarantine ground. The newspapers cried that the authorities were asleep, and the question was asked why the ship wasn't moored on the quarantine ground in the first place. Medical historians say the cholera of 1854 was brought to St. John's by foreign sailors. This would seem to indicate that the shipwrecked persons on the brig *Edward* were the culprits.

In late June the *Patriot* was using its pages to bemoan the fact that the highways and byways of the town were strewn with dead dogs at a time when the season of pestilence was at hand. In an effort to circumvent an epidemic, Dr. Stabb was in front of the Market House on Water Street, bright and early every morning at 7:00 a.m., inspecting, by government order, green fruit and all vegetables.

That summer of 1854 people suddenly found themselves seized with violent vomiting, diarrhoea, severe cramps, and collapse leading to death often within hours. On August 29 the governor gave an order for tents to be erected as a preventive measure to preserve the public health. Certain healthy families were to be removed from the infected locality of the town to these tents intended to house forty persons. Biscuits enough for three days were to be provided and the inmates of the sheds, on the parade grounds at Fort Townshend, were to be moved to lodgings in the town to make room for the persons in the tents.

The cholera raged through the autumn into early winter when it began to die down. By Christmas it was all over. Estimates of the dead range from the eighty-eight mentioned by one source to P. K. Devine's total of eight hundred. It is certain that at least a hundred townspeople were in their graves as a result of the epidemic. On 2

January 1855 Governor Darling wrote Bishop Mullock to say that January 18 had been named as a day of thanksgiving to the Almighty for the deliverance of the populace from cholera. A collection was taken up, and with it a thanksgiving fund was established, and this became the start of a building fund for the General Hospital.

It was during this terrible epidemic that the few Mercy nuns then in St. John's distinguished themselves by going into cholera-ridden homes to tend the helplessly sick and haul out corpses that nobody else would touch so that they could be placed in coffins that were dumped on the streets. In 1847 Sister Joseph, one of two Mercy nuns in the town, died of typhus she had contracted from a sailor she was attending at the St. John's Hospital.

In March 1859 diphtheria broke out in Burin district. By April it had spread to Placentia and St. Mary's Bay in spite of all precautions. It did not take long to reach the capital and this time hundreds died before the disease passed from the island.

A smallpox epidemic broke out in the outports in 1863. In June, a case was reported in an isolated house at Harbour Grace and a family was found to be infected at Portugal Cove. Everyone feared an epidemic. On official orders, the family at the Cove was removed to St. John's Hospital, and vaccination of the town and outports followed. This checked the spread of the disease. That year the governor directed that a suitable site should be found for a smallpox hospital. There had been one, apparently, in the east end, but it had burned in 1856. Some believe the 1863 hospital was the one located on the south side of Water Street, just west of Patrick Street, in an area later occupied by the gasworks. This would make it convenient to the hospital across the way.

Dr. Harper, in his historical notes on the General Hospital, says that St. John's in the 1850s was in step with the times. Heroic battles were being waged on both sides of the Atlantic to try to convince governments of the need for hospitals. Between 1854 and 1856 Florence Nightingale was fighting her own war against the army brass in the Crimea to try to improve the appalling neglect of the British soldiers who were wounded.[16]

In the meantime improvements were being carried out at the old institution. There were fireplaces and some additions that made room for eight wards, with sixty-six beds, and accommodation for a hundred patients without overcrowding. The male and female patients had their own wards, and fever patients were isolated. In 1856 water and gas mains were installed. Charles Fox Bennett took the directors of the hospital to court, to try to stop the institution from using the river that ran past his brewery to flush away sewage, but he lost the case.

Mention has already been made of the sheds at Fort Townshend parade, known as "The Camps." These rows of flimsy wooden structures, erected to provide temporary housing for victims of the Great Fire of 1846, became a kind of poor house when the fire sufferers moved out. R. J. Parsons, in speaking of The Camps in the House of Assembly in 1852, said, "There are 40 paupers in the camps. Six sleep in a room. Each person is allowed half a pound of soap. They drink kiln-dried tea without molasses and get one pound of beef on Sundays. They sleep on canvas cases filled with straw."[17] The war department made a number of attempts to have them removed and claimed rent for the property from the governor.

In 1859 it was decided to remove the paupers from "The Camps" and the destitute cases from the hospital. James Tobin, a well-to-do merchant and holder of government posts, wrote to His Excellency, offering a very eligible portion of Monkstown Field, which he had named for his birthplace, Monkstown, now a suburb of south Dublin, on lease forever at an annual rent of fifty-two pounds, with an option to buy. The lot measured 250 feet along Monkstown Road, and 150 feet back to Barnes Lane in Turbid's Town. He felt it was especially suited to the purposes of a home for the aged because of being close to the various churches and to the downtown area. Tobin named three of the streets in the area after his children—Catherine, William, and James. As the Irish landowner was not in favour at the time, his offer was refused, and a plot of land in the west end, behind the St. John's Hospital, was acquired. In October 1805 the land had been granted to Janet Cormack, who is believed to have been the mother of W. E. Cormack. The pauper's home was erected on this site at the east side of what was to become known as Poorhouse Lane.

A large building was constructed, and on 19 September 1861 the Board of Works was instructed to remove into it immediately, the inmates of the camps on the Parade Ground at Fort Townshend, and to admit persons wholly friendless, having no property. A matron was to be selected from among the inmates and paid a small salary. It was suggested that possibly the keeper of the sheds might be hired for the role of matron. She was to be permitted one assistant but only if absolutely necessary.

Under the low-beamed ceilings of the Poorhouse the aged and infirm of St. John's lived for over a hundred years. By the time of its demise conditions there had become quite primitive. It was pounded into oblivion in 1965 when Hoyles Home was opened on Portugal Cove Road. Again a building of great antiquity, one that was possibly as old as the United States of America, was razed with little outcry from an unconcerned public.

By 1864 things were looking up at the old hospital, though the matron and domestics, who slept in the basement where water soaked into the rooms through the foundation walls, causing considerable damp, complained of rheumatism and other diseases. Four years later a cook gave some engaging disclosures to the inquiry, then in its eighteenth year. In speaking of Dr. McKen she said:

> ... he never missed one day for the past 4 years. He come to the hospital never later than 10.00 a.m. and never remains later than 12 midnight. We go to bed at 10, rise at 6. There are two night nurses, two up and down, two in the fever wards.... The keeper leaves when the doctor leaves—he lives near St. Patrick's chapel. I sleep in the basement storey. There are 3 beds in the room. It is not wholesome. The fever nurses sleep upstairs. 6 sleep in the room.... Bennett, the messenger is there to go for the doctor if required—and Michael Avery also acts as a messenger. They sleep in the Long Room among the chronic patients.[18]

It is obvious from evidence given by Dr. McKen that the place must have been known as the pest house. He testified: "Bad as the hospital is as an institution for the treatment of the sick, it is by no means deserving the designation of a 'pest house'. The whole mortality out of 705 patients admitted into the hospital for 1866 was 14½%." The inquiry also turned up the information that some patients had to sleep two to a bed. The fever wards, which could accommodate eight, sometimes had forty cases. There was one nurse to thirty patients. Some of the nurses were former patients who stayed on to help. The only communication was by shouting as there were no bells. An offensive, suffocating, and poisonous smell pervaded the whole building from want of drainage, ventilation, and overcrowding. The floor seams had opened so much that in scrubbing the upper floors the water drained down on those in the beds below. Defective chimneys filled the wards with smoke. The stench from patients suffering loathsome diseases was so bad that those who were able to move fled, and several almost fainted. In spite of these apparent drawbacks there was an average of a hundred patients in the institution.

When the garrison was withdrawn in 1870 the military vacated the hospital on Forest Road and it was taken over for temporary use by people of the town. Because of its limited size only male patients could be accommodated. There were defects in the drainage and the water supply was such that it could be dangerous to a large number of users. It was soon apparent that alterations would have to be made. On 7 March 1871 the patients were sent to St. George's Barracks at Walsh's Square on Signal Hill. By winter they were back in their remodelled quarters which now had twenty beds, in three wards, and the novelty of indoor toilets. In 1874 two wings were added for male patients, with fifteen beds in each. There were also two small isolation wards. Two years later another wing was opened for male patients and the old wing set aside for the use of females.

The walls of this old wing were still unplastered and it was impossible to remove the dust from the crevices without hauling down a shower of whitewash. The rough beams in the walls were uncased and the unpainted windows had never gone beyond priming. Altogether, there was room for between fifty and sixty patients of both sexes. Prisoners, from across the way, helped build a road to the place that was finished in 1885.

In spite of the primitive conditions, by today's standards, not one of the unusually large number of surgical operations in 1879 resulted in the death of the patient. There were, however, a number of instances of blood poisoning following operations, which were performed in the ward, behind a baize screen and it was impossible to separate the septic from the nonseptic cases. It was decided to provide the new hospital with an operating room.

In 1880 an ice house was added, trees were planted on the grounds, and a carriage house was erected to protect the doctors' horses and carriages from the rain on a wet day. A porch was built over the southern entrance. In 1881 the growing complex was first called the General Hospital.

When the male patients were moved from Riverhead to Forest Road in 1871, much of the old building was converted to use as a fever hospital. It continued to serve in this capacity until 1888 in which year the authorities decided the building was a menace to the health of the town and ordered its destruction. It vanished in smoke and flame on December 28 after nearby houses were first hosed down to prevent a general conflagration. Old-timers claimed that, as the building was put to the torch, the bacteria could be heard groaning a long, long distance away.

That day the *Evening Telegram* published the following account of the burning:

> The Old Hospital at Riverhead, this morning between 4 and 7 o'clock, went up in fire and smoke. There was no large collection of spectators. The roof was removed. The fire companies, with several streams of hose, surrounded the pile to prevent the generation of too great heat. So with the close of the old year, this old landmark is gone, but contrary to the prevailing sentiment which regrets the disappearance of old landmarks, no one will be sorry to see that this one is gathered among the memories of the misty past.

Time has negated the *Telegram's* opinion and the old building, today, would have been a curiosity that could give us priceless insights into the medical treatment of a hundred and fifty years ago. It would have made an interesting museum, with the implements and memorabilia of the Carsons, Kielley, Warner, Bunting, Crowdy, Stabb, McKen, and the others who walked its corridors and became the legends of the past.

One cannot help wondering what these doctors of old would think of their profession today. Included in the 1971 Medicare Report are over 460 doctors and about 60 dentists in the province. Nine of the doctors earned between $90,000 and $150,000. The average gross fee for service payments to doctors in 1971 was $40,000 to $50,000.

A tragic example of medical neglect occurred on the evening of 17 September 1910. A man named Dillon, who lived on the southside, came home in drink, as they used to say. He upset an oil lamp and caught himself and his house on fire. He was removed from the burning building, to a neighbour's house, in great agony. A telephone at Bowring's mill, across the way, was utilized at once to call up several city doctors but none responded. For more than an hour and a half the anguished man lay on his neighbour's floor and was finally taken to hospital without any medical aid being procured. He was met on the way by Doctor Rendell, who had answered the call, but he died a few hours later in hospital. The *Evening Chronicle* called the incident "deplorable."

The fashionable disease among courtesans, around the turn of the century, was consumption. In theatres encircling the globe, audiences watched entranced as Dumas's Lady of the Camellias coughed convulsively, and in opera houses they listened breathlessly as Violetta hacked away on her deathbed to the strains of Verdi's music. In real life, tuberculosis was a tragic infirmity. Many thousands of Newfoundlanders died before it was brought under control.

The first sanitarium for the treatment of the disease in St. John's was probably the old Signal Hill Hospital. Built as a barracks, supposedly in 1792, the stucco-covered brick structure stood on the site of the present Cabot Tower parking lot at the edge of Ross's valley, on the ocean side. Both smallpox and consumptive patients were sent there in 1898. It averaged between twenty and thirty tubercular cases, which appear to have all been men.

On 16 August 1910 the I.O.D.E. opened a cottage hospital for women sufferers. Located in a small house on Blackmarsh Road it had six beds, but the demand soon increased this number to sixteen beds. The following year, Dr. H. H. Rendell, was appointed superintendent of a new sanitarium for both sexes that was in the planning stages. In June 1912, W. D. Reid, a son of the railway magnate, offered to build and equip a sanitarium in St. John's, for fifty thousand dollars, but his offer was not accepted.

Bowcock's Farm, on Topsail Road, was occupied as a sanitarium, by fifty-two patients in 1916. The men came from Signal Hill Hospital and the women from the I.O.D.E. Hospital. Extensions were added to the sanitarium and a proper tuberculosis centre was developed for treatment of the disease. In 1928, X-ray equipment was installed. Around 1957 patients were moved next door, to the recently abandoned Royal Canadian Navy Hospital, built in the meadow west of the sanitarium, during World War II. The buildings on Bowcock's Farm were then taken over for use as an annex by the Hospital for Mental and Nervous Diseases.

The old R.C.N. wartime structures finally closed their doors to tuberculosis patients on 7 May 1973, and on May 8 the sanitarium began a new phase in the former St. Clare's Hospital building, opposite Patrick Street, as a treatment centre for non-tubercular respiratory diseases, such as emphysema and asthma, as well as the centuries-old enemy of Newfoundlanders.

Early in 1917 a place for the care of ex-servicemen, suffering from tuberculosis, was opened beyond the northern suburbs of the city. It was begun with funds raised from lectures given by Phil Jensen, a returned soldier with an adventurous story to tell. Called Jensen's Camp, it was abandoned when Escasoni Hospital, for the treatment of all ex-servicemen, was opened in Archibald Emerson's former residence, "Escasoni," on Portugal Cove Road between Hoyles Home and MacDonald Drive. The place was named for the Emerson ancestral residence in Nova Scotia.

Saturday, 18 December 1920, around 4:45 p.m., a defective chimney caused an outbreak of fire at the Signal Hill Hospital. The caretaker and his wife fled. A nurse and two nursing assistants, who were off duty and resting, only just managed to escape. There were no patients in the building. Firemen were unable to get up the hill to help fight the fire, because of the condition of the road bed, so the building burned until nearly midnight when there was nothing left. This blaze not only destroyed an ancient barracks, but it also wiped out one of the most historic places in the world, for it was in a downstairs room, at the northwest corner of the old hospital building, that Marconi had received the first wireless message to span the Atlantic.

Following World War I there was another hospital for wounded ex-servicemen in the reconverted Empire Barracks, on Water Street, fronting the east side of Hill o' Chips. This brick building was originally the Empire Woodworking Factory. The hospital occupied the upper floor of the two-storey structure, with a reception hall and cloakrooms on the Water Street level. The basement housed 1,000 rifles, 700 German guns, and 150,000 rounds of ammunition. Early on the afternoon of 19 November 1919 the hospital was discovered on fire by Surgeon Major Knight, the physician in charge. The fire was then a tiny blaze in the northeast corner, caused by badly insulated wiring igniting the woodwork. The fire hall was not fifty yards away, but by the time the firemen got there the place was beyond saving. Invalid soldiers, who were stretcher cases, were carried out with great difficulty by soldiers working in the various departments, and by the nurses under the watchful eye of the matron, Nurse Catherine Fitzpatrick, one of the famous Fitzpatrick sisters, of Placentia.

The only person injured in the Empire Hospital blaze was a cook who got his hands burned. A bakery, located at the back, caught fire but the blaze was quickly extinguished. The hospital building, which had been purchased for twelve thousand dollars, had an additional value of thirty thousand in hospital equipment at the time of the fire. Only ten thousand of this total was covered by insurance.

Sudbury Hospital opened in a building set back from Water Street, behind the small West End Post Office, in 1923. Originally called Sudbury Hall, the house was erected on the site of the residence of Captain Blaney (later Edward L. Moore's Exmouth Cottage) by C. R. Thompson, manager of the Newfoundland Boot & Shoe Factory.

It was taken over in 1923 by the Government of Newfoundland and became Sudbury Hospital, a physiotherapy treatment centre for disabled servicemen of World War I. An unfortunate extension was added to the house at the back, which destroyed the impressive Victorian lines of the Thompson home. Sudbury Hospital continued to rehabilitate veterans until 31 December 1927 when the building was closed. Under the direction of Dr. N. S. Fraser, it became the first children's hospital in Newfoundland.

During World War II a Merchant Navy Hospital opened in the basement of the King George V Institute with Nurse Elizabeth Moore, of Bay de Verde, as matron. This unit was later moved to Sudbury Hospital where it continued for many years. Nurse Moore died suddenly at the hospital in 1953 and eventually the institution was closed and became a custodial home for seriously retarded children.

Ex-servicemen had to wait thirty-four years for another hospital. It was not until February 1961 that plans were prepared for a Veterans Pavilion to be attached to the General Hospital on Forest Road.

In 1892, at the instigation of Judge Prowse, a smallpox hospital was constructed, down in Ross's Valley, between Signal Hill and the sea. The valley was named for Captain Ross, R.E., commanding the Royal Engineers in 1806. If it was the judge's intention to completely isolate those suffering from the pox he certainly succeeded admirably, for the building was so totally inaccessible, either by land or sea, that it was used only twice. Three sailors from the brigantine *Grace* were quarantined there in 1899 when their vessel arrived from Europe with the disease on board, and a servant girl from the Crosbie Hotel became a patient, in 1903, when a guest at the hostelry was found to be infected.

Known as "Prowse's Folly," one newspaper said of the hospital, "It would take a man of great nerve to go to the place after dark." It was abandoned and fell into ruin. By 1911 the doors sagged open and all traces of window glass had vanished. On May 6, of that year, it was believed some boys entered on Saturday afternoon, and lit a fire in one of the rooms. By 9:30 p.m., the whole of the structure was in flames. There was no way for the fire department to reach it, so the place burned unmolested until midnight, watched by numerous people who lined the wharves of the city to marvel at the scarlet spectacle that illuminated the Narrows.

As mentioned, most smallpox patients were housed in Signal Hill Hospital, near Cabot Tower, until 5 April 1906 when a fever wing was opened in a building next to the General Hospital and all infectious diseases were sent there. From 1871 to 1888 old St. John's Hospital, on Water Street West, had housed fever patients. The hospital for consumptives, near Cabot Tower, also took fever cases for brief periods.

Epidemics were not confined to the early days of St. John's. The age-old scourge of typhus broke out again in January 1911. Two boys on Pope Street had been reported ill on 24 December 1910. On Boxing Day, December 26, the lads were taken to Signal Hill Hospital, where it was discovered that several members of the family had died before the disease was diagnosed. It was the first outbreak of the malady in twenty years. The lice and fleas that spread the contagion were busy vermin. By January 24 there were thirteen cases in hospital, and some suspected cases were discovered at Witless Bay.

The residences of the stricken were placed under interdict and guarded by watchmen to make sure nobody entered or left. A fireman on the S.S. *Portia* returned home to find his house forbidden to him. He fortified himself with drink and, attacking the guard at his door, entered the house. Reinforcements appeared from the police and the man was not permitted to leave the place until the quarantine expired. By the end of March the worst seemed to be over. In February there were reports of smallpox around the bay, and a case was discovered on the S.S. *Bruce*, but the disease was kept out of the city.

In 1918 the pandemic scourge, known as Spanish influenza, added a large number of Newfoundlanders to its toll of twenty million deaths around the world. Within weeks after the first of the flu bugs reached St. John's, thousands were afflicted. All theatres and places of public amusement were closed from October 9 by special order. Then, on October 21, Dr. N. S. Fraser, acting Medical Health Officer, published the following order: "Notice is hereby given that owing to the epidemic of influenza it has been considered advisable to close the city churches until further notice." All houses of worship were still closed on Sunday, November 10, the day before the Armistice, when many would have liked to offer a prayer of thanksgiving.

By Armistice Day it was reported that the worst was over and theatres, churches, and other public buildings were permitted to reopen on November 18. The Star used the period of enforced closing to renovate. The Casino had to delay the opening of the Klark-Urban

302

to the non-arrival of the express. The play opened on Tuesday night with the added attraction of the Catholic Cadet Corps band.

The city seemed to be rid of the bug by mid-December, but hundreds had died in the island. St. John's counted sixty-two deaths from the flu and the average age of the victims was twenty-four years. For some reason the virus was more attracted to youth than age. There were nine deaths on October 24 alone, when the epidemic was at its height. For the week of October 28 a total of twenty-eight influenza deaths were reported in the city. Many thousands were left with bad hearts and rheumatic fever, which contributed to their deaths in later years, so that the actual total was many hundreds of lives.

One of those who died, on October 26, was a Newfoundland nurse on leave from England. Ethel Dickinson was a teacher who volunteered to nurse overseas in World War I. In August 1918 she came home for a rest. While she was in St. John's the Spanish influenza epidemic reached the city. The hospitals did not have enough beds for the victims so an emergency unit was set up in the King George V Institute on Water Street. We are told that nurse after nurse caught the infection but all survived save Ethel Dickinson. She devoted herself wholeheartedly to serving the sick in the wards, often going without food and sleep. She tended hundreds until she caught the germ and died.

Those she nursed, and others, felt Miss Dickinson's sacrifice should be commemorated. On 26 October 1920, on the second anniversary of her death, a monument was unveiled at Cavendish Square, opposite the Newfoundland Hotel, by Governor Harris. The cross of grey Aberdeen granite cost four thousand dollars which was given in small amounts. On the base was the inscription: "This shaft, surmounted by the world emblem of sacrifice is set up by a grateful public in memory of Ethel Dickinson, volunteer nurse, who in the great epidemic of 1918 gave her life while tending patients at King George V Institute, St. John's."[19] At the back were the words: "In honour also of those who nursed with her in the imminent shadow of death." Imprinted on the north and south sides of the memorial are two quotations: "And I will give thee a crown of life" and "Be faithful unto death."

In 1898, Margaret Rendell, a graduate of Johns Hopkins in Baltimore, became Newfoundland's first trained nurse and was appointed matron of the General Hospital. That year, Mary Southcott, another native Newfoundlander went to train as a nurse in England. Within a year Miss Rendell married George Shea, a mayor of St. John's, and retired. They were the parents of Captain Ambrose Shea, private secretary to several lieutenant-governors. Other matrons followed Miss Rendell until 1902 when Mary Southcott returned from

England and took charge of the female staff at the General as Nursing Superintendent.

In 1903 Miss Southcott opened the hospital's first School of Nursing. Her pioneer work bore fruit and on 22 June 1911 she had the pleasure of seeing the foundation stone for a nurse's residence laid behind the old General Hospital as part of the coronation celebrations for King Edward VII.

Mary Southcott again saw history made on the afternoon of Saturday, 13 June 1913, when she took the chair at a meeting of nurses and an association was formed of which she was elected the first President. It died out but was later revived as the Newfoundland Nurse's Association. In 1914, as a result of differences with the hospital superintendent, Dr. Leonard Keegan, she resigned from the General and opened a private hospital at 28 Monkstown Rd.

The father and uncle of Mary Southcott were house builders who came from Exeter, Devon. They built and occupied Exon House, a large mansion on Strawberry Marsh Road that became an Anglican orphanage. Mary's parents, John and Pamela Southcott, moved to 28 Monkstown Road, a house which her father built. The pioneer nurse died on 29 October 1943. In 1946 a new thirteen-storey nurse's residence at the General was named Southcott Hall in her memory.

Another St. John's girl, Marion Stone, made medical history when she became the first nurse in the world to have a patient in an iron lung. In 1929 Miss Stone was nursing in Boston when Harvard's Dr. Philip Drinker invented the iron lung for a boy in New York who died of infantile paralysis before it could be used. Instead, an honours student at Harvard, Barrett Hoyt, contracted the disease and was taken to Peter Bent Brigham Hospital in Boston where a floor was devoted to his care. The nurse placed in charge of this first iron lung patient was Marion Stone who found herself part of an international story when stars like the Marx Brothers came to the hospital to perform for her patient. Miss Stone became a calendar girl when the First National Bank of Boston used a painting, on its 1929 calendar showing Dr. Drinker standing by young Hoyt in the iron lung while Miss Stone adjusted an apparatus in the background.

In the late years of the last century John and Margaret English lived in a house on the south side of Water Street, opposite St. John's Lane. Mrs. English accepted what were then called "paying guests." On 3 May 1888 their daughter, Mary Theresa, entered the Presentation Convent at Cathedral Square under the name of Sister Clare.

One day this nun was visited by a man named John Funichon who had been a boarder with her mother. Funichon had fallen in love with Mary Theresa's friend, a Miss Summers, and had returned from the gold rush in the Yukon, where he struck it rich, to claim his heart's desire. The bride and groom visited Sister Clare and Funichon gave her a gift of a rosary made of forty gold nuggets[20] and an interest in a Klondike claim.

The sister had been dreaming for some time of establishing a home in St. John's that would serve as a hostel for outport girls with nowhere to go in their off hours. She decided to sell the rosary to earn funds for the hostel, and an American master in the Knights of Columbus, John H. Reddin, who was visiting St. John's, from Denver, Colorado, offered to buy the prayer beads as a jubilee gift from the Knights to Cardinal Gibbons of Baltimore. Sister Clare asked a hundred dollars. J. J. Flaherty, supreme knight of the Knights of Columbus, visited St. John's on vacation the following summer and gave Sister Clare, to her astonishment, a cheque for a thousand dollars.

A piece of property named Father Waldron's Farm, on LeMarchant Road, had been left to another Sister Clare, a niece of the priest, and through her it came into the possession of the Presentation Order. A corner of the property had been sold to Hon. E. M. Jackman, a Minister of Finance and Customs better known as Jackman the Tailor. On his piece of land, at the corner of LeMarchant Road and St. Clare Avenue he erected an elegant private home which he called "The White House." On 11 July 1912 Sister Clare is said to have used some of her funds to purchase land on LeMarchant Road adjoining Father Waldron's Farm and the Jackman property. However, before she could proceed any further with her plans she was called to a lengthy private meeting in the convent parlour with Archbishop Howley.

When she returned to her room it was obvious from the crestfallen look on her face that something unpleasant had transpired. She turned to her secretary and said, "Send it all to the Mercy Order." When the secretary protested packing up the receipts, funds, and papers and sending them to the Mercy Convent she was told it was the Archbishop's wish and she must obey. Despite the fact that Sister Clare had drawn from the prelate the promise that her original purpose would not be forgotten, the order seems to have come as a severe shock to her. Already in poor health, she began to fail and died shortly afterwards.

The Archbishop's motives are not easy to understand. His happy relations with the Presentation Sisters as a priest seem to have soured soon after his elevation to the purple. Perhaps the young Irish Superior of the order, Sister Mary Cecilia Buckley, did not make the proper fuss over him on his attainment of churchly rank. Great men have been known to be hurt by insignificant slights. When it came time to elect the successor to Sister Buckley the Bishop asked that he appoint a Superior and the request could not be denied. He gave the nod to Sister Mary Theresa Halpin and a more unpopular choice could not have been made.

Dr. Howley later acquired The White House from E. M. Jackman for five thousand dollars and began to renovate it as a hostel for working girls. His Lordship had acquired a particular fondness for the Mercy Order and it was to these sisters that he entrusted the operation of The White House. The residence opened on 29 September 1913 but it did not draw the young ladies from the dances at the British Hall and the movies at the Nickel and Casino. After half a dozen years it was obvious the hostel was a financial failure and would have to be abandoned, as happened to a similar venture by the Sisters of Service on Garrison Hill in the 1960s.

On the death of Dr. Howley, Edward Patrick Roche, a sickly priest whom many feared would not live to be consecrated, was appointed Archbishop. He decided the time had come for the opening of a Roman Catholic hospital in St. John's and several Mercy sisters were sent away to prepare for the task of administering such an institution. On 21 May 1922 Archbishop Roche, in a private and informal ceremony attended only by sisters of the Mercy and Presentation Orders, dedicated the building as St. Clare's Hospital[21] in memory of Sister Mary Clare. It boasted an operating room and accommodation for thirty patients. The place was open to all sick persons of any religion, recommended by a physician and prepared to pay the fees. The first patient was Sister Mary Benedict McKenzie of the Presentation Order.

In 1939 a four-storey concrete building was opened on the farm property, opposite Patrick Street, boasting a hundred beds. A seven-storey brick structure was added to the complex on St. Clare Avenue on 8 January 1962, at a cost of $2,652,000. It contained 208 beds and a new maternity floor. In 1967 further expansion was announced and work was commenced on a huge extension, to the west of the existing buildings, at a cost of approximately fourteen million. Labour strikes, and a fire in the shell, retarded completion of the project. The three hundred-bed addition was finally opened on 8 September 1972.[22]

Next day the Government of Newfoundland announced that the 1939 building at St. Clare's would be vacated by the patients and it would replace the old Hospital for Chest Diseases on Topsail Road sometime in the spring of 1973.

Around 1920 Sir Marmaduke Winter headed a campaign to raise money for the building of a maternity hospital on the west corner of Pleasant Street and LeMarchant Road, to be operated by the Salvation Army. The cornerstone was laid on 20 December 1921 and Grace Maternity Hospital opened in 1923, with twenty-two beds and a staff of fifty people, under the supervision of Staff Captain E. J. Fagner. In December 1954 a new wing was opened and this added more beds. A seven-storey annex, containing beds for an additional four hundred patients, opened on 26 August 1966. The small maternity hospital, begun fifty years earlier, had grown into an important general hospital medical complex.

With the departure of the United States armed forces from St. John's, in 1961, and the closing of Fort Pepperrell, the base hospital was turned over to the Newfoundland government and reopened in 1966 as a hospital for sick children. The premier had hoped to name it in honour of President Kennedy's daughter, Caroline. However, the American Royal Family frowned on such practices where the progeny were concerned, and the institution was named instead, for a Boston physician, Charles H. Janeway, who had advised on the setting up of the children's centre. While not negating Dr. Janeway's contribution, many felt the hospital should have been named for one of the famous medical men in Newfoundland history, such as Dr. Cluny Macpherson.

Born in St. John's, Cluny Macpherson was the epitome of the old-fashioned family doctor who dedicated his life to the treatment of his patients. He did everything from treating mumps, to sewing up wounds, to delivering babies. At the time of the outbreak of World War I he was a captain in the Methodist Guards and head of the St. John Ambulance Brigade in Newfoundland. He was placed in charge of a team of eight local doctors who examined the first recruits for the Royal Newfoundland Regiment. They won fame as the Blue Puttees, or the "first 500." Enlistment was begun on 21 August 1914 at the Church Lads Brigade armoury, and on that first night Dr. Macpherson and his team examined seventy-four volunteers.[23]

Captain Macpherson later joined the regiment in England. It was a proud day for the Scottish-Newfoundlander when he accompanied the Royal Newfoundland to Edinburgh in March 1915 to garrison the ancient castle.

Shortly after midnight on 22 April 1915 at Ypres the Germans released the first poisonous fumes of chlorine gas over the British and Canadian lines. The result was that thousands of unsuspecting soldiers died in terrible agony. The first mask to combat the dangers of gas attack was invented in May by Cluny Macpherson. It consisted of a hood of khaki flannel cloth with a mica-covered opening for the eyes. Worn beneath the helmet it covered the entire head and was tucked into the neck of the uniform. In June, film was substituted for the less substantial mica eye opening. The development of the tube gas helmet followed, and finally, the box respirator was evolved. The original mica gas mask, invented by Captain Macpherson, is on display today in the Military Museum at the top of the Confederation Building in St. John's.

In 1957 Dr. Macpherson's son, Campbell, became Lieutenant-Governor of Newfoundland. The old gentleman was honoured by Memorial University in 1962 when he was awarded a doctorate in

307

Science at the convocation. With Sir Thomas Roddick, a native of Harbour Grace, he shares the honour of being one of the two most distinguished Newfoundland-born medical men.

In 1967 a Faculty of Medicine was established at Memorial University with Dr. Ian Rusted as Dean. It received its first students in 1969. A preliminary study in 1963 had advised that a medical school in Newfoundland appeared both feasible and desirable. The Mac-Farlane Commission, appointed by the University in 1965 to do a formal Feasibility Study, recommended that a Medical School and Health Sciences Centre should be developed at Memorial. Overlapping with this study was Lord Brain's Royal Commission on Health Services for Newfoundland which reported that "the provision of adequate medical services for Newfoundland in the future cannot be achieved without a medical school in the province."

In the spring of 1972, work was begun on the construction of a Health Sciences complex, on the university campus, north of Prince Philip Drive. The forty-five-million-dollar project was an undertaking of the provincial and federal governments. The plan included a large four-hundred-bed university hospital to replace the aging General Hospital. The complex was expected to be occupied fully by 1976, and it was estimated that patients, visitors, staff, and students would total approximately four thousand persons.

The University's Faculty of Arts and Science opened a school of nursing in 1966. The curriculum, leading to the Bachelor of Nursing degree consisted of one year of pre-professional courses followed by four years of professional study. Grace Hospital had established a school of nursing in 1929, followed by St. Clare's in 1947.

The Newfoundland Medical Care Commission, which ended its first year of operation on 31 March 1970, pays for all doctors' visits, whether office, home, or hospital; all X-ray and test fees; and all ward rates for hospitalization for every person living in the province. In 1971 the commission and the provincial government paid out nearly fifteen million dollars to doctors in Newfoundland for an average of thirty-two thousand each. The profession had come a long way from the days of Major Lloyd's "barbarity to the surgeon," less than two hundred years before on that October day in 1811, when Drs. Pennell and Tullidge decided to raise their fees from two-fifty to five dollars per annum.

7

By Sports Like These

Rennie's Mill on the banks of Rennie's River around 1890. Visible in the background are the Colonial Building and Government House. The small round pool in the foreground became Rennie's River Swimming Pool. (Courtesy St. John's City Hall)

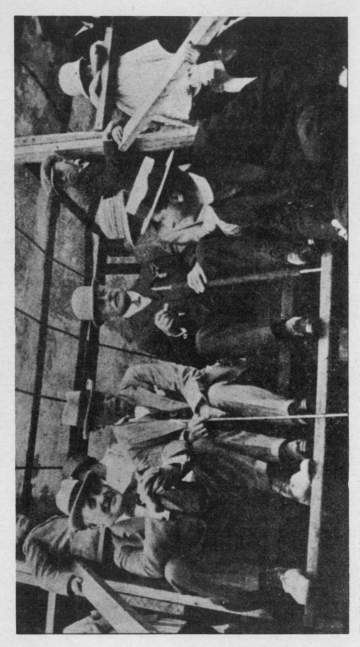

The Haig Regatta of 1924. Watching the boat races from the steps of a pavilion on the shores of Quidi Vidi Lake are Hon. W. J. Higgins, K.C., Governor Sir William Allardyce, Earl and Countess Haig, and Father T. Nangle, Chaplin to the Royal Newfoundland Regiment in World War I. (Courtesy Provincial Reference Library - Newfoundland Section)

This photograph is captioned "The Races—Quidi Vidi—1885". Three boats are seen at the start of a race. The tents along the north shore of the lake offer side-show attractions. (Courtesy Newfoundland Provincial Archives)

313

The Feildian team which won the third Boyle Trophy in 1906. The team members are—(front) Jim Simms, (Justice) J. Alex Winter, Bob Simms (father of Drs. Bob and Doug), C. E. A. Jeffrey (editor of Evening Telegram), Harry Dickinson (brother of Ethel). (Back) Gordon Boone, W. W. Blackall (remembered in Blackall Academy), Hal Hutchings. (Courtesy Newfoundland Provincial Archives)

While the boys were away in World War I the oldtimers returned to play cricket. Here is the Shamrock Team of 1917. (Front) Gus Stafford, Nix Vinicombe, E. T. Furlong, and a man Ryan. (Back) Gerry Savage, Unknown, Unknown, Unknown, Pat Berrigan, Ken Trenchard, John Donnelly and John S. Keating. (Courtesy Newfoundland Provincial Archives)

The finish of the championship race of the day at the annual regatta on Quidi Vidi Lake, 4 August 1875, as depicted in the Canadian Illustrated News. (Courtesy Public Archives of Canada)

316

By Sports Like These

By sports like these are all their cares beguil'd ...
OLIVER GOLDSMITH, *The Traveller*

One of the most unusual sports events to take place in St. John's is mentioned in an early issue of the *Royal Gazette* which began publishing in 1807. A notice for Robert Brine's Tavern, at his farm between present-day Brine Street and LeMarchant Road, advises: "A main of cocks will be fought on Tuesday next the 29th inst., at 3 o'clock in the afternoon, for five guineas a battle or five guineas the main or odd battle. Rules in every respect conformable to those practised at the Royal Pit and Newmarket." Cockfights were probably not unusual in the days before newspapers.[1] The ancient name for Craigmillar Ave., starting at the Crossroads, was Cockpit Road, which suggests there was a pit somewhere in the area.

In his book, *When Was That?*, Dr. Mosdell claims that the even more peculiar sport of bull-baiting took place near Quidi Vidi Lake on 14 August 1831 and that it was forbidden by official notice the following day.[2] A most diligent search of newspapers and official documents has failed to substantiate this claim. However, the following notice was published on Tuesday, 15 October 1830:

> Whereas information has been given to the magistrates that a tumultuous assemblage of persons took place near Quidi Vidi Pond on Wednesday last for the purpose of bull-baiting and whereas such practice is not only dangerous and cruel but a violation of the law notice is therefore hereby given that any person or persons who shall after this public notice, bait or cruelly treat bull or other animal ... [shall be] liable to fine and imprisonment.[3]

Sports such as fencing, rounders, and darts, all dating back long before the discovery of Newfoundland, must have been played by thousands of soldiers and sailors who frequented St. John's in its early history. However, little or no record of such events exists.

We can be sure there were billiard tables in many of the colonial

317

taverns scattered about the port. There is a story told of William, Duke of Clarence, afterwards King William IV, who was stationed in St. John's as a midshipman with the convoy. It seems His Royal Highness was playing billiards in a tavern on Water Street, somewhere opposite Telegram Lane, when he chanced to look up and see Dr. O'Donel, who that year became the island's first Roman Catholic bishop, pass the window. Either from bravado, drink, or the taunts of his cronies, the prince, who had an undisguised hatred for all things Irish, dropped his billiard cue, rushed into the Lower Path and attacked the Bishop. Some accounts have him merely knock the cleric into the gutter, while the historian, Philip O'Connell, writing in the *Irish Ecclesiastical Record*, claims the Duke threw a small dagger which inflicted a slight wound.[4] To avoid a riot, as news of the outrage spread, the governor, already driven to distraction by the unsavoury antics of his royal charge, sent a guard of marines to convey the heir apparent on board his ship which was ordered to sail immediately for Placentia where, according to local tradition, the imperial bloodline was extended to a score of pretty maidens.

The London Tavern, the leading hostelry of the early 1800's, boasted a billiard table about which many of the foremost townsmen of the day gathered. In 1838 the refitted commercial hotel advised that "There is an excellent billiard table kept on the premises." By midcentury, gentlemen were to be seen bending over the green baize in Merchant's Club, at the foot of McMurdo's Lane, where billiard tournaments were held in a room on the second floor. On 21 December 1882 the *Evening Mercury* advised: "The bowling alleys and billiards in connection with the Temperance Saloon and Bavarian Beer Depot will be opened to the public this Thursday evening next, 21st inst. at 7 o'clock." This building was on Duckworth Street, west of Hill o' Chips.

In announcing the opening of the New Fieldian Club, in the Board of Trade Building on Water Street East, 24 January 1910, much was made of the fact that its new billiard table was purchased in England. That same winter the billiard tournament for the city championship was staged in the Star Hall. These civic competitions continued into the twenties and thirties with such groups as the Benevolent Irish, Masonic, Star of the Sea, Guards, Total Abstinence, and City Club members taking part.

Horse racing appears to have established its popularity very early, possibly in the 1700s. J. W. Withers, an editor of the *Newfoundlander*, has given us a few examples from that paper of the high stakes offered early in the nineteenth century. They are taken from old issues which appear no longer to exist. "A race to be run on Monday next on the Circular Road, between the mare Lady Betty Piper and Moll Trip, the best of three heats for 100 guineas."[5] A guinea at that time was worth about $5.00 or a little more. Another notice reads: "To be run on Wednesday 27th inst., Nicholas Phelan's Bright Angel and Bennett Routledge's Phoenix, for fifty guineas, to start at Mr. Routledge's house at 12 o'clock, taking the full course of the Circular Road."[6] Mr. Routledge's estate was on the west side of Kenna's Hill. It has been suggested by J. W. Withers that "the full course" might have been along present-day Circular Road to Fort Townshend and back by way of Fort William. At the time there was also a track around the parade ground at Fort Townshend known as the Circular Road and part of this later became a race course called the Era Gardens. The College of Fisheries, formerly Memorial University College, now occupies much of the area. The parade ground would have been admirably suited to use as a track.

In a horse race held on 21 August 1818 the competing animals were owned by Drs. Carson and Kielley who were later to become engaged in a momentous political duel, which is covered in Chapter 5. Carson kept his horses at a west-end country residence named Craigmillar, after Mary Stuart's castle in Scotland. The estate later gave its name to an avenue in the vicinity. The doctor sold out in December 1852 and barns, carriages, and horses were destroyed by fire in 1858.

The St. John's Races of 8 September 1818 were a major event, to judge from the size of the newspaper ads. They were held at Best's Farm on Topsail Road; light refreshments were served and dogs were not permitted on the course. The stewards were Lieutenant-Colonel Manners, Captain Bowker, R.N., and the Chief Justice. The following summer, one read in the *Mercantile Journal* for July 18 that "The gentlemen amateur admirers of horse racing propose dining together on Monday next at the Crown & Anchor Tavern." The Thomas farm on Topsail Road was another popular track of the period.

On Thursday, 25 January 1821, the *Mercantile Journal* again carried news of interest to the "amateur admirers" under the heading, "A Sleigh Race": "We understand that a sleigh race will take place at 2 o'clock tomorrow, on Quidi Vidy [sic] Pond (weather permitting) between the White Foot and Black Dwarf—as these ponies are well matched it is presumed they will afford much amusement." Sleigh races were still taking place on the frozen surface of Quidi Vidi early in the present century. In 1903 A. B. Morine's horse won the silver trophy.

In the summer of 1833 the Turf Club was formed at a meeting held in Perkins's Hotel and in August it was announced that "Tenders having been received from the proprietors of the AVALON and FLOWER HILL RACE COURSES, the Turf Club determined that the races should take place on the FLOWER HILL COURSE on Thursday, the 19th, September, next."

Dr. Carson's Blucher won over three other horses in the main race. The doctor donated a part of his winning purse to the B.I.S. Orphan Asylum, a schoolhouse on Queen's Road.

The following social note was published the next day in *The Public Ledger*: "The races commenced yesterday (Thursday) and four horses started for the St. John's Plate, 80 dollars. . . . The weather was unfavourable, heavy showers falling during the greatest part of the day, thereby drenching the beaux and belles to the great disparagement of their gay habiliments."

The city races became the sport of princes, if not of kings, on 12-13 April 1845 when, under the patronage of Governor Harvey, the much-used track at Mount Pearl, still popular early in the 1900s, welcomed the visiting Prince Henry of the Netherlands. The purse for the Tradesmen's Race was $150 and that of the St. John's Turf Club $50. There were a number of lesser purses on both days. The band of the Royal Newfoundland Companies was in attendance.

The year 1919 saw the formation of the Newfoundland Horseman's Association, a resurrected version of the St. John's Turf Club of nearly a century before. On 18 July 1934 Mayor Carnell opened the excellent race course at Bella Vista Fair Grounds on Torbay and Logy Bay Roads. This venture, by P. C. O'Driscoll, was doomed by the government's refusal to allow betting which considerably decreased the availability of funds. The track was located off Logy Bay Road and the houses of Derby Place now sit on land where the hoofs of thoroughbreds once pounded. Today the Avalon raceway at the Goulds is a popular track with modern stables, stands for two thousand fans, a floodlit course, and pari-mutuel betting. A track for racing stock cars, Lakeside Speedway or Spence's Speed Bowl, opened nearby in 1964. A second stock-car track, Knight's Speedway, opened in 1971 at the crest of a hill leading into Pouch Cove.

Bathing, if not swimming, dates to the opening of Blackwoods Hot, Warm, Cold and Shower Bathing Establishment, first tested by a hesitant clientèle on 3 January 1852. According to the ads, "Those who know the value of a hot bath may have it in all its degrees. . . . The want of such an establishment has long been felt in St. John's." A. and R. B. Blackwood imported their heating apparatus from Greenock, Scotland, and the baths were open every Tuesday. Their location is unknown. The proprietors promised, "Nothing shall be wanting . . . either in the character of the baths or the nature of the charges."

S. G. Archibald opened the first indoor swimming baths in St. John's on 17 July 1860. They were located on the south side of Water Street, almost halfway between Temperance Street and Hill o' Chips. The day following the opening, hot baths were introduced. A newspaper ad grandly announced that the Prince's Baths, as they were called, were under the patronage of the Governor and Lady Bannerman. The advertisement proclaimed:

> The public of Newfoundland, visitors and travellers are informed that the town of St. John's is at length supplied with that great desideratum of comfort—Hot, Cold, Vapour and Shower, Salt and Fresh Water BATHS: also, Salt Water Swimming BATHS. This establishment is fitted up with separate departments for Ladies and Gentlemen. . . . Open from 6 a.m. until 9 p.m. summer and from 8 a.m. until 6 p.m. winter. Open for Cold Baths only from 6 to 9 a.m. and from 3 to 6 p.m. on Sundays. A female superintends the Ladies department.[7]

The first swimming hole used in St. John's was probably the harbour itself. We can be sure it did not take early settlers and visiting seamen long to discover Quidi Vidi Lake, Long Pond, and the Waterford and Rennie's Rivers. Popular places for swimming early in the present century were Silver Pool on Rennie's River, just above the Elizabeth Avenue bridge, and No Bottom, on the Virginia River, flowing through Pleasantville. The first pools constructed by the municipality were built around the turn of the century at Long Pond and on the south shore of Quidi Vidi where the present roadway ends, beyond the boathouse.

In 1927 the Rotarians decided to build a pool closer to Bannerman Park. A site was chosen on Rennie's River opposite Reeves Place, at a spot known as Freshwater. It was here that David G. Rennie had erected a dam to feed the waterwheel of his mill. A visitor to Rennie's in 1846, J. J. Broomfield of the Phoenix Fire Office, describes it as a water and cornmill working three stones and having no oatshelling and no kiln. There were two ovens in the bakery for sea biscuits and three stills in the distillery. The cornmill was worked by day only except in case of pressure of business. The sawmill contained one circular saw and one vertical saw and was used only for purposes connected with the mill. No sawing was done for the public.[8] The concrete buildings were located on the riverbank opposite Reeves Place.

The sum of three thousand dollars was raised to convert the old dam, where thousands had learned to swim, into a first-rate pool. The Highroads Commission assisted in the planning and construction. It cost six hundred dollars less than the sum raised. The pool measured two hundred and ten feet long by fifty feet wide with a depth from four and half to seven feet. Changing houses were erected on shore. A wading pool with seats for watching mothers was constructed a short distance up river at what was known as Little Dam. Both pools were opened in a special ceremony on 3 July 1928.[9]

About the same time the Waterford River was dammed in Bowring Park to provide safe swimming for people in the west end of the city. The Bowring Park pool was just above the tennis courts. It had changing rooms and toilet facilities on the bank and lifeguards were always on duty during the season. Modern pollution put an end to the use of these two pools, and to Quidi Vidi and Long Pond, as swimming haunts. For several years following World War II there was no safe place to swim in St. John's except the Y pool indoors at the King George V Institute. When this building was put up by Sir Wilfred Grenfell, as a fishermen's and working girl's home, a pool had been built in the basement. It has served the public since 19 December 1912 when the place opened.

The Lions' Club decided to put an end to the city pool shortage and on 6 September 1959 a large, heated outdoor pool was opened in Bannerman Park. On 2 July 1963 a second Lions' pool opened at Victoria Park. The city followed these generous gestures by the service club and opened two very large, heated outdoor pools in Bowring Park on 5 August 1968. One was for swimming and one for wading.

With the construction of the Memorial University indoor pool in the gymnasium building on Westerland Road in 1961, swimming made great strides in St. John's, for not only were students able to avail themselves of its use but through extension courses many older people learned the joys of swimming from professional teachers. By 1970 there were other indoor pools available to the public at Torbay Airport, Mt. Cashel, and St. Bride's College. Pools had also begun to sprout on the back lawns of private homes throughout the city.

On 7 August 1807 Governor Duckworth gave William Best permission to erect a tennis court. Lawn tennis, devised in 1874, seems to have found instant popularity in St. John's, for on 18 May 1876 the name of the tennis club already in existence on Forest Road was changed to the "Newfoundland Archery and Lawn Tennis Club." A short time later it was changed to the "Newfoundland Lawn Tennis and Croquet Club" and it continued by that name until around 1920. Its courts were in frequent use by the officers of visiting warships. The Newfoundland Lawn Tennis Association of our day was organized in St. John's in 1935.[10] The game has been played over the years on courts throughout the city. Especially popular were those behind the Newfoundland Hotel and on St. Bonaventure's College Campus, at the corner of Bonaventure Avenue and Mullock Street.

A suburban favourite was Smithville close to the present St. Pius X courts. Smithville itself was a catering establishment with a large dining room and ballroom. A verandah ran the length of the building. It stood at the south end of the present parish rectory and was much frequented, not only for weddings, afternoon teas, and a variety of receptions, but by tennis players in summer and by skaters and ski enthusiasts in winter.

Sergeant Smith, who gave his name to the place, died on 16 October 1897, leaving the courts to the church. The property was leased to Lawrence Furlong in November 1898 and his family ran it as a catering establishment and bakery until it was torn down in the late 1950s to make way for the Jesuit rectory. The tennis action has since been centred on the Riverdale courts on the banks of Rennie's River, at the south end of Fieldian Grounds, and at the Bowring Park courts on the north slope of the Waterford River.

The game of ninepins, skittles, bowls, or bowling was probably first played on bowling greens in St. John's in Tudor times. Before the Dutch brought it to America as an indoor sport, it was always played in the open and is still played out of doors on the French Island of St. Pierre. Prior to the 1892 fire there were at least four indoor alleys in the town including the previously mentioned Temperance Saloon alleys. In the 1870s and eighties there was a "skittle alley" behind Water Street, opposite Holloway Street. The South West Street Skating Rink was converted to bowling when the ice thawed and skating was over for the season. South West Street eventually became Colonial Street, and the rink property was taken over by the Church of England for the erection of Bishop Field College. Foran's and Lindberg's were the other two alleys. For some years after the fire the game went into a decline. It was not long, however, before new alleys began to attract another generation.

Besides the swimming pool, Sir Wilfred Grenfell made a bowling alley part of the sports facilities at his Institute. In 1927 the Holy Name Society opened one in their new club on Harvey Road and this became the headquarters for all league games. The oldest of these, the Commercial League, was formed of twelve teams in 1922; the Bankers' League and Civil Service League were begun later that same year; the Inter-Club League was started in 1923; and the winter of 1934-35 saw the formation of the Ladies' League.[11]

Commercial alleys such as those in the Duff Building, west of Queen on Water Street, and the Radio Building, west of Barron on New Gower Street, were immensely popular. In the forties and fifties alleys sprang up all over the city and everyone from school pupils to the aged seemed to be bowling. During the 1954 Regional Drama Festival, held in St. Patrick's Auditorium on Bonaventure Avenue, playgoers and performers were disconcerted by the thunder of rolling balls that permeated the theatre from the alleys beneath the hall. During the 1957 festival it was the turn of the bowlers to be disconcerted when they were not permitted to roll until the final curtain fell each evening.

The bicycle was invented in 1868 and fifteen years later the Newfoundland Cycle Club was formed on Monday, 13 August 1883, by a number of young men who banded together "for the purpose of encouraging the use of bicycles in St. John's." The club adopted a uniform of dark blue serge piped with red. It held its first races at Pleasantville on 13 July 1896 and both the gold and silver medals were won by T. McNeil. The organization disappeared with time but was revived again in the spring of 1972.

In 1883, on the evening of Tuesday, March 8, there was a large and enthusiastic turnout for a meeting held in the Commercial Buildings for the purpose of considering the advisability of erecting a gymnasium in the city. A committee was organized to investigate the suitability of existing structures for conversion and to cost the building of a new gymnasium. Whatever the findings of the committee were, the hoped-for gymnasium did not materialize in either an old or new edifice. In the late 1960s the former RCAF gymnasium at Torbay airport was converted to public use.

We know that curling was popular in St. John's as far back as the 1830s and possibly earlier. The Grand Royal Caledonian Curling Club was formed in 1838 for the purpose of uniting all curlers into a "brotherhood of the rink." It was noted that the game brought together persons of every shade of society—clergy, merchants, tradesmen, and private gentlemen—"for in Curling there is no aristocracy of feeling. . . ." The Avalon Curling and Skating Rink, which was opened in Bannerman Park on 4 January 1870 by Governor Hill, offered 4,200 feet of ice for the use of curlers, and 8,400 feet for skaters.

Before the Avalon Rink was built, curling matches took place on Quidi Vidi Lake. The *Newfoundland Express* for 22 January 1863 carries the following item: "The Terra Nova Curling Club held a match on Quidi Vidi yesterday, a challenge having passed between Captain Murray, R. E., and Smith McKay[Discoverer of the Tilt Cove copper mine in 1857]. . . . The game was closely contested, resulting in the success of Captain Murray's party by one."

Seven years before construction of the Avalon Rink, on 4 February 1863, with the thermometer registering 8 below zero, Professor Prime opened a gymnasium near what was to become the Avalon site. On 4 January 1866 the reconstructed gym was reopened, as St. John's first skating rink, the Victoria. It was given an "extended promenade and gallery." Both these alcazars were destroyed by fire on the night of 17 July 1878. At the time, they were leased to Professor Danielle who was using one for storing and renting costumes and the other as a palais de dance for his popular costume balls. These rinks were replaced a few years later by the South West Street Skating Rink. As early as 1868 Lundberg's advertised skates for sale that were "The best, cheapest, and most comfortable skate ever invented, requires no straps or plates, and fits any boot."

On 8 October 1882 the cornerstone was laid for a new indoor

curling and skating rink, on the southeast corner of the parade ground at Fort Townshend. Smith McKay, was elected president of the shareholders, who put up a capital investment of $6,800 to erect a building two storeys high, with a gallery all around. The rink was to be two hundred feet by seventy feet with curling in the centre and skating in the outer circle. The St. John's Curling and Skating Rink on the Circular Road of the Parade Grounds opened 10 January 1883. The building was brilliantly lit and Professor Bennett's Band supplied what the *Evening Telegram* foretold as "Music for the multitude from 8 o'clock till 10, if not longer." The *Evening Mercury* promised that the event would "echo with music's voluptuous swell" and that the rink would be "thronged with youth and beauty of the city and not be without its fashion as well." In time this building became known as the Parade Rink. It stood on the site of the Paramount Theatre of our day. A curling rink was opened at Bally Haly in the fall of 1962.

The cornerstone for the Prince of Wales Skating Rink was laid on 15 December 1898 by the governor, Sir Henry McCallum, on part of the site of Fort William. It was formally opened on 21 January 1899 and the first hockey match took place on its ice, February 2, between a visiting Canadian team and some city all stars. The visitors won by a score of two-to-one. The new rink had dressing rooms 36 x 20, a smoking room 43 x 20, and a skating surface of 184 x 73 feet. It also boasted committee rooms and lavatories.

The establishment was later taken over by the St. John's Skating Rink Company and the name was changed to the Prince's Rink. In the summer of 1929 the owners decided to sell out. The rink was advertised but no purchaser could be found. Much concern was shown regarding the fate of winter sports in the city, and various groups and organizations were asked to come forward. Finally in 1933 the building was purchased by the Guards Athletic Association and skating and hockey were resumed. In 1937 the property was purchased by the Arena Rink Company and the name was changed to the Arena. An artificial ice plant was installed by the new owners, which meant ice sports no longer depended on the whims of the weather.

On 28 November 1941 the Arena was totally destroyed in a $100,000 fire. While a skating party of between twenty and thirty people was on the ice, fire broke out in the boiler room at 7:25 p.m. Three minutes later the alarm was rung but there was no saving the building. After the collapse of the high roof the flames spread to the curling rink next door and it, too, was gutted.

The Avalon Curling Rink, as it was known, had been officially opened on 15 January 1910 by Governor Ralph Williams who was the patron of the Mic Mac and Terra Nova Curling Clubs scratch match which was held after Sir Ralph threw the first stone at noon. In 1916 the curling rink became the headquarters for the Newfoundland Regiment with 750 men in barracks there.

Following the destruction of the Arena and Avalon rinks in 1941 the *Evening Telegram* of December 2 lamented that "Chances that the city will ever have another Arena appear very remote. . . ." The curling rink was quickly renovated, extended, and reopened, but the wait for a new Arena was to be a long one. Barbara Ann Scott, Canada's first Olympic Gold Medal Skating Champion, journeyed to Newfoundland in 1950 and on St. John's Day, June 24, laid the cornerstone for Memorial Stadium on the vacant site between King's Bridge Road and Quidi Vidi. Even then haste was made slowly. It was not until 24 February 1954 that construction on the building was at last begun. It opened the following year under civic administration.

St. John's Memorial Stadium hosted the Canadian Men's Curling Championship, known as the MacDonald Briar, in March 1972. Competing for the MacDonald Cup were championship teams from all the provinces and territories of Canada. For the Briar the ice surface was divided into a series of rinks.

Hockey was introduced to the town in 1896, about fifteen years after the game was invented in Montreal. It came to Newfoundland with Canadians in the employ of the Bank of Montreal and others who were employed by the Reid-Newfoundland Company in running the railway. In February 1896 a part of the ice on Quidi Vidi was cleared for players using inverted walking sticks and a cricket ball. Dr. Grenfell was a member of one of the teams.

In 1898, the year construction was begun on the Prince of Wales Rink, an ice-hockey rink called the Victorian, was hastily constructed on King's Road just above the Bishop Field College property. Inter-school hockey began with the opening of this rink and the first matches were played between Bishop Field and Methodist College. The rink was later used as an armoury by the Highlanders and finally as a garage. In the 1940s it was torn down and replaced by a concrete building that is now a wholesale grocers. From then on St. Bonaventure's College dominated the sport for several decades.

The first regulation sticks, brought in from Halifax, were of soft wood and did not stand up for long. A local source was sought and carriage shafts from city wheelwrights, ripped in two, became the regulation sticks. Early skates were either fastened to wooden soles or were held to the boot by straps. Pads were magazines stuffed into stockings until football shinpads came into use. Old kid gloves were worn with the fingers cut out. The price of skates in St. John's at the turn of the century was twenty-five cents per pair for skeleton and forty-eight cents per pair for Acme. Curling stones were $13.30 and $14.20. Until 1910 goal posts were two stakes stuck in the ice. In 1904 netting had been added to catch the puck.[12]

The first St. John's team to play outside Newfoundland went to the Maritimes in 1901. Two years later Sir Cavendish Boyle donated the famous Boyle Trophy. It was the intention of His Excellency that his Inter-Colonial Trophy be competed for by the finest teams in Newfoundland and the Maritimes. When this proved impossible to organize it became the City Championship Trophy.

No rink was available for hockey on any kind of regular basis until 1904, and players had to buy regular season tickets and play their games at 6:30 p.m. before general skating commenced. In 1910, the year regulation goals were introduced locally, the Prince of Wales Rink provided players with dressing rooms for the first time and games were switched to a more convenient 7:00 p.m.

An important year in St. John's hockey life was 1935. That year saw the creation of the St. John's Senior Hockey League and the first all-Newfoundland championship series. Teams from Bay Roberts, Corner Brook, and the Guards, representing the city, took part in the series which was won by Corner Brook. The cup for the series, known as the Herder Memorial Trophy, was donated that year for the first time by the *Evening Telegram* in memory of hockey-playing members of the Herder family.

During the lean years between the destruction of the Arena in 1941 and the opening of Memorial Stadium in 1955 hockey was kept alive in the city at a little wooden rink on Mullock Street known as the Forum, owned by St. Bonaventure's College. At the time of the Arena fire the Forum had a dirt floor that was flooded after the first frost in winter. A wooden floor was put down and this improved the level of the ice surface. Later an artificial ice plant was installed and the game was enabled to survive without the loss of a whole generation.

The Roman Catholic school was not the only one to have its own rink. The United and Anglican denominations also built stadiums to serve the skating and hockey needs of their people. The Prince of Wales Arena on Pennywell Road (not to be confused with the Prince's Rink and/or Arena), just east of the junction with Prince of Wales Street, officially opened 20 January 1956. Much of the interior of the administration and dressing-rooms area was gutted by fire on 8 January 1971. The remainder of the pre-fab metal building was torn down and the whole replaced by a brick building which opened in the fall of 1972. The Church of England venture, Fieldian Gardens, was constructed in a field between Pennywell road and Grenfell Avenue, east of Smith Avenue. It was officially opened by Premier Smallwood on 3 February 1966.

In 1958 a former National Hockey League player with the Toronto Maple Leafs, Howie Meeker, settled in St. John's and as coach of the Guards gave the game new life. Alex and George

Faulkner, two brothers from Bishop's Falls, brought their experience to St. John's in the late sixties. Alex, the first Newfoundlander to play in the N.H.L., was a former Detroit team member and had played with San Diego for several seasons before coming to St. John's. In the semi-finals and finals of the 1963-64 Stanley Cup series he scored five goals for Detroit. George became the first Newfoundlander to take part in world championship hockey when he played on the Canadian team at Ljubljana, Yugoslavia, in 1966.

In the days before the popularity of hockey the favourite competitive sport in winter was the skating race, because not everyone could afford curling. Many a local Hans Brinker found a fleeting moment of glory by outskating his fellows. In 1887 the prize for winning the three-mile race at the City Rink on March 3 was a silver watch. On 8 March 1900 the three-mile race in the Prince's Rink ended in a hotly disputed dead heat. In a six-hour contest at the same rink on 30 January 1905 the competitors covered a distance of seventy-one miles.

The City Rink was off Prescott Street on a height of land occupied for the latter half of this century by the Atlantic Films studios. This sixteen-sided, tent-like structure was erected on pilings by John Foran, of Atlantic Hotel fame, and during the night of the 1892 fire it crashed in flames into Duckworth Street. The rink had known a previous disaster on a Saturday, after ice skating, when one-third of the roof fell in, just one hour after the customers had left the building. The collapse carried with it the bandstand which was located in the centre of the skating area. A pole up through the bandstand held the roof aloft like an umbrella. Had it fallen in an hour earlier the results might well have been tragic for band members and skaters.

Vague mention is made in some papers of a small indoor rink at Fort William. This was not the Prince's Rink but possibly a drill hall or some other open-floored building. The place was later enlarged and used as part of the railway station, perhaps the freight-storage shed. One old sports fan, writing to the newspapers, says the rink building was destroyed by fire. We know the freight shed at Fort William was heavily damaged in a blaze.

A third rink on the site of Fort William was the Winter Garden. With the coming of frost, the Newfoundland Hotel tennis courts were flooded and the music of "The Skater's Waltz" and "Over the Waves," blaring from the loudspeaker by day and by night, indicated that a general skating session was in progress. The Winter Garden went out of existence during World War II when the total blackout of the city made it impossible to light an outdoor rink at night.

Roller skating made its appearance at the Prince of Wales Rink on 2 September 1901. Admission to the three daily sessions was ten cents for each time and fifteen cents for the skates. Professor Bennett's ten-piece band supplied the music. On opening night four hundred pairs of skates were all gone by 8:30 and a further supply was telegraphed for by the management. There was a later roller rink off Merrymeeting Road at 1 Rankin Street, which operated from 1933 to 1956. When this roller and ice-skating rink first opened it had a concrete floor but this was found unsatisfactory for roller skating and the concrete was covered by a maple floor.

The first mention we have of soccer is the formation of the St. John's Football Club, 21 March 1873. Fourteen years later there was only one team in the city. It was made up of workers at the Terra Nova Foundry and played visiting teams from warships in the harbour. The Scottish drapers in our Water Street stores formed the next team and after that came Knowling's, Star of the Sea, B.I.S., and others so that the Football League became a reality. The first cup donated by George Knowling, was won by the Scottish lads of the St. Andrew's team. The first tie cup was won in 1890 by the Star of the Sea players.

The golden days of football ended with World War I after which there were new games to interest the sports minded. Interschool soccer competitions did, however, manage to keep the game alive down through the years. The winning of the collegiate championship for the city was always a great event in a student's life. The popular playing fields were Fieldian Grounds, at the eastern foot of Robinson's Hill; Shamrock Field, on the east corner of Merrymeeting and Newtown Roads; St. George's Field, off Newtown Road, almost opposite Shamrock Field; and Buckmaster's Field, behind LeMarchant Road, between Golf Avenue and Prince of Wales Street. Shamrock and Buckmaster's Fields were taken over for military camps during World War II, the former by the Newfoundland Home Defence and the latter by the Canadian Armed Forces.

Whatever may be said about the playing fields of Eton, many of the boys who tested their courage on the playing fields of St. John's were soon called on to test it again, on the larger field of battle, in World War II. A portion of them never returned. The same was true of a number of the leading hockey players of the twenties and thirties.

After Confederation in 1949 attempts were made to introduce the North American game of football. In spite of the fascination of the Canadian Grey Cup play-off on television, however, efforts to organize the sport in St. John's met with indifferent success and soccer remains an attraction at the field in King George V Park on the north shore of Quidi Vidi, and at Wishingwell Park on Empire Avenue. St. Pat's Field on the east side of Carpasian Road, at the foot of Johnny's Hill, had a brief moment of glory but for much of the fifties, sixties, and seventies it was mainly used by fishermen from the Portuguese and Spanish trawlers visiting the port.

On 20 August 1972 the first World Cup Series soccer match was

329

played in St. John's when teams from Canada and the United States faced each other. It was one of two games played in Canada that year by the national team. The referee and linesmen were from Bermuda. Hosting the game cost in excess of ten thousand dollars with the City Council providing the seating for 7,070 fans. The game was played in the King George V Park which could normally seat twelve hundred spectators. It was hoped that the World Cup game would be the start of introducing professional soccer to Newfoundland.

It is impossible to say when cricket was first organized in St. John's. Known before 1600, the game was probably brought to the island in the early days by men of the garrison or of the ships that frequented the harbour. It reached the height of its popularity in the town during the late nineties of the last century. An item in the *Mercantile Journal* for 16 September 1824 mentions a club but, unfortunately, fails to say when it was founded. The newspaper report states: "On Tuesday last the members of the St. John's Cricket Club entertained a large and respectable party at the Navy, Army & Commercial Hotel to celebrate the anniversary of the institution. They sat down to an excellent dinner at half past five o'clock—after the cloth was removed toasts were drunk and the party broke up at a late hour." This club was revived, after many years, at a meeting in Hotel Newfoundland in the winter of 1964, with Malcolm McLaren as president, and its first games were played on the traditional pitch at Pleasantville in 1965.

The day of the week, or the time of the day, when a sporting event took place in the nineteenth century seems to have no relation to working hours. Perhaps it was the practice to close things down for a match. In any case, most business houses were open until nine or ten o'clock at night. On 17 July 1860, for example, in what one would imagine to be the height of the fishing season, the papers carried notice of a game of cricket to take place on the Parade Ground commencing at 12:30 p.m. In the summer of 1871 the community sent a team to Halifax to compete in the First Intercolonial Cricket Match. They lost.

In October 1874, on the complaint of Captain Rogers of the Newfoundland Regiment, Governor Campbell ordered the plantations of Captain Pitts and Colonel Williams, which had encroached on the common pasture for cattle on the north bank of Quidi Vidi, restored to public use. John Williams's farm, "Golden Grove," was just west of Virginia River. During the 1890s the common pasture became the St. John's cricket grounds. They were located on a flat stretch of land later used as a drill field by the Newfoundland volunteers, in World War I, and by pioneer aviators, after the war.

By horse-drawn victoria, and on foot, crowds followed the road from King's Bridge, once called King's Pinch, past Ross's Farm, formerly Jocelyn's, to the grounds. The journey ended at the wayside inn of Peter Rutledge overlooking the pitch. This hostelry was located on Pour's Hill just above the site of the Pleasantville fire hall. There was a Charles Pour living in Maggotty Cove in 1819 and he may have given his name to the path. Rutledge purchased the place from Robert Parker Jones of Norwood, England, in 1881.

At "Peter's," patrons could wash the dust of the road from their throats with liquors, beer, or milk. The two-storey building was enclosed on all sides by a verandah where those with picnic baskets found shade. Inside, luncheons were served to the teams, umpires, and scorers during an interval in the all-day matches. The return to the grounds of the elevens, led by the umpires, would be the signal for a ripple of applause from the spectators. The Rutledge establishment was assigned to John M. Dooley, for $575, on 23 April 1903. Dooley served "Teas, Dinners and Temperance Drinks."

Around 1900 the Pleasantville grounds had to be abandoned and the game was moved to St. George's Field. The new pitch proved a poor substitute and very soon interest in the sport began to wane. The shortness of the season and the emerging popularity of football as a summer game, combined with the fact that there was no ground in the really excellent condition called for by first-class cricket, meant that by the close of the first decade of the century the game had all but disappeared. Some cricket was attempted at Llewellyn grounds, on the west corner of Empire Avenue and Forest Road. An effort was made in 1911-12 to revive interest but it did not succeed. A sportsman of the time observed that in the old days, when there was one mail a month, it was possible to play cricket, but with a daily mail service in St. John's, businessmen could no longer afford to take the time off.

Baseball, the heir to cricket, did not find immediate favour. An *Evening Telegram* reporter sneered at it as a glorified game of rounders, as played in his schooldays. He was taken to task by a reader who assured the public that, while this might appear to be the case, there was more to baseball than cricket, billiards, or hockey put together.

This game was introduced to the town in much the same way as hockey. Canadians who were locally employed brought baseball with them to St. John's. At the time, it was observed in the press, "Some may deprecate the starting of what is obviously an American game in a colony so essentially British as Newfoundland but it has been definitely demonstrated that cricket will never be revived here." The year was 1913.

A number of baseball games had been played in years previous to 1913 but attempts to establish the sport on a regular basis were unsuccessful. In that year the St. John's Amateur Baseball League was formed, thanks mainly to the efforts of Canadian employees of the

Imperial Tobacco Company, the Bank of Montreal, and the Reid-Newfoundland Railway.

The league, that first season, consisted of four teams. The Wanderers, who became the eventual champions, were mostly bank employees augmented by other transient residents of the community. The Red Lions were a team of railway employees. There were two Irish groups—the B.I.S. and Shamrocks. By then Wednesday afternoons had been declared a commercial half-holiday by law and two rounds of games were played each Wednesday afternoon, for the Silver Cup presented by G. G. Allen, Vice-President of the Imperial Tobacco Company (Nfld) Ltd. It had to be won three separate years before possession. There was another reward of a silk waistcoat for the first player to secure a home run in any league game. It was offered by Mark Chaplin, the "King of Tailors."

During the years between the wars Shamrock Field served as the city ball park. World War II put the game into a decline in spite of the presence of so many Americans in St. John's. Shamrock Field was a military camp and there was no other suitable place available. The sport began to recover in 1947 when St. Pat's opened a modern ball park in the valley below the northeast corner of Empire Avenue and Carpasian Road. Equipped with an up-to-date diamond, dressing rooms, dugouts, floodlights for night games, and bleachers for fans, city patrons were treated to some exciting events. In 1948 the McCormack Trophy was donated for the first time and won by the team from Corner Brook.

In the spring of 1969 the game moved to Wishingwell Park on Empire Avenue West. This very modern facility was built at civic expense on ground that served as the city dump until the middle of the twentieth century when the dump was moved to Robin Hood Bay. St. Pat's Field fell into ruin soon after it was abandoned, and the ball park and adjoining football field were offered for sale and real estate development.

There was another well-used pitch in Bannerman Park, at the corner of Circular Road and Bannerman Road, as well as one at Pleasantville, which had been used by the Americans stationed at Fort Pepperrell. This was the former cricket grounds of another century and located on base property. Minor league games were played at Churchill Square and Holy Cross Field, off Leslie Street.

Softball was almost an unknown sport in Newfoundland before the arrival of the Americans in St. John's. With the opening of Fort Pepperrell in 1941 the game was introduced, but local interest was not on an organized basis until 1962 when the Newfoundland Softball Association was formed. Eventually there were sixteen teams competing and there was a seven-team junior league for boys under eighteen, as well as a two-team ladies' league.[14]

The Catholic Cadet Corps (C.C.C.) introduced basketball to St. John's about twenty years after the sport was invented in the United States. The first league series game took place in the C.C.C. Armoury just off Harvey Road, east of the lane leading to Fort Townshend. On Monday night, 17 January 1910, two cadet teams, known as the Pink Uns and the Slugs, faced each other. By a score of four-to-two the Slugs won. A reporter covering the event observed: "This interesting game has become very popular among members of the brigade and will be continued throughout the winter." Its permanence did not become assured until basketball courts were added to high school gymnasiums. The courts in the Grenfell Seaman's Institute on Water Street, and the Memorial College on Parade Street, also gave the game a boost in popularity. Interschool series were played after school hours in the C.C.C. Armoury and in the Church Lads Brigade (C.L.B.) Armoury, until the modern high schools of the fifties and sixties were built.

Boxing became popular as a sport in the British Isles in the early part of the eighteenth century when James Figg, the first British heavyweight king, opened his amphitheatre for exhibitions of boxing skill in 1719. We do not know when the sport reached Newfoundland but we can be sure the start of fist fighting coincided with the arrival of the first white men. By the end of the nineteenth century boxing and wrestling matches between the sailors of visiting warships and local notables had become commonplace.

In 1845 St. John's witnessed the birth of a boy who was destined to become the professional heavyweight boxing champion of North America, Johnny Dwyer. The championship match took place on 8 May 1879 in Canada. Jimmy Elliott, the defending champion, was knocked out in the twelfth round and the St. John's-born winner retired soon afterwards as undefeated champion of North America.

Professional boxing was introduced in 1930 but the hoped-for public interest did not materialize. It was abandoned after 1934 because of the failure of local professionals to draw attendance. One crowd getter was Frank Stamp, a policeman who packed them in at both the Majestic Theatre and the Prince's Rink. After securing a record knockout in Halifax he had joined Jack Sharkey's Camp in Boston and turned professional. While he did well, his career was a financial failure because of his age and he returned home two years later.

Sam LaFosse was a promising "south-paw" who held the local bantam-weight boxing title for ten years without defeat. It was decided to send him as Newfoundland's representative to the 1930 British Empire Games at Hamilton where he did extremely well until suddenly stricken with severe arthritis. There was nothing doctors could do to help him. In spite of his suffering he went through with a

333

match, but was outclassed on points and his career was at an end.

In 1934 two first-class lightweights were brought in from Boston but in spite of good work they failed to draw the necessary crowds and the backers took a financial beating. After that, the attempt to push boxing as a professional sport in St. John's was abandoned.[15]

In 1922 the C.L.B. had organized boxing and wrestling classes, and an autumn tournament and a spring championship match were held. The Guards and other clubs also began giving instructions and these amateur tournaments became so popular it was necessary to hold elimination nights.

The year 1908 had seen the organization of the Avalon Athletic Club and it was here that the city's first wrestling bouts took place. A year or so later, a German employed by W. D. Reid as chauffeur, took up the challenge of Pius, a famous handcuff-king, in a local theatre. Well within the allotted time he had the wrestling magician senseless and in handcuffs. That was the beginning of the professional career of Otto Oppelt who was known in the ring as Young Hackenschmidt. Oppelt opened a club in St. John's and soon a number of imitators were flourishing, in such clubs as the Avalon Green Spring, Shamrock, and Terra Novas.

During the autumn of 1909 the first Newfoundland Amateur Wrestling Championships were held in the Prince of Wales Rink. Young Olsen from Sweden, who was lightweight champion of the world, was referee before a capacity crowd. That night Olsen successfully defended his title in a world championship match when he defeated Fred LaPointe, lightweight champion of Canada. Olsen stayed on in St. John's to teach wrestling and physical culture at the Avalon Athletic Club. At the Alhambra Tournament, in London, Olsen competed as lightweight champion of Newfoundland but he was disqualified. He later left the city to take up a position as wrestling instructor at Harvard University and after that as Professor of Physical Culture at Ohio State University. In later years he returned to the ring as Young Reiss, but despite the name, his age was showing.[16]

Tom "Dynamite" Dunne was a St. John's youth making a name for himself in wrestling circles in the United States in 1940 when a serious leg injury in the ring sent him home to stay. In 1955, when Memorial Stadium was opened, Tom Dunne turned to promoting. His involvement came about because of the wrestling match refereed by Maurice "Rocket" Richard, then the greatest hockey player in the world. Despite "Rocket's" presence the event looked like a financial disaster. Tom Dunne stepped into the breach and not only saved the day but made wrestling the most popular sport in the city for years to come. Television was just beginning and the tube quickly turned the population into wrestling addicts. From 1955 to 1964 the city witnessed the golden age of wrestling. And golden it was in every way, from the cash drawer to the great name attractions on the Stadium mat, Whipper Billy Watson, Gorgeous George, Hard-Boiled Haggerty, and world champion Gene Kiniski.

When wrestling was taken off television the craze for live bouts quickly died but the name of promoter Tom Dunne lives on in the St. John's Athlete of the Year award which he instituted by donating the first trophy in 1951. The first winner was Ferd Hayward. In 1969 the award was split between male and female winners. The first female Athlete of the Year was Maria Fitzpatrick.

Memorial University revived an interest in wrestling. In 1967 Gus Jones of St. John's won a gold medal for the sport at the Canada Winter Games. As president of the Newfoundland Amateur Wrestling Association he was one of those instrumental in seeing that the Canadian wrestling championships, and the Olympic Trial for the summer Olympics at Munich, were hosted by the N.A.W.A. and the Department of Physical Education and Athletics, at Memorial University, in March 1972. Facilities for the three-day event were provided by the university.

No doubt trout were being caught in the rivers and ponds around St. John's for centuries before the arrival of the white man. We can only look back with envy to the first pioneers who dropped their baited hooks into waters that teemed with millions of fish. The first city anglers' competition was instituted by Ayre & Sons Ltd. on 26 June 1908. Prizes were offered for the largest trout caught on that date and first place went to W. Skeans for a rainbow trout weighing two pounds one ounce caught with a Riverside steel fishing rod. The Queen's Birthday, May 24, was the big fishermen's holiday for the year. Thousands took off for cabins and shacks in the woods and for many years the railway laid on a special train to carry fishermen to their favourite haunts along the tracks. This train, called the Trouter's Special, ran for the last time in 1970. It is remembered now in the brand name for a locally bottled rum.

One of the first track and field events to take place in the town, to our certain knowledge, was a walking match from King's Bridge to Torbay and return, which was held on 20 May 1860. A fifty-mile "go as you please" walking and running meet was held in the Parade Rink on Harvey Road on 14 September 1885. From 1906 to 1911 spectators turned out to watch a twenty-mile walk from Victoria Hall on Gower Street at Long's Hill, along Queen's Road, Rennie's Mill Road, Portugal Cove Road, around Windsor Lake, and back to the start.

The Amateur Athletic Association, which came into being in 1921, concerned itself with organizing track and field events. That year four St. John's lads were sent to Halifax to compete against the best athletes in Eastern Canada in the Wanderers' Sports. Every man came home with a trophy and the team secured second place.[17]

The first marathon in St. John's was run in 1908. The course was from Octagon Pond to Cavendish Square. In 1921 the *Evening Telegram* instituted its ten-mile road race, from the Octagon to the newspaper office, and the winner was Ron O'Toole. The first running of the Royal Stores ten-mile walk was in the summer of 1924. The exact day is unknown as the records are lost. For many years the prize for this event was the Philco Cup. On 22 September 1969 the annual Thompson's Jewellery ten-kilometer run was begun.

In 1930 Newfoundland was represented in track and field at the British Empire Games in Hamilton, Ontario. Other national and international competitions were entered by city athletes including the Boston Marathon and the Olympics. Pat Kelly competed in the former, and Ferd Hayward in the latter, at Helsinki.

Golf, which originated in Scotland as far back as the fifteenth century, was represented in Newfoundland before 1900 by a golf course in the west of Buckmaster's Field, commemorated today by Golf Avenue. There was no suitable course in the town, however, until 1908 when a group of people purchased Colonel Haly's farm on Logy Bay Road. The Colonel, who was an A.D.C. to Governor Cochrane, started Bally Haly in 1825. A memorial plaque to him in St. Thomas's Garrison Church, Military Road, reads:

> In memory of Wm. Haly Esq. of Bally Haly near this town a Lieut. Colonel in the Br. army and President of the Council of Newfoundland. He was a member of an ancient Irish family, who, after a distinguished military career, settled in this colony where he died, respected and regretted by all classes 14th September, 1835, in the 65th year of his age.

The memorial mentions his wife, Anne, a daughter of George Hutchings, and eight children. One of these, a magistrate in Taabinga, Queensland, died at sea in 1861 on his way back to Australia after a visit home to Newfoundland.

In the early 1860s Bally Haly was in the possession of John Deakins; in the late seventies Mr. LeDrew was taking boarders anxious for a "country retreat." The most flamboyant tenant, according to John Maclay Byrnes in *The Paths to Yesterday*, appeared in St. John's early in the 1890s and seems to have called himself after the place, Haly Hutton. This peculiar person's origins are obscure. In earlier life he was said to have been a magistrate in British Africa where he suffered a sun stroke which impaired his mental ability. He took up residence at Bally Haly with a body servant named McGin.

He threw up ramparts, in the field around the house, and fortified them with imitation cannon made from wood. On Sunday afternoons he would conduct tours of the battlements, explaining the tactical reasons for the various emplacements. He also liked to spend hours in his carriage, driving up and down Water Street, bowing and smiling, with courtly dignity, to the ladies on the sidewalks.[18]

In 1917 Bally Haly was organized as a proper golf club. The first clubhouse was destroyed by fire in December 1937, and was replaced by a huge, rambling, colonial-style house with a wide verandah in front. This also went up in flames on 12 August 1957. Several of the help, who were asleep at the time, barely escaped with their lives. The present clubhouse was erected in the late fifties.

Professional golf was introduced to Newfoundland at Bally Haly in 1968 when the Newfoundland Open Golf Tournament was held for the first time. By 1972 pros were competing from as far away as Mexico for the eight thousand dollars in prize money that was being offered.

A sports activity to achieve recent popularity in St. John's is skiing. It was almost unknown until around 1920. The slopes of Bally Haly and Mount Scio, above the shores of Long Pond, were favourite ski runs. During March 1936 a cross-country ski race saw thirty-six competing on a four-mile course. Governor Walwyn fired the starting gun and Ferd Hayward won the trophy donated by the Peterborough Toboggan Company of Canada.[19]

In the late 1940s North Bank Ski Club opened in a small house at the foot of Mount Scio Road. It was located in a meadow a dozen yards north of where Long Pond empties into Rennie's River. Following the demise of this club it was many years before skiing in the city again became organized. In the winter of 1970-71 a ski club was started and a slope obtained at the junction of the Marine Drive and the road to the Fisheries Research Lab at Logy Bay. The following season a small tow was installed, but there was no clubhouse.

The sport most recently organized in the capital city is one that spread from India and Persia to Europe as far back as the thirteenth century. The Newfoundland Chess Association came into being in 1969 when the Downtown Development Corporation, a group responsible for a short-lived mall on Water Street, asked Roger Langen and some of his friends to play chess on a giant chessboard painted on Water Street, just west of the top of Clift's Cove. They agreed, on condition that a trophy be donated to a chess club they were forming. A large trophy was donated to the forty-five member organization. Two knights, the emblem of victory, stood on either side of a cup.

The first Newfoundland Open Tournament, in 1969, was won by Roger Langen, who remained the champion for some years. He was also first President of the Association and taught the game at Memorial University. In 1970 the St. John's players joined the Chess Federation of Canada. That year they bid forty-five hundred dollars to host the eighth Canadian Open Chess Championship and were awarded the games.

In ending this brief résumé of the long, involved story of sporting life in our capital city we turn inevitably to the oldest continuing sports event in North America, the annual St. John's Regatta. Because of incomplete records and missing newspapers it is impossible to say in what year the contest was begun.

A search of available sources seems to indicate that the first regatta in St. John's took place on Tuesday, 22 September 1818. This claim is based on the following item from the *Mercantile Journal* of Thursday, September 24.

> Tuesday last being the anniversary of our beloved Sovereign it was celebrated by a display of colours, etc. About 2 o'clock the boats entered for the rowing match, advertised in the Sentinal of Saturday last, started 6 in number—the silver cup was won by the Custom House boat in 25 minutes, a distance of about 2 miles. The day was remarkably fine, a great number of boats attended the race which rendered the scene particularly interesting.

The Coronation of George III took place on 22 September 1761 and it was this anniversary that was being celebrated. No copy of the *Sentinal* for the date mentioned is now known to exist so that no further details are available from that source. The fact that "a great number of boats attended," and the distance was two miles, seems to indicate that the race was held in the harbour. In any case the item proves that there was a St. John's Regatta in 1818 and this makes the event 155 years old in 1973.

The Honourable Fabian O'Dea, while Lieutenant-Governor of Newfoundland, found mention of a regatta in St. John's in a report from the officer commanding the engineers constructing Government House. "Sir," the gentleman wrote to the Secretary, 21 August 1827, "I shall be obliged to you to mention to His Excellency I have been obliged to give the workmen a half holiday in consequence of a boat race which they wished to attend. I found the men would be idling their time in looking at the race instead of working. I have acceded to this request with reluctance."

The 1828 Regatta featured an Amateur Race between Brookings gig and Hoyle's whaleboat. It was won by Brookings and the names of that first known championship crew were Lash, Furneaux, Hepburn, and Winter, with Pierce as coxswain. The early raceboats were gigs, whaleboats, and punts with such names as Lallah Rook, Maid of the Mist, Red Rover, Lady of the Lake, Jenny Lind, Quickstep, Minnie Clyde, Indian Chief, and Ferryland Lass.

The first evidence we have of any race taking place on Quidi Vidi Lake is found the following year. Both the *Royal Gazette* and the *Public Ledger*, for the week of Monday, 18 August 1829, mention the event. Under the heading "Regatta," the *Royal Gazette* informs readers that "The approaching Boat Races engage much attention, and should the weather prove fine, we doubt not that the lovers of amusements will be highly gratified—as we understand several excellent matches are to take place—Thursday is the day appointed for the Rowing Matches on Quidi Vidi Lake and Saturday for the Sailing Matches on the harbour." We know for a fact that there were rowing and sailing competitions taking place on the harbour as far back as the 1700s, and probably among ships' crews long before that.

The *Public Ledger* spoke of the 1829 Regatta in these terms: "We are confidently informed that in addition to the boats which are intended to contest for the prize on Quidi Vity [sic] Lake on Thursday next there will be several bye-watches (the rowing by gentlemen) which are expected to afford a great deal of amusement." Governor Cochrane, thirty days out of Falmouth, arrived back in St. John's at one o'clock on August 12, after ten months' absence, just in time to lend his patronage to the races.

In the 1844 Regatta the Lucy Long won against five other boats. The sensation that year was not the race but the arrest of Jane Flowers. William Fogarty, who was quarrelling with two or three persons at the lakeside, stuck Jane's husband. Jane and Patrick Cowan struck Fogarty back at the same time, whereupon he fell down dead. The two were tried for manslaughter in December and acquitted when Drs. Kielley and McKen, who had failed to revive him, testified that he could not have died of the blows.

The year 1853 saw a three-day regatta, the longest in the event's history. Two years later, in 1855, the Challenge Race between a St. John's crew and a group of Quidi Vidi fishermen was won by the fishermen in the Undine. For some reason a second race was held later that summer between the city crew and the fishermen on July 27. The St. John's men rowed in the Undine this time and the Quidi Vidi men in the Lady Darling. The fishermen won the prize of fifty pounds and the victory so delighted the boat's owners that they gave her to the crew.

In 1856 the first ladies' race appears to have been rowed and it resulted in a victory for the ladies of Quidi Vidi over those from the Battery. The Prince of Wales, who was to give his name to an era as King Edward VII, was a guest at the 1860 Regatta and he offered a hundred pounds to the winners of the Fishermen's Race. Pedley writes that the prince "gratified the fishermen by honouring their regatta with his presence and the wives of some of them still more, by going away from the holiday spectacle to examine the fishing stages in Quidi

Vidi, so as to learn something of the avocations of ordinary life." Strangely enough, after this royal visit, there was not another regatta for eleven years.

Beginning with the revival in 1871, rowing times started to improve and by 1877 a Placentia crew was able to win the Fishermen's Race in ten minutes, 28 seconds. A remarkable thing about this crew was that they built their boat in Placentia and carried it on their backs to St. John's over a rough trail through the woods, since no roads existed. The eight men were all over six feet tall. They rowed against teams from Torbay, Outer Cove, Harbour Grace, St. John's, and from a British warship that was in port. Their victory was the cause of great excitement and Governor Musgrave asked to have the eight visitors brought to him so he could give each a golden sovereign. Their moment of glory over, the victorious crew hoisted their boat on their backs again and walked home with it to Placentia.

The Amateur Race in 1884 was marred by tragedy. A crew of teenage boys from Torbay were rowing the *Terra Nova* to her home stakes when she swamped and sank. Three of the crew, Samuel Gosse, John Martin, and Mogue Power, were drowned in the confusion. The *Terra Nova* was renamed the *Myrtle* after that and went on to many successes in future years.

From the sixties to the eighties the start and finish of a race was always signalled by the firing of a cannon. It was placed on a little neck of land that jutted out from the shore southeast of the mouth of Rennie's River. Mr. Brewin, the old gentleman in charge, would set off the powder-laden cannon by applying a poker, from the fire he kept burning all day, to the touch hole of the gun.[20] The last year in which it was used was 1885. The cannon was retired to Signal Hill where it became the noonday gun for many years. There is in existence an excellent sketch of the lake showing the cannon about to be fired at the start of a race.

A note of splendour was added to the event in 1891 by the celebrated character, Professor Danielle, who advertised that "The Royal Palace Tent at the Regatta will be the most unique, gorgeous, high, light, airy, cool and comfortable that ever has been or ever will be seen on the banks of Quidi Vidi Lake—where ladies and gentlemen may comfortably sit, eat, sip and enjoy . . . its height, its flag and general aspect will attract and invite you."

In 1887 the Regatta lasted two days and featured yacht races. The following year the novelty was a canoe race. No regatta was held in 1892, the year of the last Great Fire, because of the magnitude of the calamity in July and the fact that the shores of the lake were being used by fire victims who were housed there in military tents.

An Outer Cove crew won immortality in 1901 when they established the fastest time on record by rowing the Blue Peter to victory in nine minutes, thirteen and three-quarter seconds in the championship race. The names of these men, who deserve mention for their achievement, were Daniel and Dennis McCarthy, Dennis Croke, Martin Boland, John Nugent, John Whelan, and coxswain Walter Power. Some excitement was added in 1902 when the crew of the Bob Sexton broke an oar as the boat turned the buoy and still rowed home to victory.

The novelty in 1906 was a swimming race across Quidi Vidi Lake. This event was continued up to 1914 when the First World War put a temporary end to the Regatta because most of the oarsmen were in Europe fighting the war to end all wars. With the signing of the Armistice in 1918 the event was resumed and it has continued without interruption ever since. Today it is more in the nature of a giant carnival rather than a sports happening with traffic jams, fun fairs, wheels of fortune, fish ponds, cotton candy, bands, singers, folk dancers, acres of hot dogs, chips and soft drinks, and tons of litter. The rowing is often obscured or ignored by the mulling thousands.

In Come Home Year, 1966, it was estimated that nearly thirty-five thousand people attended the races at Quidi Vidi, but this seems an exaggeration. The only really sour note down the years has been that struck by the weather. Postponements due to wind, rain, or fog have been numerous.

The source of the name Quidi Vidi, which is applied to the lake and the small village at its mouth, has been disputed by various scholars and historians. One group claims it was the name of a lady called Kitty Vitty who kept a tavern on its shores in the long ago. Another group claims it came from Qui Divida because of the opening in the wall of rock that leads from the village to the sea. There are as many spellings of the name as there are theories of its derivation.

Strangely, the oldest known reference to the place uses a pronunciation still in use today. James Yonge, who was in St. John's in 1669 as a surgeon on board H.M.S. *Marigold*, states in his journal for that year: "I forgot to mention that during our being here I went once to Petty Harbour, and twice to Kitty-vitty, of which place I forbear a description, intending to leave that to the figures by and by, to be made of all the harbours I have been in in this land."[21] Today there are three accepted pronunciations for the name of the village. Besides James Yonge's Kitty Vitty we have Kiddy Viddy and Kwida Vida.

In the proposals of the inhabitants for the defence of the English settlements in 1679 the spelling used is Que de Vide. In a document dated 1680 relating to John Downing, the prominent merchant of the place who was the father of permanent settlement in Newfoundland, the spelling is Quitevide.

Aaron Thomas, in his very personal and invaluable journal of his visit to Newfoundland in 1794 writes: "You must know that there is a singular place about two miles from St. John's called Titti Whitti." The Thomas pronunciation has not survived. It is of interest to note that D'Ewes Coke, the chief magistrate, was conducting his fishing business at the village during the summer Aaron Thomas paid the place a visit. Coke may have taken over the Downing plantation.

There are several very old structures still standing at Quidi Vidi but in the absence of any regulations regarding the repair of historic buildings most of these have been stripped of their special character by the substitution of modern picture windows, for the small glass panes of the Colonial period, and wide imitation-clapboard metal siding for the narrow wooden clapboard or shingles.

The St. John's Historic Trust spent a considerable sum of money in the 1960s to restore the nineteenth-century chapel which was about to be demolished. For this effort the Trust received a Heritage Award from a national body. Unfortunately, the house directly south and in front of the chapel, the one used as a field hospital in the Seven Years' War and probably built in the middle years of the eighteenth century, was recklessly modernized and denuded of its Colonial features in the early 1970s. Before these renovations it bore a striking resemblance to a 1750 addition to the John Howland House at Plymouth, Mass. It was also not unlike the front of the Ship, a tavern on King's Beach at St. John's, shown in a painting circa 1770.

At 2 Barrows Road, near the waterfront in Quidi Vidi, stands a white house with a low roof that has fortunately preserved its distinguishing traits. Historians and architects argue over the exact age of the structure. Houses of almost identical design in New England date from the early 1700s. Even its most doubtful critics admit to construction before 1800. It is not improbable that the dwelling on Byers Road was the home of that substantial merchant, John Downing, later occupied by Chief Magistrate D'Ewes Coke. If we go by what we are told of Colonial housing in St. John's, even in the early 1800s, it must have been one of the more desirable residences in the environs of the community, erected by a man of means. Being removed from the town area, it has survived fires and redevelopment.

342

8

Up Above the World You Fly

The end of the first successful non-stop flight across the Atlantic. Alcock and Brown's Vickers Vimy lands in a bog (mistaken for a field) at Clifden, Ireland, 16 hours after leaving St. John's.

Crowds inspect Alcock and Brown's Vickers Vimy just before take-off, 14 June 1919, when the fliers became the first to fly the Atlantic non-stop. The plane is now in the Science Museum, South Kensington, London. (Courtesy Newfoundland Provincial Archives)

Alcock and Brown's Vickers Vimy plane at Lester's Field, St. John's, preparing to take off on the first successful non-stop flight across the Atlantic. The flight was from St. John's to Clifden, Ireland, in 16 hours, 14 June 1919. (Courtesy St. John's City Hall)

Hawker and Grieve's plane, the first to attempt to fly the Atlantic non-stop, prepares for take-off at Mount Pearl. The small craft crashed into the Atlantic two-thirds of the way to Ireland. (Courtesy St. John's City Hall)

Raynham and Morgan's plane "The Raymor" prepares for take-off in an attempt to be the first to fly the Atlantic non-stop in 1919. The craft crashed on take-off at Pleasantville. (Courtesy St. John's City Hall)

The United States blimp C-5 at Quidi Vidi shortly before the airship broke loose from her moorings and drifted out over the Atlantic never to be seen again. (Courtesy Provincial Reference Library - Newfoundland Section))

Arthur Whitten Brown with his hand on John Alcock's shoulder in St. John's shortly before taking off on their historic transatlantic flight, June 1919.

351

Up Above the World You Fly

How I wonder what you're at!
Up above the world you fly,
Like a tea-tray in the sky.
          LEWIS CARROLL *Alice's Adventures in Wonderland*

St. John's shares, with the Newfoundland towns of Harbour Grace and Trepassey, a unique place in the story of transatlantic flying. Many of the pioneer flights were in some way connected with the city. The story of these daring adventures, up above the world, begins with the *London Daily Mail* offer of 1919. Lord Northcliffe's influential English newspaper put up a prize of ten thousand pounds for the first non-stop flight across the Atlantic in a British-built, British-manned, heavier-than-air machine. Three groups of competitors arrived in St. John's in the spring of that year and put up at the Cochrane Hotel, on Cochrane Street. A fourth group, under Rear Admiral Mark Kerr, went to Harbour Grace to use the airfield in that Conception Bay town.

The three groups in St. John's were Harry Hawker and Ltd.-Cmdr. K. McKenzie-Grieve; F. P. Raynham and Commander Morgan; and Capt. John Alcock and Lt. Arthur Whitten Brown.

Captain Alcock and Lieutenant Brown arrived in St. John's by train from Port aux Basques on 13 May 1919, being twelve hours late on a scheduled twenty-seven hour journey. Almost immediately they hired a car and drove to Mount Pearl to look for a flying field. There was none to be had as all suitable ground had been appropriated by the other fliers who were already in the town.[1]

Besides the small group of British aviators, St. John's was playing host to several American correspondents who had come to Newfoundland to cover the departure of their country's NC flying boats from Trepassey for the Azores. This first attempt at island hopping across the Atlantic was a major undertaking of the United States government. Destroyers had been stationed every fifty miles along the ocean route to flash beacons and shoot up star shells to guide the air machines. Of the four NC flying boats that started, only one made it to Europe. The NC 2 never even left New York. Another, the NC 5, lost her way in a fog and, after flying over Newfoundland for some hours,

352

in a vain search for Trepassey, landed in St. John's harbour. The British flyers were among the crowds she attracted. They watched her take off and steer an erratic course through the Narrows, but she was soon a total loss. The NC 1 and NC 3 crash landed in the Atlantic. The NC 1 was taken in tow by a ship but the plane sank. The NC 3 was forced to plough through two hundred miles of ocean to reach the Azores. Only the NC 4 was able to complete the flight to Fayal Island, on May 20, and eventually to Lisbon, on 27 May 1919.[2]

It was this flight by the Americans that had caused Hawker, Grieve, Raynham, and Morgan to discard caution and risk everything in an attempt to win for Great Britain the honour of completing the first flight across the Atlantic.

On hearing that the NC 4 had reached the Azores, Hawker and Grieve decided to try to beat the Americans to the victory although flying conditions were decidedly unfavourable.

The first attempt to cross the Atlantic non-stop by air was begun in St. John's at Glendenning's Farm, in Mount Pearl, on 18 May 1919, at 1:25 p.m., Newfoundland summer time. Glendenning's Farm is now the Federal Department of Agriculture Research Station, on the north side of Brookfield Road.

In their Sopwith biplane, *Atlantic*, Harry Hawker, of Australia, and Lieutenant-Commander McKenzie-Grieve, of England, took off on what they pretended was a test flight under full load. This did not prevent a large Sunday afternoon crowd from collecting to watch the antics of the flyers.

The plane lumbered westward across the field and rose into the air. It passed over the city at an altitude of one thousand feet, flew over Cabot Tower, and vanished from sight. Beyond the Narrows, the undercarriage was released to lighten the load. This was later recovered by a fisherman, in the waters off Cape St. Mary's, and returned to St. John's. The plane, fitted with two Rolls-Royce Condor engines, travelled at a speed of 125 miles per hour and carried enough fuel for thirty hours.[3]

Fourteen and a half hours after take-off the *Atlantic* was forced down in the sea, seven hundred miles off the Irish coast, in the vicinity of the Danish tramp ship S.S. *Mary*. The two flyers were rescued but, due to the fact that neither plane nor ship had wireless, they were thought lost at sea until May 25 when the rescue vessel docked at Thurso, Scotland.

Their plane, complete with mail bag and contents, was discovered five days later still floating in the Atlantic. A wheel from the retrieved undercarriage is now on view in the Air Museum at Gander Airport. The flyers were awarded the George Cross for their attempt. Hawker died in an air crash on 12 July 1921; Grieve died on 26 September 1942, of natural causes, in Australia.

A memorial erected on the grounds of the Agricultural Research Station, Brookfield Road, keeps alive the memory of that May afternoon in 1919 when two fearless men climbed into a flimsy plane to gamble with fate in an attempt to conquer the unconquered. The plaque reads:

HAWKER AND MACKENZIE-GRIEVE
FIRST ATTEMPT BY AEROPLANE TO CROSS THE ATLANTIC
On May 18, 1919, the Sopwith "Atlantic" with Harry C. Hawker and Lt. Comdr. K. Mackenzie-Grieve, R.N. as the crew departed from this site on the first attempt to fly non-stop across the Atlantic Ocean by aeroplane. The Sopwith biplane, because of a faulty radiator, was forced down at sea 1050 miles out from Newfoundland and the two airmen were miraculously rescued by the Danish steamer MARY.

When word reached the Cochrane Hotel that Hawker and Grieve were taking to the air Raynham and Morgan immediately guessed what their rivals were up to and headed for their own craft, the Martinsyde biplane, *Raymor*, a word compounded of the first three letters of their two names, which was in a meadow at Pleasantville on the north side of Quidi Vidi Lake. The choice of this field was to prove their undoing. The runway was not long enough for a good run and the valley was laced with crosswinds. Around four-thirty in the afternoon, two hours after the departure of the other two, they climbed into the plane, tuned up, taxied down the three hundred yards of meadow, and lifted twenty feet into the air, as a thousand spectators cheered.

Moments after take-off a crosswind started the aircraft, heavily laden with fuel, drifting sideways. She dipped down so that her wheels touched the ground and broke off. Fifty yards from take-off she crashed. Morgan was badly injured by a piece of glass entering his head. Thus the second attempt to conquer the Atlantic by air was a failure. The plane was repaired, renamed *Chimera*,[4] and on 17 July 1919 an attempt was again made by Raynham, with another navigator, but once more the plane could barely lift from the poor runway. A crosswind swept her sideways, the undergear was wiped off, and she crashed a second time. Raynham and Morgan packed up and left for England by ship.

A plaque, which commemorates their ill-fated attempts, is situated on the Boulevard. This road, which skirts the north shore of Quidi Vidi Lake, covers part of the runway used by the *Raymor*. The historic marker, located just east of the Canadian Legion building, reads:

PLEASANTVILLE
PIONEER FLYING FIELD

In May, 1919, this site was first used by the aircraft attempting a non-stop crossing of the Atlantic ocean. The Alcock & Brown aeroplane was assembled here in preparation for the first successful non-stop crossing. The "Raymor" crewed by two Englishmen Raynham and Morgan crashed here on take-off and the U.S. Navy airship C.5 was swept away from its moorings and lost during a windstorm. In the years to follow both the lake and the surrounding meadows were used extensively by pioneer aviators.

After their arrival in St. John's, Alcock and Brown lost no time in pursuing their search for an aerodrome. They drove over hundreds of miles of bad road. Tired of hiring vehicles they bought a second-hand Buick, and used every opportunity to explore St. John's. On May 18 they drove to Ferryland, after hearing that suitable land was available in that community, but in this they were disappointed. On the way back to St. John's a passing motorist shouted at them that Hawker had left that afternoon and Raynham's machine had been smashed before he could get it off the ground.

Raynham offered the two the use of his field at Pleasantville, and thus it was that their Vickers-Vimy, which arrived in a few days, was uncrated and assembled on the shores of Quidi Vidi. They continued their search for a suitable take-off place. One was offered at Harbour Grace but the five thousand dollars the owner demanded for its hire was prohibitive. Rear Admiral Mark Kerr refused them the use of the Harbour Grace airstrip until after his own machine had left.

A Mr. Lester, who had done the carting of their planes from the dock to Pleasantville, offered the flyers the use of his meadow just below Mundy Pond. After inspection, it was found that by adding four smaller fields, on the hilltop, a run of five hundred yards could be obtained. Some thirty labourers were set to work blasting and levelling hills, walls, and fences.

On June 9 the first test flight was made and the plane was landed at Lester's Field, with the aid of a smudge fire. A second flight took place on June 12. On both tests the only real trouble was with the wireless.

The flyers saw Kerr's Handley-Page over St. John's making test flights from Harbour Grace, and they determined to get away on Friday, June 13, as they both considered thirteen to be their lucky number. However, everything could not be ready in time and so departure was postponed until 4:00 a.m. Saturday, June 14. Friday evening the flyers went to bed in the Cochrane Hotel at 7:00 p.m. and were awakened before dawn. By 3:30 a.m. they were at their machine in Lester's Field watching a large black cat saunter in front of the plane. This they considered a good omen.

During the night the tanks had been filled with 870 gallons of gasoline and 40 gallons of oil. They carried a toilet kit, sandwiches, chocolate, malted milk, and two thermos flasks of coffee. There were three hundred private letters in the mail bag.

Sightseers, thinking the attempt would be postponed because of a strong wind, kept away. Besides the mechanics, only a handful of reporters and very few of the curious were present. Then, with throttles wide open and engines all out, the Vickers-Vimy turned into the westerly wind. Take off, at 12:58 p.m., Newfoundland time, was up the slope of the field. It barely succeeded in getting airborne. There were breathless moments in which it was feared the craft would hit a roof or treetop. When the plane vanished over the hill, it was assumed she had crashed. The small crowd waited anxiously until a few minutes later when the aircraft reappeared climbing steadily and gaining speed. Only Alcock's cleverness as a pilot saved them from disaster. As they flew over the field they waved to those on the ground and passed over the city at a thousand feet. It was 4:28 p.m. (Greenwich Time). Sixteen hours and twenty-eight minutes later, shortly before 10:00 a.m., they landed in a bog, near Clifden, on the west of Ireland. The flight from coast to coast, 1,680 miles, lasted fifteen hours, fifty-seven minutes.[5] The amazing story of those sixteen hours is one of heroism and courage, in the face of great odds, and it marked the first successful non-stop flight across the Atlantic.

A feat considered to be impossible had been accomplished and transatlantic flying was born on that seemingly endless night. Fame and honours awaited the two men, as well as the nearly fifty thousand dollar prize offered by the *Daily Mail*. They were received everywhere in triumph, and huge crowds acclaimed them at every stop in Ireland and on the Holyhead-to-Euston run. When they arrived in London they were still in the clothes in which they had crossed the Atlantic.

The *Daily Mail* prize was presented Friday, June 20, at a luncheon in the Savoy Hotel. After the speeches Winston Churchill, the Home Secretary, arose and presented them with the cheque for ten thousand pounds and proclaimed that the king had authorized him to announce that a knighthood had been conferred on both flyers. Wherever they went they were lionized by an adoring public that was soon to forget they ever existed, in the international madness over Charles Lindbergh's solo flight, ten years later.

Sir John Alcock died in a flying accident just six months after his great feat. In December 1919 he was delivering a Vickers-Viking to an air show near Paris, in bad visibility, when he crashed near Rouen and was killed. Sir Arthur Whitten Brown gave up flying and returned to his first love, engineering. He died in 1948.

Mechanics hauled the Vimy from the bog in Ireland and dismantled it for shipment back to England. After repair it was given to the Science Museum in South Kensington, London, where it hangs today.

The pioneer airmen were commemorated by a memorial at London Airport, opposite the entrance to the transatlantic terminal. The Heathrow monument has two life-size statues of the airmen in flying kit. The plinth beneath them bears the following inscription: "Sir John Alcock and Sir Arthur Whitten Brown who made the first direct flight across the Atlantic. Vickers Vimy aircraft: Rolls Royce engines. St. John's, Newfoundland: Clifden, Ireland. 14th to 15th June 1919." Derrygimla Bog, near Clifden in the west of Ireland, also has an impressive memorial to mark the achievement of the flyers. The bog itself is unchanged.

There are two Alcock and Brown monuments in St. John's. One is located on LeMarchant Road, opposite St. Clare's Hospital, at the west corner of Patrick Street. The bronze plaque, almost hidden in a copse of trees, bears the following inscription:

ALCOCK AND BROWN—TRANSATLANTIC FLIGHT
On the 14th, of June, 1919, Captain John Alcock and Lt. Arthur Whitten Brown of the RAF took off nearby on the first non-stop transatlantic flight in Vickers Vimy aeroplane at 12:58 p.m. Newfoundland time. 16 hours and 12 minutes later they landed at Clifden, Ireland, a distance of 1800 miles.

The second, and much more impressive monument, is located on Blackmarsh Road, opposite Froude Avenue. Blackmarsh Road itself cuts across what was once Lester's Field. The actual place of take-off was just to the west, below the monument. The memorial itself shows a stylized bird in flight and is the work of the Dutch-born Newfoundland sculptor, Hans Melis. The inscription on the tablet, again showing the discrepancy of fifteen minutes, reads:

On June 14th, 1919, Captain John Alcock, RAF and Lt. Arthur Brown, RAF, starting from Lester's Field, St. John's, Newfoundland, made the first successful non-stop transatlantic flight landing on a bog at Clifden, Ireland 16 hours and 12 minutes after take-off. This plaque unveiled by the Hon. J. R. Smallwood, Premier of Newfoundland & Labrador on June 14th, 1969 commemorates the fiftieth anniversary of the historic event.

A reenactment of the flight was sponsored by the Royal Trust Company in 1969 to mark the fiftieth anniversary of the air victory. For the reenactment, Eugene Locke and Thomas Lee flew from St. John's to Shannon, via Clifden, on June 14-15 in a Piper Navajo.

The fourth aspirant for the *Daily Mail* prize, Admiral Mark Kerr and his crew at Harbour Grace, heard the news of their rival's victory with downcast faces. The triumph of Alcock and Brown, and a defect in his Handley-Page machine, caused Kerr to abandon the Atlantic venture.

Among other early air flights involving St. John's, and worth noting, was that of the C.5 airship. This non-rigid, twin-engine craft, with E. Coil as captain, arrived at Pleasantville, St. John's, from New Jersey on 8 May 1919, to follow the route of the U.S. NC Flying Boats. On May 15 a roaring southwest gale ripped the C.5 from her moorings on the north side of Quidi Vidi Lake. Three crew members were on the ground trying to hold her down and two were in the gondola. As the lighter-than-air craft broke away from her moorings the two in the gondola jumped from a height of about twenty feet. One sustained a broken ankle.[6] The airship was swept out over the Atlantic and, though a United States destroyer in port at the time put out in immediate pursuit, the C.5 was never seen again. A local legend has a crew member dangling from the ropes as the craft vanished from sight but this is popular imagination and has no basis in fact.

In 1920 an Australian airman, Major F. Sidney Cotton, arrived in Newfoundland with Sydney Bennett, a Newfoundlander whom he met when they served together in the Royal Flying Corps and a son of Sir John Bennett. It was their purpose in life to establish the first air service in Newfoundland. In June 1919, with the success of the Alcock and Brown venture, the Newfoundland Legislature had hurriedly given an air service concession in the country to the Imperial Aircraft Company of Britain which was operating Imperial Airways. Nothing came of the granting of this franchise.

Cotton and Bennett convinced Alan Butler, a well-to-do Englishman, to finance them in an airline venture in the island of Newfoundland. Late in 1920 their plane arrived at St. John's on board ship and was uncrated and assembled. The airmen's activities were daily reported in the press and were a cause of much excitement.[7]

In 1921 Cotton engaged the interest of the owners of the large sealing vessels in hiring his services as a seal spotter. It was his job to locate the patches. This led to some embarrassment when, on one occasion, he found what he thought to be the main patch. When the ships reached the spot there was not a seal anywhere in sight. Johnnie Burke, the great ballad writer, turned the event into a successful stage comedy, "Cotton's Patch," in which the patch turned out to be on the seat of Cotton's pants. Along with Queen Victoria, the Major was not amused.

The first passenger flight in Newfoundland took place 10 February 1922, when Major Cotton flew Mr. P. Blackstedt from St. John's to Alexander Bay (near Glovertown) in his Martinsyde plane. The round trip took two hours.[8]

Toward the end of 1922 the Post Office decided to put up two thousand dollars if Cotton could establish an airmail service between St. John's and Halifax. The hope was premature. The Major and Syd Bennett took off together from their hangar on Quidi Vidi, where the boathouse stands today, on what they thought would be a history-making flight. It turned out to be a disaster, and nearly a tragedy. They were forced down on Deer Lake, where the plane was damaged and Bennett suffered some painful injuries.[9] He died at St. John's, 3 June 1945, at the age of forty-eight years.

At one time Cotton had three planes in service but his pilots all cracked up their craft. By 1923 the attempt at establishing a local airline was deemed a failure and was abandoned. Major Cotton left Newfoundland. He returned to St. John's a few years later to demonstrate a tractor for use in clearing snow. On 9 June 1927 he again arrived in the city, on board the S.S. *Sylvia*, with a monoplane to be used in a search for Nungesser and Coli, missing French aviators. During World War II he served the Air Ministry in a valuable capacity and died in England around 1970.

It was 20 May 1927 when an unknown airmail pilot, Charles Lindbergh, took off from Roosevelt Field in New York: 3,620 miles and 33.29.30 hours later he landed in Paris, to become the first solo flyer to conquer the Atlantic. For this feat he won the Orteig prize of twenty-five thousand dollars and immortality. As a safety measure, because he had no radio, Lindbergh flew along the Atlantic seaboard from New York to Nova Scotia to Newfoundland before heading out across the ocean. He believed this to be the most practical route for, if trouble developed, he felt he could land at any time. Even if he went down in the sea, the search area would be narrowed by knowing that he was somewhere east of Newfoundland. He was also comforted by the thought that he could return and land on one of the green fields of Avalon should the engine miss or the oil pressure drop.

In a hazy sunset Lindbergh flew over the shore of Conception Bay. He saw the breakers and the railway and the roads that twisted from village to village. In his mind he was thinking of the surprise of the citizens of St. John's to see the Spirit of St. Louis suddenly sweep down from the scarlet ember of evening cloud and head out across the ocean, into the darkening sky. It was just about eight o'clock in the evening when the citizens of the town looked up to see the small aeroplane overhead.

Charles Lindbergh wrote of this historic moment in his autobiography:

> I came upon it suddenly—the little city of St. John's, after skimming over the top of a creviced granite summit—flat roofed houses and stores, nestled at the edge of a deep harbour. It's almost completely surrounded by mountains. Farther ahead, the entrance to the harbour is a narrow gap with sides running up steeply to the crest of a low coastal range which holds back the ocean. Fishing boats are riding at buoys and moored at wharves.
>
> Twilight deepens as I plunge into the valley. Mountains behind screen off the colors of the western sky. For me, this northern city is the last point on the last island of America— the end of land; the end of day.
>
> There's no time to circle, no fuel to waste. It takes only a moment, stick forward, engine throttled. To dive down over the wharves (men stop their after-supper chores to look upward), over the ships in the harbour (a rowboat's oars lose their rhythm as I pass), and out through the gap, that doorway to the Atlantic. Mountain sides slip by on either wing. Great rollers break in spray against their base. The hulk of a wrecked ship lies high upon the boulders. North America and its islands are behind. Ireland is two thousand miles ahead.[10]

As the darkness spread around him Lindbergh realized the impossibility of turning back. Even if he did reach St. John's it would only be a scattering of lights on the black earth—shoals and cliffs and vague mountains. If he had to come down after dark he would have to crash, whether on land or sea. As we all know, Charles Lindbergh did not come down until the following evening, at LeBourget Aerodrome, in Paris, and the world went mad.

Six years later, the legendary flyer was able to get a first-hand view of the little city he had seen from the air on his immortal flight. On 12 July 1933, a year after the kidnap murder of their son, Lindbergh, accompanied by his wife, Anne Morrow, landed at Bay Bulls Big Pond. The two motored to St. John's and spent the night at the Cochrane Hotel. Next day they left for Cartwright, Labrador. During a five-month period the Lindberghs logged thirty thousand miles and visited four continents studying base sites which might be established for future airfields. Their work proved a great success and later enabled Pan-American Airways to set up its international air routes.

An historical marker at Bay Bulls Big Pond commemorates the visit of the Lindberghs to Newfoundland. The marker, located off the highway, a few yards from the water's edge, reads:

BAY BULLS BIG POND
CAPTAIN CHARLES A. LINDBERGH

On July 12th, 1933, Captain Charles A. Lindbergh, with his wife Anne Lindbergh, landed on this pond during a 30,000 mile survey flight that was to assist in establishing base sites for future air routes. Six years previously, in 1927, Captain Charles A. Lindbergh had flown over the city of St. John's on his historic non-stop solo flight from New York to Paris.

On 9 October 1929 a Barling monoplane, *Golden Hind*, a remarkably small craft with an open cockpit, landed at Lester's Field in St. John's. The young German pilot, Urban Diteman, was considered foolhardy to attempt to fly the Atlantic in such a plane, but he quickly demonstrated the craft's airworthiness to the citizens of the city in a series of wildcat aerial antics. On October 22, waving a gay farewell to his onlookers the daredevil airman took off from Harbour Grace for London. He was never seen or heard of again.

The leader of another important international air expedition who came to St. John's was Italo Balbo. With his crews, and twenty-four Savia-Marchetti flying boats (as well as the blessings of Mussolini), Balbo's Italian armada took off from Orbetello, Italy, on 5 July 1933 for North America. It was a bold and fabulous event that caught the imagination of the world. On the flight west to Chicago the flying boats made one of their stops at Cartwright, Labrador. Returning to Italy from New York they made another stop at Shoal Harbour in Trinity Bay on 28 July 1933, expecting to depart again on July 31. However, the weather over the Atlantic deteriorated to such an extent that the take-off was indefinitely postponed. On August 1, Air-Marshal Balbo made an appointment with two Italian submarines and the Italian supply ship, *Biglieri*, to meet in St. John's harbour. Early the following day he departed by train for the city accompanied by twenty officers and a number of newspapermen.

In his journal Balbo describes the Newfoundland capital: "It is truly a beautiful town with a distinctly Nordic stamp about it. Its houses, made of timber, are for the most part, of dazzling whiteness and stretch away from the sea along the slopes of the hills."[11]

He goes on to say, "the Prime Minister and other representatives of the Government of the island are among the large crowd that welcomes us with vociferous cheers ... citizens who form the reception Committee are frock-coated and silk-hatted. ... This convention is mere veneer ... these islanders are charmingly naive and natural."[12]

That evening he dined with the sailors on board ship in the harbour. Later they attended a dance at the Newfoundland Hotel where "Italian airmen vied with the sailors in their skill and physical endurance as interpreters of the mazes of tangos and foxtrots."

Next morning he was driven to Cabot Tower to unveil a plaque. While at the tower he sent his famous compatriot, Signor Marconi, a message in which he said that Italians were proud of the fact that their countryman had linked the ends of the world together by his wonderful invention.

From Cabot Tower, Balbo was taken to an official luncheon with the Prime Minister, Frederick Alderdice, who was a Belfast Irishman of education and refinement. Toasts were drunk to King George, King Victor Emmanuel, and Mussolini. The affair ended with Prime Minister Alderdice raising his glass to Balbo and singing, "For he's a jolly good fellow." Members of the Cabinet joined in as the refrain went along.

That afternoon the Air Marshal was to speak to the sailors. He gave orders that all the Italians were to be assembled in a waterfront shed because of a heavy downpour. He addressed them, shook hands with them individually, and passed out autographed photos.

In the evening he was given a rousing send-off at the railway station by the Prime Minister and Cabinet. One official, Mr. Emerson, speaking on behalf of Governor Anderson who was in Trepassey, was moved to reply to Balbo's farewell speech in "faultless Italian." At 3:30 a.m. on August 7 reveille was sounded in Shoal Bay and within hours the armada was flying home in the growing dawn. Mussolini and the people of Italy gave the flyers the greatest triumphal entry into Rome since the days of the Caesars. In November, Balbo, a Fascist leader who had taken part in the 1922 March on Rome, was sent by Mussolini to Libya, where he was appointed governor. The dictator feared the popularity of the hero aviator and saw in him a rival for his job. An air crash over Tobruk, in June 1940, took the life of Italo Balbo. There was a suspicion the crash was the work of Mussolini.

St. John's citizens got a view of the ill-fated German zeppelin, *Hindenburg*, on the clear, sunny afternoon of 4 July 1936 when she cruised low over Conception Bay and circled St. John's before passing out over the Atlantic. Less than one year later on 6 May 1937, the great airship caught fire and exploded as she was being moored at Lakehurst, N.J., after a transatlantic flight. Thirty-seven of the ninety-seven people on board lost their lives in the tragedy.

Two other early flights are worth recording in this brief history of the pioneer air attempts that involved St. John's. A forty-one-year-old flying veteran of World War I, Major Wynne-Eaton, arrived in the city in 1930. He had his plane assembled and, on July 6 of that year, took off from Lester's Field for Harbour Grace where he was to launch his transatlantic flight. As the DeHavilland monoplane, *Puss Moth*, climbed steeply into the air it suddenly nosed over, crashed, and burst into flames. The badly injured pilot was unconscious when he was rescued from certain death by men on the field. Within fifteen minutes the craft was a charred mass of rubble. The Major stayed two weeks in hospital and returned to England.[13]

On a September day in 1922 one of the most fascinating murders in American history rocked the nation. Rev. Edward Hall, pastor of the fashionable St. John's Episcopal Church in New Brunswick, N.J., and Mrs. Eleanor Hall, a choir member of some years' standing, were discovered shot to death in a country lane. Their scandalous love affair had been common knowledge for some time. What made the double murder exciting was that the corpses were strewn with their love letters and one of the Reverend Hall's calling cards.

Four years later, the sensation skyrocketed back into the headlines when Mrs. Hall and her two brothers were arrested and charged with the crimes. The case had been reopened because of the efforts of Philip Payne, editor of the tabloid, *New York Daily Mirror*. Payne had gained possession of the calling card, found at the feet of the Reverend Hall, and was able to produce a fingerprint expert who swore the card contained the blurred prints of Mrs. Hall's brother, Willie. This persuaded the governor to order the arrests and trial.

The state's star witness, known as the Pig Woman, was wheeled into court on a stretcher, and after claiming to have seen Mrs. Hall kneeling over her husband's corpse she was carried out screaming hysterically at the defendant. It took the jury six hours to bring in a verdict of Not Guilty.

Mrs. Hall promptly sued the *Daily Mirror* for three million dollars, and Payne just as promptly set out for Rome. His mode of transport was a Fokker-Bristol monoplane called *Old Glory*. With an American flag painted on its wings, the plane took off from Old Orchard, Maine, on 6 September 1927. Besides the flamboyant newspaperman, the small craft carried the pilot, Lloyd Bertaud, and James Hill. The flying venture was being sponsored by William Randolph Hearst.[14]

Old Glory flew over Cape Breton, N.S., and around 9:45 p.m. passed over Newfoundland, just south of St. John's. At dawn the next day, five hours after passing near the city, an SOS was picked up from the plane by the S.S. *Lapland* and the S.S. *Carmania*, indicating trouble. Soon the radio messages ceased. When the aicraft was given up for lost on September 9, Hearst chartered the Newfoundland coastal vessel, S.S. *Kyle*, to commence a search of the Atlantic. She put out from St. John's and three days later located some of the wreckage floating in the sea five hundred miles east of Cape Race. When the ship docked at the Newfoundland capital, this wreckage proved to be part of the wing of *Old Glory*—the part with the American flag painted on it. What became of this valuable museum piece is not known, nor has any trace of the flyers ever been found.

Just before Christmas, the following year, the libel suit against Payne's paper was settled out of court, by the widow Hall, for an undisclosed sum, rumoured to be between fifty and a hundred and fifty thousand dollars.

Newfoundland Airways was organized in 1930 by Arthur Sullivan, a young Newfoundlander who had five or six flying lessons in England but no licence to fly. He engaged Douglas Fraser, a son of Dr. N. S. Fraser, to go with him to Toronto and bring back a Gipsy Moth plane. Fraser had learned to pilot a plane with Curtiss-Reid in 1928-29 and had flown with that firm in the north before returning to St. John's.

The two men spent ten days in Toronto and left to fly home shortly after noon on November 4, reaching Montreal just over four hours later. Two days were lost in that city while the young flyers enjoyed the delights it offered. They did not get away again until the morning of the seventh, a very windy day. By noon they reached Quebec City. At Rimouski they took on gasoline for the long hop to Woodstock, N.B. The small craft had a fuel capacity of twenty-five gallons and a speed of 80 m.p.h. It was mid afternoon when they circled the airfield at Woodstock, which was actually a racecourse.

An instructor for Moncton airport, who had flown ahead of them from Rimouski to Woodstock, went on to Moncton promising to see that the flares they had wired ahead to have lit were ready. There were dangerous radio towers in the vicinity of the landing field and the Gipsy Moth had no lights. At 3:30 p.m. the two pioneers left for Moncton, arriving there at 4:50 that afternoon. It was dark and no flares had been lit. They saw a farm and some cows grazing in a pasture where they decided to land. Fraser said to Sullivan, "This is goodbye to your plane." As they were heading for the cows Art Sullivan shouted that he saw some fire up ahead. Fraser aimed for the flames and they found themselves on the ground at Moncton airport.

It took nearly three hours, on November 8, to get from Moncton to Sydney, where they put up at the Isle Royale Hotel. Three attempts were made to leave Sydney and reach the beach at Stephenville Crossing where they could only land at low tide. On the second attempt they nearly made it but cloud forced them back to Nova Scotia. They finally left the Cape Breton town at 9:50 a.m., November 12, landing on the sands at the Crossing ten minutes past noon. Owing to some delays they had to postpone their departure for St. John's until the following day. It was eleven o'clock on the morning of the eighteenth before they left for the capital. A heavy snowstorm, near Grand Falls, forced them down in a vegetable garden owned by the Anglo Newfoundland Development Company (A.N.D.). The following day the journey was resumed and they landed at the Mount Pearl airstrip at 2:43 p.m., having taken fifteen days to fly from Toronto. This completed the first flight from Toronto and Montreal to St. John's. It made air history.[15]

Next day they offered anyone wanting to see the city from a plane, as a passenger, the opportunity to do so. By paying five dollars and flying over St. John's with Douglas Fraser at 3:20 p.m. on November 20, George K. Noah, a son of Kaleem Noah, became the first commercial passenger on a Newfoundland-owned and operated airline. It was the only commercial airline east of Montreal.

On the flight from Toronto, Fraser taught Sullivan to fly. Soon after their return to St. John's the two parted company and Douglas Fraser formed his own organization, Old Colony Airways, with an Englishman named Bertram Clayton as his mechanic.

Arthur Sullivan made history on 18 February 1931 when he completed the first winter airmail service by flying his Gipsy Moth as far north as St. Anthony, stopping at villages along the way to ask directions. The winter route he pioneered is flown by provincial carriers to this day. Before modern highways joined the coastal settlements of Newfoundland these flights were often the only link with the outside world for many months.

On 26 November 1931 Fraser and Clayton flew Dr. Pritchard of Bay Roberts to William Dawe's sawmill at Burlington where he operated on the foreman who was suffering from bloodpoisoning. On the way back the plane was forced down on Wigwam Pond and the travellers walked the four miles to Grand Falls where they arrived at eight o'clock that evening unaware of the concern for the missing plane, its passenger, and crew. Before they had an opportunity to take off again the water froze. Fraser waited a month until about five inches of ice had formed, hauled the pontoon plane up on the ice, and fitted her for flight.

On December 9 Fraser and Clayton attempted a take-off. As the Curtiss-Robin taxied the half-mile she began to skid sideways toward an unfrozen river. About twenty feet from shore the ice gave way shearing off the wings. Soaking wet, the two men climbed along the tail to the ice, as the fuselage settled in thirty feet of water. They walked to a nearby base shack where they changed into dry clothing. The motor was all that was rescued from the wreckage.

At 8:30 a.m. on the clear spring morning of 30 May 1932 Arthur Sullivan and Karl Kuehnert, a young dentist from Illinois visiting the Grenfell Hospital at St. Anthony to get some experience, took off for a brief joyride. At the end of a night of merriment Kuehnert had expressed a desire for a closer look at an iceberg which was grounded on a nearby cape. Sullivan was delighted to give him the pleasure and they flew off in the Gipsy Moth never to be seen again. Two nurses later reported seeing the plane fly behind the iceberg, after which the sound of its motor suddenly died.

Search planes arrived from Boston and Quebec and Douglas Fraser and Bert Clayton flew up from St. John's. Mrs. Sullivan, the mother of the missing pilot, intended to go with them but Fraser dissuaded her. On June 9 the search was abandoned. Sullivan's overnight bag washed ashore as did an interwing strut from a plane. It was later identified by the DeHavilland people as coming from Sullivan's Gipsy Moth. The strut was given to the flyer's mother.

Fraser became an airmail pilot for Mussolini on 28 July 1932 when a plane from New York arrived at Lester's Field, St. John's, after being unable to find the Harbour Grace airstrip. On board was important mail from the dictator of Italy for Air Marshal Italo Balbo, whose giant air armada was then moored near Clarenville. The plane from New York was piloted by Commander Pond, USN, who was accompanied by Lieutenant Carisi, a mechanic. The letters from Mussolini to Balbo had been landed from the S.S. *Bremen* in New York. Next day Fraser flew the American and his packet of mail to the Air Marshal who gave them a warmhearted reception at Clarenville.

Search and rescue were an important part of the Old Colony Airways operation. A selfless pioneer in this field, Douglas Fraser saved many dozens of lives, sometimes under dangerous conditions, with little or no financial remuneration. The government of the day paid him nothing. An example of his heroism was displayed on 133 January 1934 when he flew with Clayton to Carmanville, on the Northeast coast, in a blinding snowstorm and succeeded in bringing to hospital at St. John's a girl suffering from acute appendicitis from which she would have died without immediate medical attention.

When the plane got back the two men figured they were over the city because of the bright glow in the snow. During a momentary opening in the flurries Fraser spotted the Basilica towers and using these as a guide found his way to Quidi Vidi where he landed without mishap about 6:00 p.m., aided by the headlights of cars shining on the water.

In 1934 the Commission of Government decided to establish a government-owned air service. Old Colony Airways was bought out and leased to Imperial Airways of Great Britain, so that Fraser became a pilot for Imperial Airways operating in Newfoundland. He had built his own hangar at the water's edge, on the north bank of Quidi Vidi, just west of the mouth of the Virginia River. The earlier Cotton-Bennett hangar had been on the site of the present boathouse.

During World War II Captain Fraser located Stephenville and Argentia airports for the Americans and earlier played a role in the selection of the Gander site. He tried to convince a man, sent to Newfoundland by the RCAF to scout a location for an airport near St. John's to suggest it be built near Cochrane Pond. Against the local experts' advice the Canadian stranger recommended Torbay, and air

366

travellers have rued that unfortunate decision ever since because of its being so prone to fogs. Fraser, who gave up flying in 1944, was the first person to fly to the site of the air crash near Gander, which killed the great insulin discoverer, Sir Frederick Banting.

At 6:05 p.m. on the evening of 12 July 1933 Douglas Fraser was tinkering with his plane on the shore of Quidi Vidi when an aircraft landed on the lake. It was Charles and Anne Lindbergh, who had lost their way trying to find Bay Bulls Big Pond, where the reception committee and thousands of citizens, in five hundred motor cars, waited to greet them. Fraser and Tom Chalker rowed out in a small boat and gave the great international flyers instructions on how to reach Big Pond. That night the young Newfoundland aviator met them again at a reception held at Littlefield (Pringlesdale). It was Fraser who advised Capt. Ben Taverner, of the S.S. *Kyle*, where to search the Atlantic for the lost plane *Old Glory*.

In 1942 Trans-Canada Airlines, which was later given the more Gallic sounding name of Air Canada, decided to use the new airport at St. John's, built by the military for RCAF and USAF planes, to establish a commercial service between Canada and Newfoundland. Since the latter was an independent country at the time, and not a Canadian province, customs inspectors were assigned to the airport.

The first flight on a regular passenger service between Canada and Torbay Airport took place on 1 May 1942. There were five passengers on board—three males and two females. The aircraft used on these early flights were tenpassenger Lockheed Lodestars. There was one return flight daily. However, it was only for the brave. Most persons still preferred to cross 550 miles of Newfoundland by railway, and 100 miles of water in Cabot Strait by ferry, in spite of the wartime danger from U-boats, to reach Canada and destinations west. But a beginning had been made which was to end the isolation of St. John's forever.[16]

There have been several fatal crashes at Torbay Airport (now St. John's Airport), but none involving a commercial airliner. The worst of them happened soon after the flying field opened. On 6 May 1942 an RCAF aircraft crashed just after leaving the runway. In the mishap eight airmen, some of them on their way home on leave, lost their lives. Funeral services were held at the Roman Catholic Cathedral for one, and at the Church of England Cathedral for the others. The eight coffins were then paraded through the streets of the city, to the mournful beat of a military band, as far as the Railway Station where they were placed on board a train and taken to Gander for burial in the RCAF plot there.

A deplorably patched-up North American B-25, an old military aircraft from World War II, limped into Torbay Airport on 19 February 1962, carrying six Americans on an adventure junket that was intended to take them around the world. One of the six was the Hollywood star, Charles McGraw, a well-known gravel-voiced actor, noted for his many performances in gangster pictures and for his portrayal of the Falcon in a successful television series. McGraw had started his film career in the early forties and was seen in such pictures as *The Killers, Spartacus, The Birds,* and *In Cold Blood.* With him on the flight was his stunt man, Robert Hoy.

The B-25 had already been held up five days in Halifax by mechanical problems. About four minutes out of St. John's, as they were preparing to land, the cabin filled with smoke from the engine. The adventurers finally took off on February 29 for Europe. Minutes out over the ocean the radio failed and they returned to Argentia. Repairs took four or five days. During the wait a call came for McGraw to return to Hollywood to star in a new television series, *Logan's Port.* On March 2 he travelled from Argentia to St. John's. Next day Robert Hoy got cold feet and joined him, and the two performers flew back to Hollywood together. With everyone predicting disaster, the B-25 finally headed across the Atlantic. As it was coming in for a landing at Maison Blanche Airport in Algiers, an engine fell off in flames and the plane crashed, killing all on board.

In 1949 Eric Blackwood, a bush pilot who provided an air service out of Gander with Piper Cubs, sold his fledgeling airline operation to a new company which had been formed at St. John's, with Chesley A. Crosbie as president. It was called Eastern Provincial Airways. The organization expanded rapidly adding new routes and modern equipment for the transportation of passengers on regular schedules within the province. In the summer of 1954 Gander was made the flying headquarters with executive administration remaining at St. John's. A giant step forward was taken in May 1963 when Eastern Provincial Airways bought out Maritime Central Airways, a considerable passenger and freight service based at Charlottetown.[17] This made EPA of St. John's one of the major airlines operating within Canada. In 1972 its shares were offered on the stock market for the first time.

9

The People are the City

Newfoundland-born showman John Murrary Anderson, who was Broadway's greatest producer after Ziegfeld, presents scholarships to two of the most deserving students of his Dramatic School, Bette Davis and Pauline Potter. (Courtesy Theatre Collection—New York Public Library)

Peter-from-Heaven was one of the many characters who populated St. John's in the last century. He would wear three or four hats at a time and preach hell fire and damnation to all who paused to listen. (Courtesy Newfoundland Provincial Archives)

Pioneer pilot Douglas Fraser and his Curtiss Robin plane of Old Colony Airways on Quidi Vidi Lake at St. John's. (Courtesy Provincial Reference Library—Newfoundland Section)

The People Are the City

What is the city but people?
True, the people are the city.

WILLIAM SHAKESPEARE *Coriolanus*

As a village grows into a town it develops a class of people known as "characters." When a town becomes a city it begins a search for "famous sons." St. John's has gone through both stages. The past is full of tales about those romantic folk Newfoundlanders liked to call "queer sticks." Many were crippled, or stunted, or in other ways afflicted. Yet they were always shown a traditional respect. They were welcome guests who sat on the old wooden settles, by the fire, warming their bones before going on their way. The mentally retarded were said to have been "touched by the hand of God."

Among the cult of the wayfarers, none was more welcome than the fiddler. Late in the last century a favourite place for fiddlers to congregate was Leary's Bridge, which spanned Leary's Brook, not far from the Avalon Mall. In the days when Oxen Pond Road took you far out in the country, the old bridge was a favourite place for dancing on moonlit nights and young couples would stroll out from the town to set their toes tapping to such fiddled tunes as "Peggy O'Neill" and "The Banks of Newfoundland."[1]

Peter from Heaven could certainly be said to have been touched by the hand of God. A kind of harmless madman, he won his place in history by standing about, on the lower part of Pennywell Road, crying aloud quotes from the Bible while wearing three or four hats at a time on top of his head.

Trotters McCarthy's physical deformity got him into Robert Ripley's "Believe It or Not" series. A ne'er-do-well from Paradise, a community near Octagon Pond, McCarthy had something wrong with his legs so that he couldn't walk, but trotted along at a running pace. In "Believe It or Not," Ripley called him "The man who never walked."

Another person with a similar name, who became a household word during the middle years of the twentieth century was Tommy Toe. His real name was Peddle and he came from the Alexander

374

Street area, probably Gallagher's Range. A handsome youth, with black curly hair, Peddle served in the navy during World War I. On his return, he took to drink and became a familiar character along Water Street. Nobody knows where the nickname "Toe" came from. A prodigious worker when sober, he was extremely scrappy and quarrelsome when under the influence. Tommy Toe disappeared during the 1960s when Harbour Drive was under construction. It was thought he fell over the wharf and drowned, but the legend persists that he fell into one of the frames for the concrete pilings and went to sleep. Next morning, it is said, he was buried under tons of concrete without anyone knowing he was lying there.

Dr. Neal was reared by the Connolly family but his origins were obscure. It was said he was the illegitimate son of the Prince of Wales (Edward ᴠɪɪ), who visited St. John's in 1870. There is no denying he bore a striking resemblance to the monarch. The doctor, who had no degree of any sort, made the West End Fire Hall his headquarters. He walked to all the funerals he could attend, wearing a fireman's hat and carrying a cane made from an old umbrella. Neal lived in the poor house for about thirty years before he died in the early 1920s. He was then in his sixties, as far as anyone knew.

One day in the 1870s a young lad was flung ashore from an English vessel in St. John's harbour. He was called Dickie Magee and was somewhat retarded. He had been brutally beaten by the mate and ill-treated by the crew that abandoned him in a strange land. Dressed in several ragged coats and known by the name Stinky, Magee slept on cold nights curled up in front of the stove in the *Morning Chronicle* office. A blond with pink cheeks and bright eyes, Dickie imagined himself to be the reincarnation of the imaginary Sherlock Holmes. He would regale his listeners with tales of robberies and murders which he had solved for the London police. Magee was employed by the newspaper for many years without any payment other than the right to sleep by the fire. In later years he lived in the basement of the old Post Office where he was found dead one morning.[2]

Caroline Bowdin was never seen in public but that she was covered from head to toe in bows of bright-coloured ribbons. She married a fellow of her own mental stature named Flipper Smith, and the two were immortalized by Johnny Burke in a verse of his famous song, "The Kelligrew's Soiree:"

> Jim Brine, Din Ryan, Flipper Smith and Caroline
> I tell you boys we had a time
> At the Kelligrew's Soiree!

Bernard Walsh was a popular fool just after the turn of the century. Many tales are told of his wit and cunning. One April 1 he was walking along Water Street when he was hailed by a businessman named Ned Noonan, who asked him to take a note to James Baird. Noonan said it was something he forgot to tell the merchant and, as he was on his way up town, he didn't want to go back. Bernard agreed to oblige. Trying to control his mirth, Noonan slipped a hasty note into an envelope and sent Walsh on his way. As soon as he was out of sight of the sender, Bernard nipped down onto Walter Grieve's wharf, carefully opened the poorly closed envelope, and read the contents. Taking a pencil from his pocket he added something in imitation of the notewriter's hand, resealed the message and was on his way. At five o'clock that evening he was found sound asleep propped up on the sidewalk against Tom Haw's Corner on New Gower Street. The smell which emanated from him indicated he had visited many public houses in the downtown area during the afternoon. When the crumpled envelope in his hand was opened, the message contained above the well-known signature of Ned Noonan was "Send the fool farther." To this Bernard had added a second line, "and give him a drink." Unwary publicans had honoured the instruction.

Another night, Bernard Walsh's father gave him the money to go to a soiree with the stern admonition that he come home between twelve and one. Three o'clock was striking when the young man finally reached home. His father berated him the following morning. With wounded pride Bernard informed his father that he had come home as he was told. To prove he was not telling a lie he took his father to the front door and showed him the doorposts. On one side was chalked the number twelve and on the other side the number one .[3]

Probably the last touched-by-the-hand-of-God type St. John's will ever know, with the exception of the usual assortment of alcoholic panhandlers, is William Murphy, who died in the 1960s at an early age. He was popularly known as Silly Willie. It can be said that poor Willie was not always treated with Christian charity by the boys and girls of the town who sometimes taunted him until he took chase and they scattered in panicky flight. Sometimes Willie would suddenly round a corner and come upon a tormentor standing alone. Before the youth could escape, Willie would clutch him by the throat, make a Dracula face, and give a wild laugh, before allowing his terrified victim to break free and make a mad dash for home.

Willie delighted in striking terror into the hearts of shop girls who would be draping windows. He would appear out of a throng of shoppers passing by the store where the young women were working, press his face tightly against the windowpane, and when an unsuspecting girl looked up, he would twist his features into a hideous mask.

Like Dr. Neal before him, Silly Willie was devoted to the dear departed. If it could be said he had any occupation in life, it was that of mourner. In the days when coffins were borne through the streets of St. John's on horse-drawn hearses (until around 1950), the first mourner to come trotting along behind the hearse, at any funeral of importance, was Willie. Newsreel shots and newspaper photos of distinguished corpses, on their way to their eternal resting places, show Willie marching along behind, his head bowed in reverence.

Probably because it is a seaport, life in St. John's has always been enriched by the presence of true characters. Three of the most remarkable were Bampfylde Carew, the Hermit, and Count de Courcy. All arrived by ship. The first of these was known in the west country of England as the King of Beggars. Bampfylde Carew was born into a fairly well-to-do Devonshire family. However, he decided to drop out of school and live the life of a gypsy. Around 1700 he shipped on board one of Capt. Arthur Holdsworth's vessels in search of new adventures and sailed from Dartmouth to St. John's. During the voyage a French prize was captured. In his autobiography, written in the third person and published in 1745, Carew says they took it to St. John's and ransomed it to the French, at Placentia, which he describes as "a considerable place in Newfoundland."

In the book, *The King of Beggars*, the author goes on to say:

> Bampfylde, besides the French harbours, this trip visited St. John's, Torbay, Kitty Vitty Harbour, Bay Bulls, very industriously remarking their situation and anchorage, and making himself fully acquainted with the names, circumstances and characters of all inhabitants and livers of any account therein. Bampfylde and his friend Escott being arrived in Dartmouth had Ten Pounds each of Capt. Holdsworth for their service, and thought themselves very well rewarded.[4]

The carefree rogue passed himself off in England as the son of Aaron Cock, a Newfoundland planter. On one occasion he was found out to be an imposter and was chained to a parish pump in Bristol.

Bampfylde Carew made a second unscheduled visit to St. John's when he went to say good-bye to the captain of a ship sailing for Newfoundland from Dartmouth. According to his story he drank more well than wisely and was shanghaied and taken to St. John's.

The Dixie Line is a road off the Brookfield Road, near the Ruby Line. In a tilt on the Dixie Line there lived the most mysterious person ever to reside in St. John's. His name was unknown, so everyone called him the Hermit. Historians do not seem to agree on the date of his arrival in the city. Devine and O'Mara say the man arrived around 1865 and lived six years in the tilt, in Walden-like seclusion. An Irishman, he was said to be in his early forties, quite

377

handsome, with a splendid physique, and never seemed to be in want, as he was always very clean and dressed in good clothing.

The Hermit sold trout and kindling in the streets of St. John's to earn enough money to supply his wants. He is described as having a wistful look that seemed "to revert to memory that was not happy." He made no friends and allowed no one inside his door. In keeping with the superstitions of the times, the tilt of this odd recluse was considered a place of darkness and it was carefully avoided by passers-by.

He left St. John's on 2 August 1871 on board the *City of Halifax*, in company with the Bishop of Fredericton. The passenger list shows a family of Clifts, Mrs. James French, and eight in steerage. He may have been one of those in steerage. Yet, we are told that on the morning he sailed he was attired in the finest of clothes and costly jewellery. He carried a gold cane and wore a stovepipe hat and a long cloak over striped pants. French is not an unusual name in Ireland and he might well have been the Mr. James French on the vessel's manifesto.

When the Hermit was gone, a search of his tilt, by the curious, showed he left behind some elegant curios and expensive things. It was said that broken crystal and silverware were found.

P. J. Kinsella, a civil servant interested in preserving local traditions, suggested that he might have been in reality the exiled Irish patriot, Kevin O'Doherty, and the identification went unchallenged for many years. However, a check on the facts reveals that O'Doherty was a doctor exiled to Van Diemen's Land, Australia, for his part in the Irish Movement. On his release in 1854 he married Mary Eva Kelly who was known as Eva of the Nation, for she contributed prose, essays, and poems to the newspaper *The Nation*. After their marriage, O'Doherty was elected M.P. for Meath. The two subsequently went to Brisbane, Australia, where he was elected a member of both houses of Parliament in Queensland, where he died in 1905. There is no possibility that he was the Hermit whose identity remains a matter for speculation. He may well have been an exiled Irish rebel. We will probably never know.

The veil of mystery also shrouds Count de Courcy who died at the General Hospital on 28 May 1888. The *Evening Mercury* summed up his story the next day in the following article:

> The unfortunate man known as Count de Courcy, whose death was recorded yesterday, was a well known character about St. John's for the last two or three years. He had a good education, spoke several languages, and had travelled all over the world. His powers as a ventriloquist are well known to those who frequented the same places of resort as he did.

He was always willing, for a glass of grog, to give an exhibition.

Those who knew him intimately say that there is a certain mystery attached to his life which, now that he is dead, will perhaps be unravelled. They say his only fault was love of the intoxicating cup, and "drunk or sober he was always a gentleman".

On Saturday night he was in a public house on Water Street where he said he received a blow on the chest, from some one present, which affected him so much that he could not rise out of bed the next morning. His place of abode was the Sailor's Home, and, on the steward of that establishment going into his room the unfortunate man said that he was dying. Dr. Bunting was sent for and on seeing him ordered him to be conveyed to the Hospital where he died eleven hours after arriving there. Before his death, Miss Cowan, the Matron of the Institution, asked him what his religious persuasion was, he answered Roman Catholic, and she immediately had a priest in attendance who prepared him for death. Miss Cowan also asked the dying man if he had any message to leave for anyone, and he said that he would like to write his wife's address. Taking pen in hand to do so he wrote Countess De C_____ and then expired without finishing the address.

Dr. Shea made a post mortem examination on the body this morning. When the Doctor saw the deceased at the Hospital he was in bed cold and pulseless; he was dying. The Doctor administered the usual remedies, but without avail. There were no marks of violence, but the indications were that he suffered from fatty degeneration of the heart, and the condition of this organ fully accounted for his death.

The only information that can be added to the *Evening Mercury* article, after nearly a hundred years, is that the man spoke fluent French and his English was French accented. He was thought to have been the wastrel son of some French nobleman who, having reached St. John's, came ashore from whatever vessel he was on, drowned himself in drink, and remained.

Besides its characters, the old city can also claim its share of famous sons. They include the great and the small. Henry Supple, Jr., for example, was a St. John's native who is fleetingly remembered as a construction foreman during the building of the Brooklyn Bridge. On 26 August 1876 his name went down in history when he and Edwin Farrington, the foreman of the riggers, became the first people to cross the Bridge. Tens of thousands watched and cheered as the American and the twenty-five-year-old Newfoundlander were pulled across the river in a chair.

William Taylor may not be known to many today, but he made

his mark in America. Born at St. John's on 15 April 1831, he died in Boston on 6 January 1895 and was the subject of a remarkable eulogy in the *Boston Post*. In his exciting lifetime Taylor began his adventures as a sea captain sailing around the world. At the age of thirty he settled in Boston and was elected to the city council. In 1872 he was elected to the Massachusetts House of Representatives. In 1879 he was a State Senator and was the man responsible for the Massachusetts Manhood Suffrage Act. For six years, from 1883, he served as Health Commissioner. He ended his days as Superintendent of the New York and New England Railroad. Following the 1892 Great Fire in St. John's, he spearheaded the relief efforts in Boston.[5]

Lt.-Cmdr. Alastair Mars, a son of P. C. Mars, was born at St. John's in 1915 and had a distinguished career in the navy during World War II. He afterwards settled in England, took up writing, and produced a dozen books, some autobiographical, some fiction. During the war he became a legend as a submarine commander in the Mediterranean Sea. He was credited with sinking thirty thousand tons of enemy shipping. For these exploits he was awarded the Distinguished Service Order, double Distinguished Service Cross, and the Burma Star. After the war he continued to make headlines by suing the Royal Navy for money he figured was due him. He won the suit but was court-martialed and dismissed for refusing to take up a shore posting in England. Another lawsuit followed. He lost, but collected five thousand dollars in severance pay. In order to fight his lawsuits he had to go on the dole, pawn his medals, and take such jobs as driving a furniture van. In 1972 Mars's name flared in the headlines again when he was thrown off the island of Malta while researching a book.[6]

Both native sons and adopted sons of St. John's have won distinction in varying ways and in places both near and far. Their callings made them what they are and their stories are interwoven in the history and traditions of the town. The following have won for themselves particular honours or curious renown and their accomplishments have enriched all our lives. Their stories are briefly told in alphabetical order.

John Murray Anderson

A few days before John Murray Anderson died, 30 January 1954, the New York *Tribune*'s magazine, *This Week*, called him "Uncle Broadway." The greatest American theatrical producer after Florenz Ziegfeld was born in St. John's, 20 September 1886. The Honourable John Anderson was his father.

Known as the "Great Provider," John Anderson came to Newfoundland from Ayreshire in 1875 to work for James Baird as a draper's assistant. He married Amelia Murray, a sister of Andrew and David Murray, and became a Member of the House of Assembly for

St. John's West in 1901. He was appointed to the Legislative Council in 1905.

Young Anderson was educated at Bishop Feild College in St. John's, at Edinburgh Academy in Scotland, and at Lausanne University in Switzerland. John Murray then studied singing in London under Sir Charles Stanley and acting under Sir Herbert Beerbohm Tree. In 1913 he became a dancing teacher in New York and later was producer of revues at the Palais Royal. He wrote and produced his first Broadway play in 1919. It was *The World Mother* and Blanche Bates was the star.[7]

During his long career, John Murray Anderson devised and staged well over one hundred theatrical productions on Broadway, including *Irving Berlin's Music Box Revue*, with Fanny Brice and Grace Moore. The song "All Alone" was introduced in that show. *Greenwich Village Follies* featured two young dancers Anderson had discovered, named Doris Humphreys and Martha Graham, and a comedy player, Lulu McConnell, who was to become famous years later on radio's *It Pays to Be Ignorant*. *What's in a Name* featured another unknown, called Honey Kay, who afterwards changed her first name to Beatrice. *The League of Notions* had the Dolly Sisters; *Jack and Jill* had Clifton Webb and Ann Pennington; and in the first of many editions of *John Murray Anderson's Almanac* Trixie Fraganza introduced the song "I May Be Wrong, but I Think You're Wonderful."

In Hollywood, Carl Laemmle, Sr., wanted Ziegfeld to produce the first technicolor, sound-feature musical film. When Ziegfeld was not available, Anderson accepted the job and made *The King of Jazz* with the great Paul Whiteman. The year was 1930.

In London, Murray Anderson staged *The League of Notions* with the Dolly Sisters; *Bow Bells* in which Binnie Hale introduced "My Temptation"; and *Over the Page*, featuring a new comedian he discovered called Reginald Gardiner. He returned to America to take charge of a series of shows for the newly opened Radio City Music Hall in New York, and this was followed by a production for Billy Rose of the unforgettable theatrical event *Jumbo*, starring Jimmy Durante and featuring such Rogers and Hart songs as "The Most Beautiful Girl in the World." There followed *Thumbs Up* with Eddie Dowling; his wife, Ray Dooley; and Bobby Clark; and after Ziegfeld's death he staged a new *Ziegfeld Follies* with Fannie Brice, Bob Hope, Josephine Baker, Gertrude Niessen, and Judy Canova. It was designed by Vincente Minnelli, and the music, which included "I Can't Get Started," was by Vernon Duke. Ogden Nash supplied Hope's material. It was in Anderson's show that Fannie Brice introduced her immortal Baby Snooks. In London again he presented *Home and Beauty* with Binnie Hale, Jeanette MacDonald, and two young discoveries who afterwards became British film stars, Greta Gynt and Michael Wilding.

In the 1939 New York World's Fair, John Murray Anderson staged the Billy Rose *Aquacade*, starring Eleanor Holm (Mrs. Rose) and Johnny Weismuller (Tarzan). In the second edition, in the 1940 San Francisco Exhibition, Buster Crabbe replaced Weismuller.

For twelve years Anderson put on all the shows at Billy Rose's Diamond Horseshoe in New York with such stars as Fritzi Scheff, Gilda Gray, Ann Pennington, Joe Howard, Mae Murray, Nita Naldi, and Carlyle Blackwell. From 1942, he staged the *Greatest Show on Earth* each year for the Ringling Brothers, Barnum and Bailey Circus. Other Broadway shows followed, including *One for the Money, Two for the Show*, and *Three to Make Ready*. In these, he discovered and helped to stardom such unknowns as Eve Arden, Alfred Drake, Richard Haydn, Betty Hutton, Gene Kelly, Gordon MacRae, and Keenan Wynn. Back in Hollywood he staged the technicolor musical *Bathing Beauty*, with Esther Williams and Red Skelton, for M-G-M, and the production numbers in Cecil B. DeMille's Academy Award-winning circus picture *The Greatest Show on Earth*. *New Faces of 1952* introduced Eartha Kitt, and *Two's Company* had Bette Davis, a girl he first discovered in his acting school many years before. There was another edition of *John Murray Anderson's Almanac* which introduced to America the English comedienne, Hermione Gingold, and discovered an unknown folk singer, Harry Belafonte. This ended the great man's career.

On 30 January 1954 he died in New York City where *Almanac* was being hailed by the *Daily Mirror* as "a bright and brilliant show." Unlike many in show business, who are instantly forgotten, his funeral was attended by big-time and small-time actors and actresses, showgirls, dancers, writers, stagehands, producers, composers, circus performers, roustabouts, clowns, as well as stage and screen stars. It is a matter of regret that the Newfoundland government has not seen fit, so far, to honour this most famous of St. John's-born citizens by naming the theatre in the Arts & Culture Centre, the John Murray Anderson Theatre, after the beloved showman.

Donald Brian

Few Newfoundlanders, hearing somebody sing the words "Long ago I fell in love with a girl like you," or "I'm off to gay Maxim's, the Paris of my dreams," ever realize that these great songs, from Franz Lehar's immortal operetta, *The Merry Widow*, were sung to North American audiences for the first time by a popular singing star who was born at St. John's in 1875, Donald Brian.

The Merry Widow opened at the New Amsterdam Theatre on Broadway, 21 October 1907, and ran for 416 performances. Ethel Jackson was Sonia and Newfoundland's Donald Brian was the dashing hero, Prince Danilo. The popularity of the operetta is undimmed and it is still revived every year somewhere in New York City.

The star was born Dennis O'Brien, the son of a butcher, Dennis Francis O'Brien, who lived on Cockpit Road, now Topsail Road and Craigmillar Avenue. His mother was Margaret Selby. His father was not the Captain O'Brien who had a butcher shop and poultry stall just to the west of the old Market House. This man had emigrated to the United States some years before Donald was born. Donald has also been reported to be the son of Dennis O'Brien, the road inspector, who lived all his life in Newfoundland and died in his house on Queen Street, 2 January 1886.

The future matinee idol made his debut in a concert staged by the Benevolent Irish Society at St. Patrick's Hall in 1880. The five-year-old tot warbled his interpretation of "Little Widow Dunn" and "All on Account of Liza."[8] In no time at all he made a name for himself in St. John's as a concert artist and he was greatly missed in local theatricals when he moved with his family to Boston.

Dennis joined the Old Ivy League Club at Boston College and was prominent in concerts of music, singing, and dancing in the city. He made his professional debut as Hardie Grant in the 1896 production of *Shannon of the Sixth* and changed his name to Donald Brian.

Finding the theatre to his liking he embarked on an acting, singing, and dancing career in road shows and vaudeville. His New York debut took place with Joseph Arthur's Wabush Company. In such popular productions as *The News Boys, The Battle Scarred Hero*, and *The Belle of Broadway*, he worked his way to the top. Stardom came when he played the swashbuckling Captain Donegal in one of the most famous of all musical shows, *Floradora*.

Following leads in *The Silver Slipper* and *Myles Aroon*, the St. John's actor came to the notice of the great George M. Cohan. In 1904 Cohan starred him with Ethel Levey in his new musical, *Little Johnny Jones*, in which he introduced the song *Give My Regards to Broadway*. Cohan later replaced him in the part. In 1906 his name was in lights on Broadway with co-stars Victor Moore and Fay Templeton in George M.'s New Year's night opener, *Forty Five Minutes from Broadway*. When that show proved a smash hit Cohan again took over the role himself. By then Brian had few rivals in popularity and his fan mail was enormous.

George M. next gave him the lead in *Fifty Miles from Boston* but once more took over the part. This seeming setback enabled Donald Brian to grasp his chance for immortality. Because he was free, he was able to accept the leading role in *The Merry Widow*, a role subsequently played in movie versions by John Gilbert and Fernando Lamas. The show placed Brian among the greats of the

American theatre and made him the most popular star on Broadway. Over 10,000 women entered a contest which had a kiss from him as first prize. The films soon beckoned and the actor embarked on a motion picture career.

Strangely, the movies did not bring him the kind of success he enjoyed on the stage. They were silent, so his glorious voice was not heard. His acting was probably not good enough to carry him. After making such indifferent pictures as *The Voice in the Fog*, with Adda Gleason, and *The Smugglers*, with Alma Tell, he abandoned the movies. Had talkies been invented, the story might have been different.

Meanwhile, the theatre was good to Donald Brian. In 1911 he co-starred for the first time with Julia Sanderson in *The Siren*. In 1913 he was starring alone in *The Marriage Market*. Also in 1913 he again teamed with Julia Sanderson in Jerome Kern's *The Girl from Utah*. In that show he sang to Miss Sanderson "They Didn't Believe Me," and the song became an international hit. The year 1916 found him opposite Julia Sanderson once more in *Sybil*. He was starring by himself in *Her Regiment* in 1917. Wilda Bennett was his partner in the 1918 war musical, *The Girl Behind the Gun*, and in 1919 he was being co-starred with Peggy Wood and Roland Young in *Buddies*. In 1921-22 he was in *The Chocolate Soldier*. He was again co-starred with Julia Sanderson in 1925-26, this time in *No, No, Nanette*.

In 1931 Donald Brian repeated the role of Prince Danilo in a Broadway revival. By 1938 he was teaching light opera at the New England Conservatory of Music. His last appearance on the Great White Way was in the 1939 Jerome Kern musical, *Very Warm for May*, with Jack Whiting and Eve Arden. Suffering from heart disease, he retired after that show and died at his home, Window Apartments, Great Neck, New York on 22 December 1948, at the age of seventy-three.

Johnny Burke

One of the most original talents to live in St. John's was born in the city in 1851, probably at 10 King's Road. Johnny Burke's father, Capt. John Burke, was a master mariner and one of the well-known sealing captains. On New Year's Day 1865 he and his oldest son were drowned in a shipwreck at Petty Harbour Motion. His son John followed a less demanding occupation and became a clerk in O'Dwyer's firm on Water Street at the west corner of Beck's Cove, where the Bank of Nova Scotia now stands.

As a youth Johnny Burke soon gave evidence of the keen wit and eye for social satire that was to give him immortality. His song, "The Kelligrew's Soiree," is one of the most famous of Canadian folk songs and is known throughout the English-speaking world. But it is by no means the only popular ballad Johnny Burke ever wrote. Equally enjoyable are such songs as "Trinity Cake," "We Must Close Our Little Shop on Sunday Morning," "The Wedding at Renews," "Teapots at the Fire," "She's Never Been There Before," and "Cod Liver Oil." The latter has been sung around the world by Burl Ives.

Johnny Burke had numerous occupations in addition to that of clerk. He was a poet, actor, singer, and playwright. Whenever an event took place which inspired one of his ballads he could be found selling the sheets, for two to five cents per copy, from a table he would set up on Water Street, in the vacant lot east of the office. To gain attention, he placed on the table an old-fashioned gramophone with a big horn, and the sound of the wax cylinders brought him customers. These broadsheets gave him a little money and the people of St. John's a great deal of pleasure as they read his comments in verse on topical happenings. "The Kelligrew's Soiree," for example, is a masterful takeoff on the snobbery which existed among the upper classes of the day. He was uncanny in his ability to observe the lower classes, the middle classes, and the pretences of the upper classes, in St. John's life and events. He poked gentle fun and might be considered more of a funster than a satirist.

The battle which broke out in the village of Fox Trap, Conception Bay, in June 1880, when railway men tried to put a track through the community, gave him his first musical comedy. The music was shamelessly copied from hits of the day. This assured *The Battle of Foxtrap* an instant popularity when it opened at the T. A. Hall on 2 February 1881.

An English operetta, *The Runaway Girl*, inspired another of his theatrical successes. In an age when little heed was paid to copyright laws, Burke put his own words and a local setting to the popular stage show's music, and *The Runaway Girl from Fogo*, opened in St. John's to loud acclaim.

The peak of Burke's career as an operatic plagiarist was reached on 25 April 1897 when the comic opera burlesque *The Topsail Geisha: A Story of the Wash House* opened at the T. A. Hall. There were fifty performers and a full orchestra. Seats went for fifty cents in the dress circle, and forty cents reserved. So great was the popularity of this local version of the English stage hit, *The Geisha*, that it had to be held over. The setting was St. Thomas, between Topsail and St. Philips.

Burke's last musical comedy was *Cotton's Patch*, a satirical look at Major Cotton's attempts to find a patch of seals from an aeroplane. Instead, he found a patch on some long cotton drawers.

Johnny Burke was usually seen with a bowler hat on his head and a case under his arm. In the case he carried the broadsheets he sold for a penny and his writing materials. A chubby little man with a heavy moustache sagging at the corners of his lips, he always wore in the language of Sean O'Casey "a darlin' smile."[9] Of him it could be truly said "He had laughter and the love of friends." He and the sister with whom he lived resembled nothing so much as two characters out of Dickens. In the age of melodians, when people made their own entertainment, there were few homes in St. John's where the works of Burke were not known, loved, and sung.

One home where they met with little approval was the residence of Archbishop Howley. A Newfoundland magazine that published some pages of local poetry included the verse of the aristocratic Archbishop with that of Johnny Burke. His Grace took pen in hand and castigated the editor for including serious poetry, such as his own, with the nonsense rhymes of Mr. Burke. He did not object to Burke's writing it, only that it should be included with his lines, which were written for the ages, while Johnny Burke's efforts would soon be forgotten. Perhaps it is a charity that the Archbishop does not know how posterity views the work of the two gentlemen.

Johnny Burke died in 1930 at his home at 62 Prescott Street. In the nearly half a century since his passing, his wit remains undated and the implications of his satire are as enjoyable as the day he wrote them.

Archbishop William A. Carew

William Aquinas Carew was born at 155 Queen's Road, St. John's, 23 October 1922, to William J. Carew and Florence Channing. After graduation from St. Bonaventure's College he studied for the priesthood at St. Paul's Seminary in Ottawa and was ordained in St. John's by Bishop Flynn on 15 June 1947.

Six years later, in July 1953, Father Carew assumed a position on the staff of the Secretariat of State in Vatican City. He was soon elevated to the rank of Monsignior and handled all English-speaking VIP audiences with the Pope including the Queen of England and the Presidents of the United States.

The diplomatic talents of the young Monsignor did not pass unnoticed. He was only the second Canadian in the history of the church to enter the diplomatic corps. On 4 January 1970 he was consecrated Bishop and made titular Archbishop of Telde, Spain. At the same time Archbishop Carew was appointed Apostolic Nuncio (Papal Ambassador) to Rwanda and Burundi, the two leading Roman Catholic countries in Africa. He took up residence in Bujumburu, Burundi. In 1972 he headed a papal mission to Bangladesh which resulted in that country asking to establish diplomatic relations with the Vatican.

In May 1972, while Archbishop Carew was in the United States on his way home to St. John's for a holiday, civil strife broke out in Rwanda-Burundi. He was recalled by the Vatican to report on the mass genocide of one of the African tribes said to be taking place. The massacre was eventually brought to the attention of the United Nations and stopped. In 1974 the Archbishop was named by Pope

Paul vı to the highly sensitive post of Apostolic Delegate in Jerusalem and the Holy Land, with the added responsibility of Cyprus.[10] He was immediately involved in the trial by Israel of Greek Catholic Archbishop Hilarion Capucci in Jerusalem for smuggling arms from Lebanon to the Arabs in his automobile, and in the civil war which broke out on the island of Cyprus.

Maurice Cullen

One of the truly great painters in the history of Canadian art, Maurice Cullen, was born at St. John's on 6 June 1866. His father was James Cullen and his mother Sarah Ward, who lived, before the famous artist was born, on the northeast corner of Queen and George Streets. The site was afterwards occupied by Fishermen's Hall.

When Maurice was four years old, the family sailed from St. John's to Montreal where the father hoped to better his lot. The son's preoccupation with art became apparent at an early age, though as a sculptor and not as a painter. When he was fifteen he entered commercial life by taking a position with the Montreal firm of Galt Brothers, but this life did not appeal to a lad of artistic interest. Maurice wanted very much to become a sculptor and had the good fortune to become the pupil of Philippe Hébert, R.C.A., Canada's first monumental sculptor. While an apprentice with Hébert, he helped him prepare the apostle figures on the façade of St. James Cathedral.

Maurice Cullen's mother died when he was twenty-two. She left him a small legacy and this was enough to enable the artist to continue his studies in Paris.[11] He was not long at the École des Beaux-Arts when he realized that his real talent lay, not in sculpture, but in painting. In 1892 he left the École and, taking his brush and canvas, turned to landscape painting in the French countryside at such places as Moret, Giverny, and Le Pouldu.

Five of Cullen's pictures were accepted for the Paris Salon in 1894 and he became an annual contributor until he left France. In 1895 he was elected an associate of the Société Nationale des Beaux-Arts in company with such men as Rodin, Degas, and Whistler. Elected with Cullen that year were Sir John Lavery and Le Sidaner. He was propsed for membership by Gaston La Touche and this was always a matter of pride to him. It was at this time that he made his first important sale. A painting, now belonging to the museum at Pithiviers, was purchased by the French government.

James Wilson Morrice was also in France, and the two Canadian artists met and became close friends. They travelled together and painted in Venice and Brittany and later were to spend several winters painting snow scenes in Beaupré and Quebec.

Returning to Montreal in 1895, Cullen opened a studio at 98 St. Francis Xavier Street. His summers were spent at Beaupré painting the countryside and his winters passed in painting the streets and harbours of Montreal and Quebec. Since his work was radically different from the European-style Canadian painting that was popular then, he was abused and derided and it was several decades before he was to know financial security. His interpretation of Canada in personal and native terms did not suit the collections of wealthy Canadians.

After auctioning off his French and Canadian paintings in 1900, Cullen used the income to finance a trip to France, Italy, Holland, and Algeria where he stayed two years. He found the light and shadows of the African landscape especially appealing and they brought a new brightness to his work.

Back in Montreal in 1902, Cullen opened a studio at 3 Beaver Hall Square. There followed the period in which he produced his unequalled snow scenes while working at Beaupré, Quebec, and Les Eboulements. He followed the changing seasons from autumn into winter to spring, and the play of light from dawn to noon to dusk. It was his observation that "At some hour of the day the commonest subject is beautiful."[12]

It was during this period that Maurice Cullen returned to his native Newfoundland and here, where his family roots were buried deep, he found something he was able to express on canvas with sympathy and understanding. His paintings of Torbay, Petty Harbour, and St. John's now hang in the National Gallery, Ottawa, and are treasured in private collections. Especially impressive is a golden-hued picture of St. John's which he painted from a vantage point on Signal Hill. The city can be seen emerging in the morning sun from a lifting fog that hovers over Gibbet Hill.

It was on a visit to St. John's in 1909 that Cullen met a widow named Barbara Pilot whose late husband, Edward, was a son of Dr. Pilot of Queen's College. They were married the following year and Cullen adopted Mrs. Pilot's son, Robert, who was himself to become an important Canadian painter.

Robert Pilot has written of his stepfather: "He was a man of high ideals and of the greatest probity of character." He has described him as a man of rare tolerance and saving good humour who was greatly loved by all who knew him.

Cullen was commissioned in the army and sent overseas in 1918 with a group of Canadian artists to paint war scenes on the Western Front for Canadian War Memorials. He saw in war only misery and futility, and his sketches and drawings depict suffering and destruction rather than pageantry and glory. His days spent close to the fighting, in the front lines, made a deep impression on the artist.

The place of Maurice Cullen in Canadian art is secure and his name is ranked among the truly great. He brought a completely new vision to Canadian painting and was the first to interpret this country in a personal style that was reflective of Canada rather than of Europe. Inspired by the impressionists, he adapted their methods to suit Canada's region and climate.

His influence on Canadian art can be judged from what has been said about him by some of the outstanding artists of this nation. His contemporary genius, J. W. Morrice, said of Cullen: "He is the one painter in Canada who got at the 'guts' of things." In speaking for the Group of Seven, A. Y. Jackson has stated: "He influenced us more than Morrice did."[13] Others who have testified to his influence over them include Glarence Gagnon, Albert Robinson, and Arthur Lismer.

At Chambly in the Laurentians where he had a studio, set amidst flower gardens, Cullen passed away in 1934. In speaking of the need for originality, this rare and sensitive artist who had changed the course of Canadian landscape painting once counselled a young artist: "Remember, Nature is a great book with most of its leaves uncut."

Professor Danielle

With the closing of Haymarket Square to erect the War Memorial on the site, houses along St. John's Lane, to the west of the square, were torn down to widen the lane and provide greater access between Duckworth and Water Streets. One of the dwellings which disappeared was a small boarding house. In 1866 it took in, as a paying guest, a peculiar gentleman who had just arrived from the United States. His card announced "Charles Henry Danielle—Costumier and Dancing Master."

While there may have been some who wanted dancing lessons in the St. John's of the late 1860s, there was virtually no call at all for the services of a costumier. Professor Danielle immediately set about creating one. Bannerman Park had two rinks, the Avalon and Victoria. One of these he converted to his use as a depot for a costume rental agency. The other was hired for costume-dancing parties and fancy-dress balls.

On the night of 17 July 1878 the fire bell announced to the town that one of the two rinks was ablaze. Because of its proximity to the burning building, the second also caught fire and within an hour both were reduced to ashes, along with the valuable stock of costumes. The financial loss was heavy for the Professor. Taking what insurance money was coming to him, he departed our shores and was soon forgotten. Nobody expected ever to see him again.

There was genuine surprise one day in 1888 when the dapper gent was spied coming down the gangplank of the Allan Line steamer, which had just docked from Halifax. "Is the fire out?" the eccentric dancing master asked as he came ashore. Almost immediately he took a lease on Foran's City Rink, on a height of land off the east side of Prescott Street, above Duckworth Street. In recent years the studios of

Atlantic Films have been located there. On 11 September 1888 he was back in business with "a grand carnival and oriental ball."

Danielle's next venture was the Royal Restaurant on Water Street which opened in 1899. He served what he termed "dainty meals." It was required that the diner be dainty as well, for Danielle abhorred coarseness and vulgarity. He was known to order customers from the restaurant if he did not approve of their manners at table. His criticisms were hurled at the mighty as well as the lowly and no one dared contradict him because he published a little book each year in which he mercilessly exposed the ill manners and rude conduct of those patrons who would not be chastised. His motto was "Godliness Is Next to Cleanliness" and he complained of the taunt that his place was "too damned clean."

This establishment was burned out in the Great Fire of 1892. After a brief fling at running a temporary Royal in the upper part of Beck's Cove, Professor Danielle's next project was an establishment at Quidi Vidi, known as the Royal Lake Pavilion. It had a dining room, sixty by forty feet, and an overhead ballroom. With the exception of Regatta Day, business was disappointing, and vandalism was a problem. After two years he had the pavilion dismantled and, with the cooperation of the Reid-Newfoundland Railway, shipped it to a pond just beyond Irvine Station.

Of this 1895 move, the professor writes:

> Unable to endure the persecutions at Quidi Vidi Lake any longer and remain outside the insane asylum I bought this property, tore down the four thousand and five hundred Royal Lake Pavilion, carted it through town to the railway station, railroaded it and its plant to Irving Station, carted it again to the present Octagon grounds, tore down old buildings, and with a thousand more feet of lumber I erected this magnificent unsurpassed Octagon Castle. Then my real heartaches only began.

The proprietor imagined himself to be the butt of jealousy, lies, name calling, and assorted calumnies.

Octagon Castle, as the eight-sided building was called, gave its name to the nearby pond. It was opened in June 1896 by Sir William Whiteway, the Prime Minister. The curious building became a Mecca, not only for gourmets but also for sightseers. It was a four-storey structure with wings running east and west. The dining area was the full size of the rotunda with four flights of stairs leading up the octagonal walls to galleries. The railings were hung with paintings and satin banners. The ceiling was thirty feet high. Meals were served at long tables which accommodated over a dozen people, each in baronial splendour. There was a reading room and a ladies parlour, entered through a high archway elaborately hung with satin and plush draperies. These were embroidered in gold and bespangled. One of the Professor's great talents was embroidery and he was expert at crewel and petit point.

The bridal chamber was dazzling in gold and silver. It was a bower of satin, lace, and plush with a quilt valued at seven hundred dollars, embroidered with 19,732 small overlapping shells of satin which took two and a half years and eighty-five yards of material of every shade and colour to complete. There is a story told about a couple of newlyweds from around the bay who were stopping overnight at the Castle, on their way to St. John's. As the evening wore on, they made no move to go to bed, in an age when people retired early. Ten o'clock came, then ten-thirty, and finally eleven o'clock without any sign of movement by the couple. Thinking his guests too shy to ask, Professor Danielle said, "If you'll both follow me I'll show you where to find the chamber." The bridegroom looked up from the fire and replied, "That's all right, sir, just show it to the woman, I'll do mine out the window."

The building occupied 3,780 square feet of ground. It had 9,979 running feet of moulding and the Professor went over every foot with three coats of Aspinal enamel. It took 25,000 tacks to hold the 1,040 yards of wall cotton he used to cover the walls. Danielle claimed "Tub butter [margarine] has never been served on the tables of the Octagon, only good pure fresh butter." Single meals were fifty cents and "married meals" one dollar.

On the third floor of the Castle there was a room which was kept locked but was shown to every visitor. Called the mortuary room, it held the dancing master's coffin, supported on two small tables. Built in 1894, it was covered in black velvet and embroidered with gold vines, flowers, and a gold lyre on each side. The interior was upholstered with 7,800 shells of white satin. There was also a fluted satin pillow of eiderdown. A white satin shroud and a pair of golden slippers lay inside awaiting the decease of their owner. On a wall, near the head of the casket, a gilt frame held his picture and a sheet of paper on which was written: "In the back of this frame will be found full instructions to be followed immediately after my death.—C. H. Danielle." The walls were covered with two-foot diamonds of paper cut from wallpapers of numerous patterns.

Charles Henry Danielle expired at four o'clock on the afternoon of Thursday, 1 May 1902. He was seventy-two years old, having been born in Baltimore, Maryland, 1 November 1830. In a notice of his death, the *Evening Herald* said he had come to Newfoundland to teach dancing, of which art he was a master. It added "The professor was a man of varied parts and in a larger sphere might have risen to eminence. Even here he was a notable feature."[14]

According to instructions, the corpse was borne by special train, on Sunday, from the Octagon to the new railway terminal on Water Street, where the coffin was opened and the public allowed to view the remains for half an hour inside the uncompleted station. The funeral then proceeded on foot to the Church of England cemetery, where the tomb of his own design may still be seen, near the chapel. The Professor was unmarried and without relatives. His heir was Fred Brazill, a young man he had adopted, who was assisting him in the management of the Octagon.

There was a fire there on 1 March 1906, but the place was repaired. On 24 February 1915 the famous building was totally destroyed in another fire of unknown origin. The proprietor at the time was a Mr. Poole and the building was owned by R. Fowlow of Trinity. During the Smallwood era a German firm built a tool plant at the Octagon, and a house on the site of the Castle was lived in by some of the German administrators. The tool plant became McNamara Industries when the firm became insolvent.

Johnny Dwyer

A boy who was to become the professional heavyweight boxing champion of North America was born near the Crossroads, in St. John's, 15 August 1847. His name was Johnny Dwyer.

In 1879 the boxing title holder was a tough, mean veteran of the ring named Jimmy Elliott, who had been in prison for shooting and killing Jere Dunn, a notorious character and former Chief of Police of Elmira, New York, in a tavern brawl. Released with a pardon, the Heavyweight Champion was matched against Newfoundland's Johnny Dwyer on 8 May 1879 at Long Point, Canada, in a bout for the American championship.

Elliott, who was badly beaten for nine rounds, wet his hands with turpentine and blinded Dwyer. The young fighter's sight was restored with fresh water but he was so angered he clobbered his opponent unmercifully, until he stopped Elliott in the twelfth round, with an injury to his ribs and a knockout.

The St. John's native was Heavyweight Champion of North America. He retired undefeated for, strangely enough, having gained the championship, Johnny Dwyer never fought another professional bout. The following year the titled passed to Paddy Ryan who lost it, in his second title bout two years later, to John L. Sullivan. Dwyer became Chief Clerk in the Brooklyn County Court and died when probably still in his forties of unknown causes.[15]

Sir Wilfred Grenfell

On the day St. John's was destroyed in the Great Fire of 1892, a ship arrived from England carrying on board a twenty-seven-year-old doctor named Wilfred Grenfell. He was on his way to Labrador for the National

Mission to Deep Sea Fishermen. The story of his disappointments, his near fatal adventures, and his ultimate triumph is a saga of St. Anthony and Labrador.

In 1905 Dr. Grenfell decided to build a seamen's hostel in St. John's. It was his hope to make it the finest place of its kind in the world, on some land given him on the St. John's waterfront by Sir Edgar Bowring, and a building to attract the twenty-five hundred fishermen who annually visited the city was immediately begun. Grenfell, who was also an evangelist, hoped his building would prove more appealing to the men and women on the numerous coastal schooners from the outports than the taverns of the city. He estimated the cost would be something over a hundred thousand dollars and set about raising the money in Canada, the United States, and England.

The four-storey building, of dull red brick, was to be named the King George V Institute, after the monarch who laid the cornerstone in Buckingham Palace by pressing a button that sent a signal through the Atlantic cable to St. John's.

The town turned out "en fête" for the laying of the cornerstone. A direct electric connection was established between the site on Water Street and a room in Buckingham Palace. At 4:00 p.m., the King, just back from the Coronation ceremonies at Westminster Abbey, prepared to press the button which would lower the stone into place, 12:30 p.m. Newfoundland time.

At the building site, Governor Sir Ralph Williams, trusting to God and the invention of electricity, at one minute to the appointed hour had the brigades called to attention. The massed bands were made ready. Turning to the people he said, "In a few seconds His Majesty the King will touch a button at Buckingham Palace which will lower that stone in its place. He will be with you Newfoundlanders on this his Coronation Day in sympathy and in action, as you are in sympathy with him. Raise your hats in honour of His Majesty."[16]

Sir Ralph raised his hat and turned hopefully toward the stone. Within seconds a big gong signalled thirty minutes past noon. As the spectators stared in wonder, the stone descended quietly into place in the mortar the Governor had laid to receive it. A burst of wild cheering followed, the Brigades presented arms, and the massed bands rendered "God Save the King." The laying of the first cornerstone, anywhere in the world, by remote control, had been accomplished without a hitch. The event brought much publicity to the work of Dr. Grenfell. When the home was opened, 11 June 1912, congratulations poured in from all over the world, including messages from King George, Queen Mother Alexandra, and President Taft.

The final cost of the seamen's home was nearly $175,000. The New York architects, Delano and Aldrich, made a gift of their $10,000 design.[17] The place was fitted out with sleeping cubicles for men and women, a shoemaker's shop, sewing room, barber shop, hairdressers, lunch room, games room, lounge, swimming pool, and a three-hundred-seat auditorium. At last, the thousands of fishermen visiting St. John's would be spared the temptation of public houses, and the young ladies, who in their hundreds manned the galleys, need no longer tremble on the brink of moral disaster on the streets of the town. In time, the Institute closed and the building was acquired by the Newfoundland government. Part of it became a YMCA headquarters.

A bronze plaque on the building reads: "This house was built for the welfare of seamen by the gifts of many friends inspired and united by the Christian work of Wilfred T. Grenfell missionary on the coasts of Newfoundland and Labrador." The famous cornerstone may be seen to the left of the eastern entrance.

With the coming of war in 1939 St. John's once more began to fill with thousands of seamen with nowhere to go but the taverns. Unlike Sir Wilfred Grenfell's fishermen, these were the crews of allied warships and merchant ships plying the North Atlantic. On 2 October 1940 the St. John's War Services Committee was formed, following a meeting at Government House. The Committee decided to open a hostel for the armed forces somewhere along the waterfront.

Because of the facilities it contained, it was decided to seek the use of the King George V Institute. The Commission of Government gave the necessary permission. Donations of furniture, bedding, crockery, and cutlery were sought, and five thousand dollars spent on redecorating. Finally the building was ready. It was called the Caribou Hut, after the emblem of the Royal Newfoundland Regiment, and its doors were opened by Governor Walwyn on 23 December 1940.

From the day of its opening until its final closing on 17 June 1945, nearly 725,000 servicemen and women used The Caribou Hut;[18] 1,500,000 meals were served and over 4,000 beds were rented each month. In the beginning there were twenty-three beds available at thirty cents each. The number of beds soon grew to 260 and these were frequently given free of charge to men who were survivors of enemy action in the Atlantic. In addition to the facilities put there by Dr. Grenfell, there were bowling, movies, and dances (hosted by the belles of the town), and on Sunday nights there was hymn singing. His Royal Highness, the Duke of Kent, and Her Royal Highness, the Countess of Athlone, were just two of the celebrated persons entertained at the Hut. Fund raising campaigns conducted in the city kept the books balanced.

Thousands of sailors and merchant seamen from Britain wallowed in the plentiful supply of boiled, fried, poached, and scrambled eggs. Many seamen had them there for the last time. It was not unusual for a ship to leave St. John's and be lost with all hands, or just a few survivors, sometimes within hours of departure. A number of these sailors left young widows in the town. Almost all of them left friends among the

394

ladies of the Caribou Hut who had come to know their faces, if not their names.

With the peace of 1945, the King George V Institute reverted to a government office building. The third interesting period of its history was begun after the war, when part of it was converted into a Fishermen's Centre, for the thousands of European fishermen that annually visit the port.

Harold Horwood

The firstborn of Andrew and Vina Horwood was born at 140 Campbell Avenue on 2 November 1923. He was educated at Prince of Wales College in St. John's and, following high school graduation, turned to writing and journalism.

Journalism brought him into contact with Joey Smallwood, and in 1949, at the age of twenty-six, Horwood was elected a Liberal member of the first provincial House of Assembly. From 1946 to 1948 he had published a literary review, *Protocol*. He was a reporter, columnist, and editor of the *Evening Telegram* from 1952 to 1958. In 1960 he was associate editor of the *Examiner*, a weekly newspaper that lasted about one year. In its short life it won an award as the outstanding Canadian weekly of the year.

In 1966 Horwood's first novel, *Tomorrow Will Be Sunday*, was published in Toronto, and this brought him national recognition. The 1966 novel was followed by *The Foxes of Beachy Cove*, a travel guidebook called *Newfoundland*, and a Labrador novel *White Eskimo*.

Frank Knight

One of the major announcers of the United States radio and television networks was born in St. John's May 10, 1894. Frank Knight's father was Herbert E. Knight, a lawyer, and his mother was Fanny Clift. He started school at Bishop Feild but his father switched him to St. Bonaventure's College. After graduation he went to work for the Bank of Commerce leaving in 1914 to enlist in the Royal Newfoundland Regiment.

Knight was back in St. John's in 1916 suffering from shell-shock. The following year he left the city never to return. First he tried medicine at McGill but gave that up and went to New York to go on the stage. After parts in several Broadway plays, including "House Unguarded" he entered radio in 1926 with WABC in New York. The following year he moved to CBS where he became one of America's leading announcers along with such people as Graham McNamee and Milton Cross.

The rich, elegant voice of Frank Knight was perhaps best known for the many years he announced the CBS radio shows "Longine Symphonette" and "Choraliers". He later announced Longine's "Chronoscope" series on CBS-TV.

A fire in his apartment at 170 E. 77th Street in New York City,

October 10, 1973, took the life of his actress wife, Mildred Wall, who made a name for herself on Broadway in "Dark Victory" and other plays. The announcer was taken unconscious from the apartment and died October 18 without ever regaining consciousness. The President of the Longine Watch Company spoke at his funeral service which was attended by many show business celebrities.

Sergeant Mike McCarthy

Newfoundland's only winner of the United States Congressional Medal of Honour was born in St. John's in 1845, in a house on the southeast corner of Meeting House Hill (now Victoria St.) and Gower Street. His father was Charles McCarthy, a wharf manager for the coal premises of James & Robert Kent.

After graduating from Renouf's Academy, Mike went to work in the newspaper office of the *Newfoundlander*. In 1863, when he was eighteen years old, his father moved the family to Boston where the lad enlisted in the U.S. Volunteers and was later transferred to the Civil War cavalry regiment of General (Fighting Phil) Sheridan. In 1867 he worked as a printer in Arizona, but by 1869 he was back in the army. When the Nez Percé War broke out in 1877, First Sgt. Michael McCarthy was at White Bird Canyon, Idaho, on June 17 with ninety-nine men of the First Cavalry and some civilians, when the Indians ambushed the troops.

In the battle two horses were shot from under McCarthy and a third was wounded, but he survived by playing dead as the Indian women plundered the bodies. On 11 July 1877 he was in the Battle of Clearwater against the famous Chief Joseph and his Nez Percé. He was mentioned in the report of the engagement. Then, on October 4, at White Bear Canyon, he was present for the surrender of Chief Joseph.

Twenty years after the White Bird Creek engagement he was awarded the Congressional Medal of Honour for his valour in the fight. Mike McCarthy died a Colonel, in Walla Walla, Washington, 12 January 1914. His portrait may be seen in the Headquarters of the Washington State National Guard.[19]

Robert Pilot

Robert Pilot's father was Edward Frederick Pilot, a son of Canon Pilot of the Anglican Church. Dr. Pilot, who gave his name to Pilot's Hill (just as his fellow clergyman, Cannon Wood, gave his name to Wood Street), came to Newfoundland in 1867 as Vice-Principal of Queen's College. Robert was born at 2 Ordnance Street. His mother was Barbara Merchant. She was probably a daughter of Valentine Merchant, the businessman who owned Merchant's Block on Water Street. Merchant's headstone, near the main gate in Belvedere Cemetery, lists his wife's name as Barbara. She was a native of Portsmouth, England, and the similarity of

396

names seems to suggest that the Barbara Merchant who married Edward Pilot was their daughter.

Their son, Robert Wakeham Pilot, was born on 9 October 1898. Following the death of his father, the mother married Maurice Cullen in 1910. Influenced by his stepfather, young Pilot turned to painting. He studied art in Montreal and at the Academy Julian in Paris. In 1922 he was admitted to the Salon de la Société Nationale des Beaux-Arts in Paris. Winner of the Jessie Dow Prize in 1932 and 1934, Pilot became an associate of the Royal Canadian Academy in 1935.

Much of his work is seascapes but he also executed murals, decorative work, and frescoes, as well as a number of paintings of St. John's. From 1952 to 1954 he was President of the Royal Canadian Academy. He was also elected to membership in the National Academy of Design, New York, and the Institute of British Architects, London. [20] He made his home at 51 deLavigne, Westmount, Quebec, where he died on 17 December 1967.

Archbishop Francis Phelps

Francis Robinson Phelps, D.D., was born on 19 September 1863 at St. John's where his father, Rev. Joseph Phelps, held office at Queen's College. He left Newfoundland for studies at Keble College, Oxford, where he earned his M.A. in 1884. Ordained in 1887, he served in London until 1896 when he became Rector of Bishopsthorpe, Norfolk.

In 1909 the Reverend Mr. Phelps was appointed warden of St. Peter's Home, Grahamstown, South Africa. He served as Dean of Grahamstown from 1914 to 1915 when he was consecrated Bishop. The following year he became a Doctor of Divinity. In 1931 he was appointed Archbishop of Cape Town and Primate of South Africa. He retired in 1938 to Iffley, Oxfordshire, where he died on 27 June 1938 and was buried in Iffley Churchyard.

The St. John's native had risen to the highest position in the Anglican Church in South Africa where he is still remembered with affection and esteem.

Christopher Pratt

Born at Grace Hospital, St. John's, on 9 December 1935, Christopher Pratt now lives and works in St. Catherine's, St. Mary's Bay. After graduating from Prince of Wales College, he studied art for two years under Alex Colville at Mount Allison University. His paintings and graphics have placed him in the foreground of modern Canadian artists. He is one of the leading painters in Canada. While his work reflects the influence of Colville and Andrew Wyeth, it is uniquely his own and distinctly expressive of his Newfoundland environment. His dedication to detail and perfection has limited his output so that an international reputation has been slow in coming.

Until Christopher was eight years old, the Pratt family occupied a basement apartment at 216 LeMarchant Road. They then moved to 93 Waterford Bridge Road where the artist lived until he began his art studies. These were followed by a course at the Glasgow School of Art. When he returned to Newfoundland with his wife, Mary West of Fredericton, he opened a studio in the family summer home at St. Catherine's where he is still living.

Pratt's work is in the collections of the National Gallery of Canada; Confederation Art Gallery, Charlottetown; Department of External Affairs, Ottawa; Vancouver Art Gallery; and many others. In recent years, Mary Pratt has emerged as one of the most promising women painters in Canada, and she has earned herself a national reputation. In 1972 Memorial University recognized Christopher Pratt with an honorary doctorate, and in 1973 he was elected to the Order of Canada.

E. J. Pratt

The man who is generally acknowledged by critics to be the foremost Canadian poet, Edwin John Pratt, was born in Western Bay, Newfoundland, but came to live in St. John's as a very small boy. John Pratt, a dedicated Methodist missionary emigrated from the North Riding of Yorkshire to Newfoundland in 1873. In 1877 he married Fanny Knight, daughter of Captain William Knight, and their son Edwin was born at Western Bay, 4 February 1882. When Rev. John Pratt answered the call to take charge of Cochrane St. Church the family moved to St. John's.

The future poet spent some of his early years living at 24 Leslie Street. His father was minister at Cochrane Street at the time of the Great Fire of 1892. The Pratts later moved to Grand Bank where the stern preacher died 15 March 1904. His body was carried to St. John's on board the S.S. *Home* for burial in the General Protestant Cemetery.

Ned, as Edwin John became known, left school while still quite young to become a draper's apprentice. However, three years later he was happy to return to school and graduate with honours. He looked to the Methodist ministry and taught and preached in Newfoundland. After graduating from Victoria College at the University of Toronto and a year or so of preaching he turned to teaching as his vocation, ultimately joining the staff of Victoria College where he had the opportunity of becoming a major poet.

With *Titans* in 1926 Ned Pratt broke away from the romantic tradition in Canadian poetry. *Dunkirk* (1941) is considered one of the best poems of World War II. *The Titanic* and the long narrative poem *Bre-*

beuf and His Brethren, a triumphant telling of the story of the Jesuit martyrs of Huronia, are among his major works.

E. J. Pratt married Viola Whitney and their only child, Claire, the editor of this book, was born in 1921. The great poet died 26 April 1964. He was a brother of Senator Calvert Pratt of Newfoundland and a great uncle of Christopher Pratt, the artist.

Thomas Ricketts

Although a native of Middle Arm, White Bay, Thomas Ricketts lived most of his life in St. John's. During World War I he advanced his age from sixteen years to eighteen years in order to enlist in the Newfoundland Regiment. He was awarded the Victoria Cross for conspicuous bravery and devotion to duty on 14 October 1918. He was seventeen years old.

Having first seen action at Steenbeek, Ricketts was wounded by a bullet in the leg at Marcoing. After rejoining his battalion in front of Drie-Masten, he volunteered to go forward with his section commander and a Lewis gun to attempt to outflank an enemy battery. They advanced through heavy machine-gun fire and were still three hundred yards from the battery when their ammunition was exhausted. The young Newfoundland soldier doubled back a hundred yards, procured some ammunition, dashed back, and by very accurate fire with the Lewis gun, drove the enemy into a farm, enabling his platoon to advance without casualties. Eventually they captured five field guns, four machine guns, and eight prisoners. Private Ricketts's presence of mind and utter disregard for personal safety won him the Victoria Cross, one of only seventeen bestowed in the whole of World War I. He was the youngest winner of the medal in the British Army in that war. The investiture took place at Sandringham on 21 January 1919, just before the soldier was due to return home. King George V introduced him to Queen Mary and others present with the words, "This is the youngest v.c. in my army."[21] There seems to be almost a conspiracy of silence about Newfoundland's only other v.c. winner, Bernard Croke, of the Canadian Expeditionary Force who was awarded the citation for his action during the opening stage of the World War I Battle of Amiens. Little is known of him or his exploits.

F. Scott Fitzgerald once wrote: "Show me a hero and I'll write you a tragedy." This certainly seems true of Tommy Ricketts. The young man, little more than a boy, returned to an adulation with which he was not prepared to cope. A painfully shy and self-effacing outport lad, he retreated into a shell of introversion from which he never emerged. After taking a chemist's course, he opened a drugstore on Water Street, on the western corner of the foot of Job Street.

Every attempt to bring him before the public was greeted with hostility and he became a recluse refusing interviews by the press, radio, and television. He behaved almost as if he didn't even want the public to patronize his drugstore. It was seldom painted or repaired. As the years went by the floors sagged, the shelves gaped empty, and the clapboards decayed. By the time of the death of the lonely hero, 10 February 1967, the building was in such a bad state of disrepair that the Council had to issue an order for it to be torn down, as a hazard to public safety.

Sir Ambrose Shea

The first and only Newfoundlander to be appointed Governor of the Colony was born at St. John's in 1816. He was a leading figure in the commercial life of his day and Newfoundland agent for the Galway Line. Shea's office was on the north side of Water Street, a few doors west of Cochrane Street. His wharf, known as the Galway Wharf, was opposite the office.

In 1848 Shea entered the House of Assembly as representative for the District of Placentia. He was Speaker of the House in 1855. Skilled at diplomacy, he served on various delegations sent by the Legislature to England, the United States of America, and Canada.

Along with Sir Frederick Carter, he was a Newfoundland delegate to the Quebec Conference in 1864, which resulted in the formation of Canada. Because they took part in that meeting, both Carter and Shea are listed among the Fathers of Confederation. They returned to Newfoundland converted to the cause of one Dominion from sea to sea, but the idea met with hostility among their fellow Newfoundlanders.

In 1886 Ambrose Shea was knighted, and appointed Governor of Newfoundland. However, the anti-Confederates made such a fuss that the honour was withdrawn. The following year, in a face-saving gesture, Sir Ambrose was sent to be governor of the Bahamas. He left St. John's for Nassau and later a self-imposed exile in England. Twice married, to a Miss Nixon and a Mrs. (Bouchette) Hart of Quebec, he died in London at 66 Redcliff Square, South Kensington, 30 July 1905.

The remains were sent back to St. John's for a state funeral. They arrived on board the S.S. *Carthaginian* on Tuesday, August 22, and were borne to the Colonial Building for lying in state. The front of the place was draped in black bunting as was the House of Assembly chamber where the coffin was given an honour guard of police. It was uncovered, and at 7:00 p.m. the building was opened to the public, who streamed through the chamber all night. In the morning the body was carried to the Roman Catholic Cathedral where Archbishop Howley delivered the panegyric. Sir Ambrose was buried at Belvedere, August 23, as the guns at Fort Townshend fired a salute every minute during the funeral procession.

George Summers

George Bernard Summers was born in 1906 at St. John's where his father, P. J. Summers, was once Deputy Minister of Justice. At the age of twenty-three, George Summers entered the law firm of C. J. Fox, Q.C. Until 1934 he practised law in Corner Brook at which time he entered the service of the Commission of Government. In 1944 he joined the British army with the rank of Captain, and retired in 1947 as a Colonel.

In 1950 George Summers joined the External Affairs Department of the Canadian government and, within four years, became the Chargé d'Affairs at the Canadian Legation in Prague. In 1957 he was made Minister of the Canadian Legation in Teheran. When that legation was elevated to the rank of an embassy in 1961, Summers became Canada's first Ambassador to Iran. In 1962 he was appointed Canadian Ambassador to Chile, which post he held until his retirement from the diplomatic corps in 1970, at the age of sixty-four.

Major-General Sir Hugh Tudor

Hugh Tudor was born at Newton Abbey, Devonshire, in 1870. His father was Rev. Harry Tudor, sub-dean of Exeter Cathedral. He died at St. John's on 25 September 1965 at the age of ninety-five. Few Newfoundlanders realized that the old, blind gentleman was Major-General Sir Hugh Tudor, Commander of the notorious Black and Tans, in Ireland, after World War I.

Sir Hugh spent most of his life in the military before coming to Newfoundland. When he was wounded in the Boer War his close friend Winston Churchill, wired him in December 1899: "Best wishes for a Happy Christmas, swift recovery and all the luck of the war." Tudor was Commander of the Ninth Scottish Division in France during World War I and he is recognized as the inventor of the smoke screen in modern warfare. His diary, "The Fog of War," was published by himself in mimeograph form.

In March 1920 a group of out-of-work British ex-soldiers were sent to Ireland to help put down that nation's growing demands for independence. They were temporary constables of the Royal Irish Constabulary. As there were not nearly enough police uniforms to go around, the former soldiers were dressed in khaki uniforms with black belts. The sight of them put some Irish wit in mind of a famous pack of hounds known as Black and Tans. The name stuck. It was afterwards to fill Irishmen with terror and hatred.

Maj.-Gen. Sir Hugh Tudor was sent to Ireland in command of

401

the Black and Tans, the Royal Irish Constabulary, and the Dublin Metropolitan Police. He remained a shadowy figure in the background during the turmoil which followed, including the murder of MacCurtain, the Lord Mayor of Cork. His picture never appeared in the press and he was seldom seen in public. It is difficult to assess the role he played. Liam Deasy, former commandant-general of the pre-1922 IRA in the Cork area, says that the IRA intelligence, which was of the most brilliant achievement of Michael Collins, reported that Tudor, unlike other top-ranking British military men such as Crozier and Strickland, backed the excesses of the Black and Tans to the hilt. Deasy comments that perhaps Tudor believed Lloyd George sent them over to Ireland for just such a dirty job. Liam Deasy is a reliable informant, fairminded and well-educated. He retired to business after he parted company with de Valera in the middle of the brief Civil War in Ireland in 1923, when he was a member of the underground Republican executive.

On 9 February 1921, an undisciplined raid by Black and Tan Auxiliaries which, by exaggeration became known as "the notorious looting of Trim," caused £325 damage. That same night an auxiliary commander shot two young Irish prisoners in a field near Drumcondra. General Crozier went first to Trim where he summarily tried twenty-six Auxiliary cadets and held back five for trial. He returned to Dublin to find an inquiry was to be held into the Drumcondra shootings but, so he later claimed, the evidence was rigged.

General Tudor was not satisfied with General Crozier's conduct at Trim, or in the Drumcondra trial. In November he had deprived him of the power to dismiss auxiliaries. The twenty-six cadets were reinstated by Tudor, and Crozier resigned. When he reached London his charges against Tudor made front-page stories. He filled the press with accounts of his unjust treatment by the General and tales of atrocities committed by men under his command. A few years later some of the charges were repeated by Desmond McCarthy in *Lord Oxford's Letters to a Friend*. Tudor threatened an action for libel. McCarthy investigated and found that most of them were without foundation. He issued a public apology, deleted the offending pages, and wrote to Tudor: "I constantly think of my escape with amazed relief and gratitude. Think of it! If you had taken action, I should have been fighting shoulder to shoulder with Crozier. It would have been painfully true of my position then: 'His honour rooted in dishonour stood.' "

The last word on Crozier belongs to Mrs Asquith. As they strolled the lawn before lunch at Sutton Courtenay, the wife of the British Prime Minister said to him, "They tell me that you are as much a murderer as any of them, only you like things done in an orderly manner, and at Trim they were disorderly."

402

After being relieved of his command in Ireland, Tudor sought refuge in a place where the IRA would be unlikely to find him. He turned up working for Templeman's, a fish company at Bonavista. After being loaned to George M. Barr, a leading St. John's fish exporter and the man who is credited with starting the commercial lobster fishery in Newfoundland, the ex-General moved to St. John's and lived in Barr's home on Circular Road.

Sir Hugh had a wife, two daughters, and a son in England, but they never joined him in his self-imposed exile. He never discussed his service in Ireland. During the visit of King George VI and Queen Elizabeth to Newfoundland in 1938, Tudor was invited to a reception at Government House. He went with the hope that his Black and Tans service would be unknown to the monarch, but when his name was called at the reception, His Majesty looked up and inquired in a loud voice, "Are you the man who commanded in Ireland?"

Following George Barr's death, Maj.-Gen. Sir Hugh Tudor lived at Apartment 19, Churchill Square. He died in the Veterans Pavilion at the General Hospital in 1965, forgotten by even the IRA. Most persons in Ireland, who knew of him, were amazed to find he had not died years before.

Notes

It is impossible to refer here to all the sources that have been consulted or quoted. This is to be regretted as many of those not given may be important. However, in the circumstances it was not possible to do otherwise. The following abbreviations are used: Prowse refers to *A History of Newfoundland* by D. W. Prowse, Q.C., still the most definitive history of Newfoundland; *D.N.—Daily News;* *E.T.—Evening Telegram;* M.U.N.—Memorial University of Newfoundland; *N.S.—Newscene;* *N.Q.—Newfoundland Quarterly,* and N.P.A.— Newfoundland Provincial Archives. Colonial records refers to correspondence in the Governor's letter books in the Newfoundland Provincial Archives.

CHAPTER 1.

1. S. E. Morison, *The European Discovery of America*, letter, p. 206.
2. State Archives, Boston, Mass.
3. E. R. Seary, *Place Names of the Avalon Peninsula of The Island of Newfoundland*, p. 271.
4. G. R. F. Prowse, "The Origin of the Name of St. John's," *N.Q.* (June 1903), p. 5.
5. Richard Hakluyt, extra series, VIII, 9-16.
6. H. P. Biggar, *Voyages of Jacques Cartier*, p. 236.
7. Morison, *op. cit.*, p. 572.
8. D. B. Quinn and N. M. Cheshire, *The New Found Land of Stephen Parmenius*, letter, p. 171.
9. Morison, p. 578.
10. H. C. Saunders, *Jersey in the 18th & 19th Centuries*, p. 217.
11. Archives of Bristol Merchant Venturers Society, MacInnes papers.
12. G. T. Gill, *English Enterprise in Newfoundland*, p. 78.
13. James P. Howley, "The Origin of the Ships Rooms," *N.Q.* (March 1903), p. 17.
14. J. N. Kane, *Famous First Facts & Records* (New York, Ace Books), p. 217.
15. H. W. LeMessurier, "Ancient St. John's," *N.Q.* (December 1903), p. 9.
16. Prowse, p. 194.
17. *Ibid.*, p. 175.
18. *Ibid.*, p. 205.
19. "Report of Newfoundland in 1711," *E.T.* (16 July 1949).
20. Archives of Board of Trade, Waterford, Ireland.

21. *Times* (London), 14 October 1796.
22. F. L. N. Poynter, *The Journal of James Yonge*, p. 55.
23. A. Redman, *The House of Hanover*, p. 95.
24. *Ibid.*, p. 357.
25. *E.T.*, Letter, (18 March 1881).
26. L. A. Anspach, "History of the Island of Newfoundland," pp. 254-255.
27. Presentation Convent, Galway Sesquicentenary Souvenir Booklet (1965), p. 17.
28. *Ibid.*, p. 19.
29. *Ibid.*, p. 21.
30. Basilica Centenary Book, p. 210.
31. J. R. Smallwood, *The Book of Newfoundland*, II, 345.
32. P. Tocque, *Kaleidoscope Echoes*, pp. 113-114.
33. M. Preston, "Victorian Homes," British Book League article.
34. Hatton & Harvey, *Newfoundland*, p. 125.

CHAPTER 2.
1. State Papers Foreign, Spain SP 94/1 no. 106.
2. Hakluyt, *Principal Navigations*, VIII, 165.
3. Prowse, p. 133.
4. Samuel Purchas, *His Pilgrimes*, XIX, 417; pro, co 1/1, f179.
5. Prowse, p. 197.
6. *Ibid.*, p. 175.
7. Petition to the King in Council, 1669, C.O. 1: 66 no. 71.
8. Prowse, p. 214.
9. Baudoin, unpublished diary, Quebec MSS.
10. Prowse, p. 223.
11. Archives, Merchant Venturers Society, Bristol.
12. N. P. A., Richards, unpublished diary.
13. *Tyranny in St. John's: 1705-1706* (Publications of Newfoundland & Labrador Provincial Affairs), 1971, p. 8.
14. MS Collection de Documents Relatifs à l'Histoire de la Nouvelle France (Quebec), *E.T.*, (13 December 1893).
15. *Tyranny in St. John's, op. cit.*, p. 16.
16. *Ibid.*, p. 43.
17. *Ibid.*, p. 40.
18. State Archives, Boston, Mass.
19. Prowse, p. 268 (Charlevoix's account).
20. *Ibid.*, p. 270 (Section G).
21. Prowse, pp. 305-306.
22. Colville, Rear Admiral Lord, Dispatches, 1761, 1762, Occasional Papers No. 6 (Maritime News of Canada), p. 23.
23. Prowse, p. 309.
24. *Ibid.*, p. 25.
25. *Ibid.*, p. 413 (Section C).
26. Colville, Dispatches, *op. cit.*, p. 36.
27. Archives, Merchant Venturers Society, Bristol.
28. State Archives, Boston, Mass.

29.   Ray Guy, *E. T.* (17 June 1966), p. 31.
30.   N.P.A., Colonial Records, 1778.
31.   D. A. Webber, *Skinner's Fencibles*, Newfoundland Naval & Military Museum (1964), p. 7.
32.   P. Tocque, in Prowse, pp. 370-371.
33.   *Times* (London), 2 October 1796.
34.   Webber, *op. cit.*, p. 20.
35.   *Ibid.*, p. 24 *passim*.
36.   Colville, p. 32.
37.   Webber, pp. 41-42.
38.   *Ibid.*, p. 55.
39.   *Ibid.*, pp. 63-64.
40.   *Ibid.*, pp. 66-67.
41.   *Ibid.*, pp. 69-70.
42.   Webber, *The St. John's Volunteer Rangers: 1805-1814* (Newfoundland Naval & Military Museum), pp. 4-5.
43.   *Ibid.*, p. 9.
44.   *Ibid.*, p. 26.
45.   Michael P. Murphy, "Frontiersmen Held the Fort in 1914-1918," *N.S.* (1 May 1970), p. 11.
46.   "U.S. Troops Arrive in St. John's," *N.Q.* (April 1941), p. 21.
47.   *E.T.*, 16 July 1949.
48.   G. W. L. Nicholson, *The Fighting Newfoundlander*, pp. 115-118.

CHAPTER 3.
1.   Prowse, p. 163.
2.   G. Duff, "A Biographical Dictionary of the Governors of Newfoundland," MS., M.U.N. (1964), pages unnumbered.
3.   *Ibid.*
4.   *Ibid.*
5.   G. T. Wilkinson, *The Newgate Calendar*, III, 174 *passim*.
6.   Duff, *op. cit.*
7.   A. B. C. Whipple, *The Fatal gift of Beauty*, p. 6 *passim*.
8.   Prowse, p. 319.
9.   Duff.
10.   *Ibid.*
11.   *Ibid.*
12.   Prowse, p. 424.
13.   Cochrane Papers, Scottish National Library, Edinburgh.
14.   *Ibid.*
15.   Prowse, p. 462.
16.   Duff.
17.   R. C. Archibald, *Carlyle's First Love*.
18.   A. A. Parsons, *Governors I have Known*.
19.   Duff.
20.   C. L. Graves, *Hubert Parry: His Life & Works*.
21.   Duff.

CHAPTER 4.

1. Morison, *op. cit.* p. 234.
2. *Ibid.*
3. *Ibid.*
4. Prowse, pp. 40-41.
5. N.P.A., Letter from Christopher Towill (430).
6. Smallwood, *op. cit.*, I, 209.
7. N.P.A., Letterbook for 1886.
8. Canadiana, IX, 118 Ryan (*Gazette*).
9. N.P.A., Colonial Records, 1806.
10. W. J. Carroll, "The Great Wrong," *N.Q.* (December 1906), p. 13.
11. Prowse, p. 176.
12. Sir W. Eliot, *Naval Sketch Book*, p. 188 *passim*.
13. *Ibid.*, p. 187.
14. *Ibid.*, p. 184.
15. A. B. Perlin, *The Story of Newfoundland*, p. 93.
16. *Newfoundlander*, December 26, 1833.
17. G. E. Gunn, *The Political History of Newfoundland: 1832-1864*, p. 20.
18. Prowse, p. 434.
19. Gunn, *op. cit.*, p. 24.
20. *The Star*, 10 June 1835.
21. *The Public Ledger*, 2 June 1835.
22. *Ibid.*
23. Charles Pedley, *History of Newfoundland*, pp. 396 397.
24. *Ibid.*, pp. 387-388.
25. H. Clayton, *Atlantic Bridgehead*, p. 24.
26. *Ibid.*, p. 25.
27. *Ibid.*, p. 144.
28. *Ibid.*, pp. 144-145.
29. *Ibid.*, p. 146.

CHAPTER 5.

1. H. M. Mosdell, *When Was That?*, p. 148.
2. N.P.A., Colonial Records, 1750.
3. R. G. Lounsbury, *The British Fishery at Newfoundland: 1634-1763*, p. 254.
4. J. M. Murray, *The Newfoundland Journal of Aaron Thomas: 1794*, p. 187.
5. Mosdell, *op. cit.*, p. 145.
6. Prowse, p. 381.
7. Mosdell, p. 145.
8. Smallwood, *op. cit.*, IV, 453.
9. J. M. Byrnes, *The Paths to Yesterday*, p. 123.
10. *Tyranny in St. John's*, *op. cit.*, p. 3.
11. C. H. Wilkinson, *The King of Beggars: Bampfylde-Moore Carew*, pp. 92-93.
12. Colonial Records, 1867.

13. *Ibid.*, 1806.
14. Eliot, *op. cit.*, p. 172 *passim*.
15. *Ibid.*
16. *Ibid.*, pp. 180-181.
17. N.P.A., Colonial Records, 1822, pp. 260-261.
18. Archives, Phoenix Fire Office, London.
19. Dr. L. Saunders, History of the Arts in Newfoundland, Newfoundland Government Bulletin (Jan.-Mar.), p. 10.
20. Smallwood, p. 163.
21. *Evening Herald*, 14 February 1901.
22. *Ibid*, 20 February 1901, p. 4.
23. Smallwood, p. 166.
24. Brief to the Municipal Council from St. John's Symphony Orchestra.

CHAPTER 6.

1. Prowse, p. 253.
2. *Ibid.*, p. 356.
3. Colonial Records, 1797.
4. "Offbeat History," *E.T.*, 30 August 1971.
5. *Mercantile Journal*, 20 December 1820.
6. *Carbonear Sentinel*, 18 August 1838.
7. Colonial Records, 1817.
8. H. M. Mosdell, "Newfoundland Medical Association Convention," *N.Q.* (December 1926), p. 21.
9. R. W. Harper, "Notes for a Lecture on the General Hospital: 1934" MS p. 1.
10. *Ibid.*, p. 2.
11. *Ibid.*, p. 3.
12. *Ibid.*
13. *Ibid.*, p. 3 *passim*.
14. *The Trade Review*, June 1904.
15. Harper, *op. cit.*, p. 7.
16. *Ibid.*, p. 8.
17. N.P.A., *Journal of the House of Assembly*, 1852.
18. Harper, p. 11.
19. *"The Unveiling of the Dickinson Monument," N.Q.* (winter 1920), p. 8.
20. S. Gushue, "Work in Harmony with the Spirit of Their Order," *N.S.* (18 June 1970), p. 3.
21. *The Monitor*, September 1972, p. 19A.
22. *Ibid.*, pp. 20A-21A.
23. G. W. L. Nicholson, *op. cit.*, p. 105.

CHAPTER 7

1. Mosdell, *op. cit.*, p. 144.
2. *Ibid.*, p. 15.
3. Colonial Records, 1830.
4. P. O'Connell, *Irish Ecclesiastical Record* (May 1965).
5. Mosdell, p. 151.

6. *Ibid.*
7. *The Public Ledger*, 17 July 1860.
8. Archives, Phoenix Fire Office, London.
9. "Rotary: Playground's Swimming Pool at Rennie's River," *N.Q.* (October 1928), p. 23.
10. Smallwood, *op. cit.*, II, 261.
11. *Ibid.*, p. 262.
12. *Ibid.*, p. 253.
13. *Ibid.*, p. 256.
14. *Ibid.*, IV, 282.
15. *Ibid.*, II, 260.
16. *Ibid.*, p. 258.
17. *Ibid.*, p. 249.
18. Byrnes, *op. cit.*, p. 78.
19. Smallwood, II, 263.
20. John Burke, Regatta Programme, 1912.
21. F. L. N. Poynter, *op. cit.*, p. 120.

CHAPTER 8.

1. Alcock & Brown, *Our Transatlantic Flight*, **p.** 58.
2. Smallwood, I, 141-142.
3. *Ibid.*
4. Clayton, *op. cit.*, p. 165.
5. Alcock & Brown, *op. cit.*, p. 101.
6. Smallwood, I, 142.
7. Wayfarer, *D.N.* (12 January 1970).
8. Smallwood, IV, 515.
9. Wayfarer, *op. cit.*
10. C. A. Lindbergh, *The Spirit of St. Louis*, p. 278.
11. I. Balbo, *My Air Armada*, p. 239.
12. *Ibid.*, pp. 239-240.
13. Smallwood, I, 141.
14. W. M. Kunstler, *The Minister and the Choir Singer*, p. 261.
15. A. D. Sullivan, "Toronto, Canada to St. John's, Newfoundland by Air," *N.Q.* (April 1931), p. 28.
16. Perlin, *op. cit.*, p. 108.
17. Smallwood, II, 644-645.

CHAPTER 9.

1. Byrnes, *op. cit.*, p. 37.
2. *Ibid.*, pp. 64-65.
3. *Ibid.*, pp. 69-70.
4. C. H. Wilkinson, *op. cit.*, p. 25.
5. "Offbeat History," *E.T.* (30 July 1973).
6. *E.T.*, late March 1972.
7. *Who's Who in Newfoundland* (1930), p. 165.
8. M. Murphy, "Donald Brian: Matinee Idol," *N.S.* (7 November 1970), pp. 5 & 10.
9. "The Balladeers of Newfoundland," *D.N.* (27 July 1966), p. 8.

10. *The Monitor*, May 1974, p. 39.
11. *A Standard Dictionary of Canadian Biography* (1938), II, pp. 85-86.
12. M. Cullen, *National Gallery Catalogue* (first printed 1956), p. 7.
13. *Ibid.*, p. 11.
14. *Evening Herald*, 2 May 1902.
15. Offbeat History, *E.T.* (1 April 1974), p. 6.
16. G. Duff, *A Biographical Dictionary, op. cit.* (under Ralph Champneys Williams).
17. "King George the Fifth Seamen's Institute," *N.Q.* (Spring 1913), p. 22.
18. M. Duley, *The Caribou Hut*, p. 28.
19. "Rearguard Action at White Bird Canyon," *N.S.* (6 March 1970), pp. 10-11.
20. *Canadian Who's Who* (1964-1966) X, 878.
21. G. W. L. Nicholson, *op. cit.*, p. 492.

Appendix A

St. John's Old Street and Property Guide
(This list has been carefully checked against maps, deeds, and other available sources, but errors are possible in locating old places.)

STREET OR PROPERTY	PRESENT NAME OR LOCATION
Adams Plantation	New Gower St. (Vicinity City Hall)
Albion St.	Vic. junct. Monkstown and Rennie's Mill Rds.
Alfred St.	Vic. Penitentiary
Allan's Lane	Off S. side Duckworth St.
Allandale Rd. (South)	Bonaventure Ave. (Empire to Ft. Townshend)
Amherst Heights Ext.	Colville St.
Apple Tree Well	S.E. corner Pleasant St. at New Gower
Archibald's Meadow	Forest Rd.
Arundel Cottage Rd.	From Ft. Townshend to Long Pond (via Newtown, Mayor, and Bonaventure)
Avalon Terrace (Bee Orchis)	Queen's Rd. E. of Victoria St.
Baird's Cove	Clift's-Baird's Cove
Bake House (Lion)Sq.	Off New Gower St. E. of Barter's Hill
Ball Park (St. Pat's)	N.E. corner Carpasian at Empire Ave.
Barking Kettle	Vic. junct. New Gower and Duckworth Sts.
Barrens, The	Military Rd. (Vic. Bannerman Park)
Barnes Lane	Barnes Rd.
Beaver Pond Rd.	Part of Portugal Cove Rd.
Beech St.	Monchy St.
Bell's Shute	Bell St.
Belvedere Place	Bonaventure Ave. (opp. Hayward Ave.)
Bennett's Cove	S. side Water St. (W. of Steer's Cove)
Best's Farm	Off LeMarchant Rd. (Vic. Barter's Hill)
Biskin Hill	Possibly Hill o' Chips (or E. of there)
Bishop's Farm, The	Vic. Patrick St. and Plank Rd.
Blockmaker's Hall Rd.	Waterford Bridge Rd.
Blockmaker's Lane	Mahon's Lane
Boat House Lane (Clare St.)	Lakeview Ave.

Bolland's Meadow	Vic. Ft. William
Brookfield Rd. (Old)	Topsail Rd. W. from Crossroads
Branscomb's Hill	Springdale St.
Branscomb's Ridge Rd.	Pennywell Rd.
Branscomb's St.	Central St.
Brazil's Field	Beaumont St. W.
Brewery (Collier's) Lane	Factory Lane
Brine's Farm	Between Patrick and Brine Sts.
Break Heart Hill	Carter's Hill
Broom's (John) Estate	Rennie's Mill Rd.
Buckley's Lane	George St.
Buckley's Range	Ft. William N. side Plymouth Rd.
Buckmaster's Field	Between Golf Ave. and Prince of Wales St.
Bulley's Lane	Bulley St. to Duckworth, W. of Bell St.
Burke's Sq.	On Pope St.
Burst Heart Hill	Carter's Hill
Busset St. Firebreak	Off Duckworth St. (nr. Prescott St.)
Butler Place	Hamilton St. (lower part)
Cameron St.	Richmond St.
Cantfield's Lane	From Duckworth St. to Military Rd.
Carew Ave.	Barnes Place
Caul's Lane	Off Cathedral St.
Carpasian Ave.	Empire Ave. (Carpasian Rd. to Allandale Rd.)
Carter's Meadow	W. side Carter's Hill
Casey's Rd.	Mundy Pond Rd.
Castle Rennie	Signal Hill Rd. (opp. Walsh's Sq.)
Cathedral Hill	Church Hill
Chancey's Lane	Off Prescott St.
Chapel Lane	Off Duckworth St. (nr. Prescott)
Clapp's Plantation	Water St. (area W. of Prescott St.)
Clare St. (Boat House Lane)	Lakeview Ave.
Cliff Hill Farm	Glenbrook (W. side of Torbay Rd., N. of Mt. Cashel Rd.)
Cochrane's (Patrick's) Pinch	Hill on Monkstown Rd. leading to Carpasian Rd. (W. of Circular Rd.)
Cochrane's Pinch (Road to)	Monkstown Rd.
Cochrane Place	S. side Military Rd. (bet. Gower and Cochrane Sts.)
Cockpit Rd.	Craigmillar Ave.
Codner's Cove	Bishop's Cove
Codner's Lane	Off W. side Adelaide St. (N. of New Gower St.)
Cody's Lane	N. Linscott St. (Freshwater Rd. to Merrymeeting Rd.)
Coefield's Lane	W. from James St.
Collier's (Brewery) Lane	Factory Lane

Commercial Buildings (Old)	S. side Duckworth St. (E. of McBride's Hill)
Conduit Lane	Parallel bet. Duckworth and Water Sts. (orig. from McBride's Hill to War Memorial)
Congregational St.	Chapel St.
Cook's Hill (Hunt's Lane)	Water St. W. of Temperance St.
Cookstown	Area at top of Long's Hill
Cottage Farm	N. side Quidi Vidi Lake
Courting Lane (St.)	Wickford St.
Covel's Lane	Off Duckworth St. (Vic. War Memorial)
Cress St.	Off N. side of Duckworth St.
Crop Rd.	Off Newtown Rd. (Vic. Goodridge St.)
Cuddihy's Lane (River)	Off N. side New Gower St. (E. of Barter's Hill)
Cumming St.	King's Rd. to Colonial St. (N. of Gower St.)
Dammerill's Lane	Off S.E. side Adelaide St. (N. of New Gower, Site of City Hall)
Darby's-O'Gallivan's	Vic. Brazil Sq. and Casey St.
Darkuse's (Roopes) Rooms	General area of Waldegrave St. to E. of Bishop's Cove
Darling St. (Old)	Bond St. (King's Rd. to Cochrane St.)
Deady's Lane	E. of Brazil's Sq. (Leading from N. side New Gower St. to Casey St.)
Diamond March Rd.	Vic. Brookfield and Heavy Tree Rds.
Dogstown	Off Duckworth St. E.
Doolan's Rd.	Freshwater Rd. E. (to Harvey Rd.)
Dowling's Pond	Vic. Blackmarsh Rd.
Dover's Hill	Robinson's Hill
Dreeland's Well Rd.	Brazil Sq. and Casey St.
Duggan St.	Off S.E. side Flower Hill (nr. New Gower)
Duggin's Gully	Bonaventure Ave. at Mayor Ave.
Duke of York St.	Duckworth St. 120 ft. E. of Cochrane (N. to corner of Cochrane & Gower)
Dunscomb's (Pour's) Bridge	Between Duckworth St. E. and Signal Hill Rd. (nr. top Temperance St.)
Dunscomb's Rd.	Vicinty of Old Placentia Rd.
East St.	Bond St. (E. of Bannerman St.)
Edgell's (Capt.) Farm	Top Gooseberry Lane. Vic. Confederation Building
Electric Ave. (St.)	Flavin St.
Elford's (Colonel) Plantation	Vic. Quidi Vidi and Signal Hill Rds.

413

The Exchange	S. side Duckworth St. (opp. Victoria St.)
Father Walsh's Hill	From Queen's Rd. to Military Rd. E. of top of Victoria St. (now a park)
Fergus Place	Duggan St.
Finn's Lane	Off W. side Adelaide St. (N. of New Gower)
Flower Hill Firebreak	Springdale St. (Water to LeMarchant)
Flowerhill St.	Flower Hill
Foote's Lane	Alexander St.
Fortune's (Webber's) Field	Off Hamilton Ave.
Fort Waldegrave (Old)	S. side Duckworth St. at Devon Row
Fowler's Rd.	Off Empire Ave.
Freshwater	Rennie's River
Friendly Hall	Portugal Cove Rd. (nr. Gooseberry Lane)
Frog Marsh	Water St. E. of Prescott St.
Funny Lane	Scanlan's Lane (E. of Nfld. Museum)
Gallagher's (Galgay's) Range	Water St. (Alexander St. to Victoria Pk.)
Gallow's Hill	Junct. Queen's Rd. and Duckworth St.
Gambier St. (Old)	Duckworth to Water (E. of Holloway St.)
Gas Works Firebreak	Lower Patrick St.
Georgetown Rd.	Hayward Ave.
Gill's Field	Monkstown Rd. at Fleming St.
Gilmour St.	Off New Gower, E. of Flower Hill (area of City Hall development)
Gorman's Lane	Off Barnes Rd. (opp. Barnes Pl.)
Government House Sq.	King's Bridge Rd. (Lane to Gov. House)
Governor's Wharf	Clift's-Baird's Cove
Grace's Rd.	Off Freshwater Rd.
Granny Bates's Hill	Bates Hill
Greenlaw's Plantation	Vic. Portugal Cove Rd. (sometimes spelled Greenland's)
Gregory Lane	S. side Duckworth St. to Water St. (opp. Victoria St.)
Grove Farm (Golden Grove)	John Williams—N. side of Boulevard (Vic. Pleasantville Ave.)
Haggerty's Lane	Haggerty St.
Hawthorn Cottage	E. side of Carter's Hill
Hill (Samuel) Plantation	S. side Water St. (opp. Hill o' Chips)
Hogan's Farm	Newtown Rd. (Vic. Belvedere Cemetery)

Hog Island Room	N.E. side Quidi Vidi Gut
Horse Gully Farm	On Winter Ave.
Horton's Plantation	S. side Water St. (opp. McMurdo's Lane)
Hospital Lane	N. from Water St. (W. side Victoria Park)
Hospital Park	Victoria Park
Hospital Road	Bannerman Rd.
Hudson's (Ships' Room) Cove	Opp. Prescott St.
Hunt's Lane (Cook's Hill)	Duckworth to Water St. (W. of Temperance St.)
Hutching's Plantation	Vic. Waldegrave St.
Irwin Rd.	Prince Philip Parkway (Allandale Rd. to Westerland Rd.)
James St.	Mullock St.
James St.	Off S. side Carter's Hill (site of City Hall Garage)
James St.	Carew St.
Jersey Cottage (Pinkham's Farm)	Near Waterford Bridge
Job's Bridge	Long Bridge
Job's Cove	Hunter's Cove
Job's Lane	Job St.
Johnny's Hill	N. end Monkstown Rd. (leading from Circular Rd. to Carpasian Rd.)
Keen's Hill	Prescott St.
Kennedy's Lane	Off Freshwater Rd.
Kenny's Lane	Same as Duke of York St.
Kent St.	Sailsbury St.
Kerry Lane	S. side Water St. (opp. West End Post Office)
Kickham's Lane	Holloway St.
Kimberley Row	Junct. Henry St. and Dick's Sq.
King's Bridge Hill	King's Bridge Rd. (S. of Empire Ave.)
King's Wharf	Gill's Cove (opp. War Memorial)
Kitchin Place	S.W. side Job St. (bet. Water St. & Plank Rd.)
Lady's Ship Room	E. side Queen St.
Lang's Lane	Off Queen's Rd. W.
Lamb's Lane	Off Freshwater Rd. W.
Larkin's Sq.	Off Hamilton Ave. (below Carnell St.)

Law's Lane — Vic. Signal Hill
Lazy Bank — Pleasant St.
Lime Kiln Hill — Lime St.
Lindbergh Castle — Mt. Scio Rd. (later moved to Castle Rennie)
Lion's Hill — Possibly Southside and Blackhead Rds.
Lion (Bake House) Sq. — Off N. side New Gower on Cuddihy's Lane. (E. of Barter's Hill—City Hall Site
Livingston's Farm — N. end Monkstown Rd.
Llewellyn Grounds — On Forest Rd. (nr. Anglican Cemetery)
Long Pond Rd. (Old) — From Carpasian Rd. up E. side Smithville Cres. to Long Pond Bridge on Parkway
Love Lane — From Rennie's Bridge W. along riverbank into Pine Bud Ave. to Allandale
Low Back Car Rd. — City Terrace—open to traffic on Duckworth St.
Lower Path — Water St.

MacKie St. — Monroe St.
Maddock's (Maddox) Lane — Ayre's Cove and McBride's Hill
Maggotty Cove — E. end of Water St. area
Marine Parade (Promenade) — S. side Water St. (Long Bridge to opp. Alexander St.)
Market House Hill — Court House Steps
Marsh Hill — King's Rd.
McBride's Cove — Ayre's Cove
McCalman's (McCallum's) Lane — McMurdo's Lane
McCarthy's (McLarty's) Lane — Lower Prescott St. (or St. John's Lane)
McCowan St. — Quidi Vidi Rd. to lake
Meeting House Lane — Victoria St.
Merchant's Block — Water St. E. of McMurdo's Lane
Mill Bridge — Ft. Mill Lane (over Waterford River)
Mill Dam Lane — Mill Lane
Monday's Pond Rd. — Mundy Pond Rd. and St. Clare Ave.
Moore St. — Off S.W. side Carter's Hill (site of City Hall parking garage)
Moreton's (Moultan's) Lane — Same as Duke of York St.
Morley's Marsh Rd. — Shaw St.
Mount Cochrane — Mount Pearl Agricultural Station
Mount Ken — S. side Kenmount Rd. W.
Murphy Avenue — Anthony Avenue
Murphy's Field — Off Gower St. E. (behind Military Rd.)
Murphy's Range — S. side LeMarchant Rd. (W. Cookstown Rd.)
Musgrave Terrace — N. side Gower St. (E. of Cochrane St.)

Norrice Rd.	Vic. New Gower St.
North River	Waterford River (also Big Castor)
North Street	Bannerman St. N. of Bond St.
Northwest St.	Colonial St. N. of Bond St.
Notre Dame St.	Off N. side New Gower—W. of upper Adelaide St. (City Hall area)
Nunnery Lane	Holloway St. (N. of Duckworth St.)
Oak St.	Hammel St.
Old-Chapel Lane	From Henry St. to City Terrace
Old Topsail Rd.	Kenmount Road
O'Neill's Lane	Linscott St.
Ordnance Wharf	Opp. Hill o' Chips
Ordnance Yard	Duckworth St. (bet. Ordnance and Wood Sts.)
Oxenham Rd.	Vic. Aldershot St.
Palk's Hill	Old Topsail Rd. from Crossroads
Pancake (Pankham) Lane	Possibly Cathedral St. and/or Market House Hill
Parsley Bed	Water St. W. opp. Alexander St.
Parsons Lane	Water St. (Between Telegram steps and Scanlan's Lane)
Patrick's Pinch	Probably Cochrane's Pinch
Penny's Lane	From Prescott St. to King's Rd.
Plank Rd.	Deanery Ave. (from Patrick to Job Sts.)
Playhouse Hill	Queen's Rd. from Long's Hill to New Gower St.
Pleasant St. North	Campbell Ave.
Plum St.	Aldershot St.
Pokeham Path	Hamilton Ave.
Poor House Lane	Sudbury St.
Pope St.	Off S.W. side Barter's Hill, N. of New Gower St. (area W. of City Hall)
Pour's (Dunscomb's) Bridge	Between Duckworth St. and Signal Hill Rd. (nr. top Temperance St.)
Pour's Hill	Charter Ave.
Portugal Cove Rd. (Old)	Winter Ave. to Portugal Cove Rd.
Powers Court (11 houses)	Off N. side Signal Hill Rd. (opp. Walsh's Sq.)
Powder House Field	Junct. Monkstown and Rennie's Mill Rds.
Princess Cove	Water St. E. (Vic. Temperance St.)
Pringles Bridge	From Rennie's Mill Rd. to Robinson's Hill over Rennie's River
Pringlesdale	Pringle Place

Promenade (Marine Parade)	Water St. W. from Job's Bridge to opp. Alexander St.
Public Wharf, The	Clift's-Baird's Cove
Quan's (Quin's) Rd.	Off Old Topsail Rd. (W. of cemetery)
Queen's Bridge	N. end King's Bridge Rd. (opp. foot of Kenna's Hill)
Rankin's Lane	Cairo St.
Rennie's Cove	Steer's Cove
Ridge Rd.	Included London Rd.
Riverside	McGrath property S. side Elizabeth Ave. (bet. Long Pond Rd. and Rennie's River)
Riverside Drive	Empire Ave.
Rd. Across Barrens to Freshwater	Rennie's Mill Rd.
Rd. to Allandale	Bonaventure Ave.
Rd. to Wakeham's Farm	Pennywell Rd.
Rd. to Quidi Vidi	Plymouth Rd.
Robinson's Farm	Virginia Water(s)
Rocky Lane	Power St. (N. end above Patrick St.)
Rocky Rd.	Prince of Wales St.
Rogerson's Meadow	Nr. Casey St.
Roman Catholic Cemetery (Old)	S.E. side foot of Long's Hill
Rostellan Rd.	Originally from junct. Long Pond and Rennie's Mill Rds. (along E. bank of river)
Rotten Row (Pye Corner)	Prince's St. to Waldegrave St.
Roupes Plantation	Waldegrave St. to Queen St. area
St. Bon's College Farm	Area of Maple and Stoneyhouse Sts.
St. Patrick St.	S. part Patrick St.
Sclater's Corner	Water St. opp. Queen St. (W. side of Stewart's Cove)
Scanlan's Lane	Duckworth St. to Water St. (opp. Cathedral St.)
Scotland Row	W. side Church Hill
Sebastian St.	Off W. side Barter's Hill N. of New Gower St.
Shamrock Field	N.E. corner Newtown and Merrymeeting Rds.
Sheenan's (Sheehan's) Shute	Factory Lane
Sheenan (Sheehan) St.	Forest Ave.
Simms Lane	Portugal Cove Rd. (nr. junct. New Cove)

Simms St.	Off W. side Adelaide St. N. of New Gower St. (City Hall area)
Skerrett's (Gen.) Plantation	S. side Military Rd. to Gower St.
Slinking Path	S. end Quidi Vidi Rd. (behind Ft. William)
Soldier's Path	S. Freshwater and E. LeMarchant Rds.
Solomon's Lane	Same as Gregory Lane
South St.	Bannerman St. S. of Bond St.
Southwest St.	Colonial St. S. of Bond St.
Spruce St.	Cairo St.
Stephen St.	Off New Gower St. W. of Barter's Hill
Stewart's Cove	S. side Water St. (opp. Queen St.)
Stone Cutter's Yard	Water St. W. of Cochrane St. (site of Sir Humphrey Gilbert Bldg.)
Strawberry Marsh Rd. (Old)	Long Pond Rd.
Stream Ken	Leary's Brook
Street's Farm	Newtown Rd. (Vic. Belvedere)
Studdy's Lane	Henry St.
Talbot's Farm	Portugal Cove Rd.
Tank Lane	See Cuddihy's Lane
Tarahan's (Tarahin's) Town	Area bounded by Queen's Rd., Prescott St., Gower St. and Cathedral St.
Tasker Terrace	Duckworth St. (poss. City Terrace)
Tessier Place	Off Carter's Hill
Theatre Hill	Queen's Rd. from foot of Long's Hill to junct. New Gower St.
Thomas St.	N. side Water St. (E. of Springdale St.)
Thompson's Field	Thompson Place
Thompson St.	Brazil St. (S. of LeMarchant Rd.)
Thorburn Lane	Bennett's Lane
Tubrid's Town	Area of Barnes Rd.
Twysden St.	Off W. side Adelaide St. N. of New Gower St. (City Hall area)
Union Terrace	Barnes Rd.
Upper Long Pond Rd.	Bonaventure Ave. (Fleming St. to Elizabeth Ave.)
Upper Path	Duckworth St.
Vinnicomb's Hill	Signal Hill Rd.
Voy's Lane (15 families)	George St. to New Gower St. in middle of block between Queen and Waldegrave Sts.
Wakeham's Hill	Area Queen's Rd. W. (poss. Theatre Hill)

419

Walnut St.	Winchester St.
Walsh's Town	S. side Signal Hill Rd. (area Walsh's Sq.)
Watering Cove	Hunter's Cove
Waterford Place	Off Waterford Bridge Rd.
Webber's (Fortune's) Field	Vic. Hamilton Ave.
West St.	Bond St. from Bannerman to Colonial Sts.
Western Ave.	Warbury St.
Weston St.	Vic. Carter's Hill
Whiteway's Ave.	Riverview Ave.
Widow Bevil's Bridge	Poss. junct. Duckworth and Prescott Sts.
Wigmore Gully Rd.	Oxen Pond Rd.
Wilcott's Lane	S. side Gower St. (just E. of Cathedral St.)
Wildcat Hill	Area Ft. William (poss. Ordnance St.)
William St.	Cabot St.
William's Lane	Ran from Wickford St. to Water St. (present lane is only south end)
Willow St.	Malta St.
Woods Range	Water St. (E. of Temperance St.)
Yellow Marsh Rd.	Freshwater Rd. (N. of Merrymeeting Rd.)

Appendix B

Homes of Prime Ministers and Premiers of Newfoundland
(Houses they occupied at St. John's when in office)

PHILIP LITTLE (1855-1858)
  Littledale, Waterford Bridge Road (house torn down for Academy Bldg.)
JOHN KENT (1858-1861)
  2 Gower St. (house burned down in Great Fire of 1892)
SIR HUGH HOYLES (1861-1865)
  239 Duckworth St. (house burned down in Great Fire of 1892); also Beaconsfield
SIR FREDERICK CARTER (1865-1869) (1874-1878)
  Avalon Cottage, Forest Rd. (torn down for Old Queen's College) and 90
  Military Rd.
CHARLES FOX BENNETT (1870-1874)
  Water St. E. Also boarded at Union Hotel, 379 Water St. (burned in 1846
  and 1892)
SIR WILLIAM WHITEWAY (1878-1885) (1889-1894) (1895-1897)
  4 Queen's Rd. (burned 1892) and "Sunnyside," 8 Riverview Ave.
SIR ROBERT THORBURN (1885-1889)
  2 Devon Place, King's Bridge Rd. (now King's Bridge Hotel)
AUGUSTUS GOODRIDGE (1894)
  4 Park Place, Rennie's Mill Rd.
DANIEL GREENE (1894-1895)
  34 Queen's Rd. (escaped destruction in 1892 fire)
SIR JAMES WINTER (1897-1900)
  "Pringlesdale," 4 Pringle Place
SIR ROBERT BOND (1900-1909)
  Childhood home, 2 Circular Road. Stayed at Balsam Hotel, 5 Barnes Rd.
  (home in Whitbourne)
SIR EDWARD MORRIS (1909-1917)
  Beaconsfield, Topsail Rd. (now home of Roman Catholic Archbishop)
SIR WILLIAM LLOYD (1918-1919)
  Portugal Cove and New Cove Rds. (destroyed by fire) and 195 Gower St.
SIR MICHAEL CASHIN (1919)
  74 Circular Rd. (later Canada House, home of High Commissioner for
  Canada)

SIR RICHARD SQUIRES (1919-1923) (1928-1932)
  44 Rennie's Mill Rd. and "Midstream" (a lodge now in Bowring Park)
WILLIAM WARREN (1923-1924)
  3 Barnes Rd. (afterwards Balsam Hotel annex)
ALBERT HICKMAN (1924)
  48 Circular Rd.
WALTER MONROE (1924-1928)
  8 Forest Rd.
FREDERICK ALDERDICE (1928) (1932-1934)
  3 Park Place, Rennie's Mill Rd.
JOSEPH SMALLWOOD (1949-1971)
  61 Duckworth St. (Bank of Montreal now on site) and 74 Circular Rd.
FRANK MOORES (1971-)
  10 Riverview Ave, later Elizabeth Towers, Elizabeth Avenue and Mount Scio
  House, Long Pond

Homes of Lieutenant-Governors of Newfoundland
(When in office they occupied Government House)

SIR AMBROSE SHEA (1886) (Appointed Governor)
  4 Musgrave Terrace (25 Gower St.) Shea did not serve in Newfoundland
SIR ALBERT WALSH (1949)
  62 Monkstown Rd. (Interim appointment at time of Confederation)
SIR LEONARD OUTERBRIDGE (1949-1957)
  4 Pringle Place and 3 Pringle Place
CAMPBELL MACPHERSON (1957-1963)
  4 Park Place, Rennie's Mill Rd. and "Westerland," Westerland Rd.
FABIAN O'DEA (1963-1969)
  12 Winter Place
E. JOHN HARNUM (1969-   )
  19 Cornwall Cresc.

Homes of Some Distinguished St. John's Men

JOHN MURRAY ANDERSON
  3 Park Place, Rennie's Mill Rd. (probably his birthplace)
DONALD BRIAN
  Cockpit Rd., now Topsail Rd. (probably his birthplace)
JOHNNY BURKE
  Lived at 62 Prescott St.
ARCHBISHOP CAREW
  155 Queen's Rd.

422

DR. WILLIAM CARSON
Lived at what is now "Rostellan." House in trees facing the top of Rostellan St. (still standing but much changed)

MAURICE CULLEN
Family had lived on N.E. corner of Queen and George Sts. (birthplace unknown)

DR. MICHAEL FLEMING
Bishop's Palace, Henry St. S. of Dick's Sq. (burned; Star Hall on site)

SIR WILFRED GRENFELL
Had rooms in King George V Institute

HAROLD HORWOOD
Born 140 Campbell Ave. Lived at Witch Hazel Ridge, Beachy Cove.

CAPTAIN ABRAM KEAN
10 Waterford Bridge Rd. Still standing but modified externally.

DR. EDWARD KIELLEY
Cottage on Water St. W. of Job St. (torn down in recent years and replaced by a gas station)

FRANK KNIGHT
14 Circular Rd.

DR. CLUNY MacPHERSON
65 Rennie's Mill Rd. (still standing)

ARCHBISHOP PHELPS
Avalon (Queen's College), Forest Rd. at west corner of Factory Lane.

E. J. PRATT
24 Leslie Street

CHRISTOPHER PRATT
216 LeMarchant Rd. and 93 Waterford Bridge Rd.

JUDGE PROWSE
Glenbrook Lodge, (now Salvation Army home). N. of Mt. Cashel Rd.

SIR ROBERT REID
3 Forest Rd. (still standing)

THOMAS RICKETTS
Had drugstore on west corner Water and Job Sts. (marked by a monument)

DR. AUBREY SPENCER
Cochrane Place, Military Rd., first house on corner above Gower St. (burned down)

GENERAL SIR HUGH TUDOR
42 Circular Rd. and 19 Churchill Square Apts.

Addresses of Historic Sites and Buildings

BANNERMAN PARK. Oldest park in the city. Opened as a Botanical Garden, 23 July 1847. Park established 13 April 1864.

423

2 BARROWS ROAD, QUIDI VIDI. Possibly the oldest house in New-foundland. Style of architecture common in colonial British North America. Might even have been the home of John Downing. Unfortunately, no proofs of age are available.

CAPE SPEAR. Closest point to Europe on North American continent; 1,640 miles from Cape Clair, Ireland. All of North America is west of this cape. The old lighthouse, begun in 1835, is preserved.

FISHERMEN'S HALL. Oldest theatre still standing in city. Also, oldest Roman Catholic Church, excepting the Basilica. Opened 28 October 1861. Became a chapel in 1873.

FORT AMHERST, SOUTH SIDE OF THE NARROWS. First lighthouse in Newfoundland, erected here in 1811, lit in 1812. Fort built in 1763.

FORT WILLIAM, CAVENDISH SQUARE. Site of Hotel Newfoundland. Oldest regular fort in St. John's. Begun in 1697. Last remnants were destroyed around 1910.

GOVERNMENT DEMONSTRATION FARM. At Brookfield Rd., Mount Pearl, site of home of Sir James Pearl. Was take-off field used by Hawker and Grieve in first attempt to fly the Atlantic non-stop, 18 May 1919. There is a monument on the site.

GOVERNMENT HOUSE. On Military Rd. One of the oldest residences in St. John's. Begun in 1827. Completed in 1831.

GREAT FIRES. The 1817 fires began just W. of the War Memorial, near the corner of Water and Adelaide Sts. The 1846 fire began in a cabinet shop on the S. E. corner of George and Queen Sts. The 1892 fire began in a stable on the corner of Pennywell and Freshwater Rds.

KING GEORGE V INSTITUTE. Built by Sir Wilfred Grenfell. First cornerstone in the world to be laid by remote control, by King George V, from Buckingham Palace, on his Coronation Day, 22 June 1911.

LESTER'S FIELD. On Blackmarsh Rd. opp. Froude Ave. This open space, marked by a monument, is all that is left of the take-off field used by Alcock and Brown, in first successful transatlantic flight, 14 June 1919.

NEWFOUNDLAND WAR MEMORIAL. On King's Beach. Traditional site of the founding of the British Empire by Sir Humphrey Gilbert, 5 August 1583. Marked by a monument.

NICKEL THEATRE. Military Road at Garrison Hill. First movie theatre in city. Opened 1 July 1907. Closed 26 June 1960.

9 PRINCE WILLIAM PLACE. Oldest house in St. John's for which proofs are available. Known to date from 1770. It is probably the place shown in the area on a map made in 1741. Prince William (afterwards King William IV) danced at a ball in this house in the summer of 1786.

QUIDI VIDI BATTERY. At Quidi Vidi. Oldest military emplacement extant in St. John's. Constructed by d'Haussonville in 1762. Restored in War of 1812 and again in 1967.

QUIDI VIDI LAKE. Scene of St. John's Regatta. The oldest continuing annual sports event in North America, and probably in the western hemisphere. First known boat races were held in St. John's 22 September 1818.

82 QUIDI VIDI ROAD. At Quidi Vidi. This house, just S. of Christ Church, is said to have been used as a field hospital in the Seven Years' War, during the Battle of Signal Hill, 15 September 1762.

ST. THOMAS'S CHURCH. Oldest church still standing in the city. The Mall, Military Road. Opened 28 September 1836.

SHANADITHIT. Last of the Beothuck Indians. Buried in an unmarked grave in the former St. Mary's Churchyard on Southside Rd. There is a monument on the site.

SIGNAL HILL HOSPITAL. Building in which Marconi received first wireless signal transmitted across the Atlantic. Said to have been erected in 1792, it was destroyed by fire 18 December 1920. The foundation stones are still visible on the sea side of the Cabot Tower parking lot wall.

UNION BANK BUILDING, E. corner of Duckworth St. and Court House Steps, and COMMERCIAL BANK BUILDING, also on Duckworth St. 3 doors W. of Victoria Street, are the only buildings S. of Military and Harvey Rds. and E. of Beck's Cove to have survived the Great Fire of 1892. The Union Bank was erected on the site of two former Court Houses and jails. The last public hanging of a woman in St. John's took place on this corner, 22 July 1834, when Catherine Snow was hanged for murdering her husband. Last public hanging of a man took place here in January 1835 when John Flood was hanged for highway robbery.

Bibliography

The following works were consulted in preparing this book.

AHIER, PHILIP. *Stories of Jersey Seas of Jersey's Coast and of Jersey Seamen*. Huddersfield: The Advertiser Press.

ALCOCK, SIR JOHN, and BROWN, SIR ARTHUR WHITTEN. *Our Transatlantic Flight*. London William Kimber, 1969.

ANDERSON, HUGH ABERCROMBIE. *Out Without My Rubbers*. New York: Library Publishers, 1954.

ANSPACH, LEWIS AMADEUS. *History of the Island of Newfoundland*. London: Sherwood, Gilbert and Piper, 1819.

ARCHIBALD, RAYMOND CLARE. *Carlyle's First Love*. London: John Lane The Bodley Head, 1910.

AYRE, AGNES MARION. *Newfoundland Names*.

BALBO, AIR-MARSHALL ITALO. *My Air Armada*. London: Hurst & Blackett Ltd., 1934.

BAXTER, JAMES PHINNEY. *A Memoir of Jacques Cartier*. New York: Dodd Mead and Co., 1906.

BIGGAR, H. P. *Voyages of Jacques Cartier*. Ottawa: F. A. Acland, 1924.

BLUM, DANIEL. *A Pictorial History of the Silent Screen*. London: Spring Books, 1953.

BONNYCASTLE, SIR RICHARD. *Newfoundland in 1842*. London: Henry Colburn, 1842.

BUFFETT, REV. F. M. *The Story of the Church in Newfoundland*. Toronto: General Board of Religious Education, 1939.

BURROUGHS, POLLY. *The Great Ice Ship Bear*. Van Nostrand-Reinhold Company, 1970.

BYRNES, JOHN MACLAY. *The Paths to Yesterday*. Boston: Meador Publishing Company, 1931.

CARROLL, SR. MARY TERESA. *Leaves from the Annals of the Sisters of Mercy*. London: Burns and Oates, 1889.

CARSE, ROBERT. *The Seafarers*. Harper and Row, 1964.

CARTWRIGHT, GEORGE. *A Journal of Transactions and Events on the Coast of Labrador*. Newark: 1792.

CAVANAGH, MICHAEL. *Memoirs of Gen. Thomas Francis Meagher.* Worcester, Mass.: The Messenger Press, 1892.

CELL, GILLIAN T. *English Enterprise in Newfoundland: 1577-1660.* Toronto: University of Toronto Press, 1969.

CHADWICK, ST. JOHN. *Newfoundland: Island into Province.* Cambridge: University Press, 1967.

CHAPPELL, LT. EDWARD. *Voyage of H.M.S. Rosamund to Newfoundland.* London: J. Mawman, Ludgate St., 1818.

CHIDSEY, DONALD BARR. *Shackleton's Voyage.* New York: Universal Publishing and Distributing Corporation, 1967.

CLAYTON, HOWARD. *Atlantic Bridgehead.* London: Granstone Press, 1968.

COCHRANE, J. A. *The Story of Newfoundland.* Boston, London, and Montreal: Ginn and Company, 1938.

COLVILLE, LORD, REAR ADMIRAL. Dispatches: 1761-1762. Ed. Instructor Commander C. H. Little, R.C.N. Maritime Museum of Canada, 1959.

CRAMM, RICHARD. *The First Five Hundred.* Albany, New York: C. F. Williams and Son, Inc.

DAVIN, NICHOLAS FLOOD. *The Irishman in Canada.* London: Sampson Low, Marston and Co., 1877.

DAVIS, DAVID J. *St. John's and the Commissariat: 1810-1820.*

DEVINE, P. K. *Ye Olde St. John's.* St. John's: Newfoundland Directories, 1936.

DEVINE and O'MARA. *Noteable Events in the History of Newfoundland.* St. John's: Newfoundland Trade Review Office, 1900.

DEVOLPI, CHARLES P. *Newfoundland: A Pictorial Record.* Don Mills, Ont: Longmans Canada Limited, 1972.

DIBNER, BERN. *The Atlantic Cable.* New York, London, and Toronto: Blaisdell Publishing Company, 1964.

DUFF, GORDON. "A Biographical Dictionary of the Governors of Newfoundland. Unpublished thesis, Memorial University, 1964.

DULEY, MARGARET. *The Caribou Hut.* Toronto: Ryerson Press, 1949.

EDEY, MAITLAND A. *The Northeast Coast.* New York: Time-Life Books, 1972.

EGAN, FATHER BARTHOLOMEW. *Franciscan Limerick.* Limerick: Franciscan Fathers, 1971.

ELLIOTT, CAPT. SIR WILLIAM. *Naval Sketch Book.* London: Henry Colburn, 1826.

ENGLAND, GEORGE ALLAN. *The Greatest Hunt in the World.* Montreal: Tundra Books, 1969.

ENGLISH, L. E. F. *Historic Newfoundland.* St. John's: Department of Economic Development.

———. *Outlines of Newfoundland History.* London, Edinburgh, New York, Toronto, and Paris: Thomas Nelson and Sons, Ltd.

FAY, C. R. *Channel Islands and Newfoundland*. Cambridge: W. Heffer & Sons Limited, 1961.

_____. *Life and Labour in Newfoundland*. Toronto: University of Toronto Press, 1956.

FIELD, CYRUS, *Statement of Some of the Advantages Attendant upon Making St. John's, Newfoundland as a Port of Call for Transatlantic Steamers*. London: M. Lownds, 1856.

FLEISHER, NAT, and ANDRE, SAM. *A Pictorial History of Boxing*. London: Spring Books, 1959.

FORAN, E. B. *Old St. John's*.

FREEDLEY and REEVES. *A History of the Theatre*. New York: Crown Publishers, 1941.

GRAVES, CHARLES L. *Hubert Parry: His Life and Works*. London: Macmillan and Co., 1926.

GREENE, MAJOR WILLIAM HOWE. *The Wooden Walls Among the Ice Floes*. London: Hutchinson & Co. (Publishers) Ltd., 1933.

GRENFELL, WILFRED THOMASON. *A Labrador Doctor*. Boston and New York: Houghton Mifflin Company, 1919.

GUNN, GERTRUDE E. *The Political History of Newfoundland: 1832-1864*. Toronto: University of Toronto Press, 1966.

GWYNN, RICHARD. *Smallwood: The Unlikely Revolutionary*. Toronto: McClelland and Stewart, 1968.

HAITNOLL, PHYLLIS. *The Oxford Companion to the Theatre*. Oxford: Oxford University Press, 1967.

HARRINGTON, MICHAEL. *Prime Ministers of Newfoundland*. St. John's: The Evening Telegram, 1962.

HARRIS, LESLIE. *Newfoundland and Labrador: A Brief History*. J. M. Dent and Sons (Canada) Limited, 1968.

HARRISSE, HENRY. *John Cabot and Sabastian His Son*. London: Benjamin Franklin Stevens, 1896.

HARVEY, REV. MOSES. *Newfoundland in 1900*. New York: The South Publishing Company, 1900.

_____, and O'MEARA, HENRY. *The Great Fire in St. John's, Newfoundland*. Boston: The Relief Committee, 1892.

HATTON, JOSEPH, and HARVEY, REV. MOSES. *Newfoundland*. Doyle and Whittle, 1883.

HENDERSON, DOROTHY. *The Heart of Newfoundland*. Montreal: Harvest House, 1965.

HIBBS, R. *Who's Who in and from Newfoundland*. St. John's: R. Hibbs, M.H.A., 1927 and 1930.

HILL, KAY. *And Tomorrow the Stars*. New York: Dodd, Mead and Co., 1968.

HORWOOD, HAROLD. *Newfoundland*. Toronto: MacMillan of Canada, 1969.

HOWLEY, JAMES P. *The Beothucks or Red Indians*. Cambridge: University Press, 1915.

HOWLEY, VERY REV. M. F. *Ecclesiastical History of Newfoundland*. Boston: Doyle and Whittle, 1888.

JOB, ROBERT BROWN. *John Job's Family*. St. John's: Private publication, 1953.

JOHNSON, D. W. *History of Methodism in Eastern North America*. Sackville, N. B.: Tribune Press.

KEIR, DAVID. *The Bowring Story*. London: The Bodley Head, 1962.

KERR, J. LENNOX. *Wilfred Grenfell: His Life and Work*. Toronto: The Ryerson Press, 1959.

KUNSTLER, WILLIAM M. *The Minister and the Choir Singer*. New York: William Morrow and Co.

LEMESURIER, H. W. *History of St. Thomas Church*. St. John's, 1928. As amended and added to by the Centenary Committee, 1936.

LEONARD-STUART and HAGAR. *People's Cyclopedia*. New York: Syndicate Publishing Company, 1911.

LINDBERGH, CHARLES A. *The Spirit of St. Louis*. New York: Charles Scribner's Sons, 1953.

LOUNSBURY, RALPH GREENLEE. *The British Fishery at Newfoundland: 1634-1763*. Archon Books, 1969.

LYSAGHT, A. M. *Joseph Banks in Newfoundland and Labrador: 1766*. London: Faber and Faber, 1971.

McALLISTER, R. I. *Newfoundland and Labrador: The First Fifteen Years of Confederation*. St. John's: Dicks and Co. Ltd.

McGRATH, J. W. "R. G. Reid and the Newfoundland Railway." Unpublished lecture to Newfoundland Historical Society, 1971.

McGRATH, P. T. *Newfoundland in 1911*. London: Whitehead, Morris and Co. Ltd., 1911.

MacINNES, PROF. C. M. "Plan for Pamphlet on Bristol and Newfoundland: Part 1." Unpublished work.

MAGDELENE, SR. MARY. *Presentation Convent, Galway: 1815-1965 Part I*. Galway: Presentation Order, 1965.

MONCRIEFF, REV. W. M. "A History of the Presbyterian Church in Newfoundland: 1622-1966." Thesis, Knox College, Toronto, 1966.

MORISON, SAMUEL ELIOT. *The European Discovery of America*. New York: Oxford University Press, 1971.

MOSDELL, H. M. *When Was That?* St. John's: Trade Printers and Publishers, Ltd., 1923.

MOTT, HENRY YOUMANS. *Newfoundland Men*. Concord, N. H.: TW and JF Cragg, 1894.

MURPHY, MICHAEL. *The Story of the Colonial Building*. St. John's: Newfoundland and Labrador Provincial Archives, 1972.

MURRAY, JEAN M. *The Newfoundland Journal of Aaron Thomas*. Don Mills, Ont.: Longmans Canada Limited, 1968.

NICHOLSON, COLONEL G. W. L. *The Fighting Newfoundlander*. Published by the Government of Newfoundland.

_____*More Fighting Newfoundlanders*. Published by the Government of Newfoundland and Labrador, 1969.

429

O'DEA, FABIAN A., Q.C. "Cabot's Landfall—Yet Again." Newfoundland Historical Society Paper, 1971.

O'DEA, SHANE. "St. John's—Development of the City—and its Architecture." Newfoundland Historic Society Paper, 1973.

PARKER, JOHN, M. P. *Newfoundland: 10th Province of Canada*. London: Lincolns-Prager (Publishers) Ltd., 1950.

PEDLEY, REV. CHARLES. *The History of Newfoundland*. London: Longman, Green, Longman, Roberts and Green, 1863.

PERLIN, A. B. *The Story of Newfoundland*. November, 1959.

PILOT, REV. WILLIAM. *History of Newfoundland*. London and Glasgow: Collins, 1908.

PITT, DAVID G. `Windows of Agates*. St. John's: Gower Street United Church, St. John's, Newfoundland, 1966.

POWER, PATRICK. *Waterford and Lismore*. Cork: Cork University Press, 1937.

POYNTER, F. L. N. *The Journal of James Yonge: 1647-1721*. London: Longmans, Green and Co. Ltd., 1963.

PRATT, CLAIRE. *The Silent Ancestors*. McClelland & Stewart, 1971.

PROWSE, D. W. *A History of Newfoundland*. London: Eyre and Spottiswoode, 1896.

PUDDESTER, JOHN. *The Crow's Nest: 30th Anniversary Souvenir*. St. John's: The Crow's Nest, 1972.

QUINN, DAVID B. and CHESHIRE, NEIL M. *The New Found Land of Stephen Parmenius*. Toronto: University of Toronto Press, 1972.

REDMAN, ALVIN. *The House of Hanover*. New York: Funk and Wagnalls, 1968.

REEVES, JOHN. *History of the Government of the Island of Newfoundland*. London: Printed for Sewell, Debrett, Downes, 1793.

SARNOFF, PAUL. *Ice Pilot Bob Bartlett*. New York: Julian Messner, 1966.

SAUNDERS, H. C. *Jersey in the 18th and 19th Centuries*. Jersey: J. T. Bigwood, 1930.

SAVAGE, RONALD BURKE. *Catherine McAuley: The First Sister of Mercy*. Dublin: M. H. Gill and Son, Ltd., 1955.

SHERSON, ERROLL. *London's Lost Theatres of the Nineteenth Century*. London: John Lane, The Bodley Head, 1925.

SHORTIS, H. F. *Old St. John's Partial Census: 1796-1797*. Reprinted by Provincial Archives from *The Cadet*, 1916.

SMALLWOOD, J. R. *Hand Book Gazetteer and Almanac*. St. John's: Long Brothers, 1940.

_____*The Book of Newfoundland*, vols. I and II. St. John's: Newfoundland Book Publishers Ltd., 1937.

_____*The Book of Newfoundland*, vols. III and IV. St. John's: Newfoundland Book Publishers Ltd., 1967.

_____*The New Newfoundland*. New York: The Macmillan Company, 1931.

SMITH, J. HARRY. *Newfoundland Holiday*. Toronto: The Ryerson Press, 1952.

SMITH, REV. T. W. *History of the Methodist Church in British America*. Halifax, N.S.: S. F. Heustis, 1890.

TEMPLE, W. B., and HARNUM, L. J., *Information Booklet of Newfoundland and Labrador*. St. John's: Robinson and Company Ltd., 1946.

THOMPSON, FREDERIC F. *The French Shore Problem in Newfoundland*. Toronto: University of Toronto Press, 1961.

THOMS, JAMES R. *Newfoundland-Labrador Who's Who*. St. John's: E. C. Boone Advertising Limited, 1968.

TOCQUE, REV. PHILIP. *Kaleidoscope Echoes*. Toronto The Hunter, Rose Company, Ltd., 1895.

———*Newfoundland as It Was and as It Is in 1877*. London: Sampson Low, Marston, Searle and Rivington, 1878.

TODD, WILLIAM A. "Reconstructions and Evolution of Mount Pearl Park—Glendale." Unpublished Thesis, M.U.N., 1971.

TURNBULL, ROBERT. *The Story of Newfoundland*. Toronto, London, New York, and Sydney: McGraw-Hill Company of Canada, 1966.

VILLIERS, ALAN. *The Quest of the Schooner Argus*. London: Hodder and Stoughton, 1951.

WADDEN, BRIAN J. *The St. John's Electric Light Co.: 1855-1892*.

WALLACE, GRAHAM. *The Flight of Alcock and Brown*. London: Putnam, 1955.

WALSH, T. J. *Nano Nagle and the Presentation Sisters*. Dublin: M. H. Gill and Son Ltd., 1959.

WEBBER, DAVID A. *The St. John's Volunteer Rangers: 1805-1814*.

———*Skinner's Fencibles: The Royal Newfoundland Regiment: 1795-1802*. St. John's, 1964.

WHIPPLE, A. B. C. *The Fatal Gift of Beauty*. New York: Harper and Rowe, 1964.

WILKINSON, C. H. *The King of Beggars: Bampfylde-Moore Carew*. Oxford: Clarendon Press, 1931.

WILKINSON, GEORGE THEODORE. *The Newgate Calendar (3)*. London: Panther Books, 1963.

WILLIAMSON, JAMES A. *The Cabot Voyages and Bristol Discovery Under Henry VII*. Cambridge: The University Press, 1962.

WINTON, HENRY. "A Chapter in the History of Newfoundland for the Year 1861." Unpublished booklet, Provincial Archives.

WIX, REV. EDWARD. *Six Months of a Newfoundland Missionary's Journal*. London: Smith, Elder and Co., Cornhill, 1836.

PERIODICALS AND NEWSPAPERS

Annals of all Hallows, Dublin, Ireland.

"Annals of the Mount"—Private papers in the Irish Christian Brothers Archives, St. John's.

431

British Press and Jersey Times. Various issues, 1886.
Centenary Souvenir Book (Basilica of St. John the Baptist). St. John's: Robinson and Company, 1955.
Centenary Volume of the Benevolent Irish Society: 1806-1906. Cork: Guy & Co. Ltd., 1907.
Centennial Souvenir— Sisters of Mercy: 1831-1931.
Compton Castle. London: Country Life Ltd., 1971.
Daily News. Various issues.
Dublin Builder. Vol. I, 1859. Dublin: Peter Roe, Mabbot St.
Evening Telegram. Various issues.
Floes. London: Hutchinson & Co. (Publishers) Ltd., 1933.
Inter Nos. Issues of June 1942; June 1944; June 1947.
Irish Digest. Various issues.
Irish Ecclesiastical Record. Vol. II. Dublin: John F. Fowler, Dame St., 1866; Browne & Nolan, Ltd., Nassau St., 1933.
Journal of the Waterford and South East Ireland Archaelogical Society. Vol. VI. Waterford: Harvey & Co., 1900.
Maurice Cullen. The National Gallery of Canada, 1956.
Monitor. Various issues.
Newfoundland. Department of External Affairs, 1950.
Newfoundland Quarterly. Numerous old papers.
Newscene. Various issues.
Old Properties: Early Residents. Provincial Archives.
Port of St. John's. The National Harbours Board.
Program of the Presentation of Civic Symbols to the City of St. John's: Friday, October 1, 1965.
St. Bride's College Annual. Issues of June 1919; June 1947.
St. John's Newfoundland. 3rd ed. Newfoundland Board of Trade, 1955.
St. John's: North America's Oldest City. Newfoundland Board of Trade, 1961.
Story of Newfoundland: The Great Island. 1928.
Tablet. Dublin: 2 October 1841.
Twillingate Sun. 1888.
Tyranny in St. John's: 1705-1706. Provincial Archives.
Where To Go! What To Do! What To See! St. John's, Newfoundland Newfoundland Tourist and Publicity Commission.

In addition to the newspapers listed above, isolated issues of almost all St. John's, Harbour Grace, and Carbonear newspapers of the past have been consulted. They are too numerous to list here and are available at the Provincial Archives and the Provincial Reference Library—Newfoundland Section.